WOMEN CREATING CLASSICS

This is one of two companion volumes, the other being titled *Women Re-Creating Classics: Contemporary Voices.*

Also available from Bloomsbury:

Anne Carson: Antiquity by Laura Jansen

Forward with Classics: Classical Languages in Schools and Communities by Arlene Holmes-Henderson, Steven Hunt and Mai Musié

Marginal Comment: A Memoir Revisited
by K. J. Dover, Stephen Halliwell and Christopher Stray

Orientalism and the Reception of Powerful Women from the Ancient World edited by Filippo Carlà-Uhink and Anja Wieber

Tragic Heroines in Ancient Greek Drama by Hannah M. Roisman

Virginia Woolf's Greek Tragedy by Nancy Worman

Women in Ancient Greece: A Sourcebook by Bonnie MacLachlan

Women in Ancient Rome: A Sourcebook by Bonnie MacLachlan

Women's Life in Greece and Rome: A Source Book in Translation by Maureen B. Fant and Mary R. Lefkowitz

WOMEN CREATING CLASSICS

A RETROSPECTIVE

Edited by Emily Hauser and Helena Taylor

BLOOMSBURY ACADEMIC
LONDON • NEW YORK • OXFORD • NEW DELHI • SYDNEY

BLOOMSBURY ACADEMIC
Bloomsbury Publishing Plc, 50 Bedford Square, London, WC1B 3DP, UK
Bloomsbury Publishing Inc, 1385 Broadway, New York, NY 10018, USA
Bloomsbury Publishing Ireland, 29 Earlsfort Terrace, Dublin 2, D02 AY28, Ireland

BLOOMSBURY, BLOOMSBURY ACADEMIC and the Diana logo are trademarks of
Bloomsbury Publishing Plc

First published in Great Britain 2025

Copyright © Emily Hauser, Helena Taylor & Contributors, 2025

Emily Hauser & Helena Taylor have expressed their right under the Copyright, Designs and
Patents Act, 1988, to be identified as Editors of this work.

For legal purposes the Acknowledgements on p. viii constitute an extension of this copyright page.

Cover design: Terry Woodley
Cover image: 'Athena, the Protector' © Evangelia Philippidis:
https://www.theartofevangelia.net/

All rights reserved. No part of this publication may be: i) reproduced or transmitted in any form,
electronic or mechanical, including photocopying, recording or by means of any information
storage or retrieval system without prior permission in writing from the publishers; or ii) used or
reproduced in any way for the training, development or operation of artificial intelligence (AI)
technologies, including generative AI technologies. The rights holders expressly reserve this
publication from the text and data mining exception as per Article 4(3) of the Digital Single Market
Directive (EU) 2019/790.

Bloomsbury Publishing Plc does not have any control over, or responsibility for,
any third-party websites referred to or in this book. All internet addresses given in
this book were correct at the time of going to press. The author and publisher regret
any inconvenience caused if addresses have changed or sites have ceased to exist,
but can accept no responsibility for any such changes.

A catalogue record for this book is available from the British Library.

Library of Congress Cataloging-in-Publication Data
Names: Hauser, Emily (Fiction writer), editor. | Taylor, Helena, 1985- editor.
Title: Women creating classics : a retrospective / [edited by] Emily Hauser, Helena Taylor.
Description: London : New York : Bloomsbury Academic, 2025. | Includes bibliographical
references and index.
Identifiers: LCCN 2024056288 (print) | LCCN 2024056289 (ebook) | ISBN 9781350444362
(paperback) | ISBN 9781350444379 (hardback) | ISBN 9781350444393 (epub) | ISBN
9781350444386 (ebook)
Subjects: LCSH: Classical literature—Appreciation. | Mythology, Classical, in literature. |
Literature—Women authors—History and criticism.
Classification: LCC PA3013 .W66 2025 (print) | LCC PA3013 (ebook) | DDC 809/.93357–dc23/
eng/20250202
LC record available at https://lccn.loc.gov/2024056288
LC ebook record available at https://lccn.loc.gov/2024056289

ISBN:	HB:	978-1-3504-4437-9
	PB:	978-1-3504-4436-2
	ePDF:	978-1-3504-4438-6
	eBook:	978-1-3504-4439-3

Typeset by RefineCatch Limited, Bungay, Suffolk

For product safety related questions contact productsafety@bloomsbury.com.

To find out more about our authors and books visit www.bloomsbury.com
and sign up for our newsletters.

CONTENTS

List of Illustrations   vii
Acknowledgements   viii
List of Contributors   ix

Introduction   1
Emily Hauser and Helena Taylor

ANCIENT AND EARLY MODERN

1 **Women Creating History**   13
Ian Plant

2 **Classical Credentials: Women's Intellectual and Sexual Licence in Sixteenth-Century France**   23
Emma Herdman

3 **Lucrezia Marinella and Ancient Rhetoric: A Woman's Approach to Eloquence, Persuasion and Metaphor in the Late Italian Renaissance**   39
Francesca D'Alessandro Behr

MODERN

4 **'All the Allurements of Beauty and Eloquence': Aspasia of Miletus and the Intellectual Woman in the Nineteenth Century**   55
Isobel Hurst

5 **A Night in Ancient Rome: Renée Vivien's Scholarly and Literary Re-Creation of the Cult of Bona Dea**   67
Jacqueline Fabre-Serris

6 **Sofiia Parnok's Sapphic Cycle *Roses of Pieria*: Translation and Commentary**   79
Georgina Barker

7 **'Rebels Against the Tyranny of Men': *The Birds*, *The Bees* and Agitation for Degrees at Girton College 1898–1948**   107
Mara Gold

8 **'Saved with Ablatives and Declensions in the Toilet Stall': Classical Learning and the Poetry of Maxine Kumin (1925–2014)**   125
Judith P. Hallett

Contents

9   'To Read, to See, to Spin, and to Turn': Reintroducing Barbara Köhler's Elektras
Lena Grimm   137

CONTEMPORARY

10   How to Be the Best: Madeline Miller's Patroclus
Jessica Lawrence   155

11   Voices of Recovery in Josephine Balmer's *The Paths of Survival*
Sheila Murnaghan   167

12   Wrongful Conviction: Odyssean Possibilities in Tayari Jones' *An American Marriage*
Justine McConnell   177

13   Animating Disability Arts and Ovidian Metamorphosis in Kinetic Light's *DESCENT*
Amanda Kubic   189

14   Passim Clouds: *Helen*, Marilyn and *Norma Jeane Baker of Troy*
Eugenia Nicolaci   209

15   Eating the Classics: Culinary Rewritings of Classical Myths in Poems by Lena Yau
Katie Brown   221

16   The Ovidian Influence on Zadie Smith
Tracey Walters   227

17   A Contemporary Medea: Alice Diop's *St Omer* (2022)
Fiona Cox   243

References   255
Index   277

ILLUSTRATIONS

7.1	Effigy of woman undergraduate, 21 May 1897 (UA Phot.174/4), Cambridge University Library	112
7.2	Printed version of the play text. GCRF 1/3/5, Girton College Archives	118
7.3	The original handwritten cast list. GCRF 1/3/5, Girton College Archives	119
7.4	Hand-illustrated programme for *The Bees*. GCRF 1/3/5, Girton College Archives	119
8.1	1942 *El Delator,* Cheltenham High School yearbook photo and personal description of Maxine Winokur, Alumni Association of Cheltenham High School, Wyncote, PA (USA)	129
11.1	Ashes of books in the Iraqi National Library, Baghdad, April, 2003, photo © R. Lemoyne	172
13.1	Rodin, *Toilette of Venus and Andromeda*, modelled after 1890, Musée Rodin cast 1987, Bronze, 20 × 14 ½ × 23 ½ in. (50.8 × 36.8 × 59.7 cm). North Carolina Museum of Art, Raleigh, Gift of the Iris and B. Gerald Cantor Foundation, 2009.1.14	195
13.2	Laurel Lawson and Alice Sheppard in Kinetic Light's performance of *DESCENT*. New Brunswick Performing Arts Center, New Brunswick, New Jersey. Presented by the Dance Department, Mason Gross School of the Arts, Rutgers University-New Brunswick, 2022. Photo by Jaqlin Medlock	198
13.3	Laurel Lawson in Kinetic Light's performance of *DESCENT*. New Brunswick Performing Arts Center, New Brunswick, New Jersey. Presented by the Dance Department, Mason Gross School of the Arts, Rutgers University-New Brunswick, 2022. Photo by Jaqlin Medlock	202
14.1	Marylin Monroe in *The Misfits*, 1960. Photo by Eve Arnold. Courtesy Magnum Photo	210

ACKNOWLEDGEMENTS

We are extremely grateful for the support of so many people whose enthusiasm and generosity made it possible to bring this and its companion volume together. We would like to thank the Leverhulme Trust and the Classical Association who helped to fund the initial conference, 'Women Writers and Classics', which took place in June 2021 online (during Covid), from which these volumes have grown. We would additionally like to thank the University of Exeter for further financial support, including the 'HASS Faculty Monograph Fund' and the Department of Languages, Cultures, and Visual Studies fund; thanks also to the Department of Classics, Ancient History, Theology and Religion. We were incredibly fortunate that the Classical Association agreed to run our creative writing competition for girls, women and non-binary people under nineteen: for their energy, creativity and enthusiasm, thank you to Katrina Kelly, the CA engagement officer (whose tireless work made it all possible), and Anastacia Holding, the EDI officer; thank you also to competition judges, Brenna Akerman, Emily Hauser, Rani Selvarajah and Holly Smith for so generously giving their time and expertise, to the schools and teachers who took part in the competition and particularly all the students for their wonderful, wildly imaginative entries. We want to express our sincere thanks to the Bloomsbury Classics team and in particular Lily Mac Mahon, Zoe Osman, and Alice Wright, without whom this book would not have got off the ground, and to our anonymous reviewers whose insights have improved what follows. Finally, we would like to thank our contributors for their engagement and creativity – it has been a pleasure, a privilege and an inspiration to work with you all.

EH & HT, 10/10/24

CONTRIBUTORS

Georgina Barker is a translator and researcher specializing in classical reception in Russia and lesbianism in antiquity. She formerly held a Leverhulme Early-Career Fellowship at UCL. She is the editor of the zine-anthology *LESBIANTIQUITY* (www.lesbiantiquity.lgbt) which collects and translates every extant text about women loving women in the Graeco-Roman world. She is the author of *SPQR in the USSR: Elena Shvarts's Classical Antiquity*, and the compiler and director of the verbatim play *Princess Dashkova, the Woman Who Shook the World*. She lives in Scotland with her wife and her parrot.

Francesca D'Alessandro Behr, a native of Italy, is Professor of Italian and Classical Studies at the University of Houston in Texas. Her interests cover ancient and Renaissance epic poetry, classical reception, love poetry, gender studies and translation studies. Her book on Lucan, *Feeling History: Lucan, Stoicism and the Aesthetics of Passion*, appeared in 2007 and another, focused on the classical reception (*Arms and the Woman: Classical Tradition and Women Writers in the Venetian Renaissance*), was published in 2018.

Katie Brown teaches Latin American Studies, Translation and Comparative Literature at the University of Exeter. She specializes in contemporary Venezuelan culture, with a particular focus on the circulation of people (travel, migration and exile) and of texts (publishing, cultural policy and translation). She is author of *Writing and the Revolution: Venezuelan Metafiction (2004–2012)* (2019) and translator of *From Savagery* by Alejandra Banca (2024).

Fiona Cox is Professor of French and Comparative Literature at the University of Exeter. She is the author of *Aeneas Takes the Metro: The Presence of Virgil in Twentieth-Century French Literature* (1999), *Sibylline Sisters: Virgil's Presence in Contemporary Women's Writing* (2011), *Ovid's Presence in Contemporary Women's Writing: Strange Monsters* (2018), and co-editor of *Homer's Daughters: Women's Responses to Homer in the Twentieth Century and Beyond* (2019) and *Ovid in French: Reception by Women from the Renaissance to the Present* (2023).

Jacqueline Fabre-Serris is Professor of Latin Literature at the University of Lille. She is the author of *Mythe et Poésie dans les* Métamorphoses *d'Ovide* (1995), *Mythologie et littérature à Rome* (1998), *Rome, l'Arcadie et la mer des Argonautes. Essai sur la naissance d'une mythologie des origines en Occident* (2008), and co-editor of *Women and War in Antiquity* (2015) and *Identities, Ethnicities and Gender in Antiquity* (2021). Her research interests focus on Augustan poetry, Seneca, mythology and mythography, and gender studies. She is co-director of the electronic reviews *Dictynna* and *Eugesta*, and of the series *Mythographes*.

Contributors

Mara Gold is nearing the completion of her PhD/DPhil in Classics at the University of Oxford, working on the thesis, 'Performing Sapphism: Classics, Community and Culture in British Women's Colleges 1890–1930'. As well as her undergraduate degree in Classics, she has an MA in Advanced Theatre Practice (Royal Central School of Speech and Drama), a Graduate Diploma in Archaeology (UCL) and an MSt. in Modern British and European History (Oxford). She is passionate about outreach and will be pursuing some non-academic writing and presenting projects on classical reception and sapphic history upon completion of her PhD. She is equally passionate about her work with museums in both research and outreach. She delivers freelance consultancy work with museums as well as workshops, training and talks. She worked as a researcher on the National Lottery Heritage-funded Beyond the Binary project at the Pitt Rivers Museum, where she undertook in-depth research into the museum's collections, creating ways to tell LGBTQIA stories and connecting people to the past by drawing parallels with contemporary activism. She has also written and performed for stage, screen and radio.

Lena Grimm is a graduate student at the University of Michigan, Ann Arbor. Her research focuses on the intersections of translation and reception studies in twentieth- and twenty-first-century German and English language literatures, with particular interests in experimentalism, visual art and literature, and the figure of the poet-translator. She is currently in the beginning stages of writing her dissertation.

Judith Peller Hallett is Professor of Classics and Distinguished Scholar-Teacher Emerita at the University of Maryland, College Park. She earned her BA in Latin from Wellesley College and PhD in Classical Philology from Harvard University. Co-founder of the international journal *Eugesta*, an online journal on gender studies in antiquity, she has published widely in the areas of Latin language and literature; women, the family, and sexuality in Greek and Roman antiquity; and the study and reception of classics in the Anglophone world. A former Blegen Visiting Scholar in the Department of Classics at Vassar College and Suzanne Deal Booth Resident Scholar at the Center for Intercollegiate Studies in Rome, she has held fellowships from the Mellon Foundation and the National Endowment for the Humanities. A 2013 collection of essays, *Domina Illustris: Latin Literature, Gender and Reception*, celebrates her academic career.

Emily Hauser is an award-winning ancient historian, author and Senior Lecturer in Classics and Ancient History at the University of Exeter. The author of acclaimed novels rewriting Greek myth, including *For the Most Beautiful*, as well as a number of academic works including *How Women Became Poets: A Gender History of Greek Literature*, her books have been published and translated across the world, listed among the '28 Best Books for Summer' in *The Telegraph* and shortlisted for the Seminary Co-Op's Best Books of 2023. She has appeared on several BBC Radio shows including BBC Radio 4 *Woman's Hour*, and has been featured in *The Guardian* alongside Colm Tóibín and Natalie Haynes. Her new book, *Mythica: A New History of Homer's World, through the Women Written Out of It*, is out in the UK and US in April 2025. Find out more at www.emilyhauser.com.

Contributors

Emma Herdman is Lecturer in French at the University of St Andrews. Her research focuses on sixteenth-century French literature and culture, with interests particularly in classical reception, women's writing and birds. Her recent publications include 'Women's Wit: Skirting Ovid in Renaissance France', in *Ovid in French: Reception by Women from the Renaissance to the Present* edited by Fiona Cox and Helena Taylor (2023); '"Les hommes ont toute l'autorité": Madeleine des Roches and the *Querelle* between Women and the Law', *Romanic Review* (2021); and 'Piercing Proverbial Crows' Eyes: Theft and Publication in Renaissance France', *Renaissance and Reformation* (2020).

Isobel Hurst is Lecturer in English and Deputy Director of the Centre for Comparative Literature in the Department of English and Creative Writing at Goldsmiths, University of London. Her research examines the reception of Greek and Latin literature in English, looking at the connection between classical education and authorship and women writers' creative engagement with the classical tradition. She is the author of *Victorian Women Writers and the Classics: The Feminine of Homer* and has published essays in the *Oxford Handbook of Victorian Poetry* and the *Oxford History of Classical Reception in English Literature*.

Amanda Kubic is a current PhD candidate in Comparative Literature at the University of Michigan, Ann Arbor. Her dissertation, 'Animating Antiquity: Classical (Dis)embodiments by Modern Women', explores the animation and reception of Graeco-Roman antiquity in modernist and postmodern works by women in poetry and dance, in English and modern Greek. Her article 'Modernist Epithalamia: Revival, Revision, and Subversion of Sappho in H.D.'s "Hymen"' has been published in *Modernism/modernity* and her chapter 'Cripping Venus: Intersections of Classics and Disability Studies in Contemporary Receptions of the Venus de Milo' is forthcoming in the volume *Reception Studies: New Challenges in a Changing World*.

Jessica Lawrence is a PhD student in Classics at Christ's College, University of Cambridge. Her research focus is on contemporary female authored receptions of classical literature, particularly Homer. Jessica returned to academia after a post-BA hiatus working in publishing, fine art and literary event management, among other careers. When Jessica is not working on her PhD, she can be found teaching Literary Yoga, a style she created, or reading myths to her baby daughter Persephone.

Justine McConnell is Reader in Comparative Literature and Classical Reception at King's College London. She is the author of *Black Odysseys: The Homeric Odyssey in the African Diaspora since 1939* (2013), *Performing Epic or Telling Tales* (co-authored with Fiona Macintosh, 2020) and *Derek Walcott and the Creation of a Classical Caribbean* (2023). She has also co-edited four volumes on the reception of Graeco-Roman antiquity.

Sheila Murnaghan is the Allen Memorial Professor of Greek at the University of Pennsylvania. Her research focuses on ancient Greek poetry, especially epic and tragedy; gender in classical culture; and classical reception in Britain and America since the

Contributors

nineteenth century. She is the author of *Disguise and Recognition in the Odyssey* (2nd edition 2011), the co-author (with Deborah H. Roberts) of *Childhood and the Classics: Britain and America 1850–1965* (2018), and the translator (for Norton Critical Editions) of Euripides' *Medea* and Sophocles' *Antigone*. Her current project is an edition with commentary of Sophocles' *Ajax*.

Eugenia Nicolaci is a PhD student in Classics at the University of Bristol (UK). Her doctoral thesis examines Anne Carson's translations from Graeco-Roman antiquity along with her use of environmental metaphors. Nicolaci is interested in world literature, translation studies, and comparative classics. Her most recent contribution 'Translating the canon, filling the absence' appeared in Laura Jansen (ed.) *Anne Carson / Antiquity* (2022).

Ian Plant is Associate Professor in Ancient History in the Department of History and Archaeology at Macquarie University, Sydney, Australia. His research is in Greek history and historiography. His publications that most closely relate to his chapter in this book include: 'Melōsa and her prize: the victory of a woman in Ancient Greece' (2022); 'Mary Hays's Classical Women and the Promotion of Female Agency' (2018); 'Women historians of ancient Greece and Rome' (2015); *Women Writers of Ancient Greece and Rome* (2004): https://researchers.mq.edu.au/en/persons/ian-plant

Helena Taylor is Associate Professor of French and Comparative Literature at the University of Exeter. She is the author of *Women Writing Antiquity: Gender and Learning in Early Modern France* (2024), joint runner-up in the Society for the Study of Early Modern Women and Gender book prize (2024), and *The Lives of Ovid in Seventeenth-Century French Culture* (2017), and co-editor, with Fiona Cox, of *Ovid in French: Reception by Women from the Renaissance to the Present* (2023) and, with Kate Tunstall, of a special issue of *Romanic Review* entitled *Women and Querelles in Early Modern France*.

Tracey Walters is Professor of Literature in the Department of Africana Studies at Stony Brook University, New York, where she also holds an affiliate appointment with the Department of English, and Women's and Gender Studies. She is an interdisciplinary, transcultural scholar of Africana Studies, and writes about the experiences of African diasporic women through the lens of feminist studies and cultural studies. She is a leading scholar of Black British literature and Classica Africana, a subfield of classical studies. Her articles can be found in numerous journals and anthologies. She has published two monographs: *African American Women and the Classicists Tradition: Black Women Writers from Wheatley to Morrison* (2007) and *Not Your Mother's Mammy: The Representation of the Domestic in Transatlantic Media* (2021), and a reader: *Today's Writers and Their Works: Zadie Smith* (2012). She also edited *Zadie Smith: Critical Essays* (2008) and was a guest editor for *Open Cultural Studies Journal*. She is co-host of the *Black Girls with Accents* podcast and a member of Alpha Kappa Alpha Inc.

INTRODUCTION
Emily Hauser and Helena Taylor

Women Creating and Re-Creating Classics: A manifesto

The last few years have seen the start of a seismic culture shift: women's retellings of classical myths and texts have generated an entire – and massively popular – sub-genre that has brought the spotlight onto women's recreations of Classics and has taken the world by storm. We do not say it is 'astonishing' or a 'trend', as critics and journalists alike have: it is only astonishing in that it has taken so long to become mainstream, and only a trend in that it is happening now.[1] As Emily Greenwood writes in her Epilogue to our companion volume, *Women Re-Creating Classics* (p. 292), this has in fact 'been a long, long, long time in the making', and is, we hope, the start of a turn that is set to become standard practice. If the generativity and global fandom it's given birth to is anything to go by: it is.

In the last few decades, women have laid claim to Classics, calling out a set of historical cultures that marginalized women, and challenging a discipline that has traditionally ignored women's experiences and sidelined women from the profession. This is nothing new – for as long as women have been writing for a reading public, they have been engaging with ancient Greek and Roman culture – but there has recently been a radical and rapid shift towards women creating, and re-creating, Classics – in unprecedented numbers, and with shattering impact. In the last few decades, there has been a major and unmissable surge in (largely, but not only) anglophone women writers, academics, translators, poets, film-makers and critics intervening in Classics in ways that have not just shaken up the field, but that have put women's creations of Classics centre-stage. Women – Emily Wilson (2017) and Caroline Alexander (2015) – have produced historic first-ever English translations of the traditionally male-preserved Homeric epics, the *Iliad* and *Odyssey*. Women have fuelled diverse, revisionist takes on the ancient world, with global record-breaking novels like Madeline Miller's multi-million-copy-selling, Orange-Prize-winning *The Song of Achilles* (2011), along with award-winning contributions from Bernadine Evaristo (2001), Lilliam Rivera (2020) and Han Kang ([2011] 2023; recipient of the Nobel Prize in Literature in 2024). Women – Tiffany Atkinson (2011) and Roz Kaveney (2018) – have successfully taken on, and taken apart, the hostile sexual aggression of Roman poets like Catullus. Women – above all, Mary Beard (2017), not only an eminent academic but a national voice – have led the charge to reassess the ways we read women's silencing, ancient and modern. And organizations like the Women's Classical Caucus have championed the representation of women and non-binary people online, with editathons under the banner of #WCCWiki dedicated to redressing the gender bias in biographies of classicists on Wikipedia. All this has garnered serious public interest, with a sweeping range of recognitions spanning from fiction bestseller lists to high-profile criticism to viral TikTok and Bookstagram sensations. The re-visioning of Classics by women – and what's at stake in that re-visioning – has entered firmly onto the public main stage.

To me (Emily), as both a novelist who is part of the shift – my first novel, *For the Most Beautiful*, a retelling of the *Iliad* and the Trojan War through the women in the Greek camp, was published in 2016 – and a critic who comments on it, what's particularly striking about this explosion of work isn't just that it's happening now (as we'll see below, there's a long history that complicates any narrative that this is 'just a moment' for women's revisionist mythmaking). Above all, it's how women's public-facing creativity, across a whole range of media, languages, formats, cultural contexts and perspectives, is constructing a powerful intervention in a traditionally elite, 'male, pale, stale' academic discipline. Behind the new translations, the bestselling novels, the poetry collections, the documentaries and plays, are urgent, driving questions: Who gets to write the story of the past? What happens (as Madeline Miller asks in her essay in the companion volume) when the bedrock, what we think the foundation is, gets shifted, when we tell tales that have held authority in different ways? How can creative reworkings open up new avenues into the archival silences of history that have marginalized the narratives of so many? What are the mechanisms behind women's silencing and how can we right those wrongs to tell women's stories, and look ahead to a future where all voices can be heard? The classical past is no longer the preserve of white men gripping onto the orthodoxy in academe: it is a vivid, dynamic, public phenomenon, re-imagined in stories, restructured in translations, revoiced on social media.

The interventions that creativity can make in recovering women's voices, and in challenging traditional academic modes, forms the first, central strand of these volumes: the power of creative acts in re-creating Classics, particularly when it comes to communicating values of diversity and inclusivity and recovering silenced voices. The capacity of creativity to challenge the authoritative narrative of the male classical canon, to re-imagine women's stories, and to re-voice women's silence, is a powerful tool that we need to recognize and think through – particularly in academic Classics, where creative acts are (still too often) looked down on as less rigorous, or (worst of all) unphilological (Hauser 2019). As Tom Geue, Daisy Dunn and I put forward in our roundtable in the companion volume to this one, creativity isn't only for novelists, poets and trade historians: it can also foster new ways of thinking and writing at the boundary between academia and practice. Creativity, in other words, isn't a parallel mode to critical thinking: it's a complementary tool in the methodological toolkit we bring to approaching the past, as well an invitation to shake up scholarship, to look, think and write in different ways – particularly when we're uncovering the lost voices and marginalised stories of the past.

At the same time, the current upswing of feminist revisionist mythmaking is just one part of a wider culture shift – both critical and creative – that dismantles mainstream androcentric, white, heteronormative, binary-gender, transphobic, ableist and/or colonial narratives through creative acts: from (to give only a couple of examples) Saidiya Hartman's call to 'critical fabulation' to grapple with 'the power and authority of the archive and the limits it sets on what can be known, whose perspective matters, and who is endowed with the gravity and authority of the historical actor' (2019), to non-binary poet and rapper Kae Tempest's all-female-cast reworking of Sophocles (2021), to disability arts ensemble Kinetic Light's *DESCENT* (2018), to Maya Deane's transgender Achilles in *Wrath Goddess Sing* (2022). We see the vitality and dynamism that we trace in the creative reworkings of Classics by women and those with gender non-conforming identities, explored in these volumes, as just the beginning of an exploration into a much bigger picture with which they intersect – one voice among many, that seeks to celebrate the vibrancy of creativity as a way to reclaim suppressed and marginalized identities, past and present.

Speaking of bigger pictures, this brings us to the second strand weaving through these volumes: how women have responded creatively to Classics across the centuries, and in different cultures and languages. And this is where I (Helena) come in. As often as the bylines of the latest feminist myth-revisionist novels and titles of book reviews like to claim that this is 'the first time' that women's voices have been reclaimed from antiquity, and the first time that women have rewritten their own stories, the fact is that women have been creating and recreating Classics for hundreds of years, across many different time periods, and multiple cultures – starting from within the ancient world. We see this as a crucial point – not to diminish the power and importance of the cultural shift that is happening now, but because it circles back to what we wrote at the opening: this isn't a moment: it's here to stay. Female authors have been reshaping the canonical myths about men and male-authored texts of the classical world since women started writing Greek (see Ian Plant in chapter 1 of this volume). Women from Renaissance Italy (Behr, chapter 3) and France (Herdman, chapter 2) to early twentieth-century Russia (Barker, chapter 6) created and re-created Classics through their own lenses and in their own creative ways, as a way to think through their identities and intellectual endeavours, to legitimize their intellectual practice by engaging with the prestige Graeco-Roman culture represented, and to intervene in some of the fiercest debates of the day over who had access to knowledge, and why a knowledge of the worlds of the Romans and Greeks mattered, if indeed it did at all. Meanwhile, the apparent explosion of anglophone women's re-creations of Classics in the last decade can be more accurately reframed as a gradual build-up of women's dominance in fictionalized Classics, from the early modern bestselling 'romances' of Madeleine de Scudéry, to the nineteenth-century historical fictions of Lydia Child and throughout the twentieth century: from hugely successful fiction writers like Mary Renault, Laura Riding, Rosemary Sutcliff, Colleen McCullough, Lindsey Davis and Toni Morrison (Hoberman 1997) – building on and interacting with the work of pioneering poets and critics like Alicia Ostriker and Adrienne Rich, whose essay 'When We Dead Awaken: Writing as Re-Vision' (1972) is a half-a-century-old manifesto for taking a feminist point of view on old texts. While reworking Classics as a woman might seem a hot topic now, prolific women writers from across history and across linguistic and cultural contexts like Christine de Pizan, Beatriz Galindo ('La Latina'), Sofiia Parnok, Virginia Woolf and Fran Ross (to name only a few), would beg to differ.

These volumes are therefore intended both as a celebration and an investigation of the ways in which creative acts by women are re-creating Classics now – at the same time as they contextualize women's creativity in relation to the classical world across the centuries, across different languages, different cultures, different identities. The two volumes fall broadly along the lines of these two strands. This volume centres around the latter, investigating a range of women and gender non-conforming creatives' reworkings of Classics across the centuries and in different cultures and languages, as well as how these responses might resist or unpack the tensions inherent in notions of gender, race, canonicity and cultural heritage. The companion volume, meanwhile, embraces the former, exploring contemporary creativity and its intervention in re-creating Classics, asking us to consider what creativity can do to foster new ways of thinking and writing about Classics at the boundary between the creative and the critical – as well as, in the final section, building on this work to address wider questions of inclusivity, access and pedagogy through creativity in the discipline of Classics. And yet, we see the two strands intertwining with, and informing, each other throughout in ways that make this a continual and extended dialogue. Thus, while this first volume foregrounds the mode of scholarship as an access point to analysing creative responses past and present, original translations nestle alongside academic commentaries written with artistry and flair, reflecting on and celebrating the creativity of the scholar in their own right. And while the companion volume offers original creative pieces from some of the most exciting voices working to re-create Classics now, these are interwoven – and are often in direct dialogue – with critical reflections and contributions that break down non-traditional formats: interviews, creative-critical medleys, personal essays. Far from being a surrender to eclecticism, we believe that this range and diversity of offerings demonstrates – in actual practice, rather than theory – what creative approaches to Classics can do to broaden thinking, enliven criticism, and privilege inclusivity. We are not aiming for comprehensiveness (indeed, the idea of a comprehensive or canonical 'classical' is one part of what we are aiming to dismantle), but are rather guided by the lodestones of exploration and conversation. Our aim is to begin, rather than to complete, the discussion around how creativity can be part of a larger dialogue shaping and pushing back against the hegemonic thrust of Classics, and to open gaps for new thoughts, new voices, and – above all – new and diverse narratives.

Creating *Women (Re-)Creating Classics*

'Classics' as a discipline, and as cultural and economic capital, has represented – and continues to represent – a fraught site of both exclusion and legitimation for those outside its elite walls; but those struggling to get in have also torn down the edifices and challenged its exclusions. Battles over who gets to do reception and how, over its politics and ideologies, its relationship to taste and literary value, and its purchase on authorial strategy and professional success, have a long history, longer even than the discipline itself.[2]

With this study, we aim to be critical of the structures of Classics and classical reception that create or promote exclusion as we focus on diverse forms of creativity by a range of practitioners and writers, past and present. We want to challenge some of the historically 'masculinist' hierarchies value that can structure reception studies – between faithful and adaptive translations; between Latin-literate writers and non-philologists; between translation and historical fiction; between elite members of institutions and those denied access, acknowledging also that some barriers are more violent, more oppressive than others. Where a philologist like the French Anne Dacier (1647–1720), celebrated Hellenist of her age and first translator of Homer's *Iliad* and *Odyssey* into French, might be relatively well known in the history of classical reception (though not as well known, we would wager, as Alexander Pope who based much of his English translation of the *Iliad* on her French version and *its* translations), marginalized scholars – such as the nineteenth-century African-American classicist, Frazelia Campbell, or novelists such as the nineteenth-century American Lydia Child – are not.

By calling these hierarchies into question, we hope to add to work that is trying to open up classical reception studies and to think critically about how 'Classics has been a standard bearer for elitism and a source of authorization for what the Association of Critical Heritage Studies calls "Western narratives of nation, class and science"' (Hanink 2017). Meanwhile, in celebrating the diverse forms of reception by a range of creatives explored here, we are wary of what Holly Ranger describes as the white feminism that has sometimes been implicit in equating re-writing Classics with empowerment, if it means an uncritical acceptance of the ways in which Classics has been used to oppress (2023: 215–16). We suggest that it will do Classics good, that it will empower the discipline, to be vitalized by a diverse set of voices – to be renewed by creativity, reinvention and inclusion. As Aimee Suzara puts it in her intervention in the second volume of this study, 'I knew one thing: I didn't just want to keep telling the same story. I wanted to tell something that both honored the spirit of the original Lesbian Sappho and invoked a Sappho whom we could look up to: a queer feminist BIPOC icon' (p. 89).

We take gender to be one category of analysis among many others, such as race, ethnicity, sexuality, class, as intersectional feminism teaches us. Not all women wrote from a position of marginalization – Anne Dacier is a case in point, educated and enabled as she was by one of the most prominent Classicists, and teachers, in France (her father) – and not all forms of marginalization are the same. Our understanding of woman is an inclusive one – that is, it includes anyone who identifies as a woman. And although most of the creatives in these volumes identify as women, have gender non-conforming identities: we do not intend to flatten those complexities, nor to reinstate a gender binary or claim anything essential about classical reception by women – nor do we claim that women have all historically written for a collective identity, or a feminist one. What is revealed by looking at reception by women over a long period of time, in fact, is precisely the difficulty of constructing anything like a tradition of women's reception: women did/ do not write from the same positions; they are not necessarily always trailblazers or pioneers, and not necessarily always critical of systems of exclusion.[3] Rather, we want to shine a light on histories of reception that are less well known and to spotlight a range of contemporary voices.

We therefore make every effort to be inclusive and showcase the energy, dynamism, and diversity of voices with work that also directly addresses intersections between

Classics and racism and histories of oppression; sexual or gendered violence in Graeco-Roman texts and culture; and the white and Anglo- and Euro-centric nature of the discipline of Classics and classical reception studies. The challenge is considerable. We also want to take steps to divest Classics of its association with elitism: this is an association driven, in the UK at least, by the fact that subjects that come under the umbrella of Classics (ancient Greek, Latin, ancient history, classical civilization) are rarely taught in state-funded comprehensive schools but reserved for the private sector; as a recent damning report from the Classical Association shows, barriers of class intersect with other 'axes of exclusion, such as gender identity, sexual orientation, race/ethnicity, and disability' (Canevaro et al. 2024: 74). Our school-age competition aimed at school-age girls, women and non-binary young people – the winner of which is published here (Kremenstein, in our second volume) – intended to address in a small way this 'pipeline issue' for the next generation and open up routes towards a more diverse Classics, attracted nearly 350 entries from a wide range of school backgrounds thanks to the energy and attention of the EDI and engagement officers of the Classical Association (runners-up and shortlisted entries can be found on their website, https://classicalassociation.org/competition/). But this is a work in progress: more can and should be done.

The range of chapters across both volumes hopes to speak to this dynamism, creative energy and diversity of receptions of Graeco-Roman culture, both of the present time and historically. It also adds to the variety of approaches being taken in reception studies, from disability studies to sociological methods (Silverblank and Ward 2020); and we benefit from the scholarship that has tackled questions of classical reception and women from a range of angles – whether philological and scholarly (Stevenson 2008; Wyles and Hall 2016), in relation to institutions (Prins 2017), race (Walters 2007; Moyer, Lecznar and Morse 2020), twentieth- and twenty-first-century feminism (Cox 2011, 2018; Cox and Theodorakopoulos 2019) and creativity (Cox and Theodorakopoulos 2013), to name but a few. We also benefit from the work that has treated the oppressive and violent deployment of classical reception (for example Zuckerberg 2019) and several of the chapters across both volumes tackle the different forms of violence and aggression present in ancient texts.

As we have already noted, ours is not an exhaustive, comprehensive or representative selection, but rather an exploration. As editors we were committed to following contributors' expertise in terms of the writers they chose to foreground, reluctant to create or impose an alternative canon with what's on offer here. We have primarily focused on literary re/creations, but are aware that this occludes art, multimedia, film, videogaming culture: doing so is not intended to ascribe value to the literary over other forms of culture, but rather to respond laterally and creatively to the current cultural – and market – phenomenon of historical fiction by women.[4] There are so many authors and works not covered here – from Virginia Woolf to Toni Morrison; Pat Barker to Costanza Casati; Anne Dacier to Emily Wilson; Han Kang to Rita Dove; Margaret Atwood to Sarvat Hasin; Kamila Shamsie to Ali Smith; from MarleneNourbeSe Philip to Sarah Kane; Stephanie Burt to Marie Darrieussecq; Saviana Stănescu to A. E. Stallings, and many others, and despite our attempts to move beyond Anglo- and Euro-centrism, with translations from Russian, Venezuelan Spanish, and German, most of the chapters either study, or themselves constitute, works written in English. This is, we hope, a contribution towards seeking out greater diversity and more inclusivity in creating and re-creating Classics.

We hope to add to the scholarship that has so deftly looked at a range of voices in classical reception with our emphasis on creativity and our attempts to break down the barriers between scholarship, public writing and creative writing, and that has interrogated the values, practices, identities and histories we ascribe to classical reception.[5] The volumes endeavour to be an example of what James Porter (2008) calls 'live reception': situating Classics between scholarship and creativity, the academy and the public, while also – we hope – challenging those binaries.

A guide to this volume

For hundreds of years, if not thousands, Classics has been confined to the ivory tower, studied by men and men alone in pursuit of an understanding of the 'great men' of history. As late as 1925, Virginia Woolf could complain about being denied access to classical learning and 'not knowing Greek'. This volume unpacks creative responses to ancient Greek and Roman culture across time, following creatives who have reworked the classical past in their own voices as a way into thinking about issues of access, identity, and the classical literary canon. The majority of this volume attends to contemporary writing and creative arts across a range of genres – and so speaks to the contemporary momentum of women revoicing Classics as demonstrated in the companion volume, *Women Re-Creating Classics* – but the historical narrative of its opening chapters gives us an, albeit partial, indication of the long history of this phenomenon. The chronology represented here is not intended to form any sort of teleological or linear reading, but rather to demonstrate the extent of women's receptions of Graeco-Roman culture, all the while acknowledging how progressive shifts in scholarship, particularly feminist scholarship, have made this work more visible. This volume takes us to France, Italy, Venezuela, Senegal, Germany, Russia, the USA and the UK, via fiction, film, theatre and translation: this is not an exhaustive or even representative account, but it does, we hope, model the interplay between criticism, scholarship, translation and creativity that underpins the interrelation of the two volumes.

This volume opens with Ian Plant's analysis of the classical reception by ancient women: he argues that although the first recognized historian in the west is Anna Comnena in the eleventh century CE, ancient women writers (e.g. Sappho, Corinna, Aristodama, Myrtis) actively engaged with accounts of the past much earlier to provide their voice on history. We then jump forward to Renaissance France as Emma Herdman examines how three sixteenth-century women poets (Marguerite de Navarre, Louise Labé and Madeleine de l'Aubespine) negotiated the impropriety of scholarship for women by drawing on classical female figures (Diana, Semiramis and Messalina) in their

7

work. Turning to Renaissance Italy, Francesca D'Alessandro Behr analyses Lucrezia Marinella (1571–1653), well-known as the author of a proto-feminist treatise, but less known for her hagiography, and shows how she turned to classical, not religious, authorities to develop her rhetorical style in the preface to her *Life of the Virgin Mary, Empress of the Universe* (1602).

Four chapters then look at the nineteenth and early twentieth centuries: Isobel Hurst considers the tensions between writing and propriety in the historical fiction of two novelists, the American Lydia Maria Child (1802–80) and the British Eliza Lynn Linton (1822–98), and their ambivalent reception of Aspasia, a figure too far outside restrictive norms of Victorian feminine behaviour to be embraced wholly by these authors. Jacqueline Fabre-Serris explores the interactions between creativity and scholarship as she demonstrates how French poet Renée Vivien (1877–1909) recreated the Roman cult of the Bona Dea to attune with her own feminism and mysticism. Switching to translation from Russian, Georgina Barker gives us the first translation into English of Sofiia Parnok's (1885–1933) cycle of Sappho-inspired poetry: 'Roses of Pieria' (1922). In her accompanying commentary, Barker explores Parnok's relationships with Sappho, her lover Marina Tsvetaeva, Russian classical scholarship and classical and pseudo-classical influences (Sappho, Asclepiades, Ovid, Pierre Louÿs). Mara Gold then examines the archives of women's colleges, particularly Girton College in Cambridge, to show how little-known performances and adaptations of Greek comedies, notably the 1904 Girton production of *The Bees*, an adaptation of Aristophanes' *The Birds,* constituted important instances of political activism for women's education, where scholarship has tended to focus primarily on later suffrage comedies as early examples of political use of Greek comedy by women.

Poetry from the later part of the twentieth century is the subject of the next two chapters: Judith Hallett brings to light the classical allusions in the poetry of the American Jewish feminist poet and Pulitzer Prizewinner Maxine Winokur Kumin, interweaving explorations of the richnesses of Kumin's classical engagement in her poetry with reflections on her high-school Latin education. Lena Grimm breathes new life into Barbara Köhler's early work, 'Elektra. Mirrorings' (1991), with her translation from its original German. In her accompanying essay, Grimm explores how Köhler's poem offers Elektra a life beyond Orestes, unlike the Greek tragic sources, asking both through her analysis of Köhler's language and her reflections on her translation 'What language, then, is there for Elektra? How can it be brought outside of the space of tragedy, and how might it be translated?' (p. 140).

The second half of this volume turns to a wide range of contemporary art forms: novels, poetry, dance, music theatre, theatre, film scripts and translation. Jessica Lawrence demonstrates how Madeline Miller's reworking of Patroclus in her Orange Prize-winning historical novel *The Song of Achilles* (2011) recentres the moral values of the *Iliad*, and specifically asks what it is that makes a man the best of the Achaeans, through close engagement with the Greek text. Sheila Murnaghan reads Josephine Balmer's *The Paths of Survival* (2017), a poem sequence evoking the ways Aeschylus' *Myrmidons* was transmitted to the present day, in light of a tradition of feminist revisions. Although the

Myrmidons, a male-authored work of classical literature containing only male characters, might appear to have little in common with classical revision as a form of survival as championed by Adrienne Rich, Murnaghan explores the ways in which Balmer interjects a feminist revision through her creative translations. Turning to Tayari Jones' Women's Prize-winning *An American Marriage* (2018), Justine McConnell also uses Rich as a lens to explore how this text is a feminist 're-visioning' of the *Odyssey* in which the 'reverse simile' that gives us a glimpse into Penelope's perspective and an imagined gender equality in Book 23 is expanded to throw off restrictive gender roles. Setting this story in the context of the mass incarceration of Black men in contemporary America means that, as McConnell argues, Jones uses the Homeric myths to comprehend and confront difficult social and political realities. Moving from narrative to theatre and from Homer to Ovid, Amanda Kubic looks at how *DESCENT*, by the disability arts ensemble Kinetic Light, interrogates the presence of white supremacy, ableism and heterosexism in Graeco-Roman mythology and its reception through a layered engagement with Ovid's Andromeda from his *Metamorphoses* and Auguste Rodin's bronze sculpture the *Toilette of Venus and Andromeda* (1886). By re-imagining of Venus and Andromeda as visibly disabled queer lovers, by 'visually restor[ing] the racial heritage' of Andromeda, the Aethiopian princess, and with an innovative set design and light show, Kinetic Light 'turns to Ovid to transform Ovid', and 'challenges notions of an idealized, normative and bounded classical body and opens up new possibilities for dance choreography and access' (p. 190). The able body, particularly in the notion of beauty, is the subject of the next chapter as Eugenia Nicolaci turns to Anne Carson's *Norma Jeane Baker of Troy*, a version of Euripides' Helen, a partly spoken, partly sung performance for stage. By examining Carson's reference to the alternative story of Helen in Egypt as told in Euripides' tragedy *Helen,* Nicolaci shows how Carson parallels Helen and Marilyn Monroe to interrogate ancient and modern myths of female beauty and its destructive power.

Taking us to South America, Katie Brown provides an original translation from Spanish of previously untranslated poetry by Lena Yau, one of Venezuela's foremost contemporary writers, now living in Madrid as one of some eight million Venezuelans who have left the country during the 'Bolivarian Revolution'. Brown shows how Yau engages with the traditions of food cultures and hospitality in ancient Greek and Roman poetry as a way of exploring her own experiences of multiculturalism, diasporic identity and memory. In the next chapter, Tracey Walters considers the nods to Ovid in Zadie Smith's work, notably through her reworking of Chaucer, himself highly influenced by Ovid, in her 2021 play *The Wife of Willesden*. Walters shows how, writing within a tradition of Black classicism, Smith brings a contemporized perspective to Graeco-Roman myth and reworks her sources to problematize their sexual violence, blending British myth with Jamaican and Greek mythology and examining Britain's postcolonial present. Turning to film and to screen-play, Fiona Cox looks at the recent French film, *St Omer* (2022), based on true events, directed by Alice Diop and with a screenplay co-written by Diop, Amrita David, Zoé Galeron and the award-winning novelist Marie Ndiaye, which follows the writer Rama as she attends the trial of a Senegalese woman accused of killing her daughter, and as she plans to retell this story as a version of Medea. Cox examines how the Medea myth is used throughout this film – and in the real-life responses to the trial it documents – to explore how Diop fashions a twenty-first-century Medea, whose story might help us to understand the rage and the pain of an isolated immigrant.

Notes

1. The first quote is from Goff (2022) (as is 'laying claim to the discipline' below); see her nn. 1–3 for discussion of the profession of Classics. The second ('trend') is from Knowles (2024).
2. For one example, see the late seventeenth-century Quarrel of the Ancients and Moderns in France: see DeJean (1997) and Taylor (2024).
3. As is evident in any attempt to argue for a 'women's tradition' in ancient Greece: see Hauser (2023: 281–5).
4. For intersections between antiquity and contemporary art, see Holmes and Marta (2017).
5. Such as Walters (2007); Cox and Theodorakopoulos (2013); Hall and Wyles (2016); Fradinger (2023); Taylor and Cox (2023).

ANCIENT AND EARLY MODERN

CHAPTER 1
WOMEN CREATING HISTORY
Ian Plant

History and the writing of history have traditionally been considered the sole domain of men. The conventional view is that there was no significant engagement with history-writing by a Greek woman before Anna Comnena, the eleventh-century Byzantine princess. Where a work of prose history by a woman was known in antiquity, her authorship was dismissed as spurious: the historical anecdotes by Nicobule were assigned to a man (Athen. 10.434c); Pamphile's historical commentaries were said to have been written by her father or husband (Plant 2004: 67, 127–9).[1] However, examination of other work by women in antiquity reveals that women actively engaged with accounts of the past well before Anna Comnena, responding creatively to *Classics* in the form of traditional tales and offering individual retellings in their own voices. This chapter will review the work of creative writers such as Sappho, Corinna, Myrtis and Aristodama, asking how their receptions of the past negotiate the boundary between history and fiction, and provide a woman's voice on the past.

Sappho

Sappho, perhaps the most famous Greek lyric poet, was born on the island of Lesbos around 630 BCE. She has rightfully been remembered as a creative genius, a poet whose melodies were sublime, her lyrics musical and smooth.[2] We now only possess one complete poem from the nine books of her work that were available in Alexandrian times and none of her music.[3] Yet from the numerous quotations of her work that were made in antiquity and various scraps of papyrus that have been found with precious fragments of her songs, we can see that as well as saying something about her own life and about those close to her,[4] she also addressed stories from Greek myths and epic poetry. These included myths of Leda, Leto and Niobe, Adonis, Hermes, Artemis, Hector and Andromache's wedding, Helen and her daughter, and the sons of Atreus.[5] Traditional tales such as these supplied the Greeks with their early history, accounts of the founding of their cities, tales of their heroes and stories about their gods. Homer's epics and the Trojan Epic Cycle in particular, but also other national and local myths, were treated as sources for the early history of Greece that even rationalizing historians such as Herodotus and Thucydides drew upon.[6] While they recognized poetic exaggeration and largely removed the direct intervention of gods from their retelling of early Greek history, both nevertheless repeat mythical traditions as history.[7] Both of these long-acknowledged historians blur the lines between myth and history, accepting epic poetry as a source for their accounts of the past.

Sappho engages with the mythological past in a number of her poems too, articulating what she does with the first attested use of the word *mythologēsai* (telling mythological tales: F. 18.2).[8] This word is found incomplete in a papyrus fragment; it is possible that we should instead restore the text with the similar word *mythologeusai*, the verb Odysseus uses in Homer to describe his own account of his (mythological) adventures (*Od.* 12.450, 453).[9] In the same passage Sappho uses the word *ennepēn* (to tell; F. 18.1), a word Homer often uses too. Significantly, it is the verb he uses in the opening line of the *Odyssey* to call upon the Muse to tell him the tale of Odysseus (*Od.* 1.1). Whichever reading we adopt for *mythologēsai/mythologeusai*, we find Sappho here consciously pointing to the mythological story-telling traditions in epic that she addresses in her songs.

Taking F. 17 as an example, we can see how Sappho adapts the mythical past to suit the local – and present – context. This lyric poem recounts the visit of the sons of Atreus (that is, Agamemnon and Menelaus) to Messon on Lesbos where they sacrificed to Hera, Zeus and Dionysus. The story of this visit provides a charter for a festival that was celebrated there by the women of Lesbos, including Sappho herself. Significantly, her retelling of part of this epic differs in detail from what is found in the *Odyssey* about the return of these heroes (*Od.* 3.141–83, 278–85, 4.512–23). Sappho brings those heroes, as well as the gods they call upon, to Messon, her local sacred site.

What remains of this poem is not complete, but what we do have demonstrates that the song provided a foundation myth for the festival of Hera and was probably composed to be sung during the celebrations themselves (Obbink 2016: 19–21; Nagy 2007: 125–32). It was believed, no doubt from the evidence of her poems, that Sappho participated in local festivals, leading the singing herself, as attested in a short poem in the *Palatine Anthology* (*AP* 9.189). Many of Sappho's songs were written for choral performance and we also know from Sappho's contemporary Alcaeus that women sang in Hera's precinct at Messon (Alcaeus F. 130B.17–20). Sappho's version of her local history, the narrative she presents in songs such as F. 17, was therefore embraced in particular by the young women of her choirs who learnt her words and music, and then performed in this public space.[10]

Sappho reframes the journey of the sons of Atreus, heroes otherwise celebrated elsewhere in epic, to bring them to her community. She takes an episode from the story of the return of the heroes from the Trojan War, understood by the Greeks as their shared past, and retells events to engage with and so recreate in performance her local history. In so doing she shapes the past to validate current cultural practices. Sappho regularly attributes her inspiration to the Muses (e.g. F. 124, 127, 128), yet we see in her retelling of traditional stories like this one her interplay of local occasion and aetiology. The poet brings the traditional epic heroes and the gods into her community and into the celebration of her local religious festival through the voices of her choir. Sappho the poet is also Sappho the historian.

Corinna

Corinna wrote songs for choirs of girls to sing at festivals too (Skinner 1983).[11] She, like Sappho, invokes a Muse as authority for the tales she told.

Terpsichore calls me
to sing lovely tales
to white-dressed girls of Tanagra,
and the city is filled with joy
at my gossipy-clear voice.
For whatever great [deeds were done]
[still greater] lies [decorate]
the wide-dancing earth;
and stories from our fathers' time
I adorn with my own words
for our own girls and begin.

Corinna 655 1–11[12]

Corinna's words in this fragment may be taken as programmatic (West 1970: 280). She tells us that she intends to adorn traditional legends, ones that are inspired by the Muse Terpsichore ('Enjoying choral dance'), for the local community, in particular for the girls who sing her songs and dance to her music (Collins 2006: 22). Her vocabulary is unusual. The term she uses for the subject matter for her songs, *weroia* ('tales'), is found only here and as a title for her work.[13] Its meaning has been much discussed, with the conclusion that it denotes traditional tales (Heath 2017: 100–2). In addition, Corinna coins a new compound word for her poetic voice, *ligourokōtilus* (gossipy-clear), the word connoting both chattering and the idea of clarity.[14] This new adjective says there is something different about her poetic voice. This word emphasizes the presentation of a female version of a myth, alluding to an oral tradition of women's storytelling in song, one that has been largely neglected in the historical record (Heath 2017: 108–14).

One major fragment of Corinna's work (654a.i) recounts a story of a musical contest between Helicon and Cithaeron. These two mountains were important in Greek myth, with Helicon a traditional home for the Muses (Hesiod, *Theogony* 1–8). Cithaeron features in several mythic stories (Acteon, Pentheus and the Bacchae, Oedipus, rites of Dionysus and the Daedala festival of Hera), although the mountain is not otherwise noted for its musical ability. The fragment that we have includes a description of the judging process in which the gods cast a secret ballot (19–28). There were many musical competitions in the Greek world in Corinna's day that may have provided the model for this. Such competitions were held at religious festivals (Plut. *Mor.* 674d–5d) and provide the most likely occasions for the performance by local girls of Corinna's choral songs.[15]

Yet, Corinna is not merely composing, she is also engaging with older traditions, interrogating and altering them, and making them real for her own community. The innovations she brings to the traditions, as can be seen in her versions of the myths, reinforce the idea that she specifically tailored them for her fellow Boeotians (McPhee 2018: 199). In the Asopus poem (654a.ii 12–40), for example, Corinna lists nine daughters of Asopus, eponymous heroines who became mothers of heroic lines. Corinna's innovations in her telling of this myth include the elimination of conflict between Zeus and Asopus over the seizure of his daughters, the resolution of the seizure of the women by marriage to gods (facilitated by Eros and Aphrodite), and the prophecy that the women will bear a race of demi-gods. The importance of the women in these heroic lines is a point of difference with the traditional patrilineal genealogies offered in Homer (as Larson 2002: 50). Corinna also adds Thespia, Tanagra and Plataea to other versions of the Asopids, integrating the ancestry of other important Boeotian city-states to the places important to her, as well as to the local choirs who sang her song and danced to it.[16]

In addition to innovating in her retelling of local myths, Corinna also engages with 'the Classics' through criticism of earlier poets.[17] Her reproach of the earlier Boeotian poet Myrtis for 'entering into competition with Pindar, even though she is a woman', comes in a fragment quoted by Apollonius Dyscolus (664a). In a grammatical treatise on pronouns Apollonius uses the extract from Corinna as an example of the word 'I' in the Boeotian dialect. We lack the context to understand what Corinna meant here by *eris* ('competition'). She could mean that Pindar and Myrtis took part in an actual musical competition against each other, but this is unlikely. She may be speaking more generally of rivalry or even metaphorically of literary differences between their works.[18] That Corinna's songs were performed by choirs of young women from Tanagra further complicates our understanding of the expression of these sentiments: the first person 'I' would have been voiced by the women in the choir.[19] Hauser (2023: 267–70) suggests that the criticism is meant to be taken ironically: far from actually attacking Myrtis, Corinna is articulating and dismissing a common criticism made by men of women writers. In addition, the quality of her own work demonstrates the irony of the gendered criticism (see Hauser 2023: 269). That the sentiments were mouthed by female performers, the women in the choir, strengthens this irony. It is significant that Corinna marks out a space for herself within the body of Boeotian poetry, while also referencing another female poet within this cohort. Corinna links both herself and Myrtis to the classics of Boeotian literary history, in the persona of Pindar.

Such explicit reference to the works of Myrtis and Pindar is no doubt what led readers in antiquity to link her personally to these other Boeotian poets. In doing so they were following the common trait in Ancient Greek biography of one poet being taken as the pupil of another who wrote in a similar genre. Hence both Corinna and Pindar were considered the pupils of Myrtis.[20]

Corinna's engagement with Pindar's work is well attested, with *Suda*, Plutarch, Aelian and Pausanias all reporting that she won victories over Pindar; we are even told that she advised him as a young up-and-coming poet on how to improve his work (T. 1–4). While not referring to a literal competition, her criticism of Pindar, which readers must have drawn from her poetry, can instead be read as a literary response to work by the most famous local poet from two centuries before her time. Indeed, Clayman (1993) has seen in her poem about the clash of two mountains (654a.i) an allegory for different approaches to poetry, in which her poetry comes out as victorious. Her engagement with the work of both Pindar and Myrtis shows that she wanted to frame her poetry within the domain of her creative forebears. Corinna situates her work within the genre of mythological history, for which she makes programmatic statements (655.6–10, 664b), and in creating her individual version she finds a way to be critical of her 'rivals' too (Larmour 2005: 44–8; Collins 2006: 21).

Corinna composed narrative poems, songs about local heroes and heroines (664b). She wrote in a Boeotian dialect, albeit a literary one rather than her own vernacular. Her work was particularly noted for her choice of her own dialect: Pausanias considered that her victories over Pindar at Thebes could be in part attributed to her not using the Doric literary dialect he adopted (Paus. 9.22.3). Indeed, a scholiast on Aristophanes' *Acharnians* records her criticism of Pindar for using an Attic word (688). In addition to the use of dialect to characterize her work as local, there is a preponderance of Boeotian topographic references with very few references to the world outside Boeotia (Berman 2010: 44–7). Corinna focuses on the locale in which she and her performers were situated and makes it the heart of their mythological world. She provides historical and religious framework for that world.

Plutarch tells us that Corinna characterizes myths as being the essence of the art of poetry (*Mor.* 347f–8a). She remakes traditional myths to focus them on local places, giving prominence to heroes who had local importance in a process of mythological innovation (McPhee 2018). By composing local versions of the myth for the young women of Tanagra to sing, she includes them in the creative process. They were the ones who performed her version of Boeotian mythical history to their community, both singing her narratives in their own dialect and dancing to them. So, at least in part, they learnt their local history through the songs of Corinna. In their performance of these songs, they contributed to the recreation of the more immediate and distant history of their community too.

Myrtis

The Boeotian poet Myrtis was remembered (whether truthfully or not) as the teacher of both Pindar and Corinna (*Suda* Pindaros Π 1617, Corinna K 2087), as well as a poet criticized by Corinna (as mentioned above). Corinna's engagement with Myrtis' work, in addition to the fact that all three poets came from the same part of Greece, will certainly have contributed to them being linked in the historical record.

Corinna describes Myrtis as *ligoura* (clear) (664a), one of the elements of the compound word *ligourokōtilus* Corinna uses to characterize her own work. *Ligoura* is a positive adjective to use of a poet: it recalls the alluring song of the Sirens (Hom. *Od.* 12.44, 183) and Hesiod uses it to describe his own song (Hes. *Op.* 660). While we know very little about Myrtis, Plutarch (who was also a Boeotian, though much later) knew her work well enough to tell us that she was lyric poet from Anthedon and to summarize one of her poems.

According to Plutarch, Myrtis retold an aetiological myth about a site at Tanagra sacred to the hero Eunostus (Plut. *Mor.* 300d–f =716 *PMG*). While he tells us that she was poet, he also describes her retelling of the myth using the verb *historeō*. This verb encompasses the ideas of both inquiring about and recording what one has discovered, and Plutarch uses it frequently when he cites other historians (e.g. Plut. *Thes.* 14.3, 19.4, 23.5; cf. *Thes.* 30). So, while Plutarch acknowledges that Myrtis was a poet, the Greek word 'poet' itself implying creation, his use of similar language to describe male historians indicates that she too was considered an historical authority.

Plutarch paraphrases Myrtis' work to explain a cultural custom observed at Tanagra, where women were barred from the sacred grove of the hero Eunostus. He takes a song by Myrtis as an historical record of the events that led to this prohibition. Here, Myrtis' treatment of the past in song, a creative mode of literature, stands as an authority for local history. Plutarch places her interpretation of the cultural custom alongside information he draws upon from the historian Diocles, who recorded a Tanagran decree about the shrine of Eunostus in his work *Shrines of Heroes* (*Mor.* 300f–301a). Historian and poet are both observed in the act of inquiring and recording.

While we do not have Myrtis' original song, her religious subject matter, focus on a local hero cult and the particular significance of this myth for females, are strong indications that she composed her work for girls to sing at a local festival. This choral genre and her Tanagran interests further align her with Corinna. Choral songs such as these testify to the active role that women took in the religious history of their city-state. Women held leading roles in religion, which was itself of paramount importance in the Greek world. Through the work of poets like Sappho, Corinna and Myrtis we see examples of the sort of songs that women would perform with dance and music on public occasions, where creative expression took on multiple modes within the festivals that honoured their gods.

Aristodama

A woman who may well have been a contemporary of Corinna, Aristodama of Smyrna was honoured as an epic poet by both the city of Lamia in Malis and Chaleion in Western Locris.[21] She visited Lamia in the year 218/217 BCE where she performed original compositions in which she remembered their ancestors and lauded the Aetolian race. In Chaleion she presented something similar, while nevertheless making her epic specific for her audience there too.

We do not know if any of her work was written down. If it was, none of it remains. Instead it is through two inscriptions, which detail the awarding of honours to her for her compositions, that we gain some information about her epics (Siekierka, Stebnicka and Wolicki 2021: 28–9, 379–82). Both cities were part of the Aetolian League at the time, and so her treatment of Aetolian ancestors would have served both audiences well. In addressing local traditional history, as epics were seen to do, Aristodama follows earlier poets such as Sappho, Corinna, Myrtis and even Homer. As epic historian, it is the comparison with Homer that particularly resonates here, since he is the paramount epic poet and was long seen as an historical authority. However, since we have no remaining texts or even fragments, the extent to which she covered more recent history and individualized her performance for her various audiences cannot be determined.

The decree recording her honours at Chaleion suggests she tailored the epic she performed there in particular to that city's most important god, Apollo *Nasiotas* (Islander). That decree was copied and erected at Delphi (where the extant copy was found) as well as near the temple of Apollo at Chaleion. Erection of the decree in these two places not only honoured Aristodama locally at the Chaleians' most sacred site, but internationally at the most important religious centre for Apollo in the Greek world. We can infer the degree of her renown from this.

The rewards she was given by these cities included status, land rights and, in the case of Chaleion, religious honour (rights to a share of sacrificial meat, a privilege usually granted to important priests) and a generous cash gift. Lamia even bestowed citizenship on her, a high honour and an extraordinary one rarely bestowed on a woman (Rutherford 2009: 244). That this woman was not local, but came to the city to perform, reflects the increasing internationalization of musical artists in the Hellenistic world. In the third century BCE we find associations of professional artists formed to exploit opportunities to participate in festivals and contests throughout the Greek world (Aneziri 2009: 217–20). While the extent to which women were able to travel and perform alongside men is not known, we do know from the inscription that Aristodama travelled with her brother.

We are not told the context in which Aristodama performed in these cities, but it is likely that she travelled there to participate in a local festival, probably in a contest held at the festival, as this was the principal occasion for public poetry. As she references Apollo in her performance at Chaleion, the religious setting for her performance is even more likely (Siekierka 2021: 137). We might compare the performance of the daughter of Apollonius (her name is lost) who was honoured in Cos in the first century CE for her victories at the *Sebasta Olympia* (Emperor Games), the *Koinon of Asia* (Provincial Assembly) at Pergamon and other sacred festivals (*IG* XII 4.2:845; Siekierka 2021: 547). There are also examples of female harpists who travelled to Delphi to perform and were granted honours there: daughter of Aristocrates of Cyme (her name is lost: *Syll.*³:689); Polygnota of Thebes (*FD* 3.3:249; Siekierka 2021, 361–3; 365–8).

Aristodama's work can be understood to have been a city encomium, a song in praise of the locality and its people in a traditional epic metre, a genre that was popular in the Hellenistic period (Rutherford 2009: 240). In referencing the ancestors, Aristodama brings history to poetry, engaging with the past in the creation of contemporary entertainment. Her addition of a religious element to this narrative, in the person of Apollo, enhances both the genres of history and poetry, and reflects the importance of religion to the city-state.

It is unlikely that she only performed in the two cities from which evidence of her performances has survived. That each of these cities wanted the record of her performance and the city's honouring of her to be publicly displayed, and in the case of Chaleion also made public at Delphi, shows that they wanted their link to her to be widely known. In addition, the Delphic connection suggests they wanted her (and themselves through their honouring of her work) to receive recognition from the god Apollo himself. Aristodama was thus of sufficient status for her association with the city to elevate its standing.

Evidence from elsewhere shows that Aristodama was not the only female poet who travelled to perform around this time. Alcinoe, an Aetolian, from Thronion, visited Tenos in the third century BCE and was honoured there. The inscription is fragmentary, but restorations suggest she wrote a hymn in praise of Zeus, Poseidon and Amphitrite and earned herself the approbation of the people of Tenos (*IG* XII 5:812; Siekierka 2021: 137–8; 562–3). It is also significant that Aristodama was specifically honoured as a *poiētria* (poet) of epic since this is the earliest instance of the use of this female gendered term for a female poet and marks recognition of a woman as a poet in her own right (Hauser 2023: 225–8 for this idea and its importance).[22]

That women participated in musical competitions at major festivals is confirmed by the second century BCE historian Polemon, cited by Plutarch. He tells us that there was a golden book in the treasury of the Sicyonians at Delphi that had been dedicated by the poet Aristomache of Erythrae; she won the epic verse contest twice at the Isthmian games (Plut. *Mor.* 675b).[23] In a later example, Hedea of Tralles won the children's competition for playing the lyre and singing at the Athenian *Sebasteia* festival in the mid-first century CE; this multi-talented young woman also won athletic events elsewhere: the *stadion* at the Nemean and Sicyonian Games and the war-chariot race at the Isthmian Games (*FD* 3.1:534; *Syll*³ 3:802; Siekierka 2021: 368–9). These women were clearly not just participating in retelling the history of their cities and the cities they visited – the memorials created to record their successes demonstrate that they were making history, too.

Conclusions

This chapter has focused on examples of poets who have engaged with their community's mythical and literary past. That past was important to the Greeks, their myths linking, through poetry, known and local history to a time when gods, heroes and heroines were ever present in the world.

Sappho, Corinna and no doubt Myrtis too wrote for choral performance and it is difficult to distinguish what, if any, of their work may have been composed for solo performance (Calame, Collins and Orion 1997; Lardinois 1994, 1996). In creating choral performance pieces with traditional material, these poets took myths to other women who in turn became active participants in the retelling through performance, song and dance. The local past that these poets retold was mythical, religious and historical, and engaged the female performers with their history. Such performances would have honoured the gods and added to the prestige of the festival at which they were presented. While an audience heard and saw the performance, celebrating the occasion with the choir, it was the participants who contributed to the creative moment in delivering the song. The personal viewpoint of the past defined by the poet was thus localized both in the retelling of the myth to include local content, and also in its delivery through the voice of the local choir. Corinna's song of the battle between two mountains may reflect her literary criticism of Pindar's work with her own representative winning the day, but it is articulated as the view of the community who sang it. That these women wrote for choirs of young women, gave this part of the community a public role in defining the aetiological history that underpinned the religious life of their city.

The Hellenistic era also saw solo performers travel to perform in public at festivals. We have evidence that some women, such as Aristodama, Aristomache and Alcinoe were among the best: they received high honours from cities they visited. In the case of Aristodama, she received further recognition beyond the venue at which she had performed when the people of Chaleion set up a stele at Delphi to honour her performance in their city. Aristodama was recognized as a *poiētria*, a female poet, the gendered term revealing that a woman's poetic voice needed its own word to denote it. We know that women were vital to the religious life of every Greek city. What we see in the scraps of evidence that have survived is that they were important in preserving, recreating and sharing the history of a city too.[24]

Notes

1. On cultural barriers to women's engagement in political and military history, see Plant (2015: 77–8).
2. A comment attributed to Solon (T. 10); Dionysius of Halicarnassus on Sappho (T. 42); for reception also T. 43–61: Campbell's edition (1982) used in this chapter; for new translations of her extant fragments see Rayor and Lardinois (2023).
3. F.1 is the only complete poem extant; on her full output T. 2, 28; F. 103.
4. While modern scholars remind us of the distinction between the literary voice and the author (DeJean 1989: 9), Sappho's poetic voice was taken unequivocally in antiquity to be her own; on this problem see Lardinois (1994: 60–4); Lardinois (1996); Tsagarakis (1977).
5. E.g. F. 16, 17, 44, 44a, 96, 140a, 141, 142, 166. For discussion of Sappho's engagement with Homer, see Mueller (2023), Scodel (2021), Kelly (2020; 2021), Rosenmeyer (1997).
6. Homer (*c.* 725 BCE) preceded Sappho; the *Epic Cycle*, a collection of poems on the Trojan War, now only extant in fragments that may include story elements that pre-date Homer but were probably composed later; Herodotus wrote *c.* 430 BCE, Thucydides just after 400 BCE.
7. E.g. Hdt. 1.1–5, Thuc. 1.2–21; on the 'rationality' of Thucydides and Herodotus as historians in dealing with poetic traditions, see Hunter (1982: 93–115) and Marinatos (2022).
8. For later use of this word see e.g. Xen. *Sym.* 8.28; Isoc. 2.49, 6.24.
9. Both restorations are suggested by Diehl (1917: 34); Campbell prints *mythologēsai*.
10. On Sappho as a choral poet, see Lardinois (1994; 1996); on the difficulty of determining which of her poems were composed for choral performance, see Power (2020). For women participating in the Kallisteia festival in Hera's precinct, see Schol. D on *Il.* 9.130.
11. In antiquity Corinna was imagined to have been a contemporary of Pindar and Myrtis (fifth century BCE); however her work must be dated to the third century BCE on internal evidence (Collins 2006: 19–20; Larson 2007: 19 n.12; West 1970: 277–87; 1990: 553–7; Page 1953: 65–84; Lobel 1930: 356–65).
12. Campbell's edition (1992) with *PMG* numeration is used in this chapter.
13. Attested as a correction for *Geroia* ('Old Stories') by Antoninus Liberalis, *Met.* 25 = Corinna 656.

14. For discussion of the phrase, including twenty-four different translations, see Heath (2017: 86–100).
15. For the religious context of Greek choral performances, Calme (1997); for a tradition of Corinna's participation in competitions T.1-4.
16. For the idea that common cult practice helped define Boeotian identity see Mackil (2013); also Bowra (1938).
17. For Corinna's subject matter as both local heroic myth and poetic criticism, see Henderson (1995).
18. For *eris* ('strife') as musical and other contests Hdt. 6.129.2, 9.33.2, Eur. *IA* 1308; cf. rivalry and contention, Hes. *Op.* 11–26.
19. For choral performance of Corinna's work, see Henderson (1995: 31).
20. T.1 = *Suda* s.v. Corinna K 2087. For the ancient biographies of poets being derived from their works, see Lefkowitz (2012: 2).
21. Decree of Lamians: *IG* IX 2:62 (=*SIG*[4]:532); decree of Chaleians: *IG* IX 1².3:740 (=*FD* 3.3:145; *SEG* 2.263); see Siekierka (2021: 379–82) for the full texts.
22. See Hauser (2023) for exploration of the use of masculine gendered terms for female poets prior to Aristodama. Alcinoe is also identified as a *poiētria* in *IG* XII 5:812.4, but the word there is a restoration.
23. It has been suggested that Aristomache of Erythrae in Plutarch is an error for Aristodama of Smyrna (Daux 1932: 145) though this seems unlikely. Their names and homelands are distinct, Polemon was noted for his careful recording of inscriptions, and the evidence we have for the existence of other women poets means there is no reason to limit the record (see Cagnazzi 1997: 116).
24. For later historical epics by women, compare Proba's Virgilian cento on the life of Christ (fourth century CE); Eudocia's *Persian wars*, *Martyrdom of St. Cyprian*, and Homeric cento retelling the stories of creation and the life of Christ (fifth century CE).

CHAPTER 2
CLASSICAL CREDENTIALS: WOMEN'S INTELLECTUAL AND SEXUAL LICENCE IN SIXTEENTH-CENTURY FRANCE
Emma Herdman

Introduction

The recent and highly successful vogue (within anglophone publishing) for retelling classical myths from a feminist perspective is far from new. Early examples of women rewriting and repurposing classical tales include the fifth-century empress Aelia Eudocia, whose Homeric centos redeploy lines from the *Odyssey* and *Iliad* to narrate biblical episodes in epic style (Sowers 2020: 61–104), and the twelfth-century abbess Héloïse, whose self-construction, in her classically rich letters to Abélard, draws particularly on parallels with Ovid's *Heroides* (Brown and Peiffer 2000). Long before Margaret Atwood asked us to consider how the *Odyssey* might have been narrated by Penelope, or before Madeline Miller and Natalie Haynes invited us to reassess our perception of vilified and sidelined figures such as Circe, Jocasta and Medusa, early modern women were engaging with the classical world in their writing and questioning the representation of the female figures within it.[1] That engagement may be seen as part of a strategy to claim authority for their writing (at a time when women, in particular, needed to demonstrate their legitimacy as writers) by asserting their intellectual credentials.[2] Dorothy L. Sayers deploys a similar strategy in a playful lecture, 'Aristotle on Detective Fiction', delivered in Oxford on 5 March 1935, in which she demonstrates how perfectly Aristotle's discussion of tragedy, in *The Poetics*, applies to detective fiction; she thus reclaims the literary status of this all-too-easily dismissed genre by making Aristotle its master and – some twenty centuries too early – most eager would-be reader (Sayers 1946: 178). In her 1938 address 'Are Women Human?', Sayers therefore contests the view (of those who would deny women university education) that women collectively do not need to know about Aristotle by asserting that she, individually, does (Sayers 1946: 108), and Aristotle's influence can be traced in her works (Sprague 1997). Similarly, early modern women's engagement with the classics both legitimizes their writing (by lending it intellectual authority) and extends the range of subjects and genres available to them, even if it requires them to strike a delicate balance between displaying their classical learning and refraining from appearing too knowledgeable about a world whose sexual *mores* were far from compatible with the decorous expectations placed on them by *bienséance*.[3] When the classical world is written by women, it finds itself being repurposed to suit those women's writerly aims.

Women Creating Classics

This chapter focuses on three sixteenth-century French writers – Marguerite de Navarre, Louise Labé and Madeleine de l'Aubespine – who drew on the classics in poems that invite us to reconceptualize a powerful female figure, represented either overtly or covertly, according to the moral status conventionally ascribed to her. Marguerite de Navarre's *Fable du Faux Cuyder* (Fable of False Presumption) focuses on the virgin goddess and hunter Diana.[4] The fable is an expanded French version of Jacopo Sannazaro's neo-Latin poem *Salices* (The Willows), set in a classical world and narrating the transformation into willows of a group of nymphs, to save them from being raped by satyrs (Sannazaro 2009: 146–53). The first of Louise Labé's three elegies, which warns the ladies of Lyon not to judge the poet for having fallen in love, takes Semiramis, queen of Babylon, as an example of a virtuous ruler and military leader whose character was radically altered (and her reputation irredeemably compromised) when she fell in love with her son.[5] Madeleine de l'Aubespine's sonnet 'Enigme' (Enigma) is a titillating evocation of the exquisite pleasure that the solitary poet derives from what she eventually reveals is her lute;[6] the clear suggestion that her pleasure is sexual is reinforced by the reference to Messalina, the wife of the Roman emperor Claudius, synonymous since Tacitus and Juvenal with insatiable lust. While these three poems belong to different genres and use the classical world for diverse purposes, they share a common motif: the rewriting of a classical female figure to illustrate the complexity of a multi-faceted and divided self.

Marguerite de Navarre and Diana

Marguerite de Navarre's *Fable of False Presumption* was first published in 1543 and included in her 1547 collected works under a new name, the *Histoire des Satyres, et Nymphes de Dyane* (Story of the Satyrs and the Nymphs of Diana).[7] The poem's narrative is taken from Sannazaro's *Willows*, printed first in 1526 (Sannazaro 2009: 459), and then in France in 1536 (Reyff 2012: 17).[8] Marguerite's version of the tale considerably expands Sannazaro's poem (from 113 lines to 868 lines), and rewrites it as a moral fable about human frailty and the need to rely upon God.

Sannazaro's *Willows* is set in the pastoral world of Virgil's *Eclogues* which it relocates to the banks of the river Sarnus, near Sannazaro's native Naples. In the style of Ovid's *Metamorphoses*, it tells of a group of nymphs enticed by the music and honeyed words of rapacious satyrs, who invite the nymphs to approach and dance to their music, promising them that they have nothing to fear, only to fall lustfully on them. The nymphs flee and, having prayed for help to the river Sarnus that blocks their flight, are preparing to drown themselves in its waters when they are metamorphosed into willows. Sannazaro's narrative is heavily Ovidian. The nymphs' initial fear of the satyrs reflects their knowledge of tales that echo and foreshadow their own:

> They had heard of your tribulations, daughter of Peneus, and the misfortune, alas, through which the ill-starred Nonacrian maiden, the ill-starred maiden – (for

what did she not try?) fleeing Pan in fearful flight from the crest of Mt. Cyllene, Pan the god of Arcadia, though she was the most beautiful, though she was preeminent among Diana's holy bands – had once changed her tender breast into a knotty reed.

Sannazaro 2009: 149

Yet if Sannazaro's nymphs have read Ovid's Metamorphoses, which recount the transformations of Daphne (the daughter of Peneus) into a laurel tree as she flees from Apollo (*Metamorphoses* 1.452–567) and of Syrinx (the Nonacrian maiden) into a reed as she flees from Pan (*Metamorphoses* 1.689–712), this does not save them from a similar fate.

Sannazaro differs from Ovid, however, in leaving his nymphs' metamorphosis resolutely unexplained. Ovid's two nymphs are metamorphosed in immediate response to prayer:

Then she saw the waters of the Peneus: 'O father,' she cried, 'help me! If you rivers really have divine powers, work some transformation, and destroy this beauty which makes me please all too well!' Her prayer was scarcely ended when a deep languor took hold on her limbs, her soft breast was enclosed in thin bark, her hair grew into leaves, her arms into branches, and her feet that were lately so swift were held fast by sluggish roots, while her face became the tree-top. Nothing of her was left, except her shining loveliness.

Metamorphoses *1.544–52: 43*

Ovid, typically, does not quite give Daphne what she asked for (the beauty she had prayed to lose is the one thing she retains), but her prayer is answered in the transformation that saves her. Similarly, Syrinx's metamorphosis is presented as the immediate consequence of her prayer to the river gods (*Metamorphoses* 1.701–6). Accordingly, when the river halts their flight, Sannazaro's nymphs follow their two models by calling 'upon Sarnus and their sisters of the stream' (Sannazaro 2009: 151). But here the exemplarity of Daphne and Syrinx appears to end, as Sannazaro seems reluctant to accord to Sarnus the powers that Ovid affords to the rivers Peneus and Ladon: 'But what could Sarnus or those squadrons of swimming Naiads do when iron fate stands opposed and the laws of hard adamant remain unbending?' (Sannazaro 2009: 151–3). Sannazaro's nymphs look to be beyond all help: they are preparing to drown themselves when the saving transformation takes place. Where the immediacy of the metamorphoses in Ovid suggests the responsiveness of the protective deities whom the nymphs invoke, the slight delay that Sannazaro introduces adds dramatic tension to a plight from which it looks – even to readers of Ovid – as if the nymphs cannot possibly be rescued until, eventually, they are.

Marguerite de Navarre's version turns Sannazaro's tale into a moral fable on the theme, echoed widely across her writing, of the false presumption (*cuyder*) of those who fail to recognize their dependence on God. The *Fable* promises to depict firstly 'the malice of men, and their regrets when their vice is overcome by virtue' (Navarre 1547: 4), seen in the satyrs' lust and disappointment when their rape attempts fail. Secondly, through the naively trusting nymphs, the poem will show that: 'ignorance of evil, disguised by an honest appearance, often deceives women who have not learned that he who has been taken in can himself take in' (Navarre 1547: 4). This moral lesson ('Que prendre peult celuy, que lon ha pris') echoes and inverts the final line of Andrea Alciato's Latin-French emblem of 1536, 'Iusta ultio / Juste vengence' (Just Revenge), illustrated by the raven that is poisoned by the scorpion it has seized: 'Bien souvent les preneurs se preignent' (often predators themselves become prey) (Alciato 1536: [K8]^v-L[1]^r). Thirdly, the poem will show that although the nymphs' mistake lies less in naively trusting the satyrs than in straying from the protection of Diana, 'virtue guided by ignorance is ultimately often helped by the gods' (Navarre 1547: 4). This focuses the narrative upon Diana, who is mentioned only incidentally by Sannazaro, but whose responses to the nymphs' initial disobedience and subsequent prayer occupy a major part of Marguerite's poem.[9] These responses allow Marguerite to reflect upon divine-human relations and the efficacy of prayer. In the process, she significantly rewrites the Diana of Ovid's *Metamorphoses*.

Ovid's Diana is quick to take offence and liable to punish. She banishes the pregnant Callisto, raped by Jupiter (*Metamorphoses* 2.409–507), and transforms Actaeon, who had inadvertently glimpsed her bathing, into a stag (*Metamorphoses* 3.173–252), with fatal consequences. She takes violent revenge on those who fail to recognize her status, such as Niobe, for presuming herself superior to Diana's mother, Leto (*Metamorphoses* 6.165–312), Chione, for presuming herself more beautiful than Diana (*Metamorphoses* 11.301–27), and king Oeneus of Calydon, for making harvest offerings to every god except her (*Metamorphoses* 8.270–83). But she is also a passionate defender of chastity, substituting a stag as sacrificial victim for the virgin Iphigenia (*Metamorphoses* 12.27–38), whose blood she had demanded to punish Agamemnon for boasting that he was a better hunter than her (Hornblower and Spawforth 1996: s.v. 'Agamemnon'), and hiding the virginal hunter Hippolytus, restored to life by Aesculapius, from death (*Metamorphoses* 15.531–46). For as long as their virginity remains intact, Marguerite's nymphs might reasonably hope for the clemency shown by Diana to Iphigenia, but fear the punishment of (the surely innocent) Callisto.

Marguerite's Diana responds to the nymphs' prayer with an initial streak of anger that is instantly tempered by pity. In a long reflective soliloquy, she addresses the *cuyder* (presumption) that is variously a personification ('O *Cuyder*, through your pride you make foolish the hearts of poor fools', Navarre 1547: 23), a noun ('Because of this *Cuyder*, which made them think themselves equal to me, they have gone from me', Navarre 1547: 24), and a verb ('By presuming themselves – *se cuyder* – to be inviolable virgins, they strayed from me and were undone', Navarre 1547: 24). The effects of this versatile *cuyder* are to divide what ought to be unified, separating the nymphs both physically and spiritually from Diana. Moreover, the *cuyder* that misled the lusty satyrs and the naive nymphs threatens even Diana, who initially contemplates angrily killing the disobedient nymphs:

My heart, moved by anger and by love, then presumed [*cuyda*] to force me to act and to draw my arrows against them, making my maternal hands cruel, and saving them by a sudden death from the approaching evil covered in sweet attractions.

Navarre 1547: 25

Yet the anger in Diana's heart is checked by her greater love, which prefers to teach the nymphs a moral lesson:

But my love, so virtuous and lofty, and subject to no failing, drew back my hand (which already held the arrow in the bow) set to pierce their hearts, considering that it was not appropriate to punish them promptly in this way.

Navarre 1547: 25

The *cuyder* that threatens even a classical divinity, creating a division between Diana's conflicting emotions that echoes the division between herself and the nymphs, is defeated when Diana's maternal love overcomes her wounded pride, and her emotional unity is restored.

Moreover, this split Diana has a further quality that will surprise readers of Ovid. The nymphs' prayer mollifies Diana with its mix of penitence (they recognize and repent of their fault), self-defence (they are guilty of folly rather than lust), persuasive argument (it is in Diana's interests to preserve the chastity of her devotees), and flattery (they are not worthy of Diana). The prayer moves Diana to renounce the moral lesson she had intended to teach them (by abandoning them to a life dependent on *cuyder* rather than blessed with her favours), because:

seeing their distress, their grief, their lament, their sighs and their tears, their great sadness, their cries, their piteous words, their placing of their only hope in my great power, and the true recognition of their errors, I hear that each of them, invoking me, admires me for my generosity [*bonté*].

Navarre 1547: 26

This appeal to Diana's generosity (her goodness, her kindness) moves her to clemency and prompts her to reflect upon her possession of this admirable quality:

I would therefore do damage to the generosity they appeal to if I stopped it from going to their help. This generosity that they recognize in me, that is indeed held in their hearts by me, makes them feel that they have recourse to me. This generosity moves me to help them.

Navarre 1547: 26

Diana's generosity unites her with the nymphs both as a value they have acquired from her and as a means of access to her; it is Diana's own loyalty to this quality of generosity that moves her to save the nymphs: 'If they have dared to be unfaithful to their vows, I do not wish to be unfaithful to my great generosity, through which all evil is overcome by good' (Navarre 1547: 27). Diana's fidelity to her values distinguishes her from the nymphs who had so easily abandoned those values, but it also reunites her with them as she moves from punitive anger to pitying generosity. Callisto could have asked for nothing more.

If Ovid's river gods respond instantly to his nymphs' prayers, while Sannazaro's river gods, in contrast, seem powerless to do so, Marguerite's Diana reflects at length on her own emotional responses to the nymphs' waywardness and on the courses of action available to her. The *Fable*'s moral lesson is that it is in the generous divine forgiveness of repentant sinners that lies the efficacy of prayer. That moral lesson finds a striking counter-example in the *Heptameron*, which transposes the theme of human presumption from the *Fable*'s classical setting (unique in Marguerite's writing) to early sixteenth-century France. Story 30 tells the sorry tale of a double incest as a warning against failure to turn repentantly to God.[10] It starts with a substitution: a devout widow, unable to believe that her son wishes to seduce her maid, takes the maid's place at a night-time assignation with him; her disbelief in his (or her) capacity for lust, resembling the nymphs' naive trust of the satyrs, lasts until she herself feels 'a too abominable pleasure' and, 'forgetting herself a mother', is impregnated by her own son (Navarre 2000: 339). Where Diana's maternal love overrides angry instinct, the widow fails to overcome the sexual instinct that similarly separates her from her maternal self. And where the nymphs turn to Diana, the widow in her shame tries to rely upon her own resources:

> But instead of humbly recognizing the weakness of our flesh, which without God's help can only commit sin, she wanted to atone for the past by her own means and by her tears, and to avoid future evil by her prudence. She still blamed her sin on the occasion and not on her propensity to do wrong, for which there is no remedy other than God's grace. She thought she would act to ensure she would never succumb to such a misfortune in the future: and as if there were only one type of sin to bring people to damnation, she put all her energy into avoiding that one alone. But the root of pride, which external sin should cure, still grew in her heart, so that by avoiding one evil she committed many others.
>
> *Navarre 2000: 340*

She therefore sends her son away, bears his child in secret to be brought up as her bastard brother's daughter, and forbids her son to return until he is happily married; when he does eventually return, he has unwittingly married his own sister and daughter.

The tale is cast as another moral fable about (false) presumption. Although the narrator, Hircan, uses the term *cuyder* only once in the tale itself (when the widow learns her son has married their daughter, and presumes – *cuyda* – she will die of grief), he introduces it immediately into the discussion that follows: 'See, ladies, what happens to women who presume [*cuident*] that by their strength and virtue they can conquer love and nature, with all the powers with which God has imbued these' (Navarre 2000: 343).

The widow's presumption is identical to that of the nymphs. Oisille therefore moves the moral of Hircan's tale from the particular to the general: 'And it seems to me that every man and woman should here bow their heads in fear of God, seeing that so many evils have come from presuming [*cuider*] to do good' (Navarre 2000: 343). Where Hircan blames the widow for her self-reliance, Oisille emphasizes that the moral of her example is a lesson for everyone.

Strikingly, none of the *Heptameron*'s ten story-tellers condemns the widow for incest.[11] Rather, her fault lies in presuming herself first immune to lust and then capable of managing the consequences when it transpires she is not. The discussion that follows the tale focuses on human fragility without God – a lesson that comes straight from the *Fable*. Marguerite's rewriting of Sannazaro's Ovidian myth thus contributes to a sustained theme that will resonate across her works. In contrast, Louise Labé's similarly sympathetic response to incest contributes to her poetic call for unity between women changed – and made interchangeable – by love.

Louise Labé and Semiramis

In her three elegies, first published in her *Euvres* (Works) in 1555, Louise Labé responds to the challenge of inscribing herself into a literary tradition inherited from Antiquity of male-authored love poetry by drawing on the classical elegiac poets, Ovid, Propertius and Tibullus (Sterritt 2005: 15).[12] The first elegy describes the poet's service first to Love and then to poetry, as she sings on Sappho's lyre, given to her by Phoebus, of her amorous suffering (2004: 107, 1.1–16). The second elegy, written in the style of Ovid's *Heroides*, is addressed to an absent beloved two months after his promised return; it speculates on the reasons for his delay (infidelity or illness), and concludes by imagining the poet's own gravestone and inviting the beloved to appease her ashes with his tears.[13] The final elegy, describing the poet's (Ovidian) defeat to the arrows and fires of Love and praying that her love might be requited, is an apologia addressed to the poet's female readers.

Labé's first elegy echoes Ovid in its representation of the poet as a victim of Love's sure arrows, and of the effects of this upon her poetry. Ovid parodies the conventional poetic apology for not writing epic by claiming that Cupid stole one of his metrical feet, forcing him to abandon the lofty themes of hexameter and write instead in elegiac couplets and so of love (*Amores* 1.1.1–4).[14] He complains that Cupid has no right to interfere with the Muses, and speculates on the chaos that would follow should other classical gods similarly appropriate attributes and properties that are not theirs (*Amores* 1.1.5–12). He also objects that he has been made a love poet even though he is not in love – an incongruity that Cupid swiftly remedies (*Amores* 1.1.21–4). Like Ovid, Labé accepts the alteration brought about in her by love; but she also engages with the interchangeability that Ovid rejects as she makes her particular case (like that of Marguerite's widow) applicable to anyone. The love that estranges her from herself allows her to identify with other lovers, and so to warn her readers, in a direct imitation of Tibullus, not to judge her lest they too fall in love.[15] The example she chooses to illustrate Love's capacity to strike and change even the most surprising of victims is Semiramis.

Semiramis' posthumous reputation makes her exemplarity decidedly ambiguous.[16] While Diodorus Siculus' account of her life (*The Library of History* 2.4–20) praises her as a fierce warrior who builds Babylon and extends its empire, the Church Fathers condemned her for such worldly ambition and for sexual immorality, portraying her as posing as her son in order to reign, attempting to marry him, and being killed by him. She thus becomes synonymous with lust for power and blood as well as with incest. Dante confines Semiramis to the second circle – lust – of hell (Alighieri 1996: 89, 5.52–60); in contrast, Boccaccio praises her virile bravery and intelligence on the battlefield, although his admiration vanishes at a single stroke when he considers her sexual licentiousness (which he evokes in some detail): 'Her accomplishments would be extraordinary and praiseworthy and deserving of perpetual memory for a vigorous male, to say nothing of a woman. But with one unspeakable act of seduction Semiramis stained them all' (Boccaccio 2003: 10, 2.13). Semiramis' rehabilitation begins properly with Christine de Pisan, who has Semiramis as the first foundation stone of her *Cité des Dames* (City of Ladies) (Pisan 1999: 35–7). Where Boccaccio, following Orosius, has Semiramis changing the law to legalize the incest that Augustine considers against nature (Boccaccio 2003: 11, 2.15), Christine portrays her incest as according to natural law, before it was against the written law (Pisan 1999: 36–7).[17]

The rehabilitation of Semiramis subsequently depends on drawing a veil over her sexual *mores* and the incest absent from Ancient accounts but all too prominent in the Middle Ages. Symphorien Champier, in his 1503 *Nef des dames vertueuses* (Ship of Virtuous Ladies), attributes the sexual freedom of the Babylonians to their ignorance of Christian salvation, rather than to Semiramis, whom he praises for her valour (Champier 2007: 127–8). He thus follows his own advice against condemning women:

> These sins are said to come from [women]. I ask you, who say these things of them, why do you not recount their good as well as their evil? What moves you to such folly, if not the malice and ill will you bear them? Why do you not tell of ... the valour of queen Semiramis? Furthermore, do not look only at the sins of women, but think of those of men.
>
> *Champier 2007: 56–7*

Similarly, Jean du Pré, in his 1534 *Palais des nobles Dames* (Palace of Noble Ladies), praises Semiramis for her courage and good government of Babylon (Du Pré 2007: 146) and makes her a symbol of abstinence, following the legend that in infancy she was fed on milk and cheese by doves (Diodorus, *Library* 2.4), in a manner that contrasts sharply with Boccaccio's depictions of her sexual excesses. Du Pré's account of Semiramis' successful crushing of a Babylonian rebellion concludes: 'There is therefore no reason to pervert the decent order and so deprive the Lady of the virtue that ought to represent her' (Du Pré 2007: 334). The moral applies ostensibly to the rebellious Babylonians, but equally to those who remember Semiramis' sexual depravity at the expense of her virtuous deeds.

Labé's elegy is all the more striking for not condemning, justifying, or ignoring Semiramis' incestuous love, but presenting it as a reason to pity her. First she evokes Semiramis' defeat by the love that Ovid (*Amores* 1.9.1) calls a form of soldiership: 'Still having the desire to conquer all her neighbours, or to go to war with them, she discovered Love, who harried her so strongly that, vanquished, she abandoned arms and laws' (Labé 2004: 109, 1.67–70). She then asks her readers a rhetorical question that shows her sympathy for Semiramis: 'Did not her royal grandeur deserve at least to undergo a less troubling misfortune than to love her son?' (Labé 2004: 109, 1.71–3). The question invites agreement, mitigating against condemnation of the incestuous love that is introduced with casual understatement as a misfortune that Semiramis deserved not to endure. Labé then sets out a comparison between the poet and Semiramis, whom she addresses directly: 'You abandoned martial harshness to rediscover congenial sweetness. Love has so estranged you from yourself that you might be said to have been changed into another' (Labé 2004: 109, 1.87–90). In the third elegy, the poet undergoes a similar change: 'Love could not endure for long to see my heart loving only Mars and knowledge ... Love ... disguises me and makes me appear different, so that I myself cannot recognize myself' (Labé 2004: 116–17, 3.43–4 and 3.71–2). The poet's self-estrangement is foreshadowed by the self-inflicted wound through which she succumbs to Love:

Love's arms were my eyes, from which I cast so many arrows on those who looked too much at me and did not watch out sufficiently for my bow. But my own arrows undid my own eyes and made me an example of vengeance.

Labé 2004: 108, 1.28–32

The poetic justice with which Love employs the poet's own weapons against her, echoing the Ovidian theme of Love punishing those who resist him, leads to a form of self-alienation.[18] As she is unexpectedly wounded by her own arrows, the poet no longer resembles the inviolable virgin huntress Diana; instead, like Semiramis, she illustrates the emblematic moral lesson found in Alciato's *Emblems* and in Marguerite's *Fable*, and addressed here to the ladies of Lyon, of 'le preneur pris'.[19]

The poet thus enjoins her readers not to condemn lovers, since they too may be metamorphosed by love: 'So may he who sees me lament over being struck by love not despise my sad grief: perhaps Love will shortly appear no less grievously to him' (Labé 2004: 109, 1.91–4). The warning that the critical (male) reader may suffer the same fate leads into the depiction of a woman afflicted with love, painfully and ridiculously, in old age: 'I have seen such a woman, who had rejected love in her youth, then burn with passion, in her old age, and tenderly lament the harsh rigour of her late torment' (Labé 2004: 109, 1.95–8). The imagined elderly lover – echoing the poet, who similarly once scorned the love she now suffers – is borrowed, as Sterritt has shown, from Tibullus, who warns his (male) reader not to judge a lover lest he suffer the humiliating incongruity of being struck with love in old age (Tibullus 1.2.87–96). Labé rewrites Tibullus' satirized old-aged lover as a woman, and so conflates four figures changed by love: the poet; Semiramis, to whom she explicitly compares herself; the reader, who may suffer the same misfortune; and the imaginary old woman who has already done so, and is now reviled as both unattractive and ridiculous. Labé's portrait is balanced delicately between mockery and pity, as the elderly lover's alienated self fails to see the vanity of her efforts to appear enticing, although this is all too apparent to her youthful beloved:

> And the more she made herself up to her liking, the less she was noticed by her love, who ran away and paid no attention to her, so ugly did she seem to him; he felt deeply embarrassed to be loved by her.
>
> Labé 2004: 110, 1.105–9

The age disparity that also exists between Semiramis and her son heightens the humiliation of loving in inappropriate old age (Ovid, *Amores* 1.9.3–4). The poet potentially shares that humiliation, representing herself (aged twenty-nine) as thirteen years older than when she first loved (Labé 2004: 117, 3.73–6). Thus the poet's warning that her readers may also be conflated with these three figures is a generous one: as she herself identifies with both the ridiculous elderly lover and the incestuous Semiramis, she asks them to be treated with sympathy. Labé's originality lies in admiring Semiramis without ignoring her reputation for incest, and in portraying her – incestuous, old and ridiculous, and comparable to any lover – primarily as pitiable.

Madeleine de l'Aubespine and Messalina

If Louise Labé's self-identification with and sympathy for Semiramis is surprising, then even more so is Madeleine de l'Aubespine's self-identification with and celebration of Messalina. L'Aubespine, who engages with the classical world by translating Ovid, also rewrites it in her poetry, most of which was printed only after her death in 1596.[20] A notable example is her oblique reference, in a titillatingly enigmatic sonnet, to Juvenal's sixth satire, in which he attacks both marriage and women. Through this reference, l'Aubespine draws a startling comparison between herself and Messalina, the young third wife of the much older emperor Claudius, whose mock-marriage to her lover, the consul-designate Gaius Silius, led to both of their deaths.[21] The sonnet's earliest source is a late sixteenth-century manuscript anthology of poetry (BnF ms. français 1718, fol. 57ʳ); it was first printed in 1618, with some slight but significant variants, in one of the seventeenth century's most popular anthologies of erotic poetry, *Le Cabinet satyrique* (The Satyric Cabinet) (1618: 308).

L'Aubespine's self-identification with Messalina is startling both because of the sonnet in which it appears and because of Messalina's reputation: her condemnation (for treason and for the sexual profligacy that only Claudius ignored) by historians since Tacitus (*Annals* 11.12 and 11.26–38) is cemented by Juvenal's satirical portrayal of her lust and of the sexual and political tyranny she exercised over her lovers (*Satires* 6.115–32 and 10.329–45).[22] Her only place in catalogues of praiseworthy women is as a brief counter-example to Dido's exemplary chastity, and as a warning to early modern women of the immorality of their sexual behaviour (Boccaccio 2003: 89, 42.23). Proud identification with Messalina is, then, unexpected. Yet it is perhaps less surprising given the nature of l'Aubespine's enigmatic sonnet, which describes the exquisite pleasure she derives each evening in bed from a deftly-handled instrument: the retrospective revelation that the instrument in question is a lute comes only after the clear suggestion that the pleasure in question is sexual, provided either by a male sex object governed entirely by the poet's will, or by an artificial substitute – in either case, there is no question of whether this autonomous pleasure is shared by the instrument that arouses it.[23] The ambiguity over whether the enigma describes sexual or musical pleasure is sustained in French by the flexibility of the masculine pronouns (*il, le,* and *lui*), which may refer equally to a human (*he, him*) or to an impersonal object (*it*) as the source of pleasure.

The oblique identification with Messalina appears at the very end of the sonnet:

Ainsi mon bien aymé, tant que le nerf luy tire,
Me contente et me plaist. Puis de moy, doucement,
Lasse et non assouvye, enfin je le retire.

Kłosowska 2008: 191, n. 1[24]

(Thus my well-beloved, while I pluck his/its string, contents and pleases me. Then, finally, tired and not sated, I gently withdraw him/it from me.)

The last line is a direct translation of Juvenal's famous description of Messalina, whom he portrays as so sexually insatiable that even the nights she regularly spends in the brothel are not enough to quench her desire; at closing time, she departs only with reluctance: 'et lassata viris necdum satiata recessit' (she went away, exhausted by the men but not yet satisfied) (*Satire* 6.130).

Juvenal's oft-quoted phrase has become short-hand for women's lust; Charles Baudelaire's sonnet 'Sed non satiata' (a near approximation of Juvenal's line) in *Les Fleurs du Mal* (The Flowers of Evil) expresses the poet's inadequacy to satisfy his ardent mistress (Baudelaire 1991: 78). L'Aubespine stays closer to Juvenal, omitting only the term *viris* in order to emphasize the poet's autonomy over her pleasure and maintain the ambiguity over whether it is musical or sexual. Yet whereas Juvenal's Messalina withdraws from the brothel, l'Aubespine's poet withdraws the instrument that gives her such pleasure from herself. Like Marguerite's conflicted Diana or Labé's self-alienated poet, she has a double self: she is equated both with Messalina the sexual pleasure-seeker and with the brothel as the site of that pleasure. The doubling of the poet as the site and the agent of sexual pleasure both asserts her sexuality and emphasizes her autonomy over the means of her sexual satisfaction.

Small but significant textual variants in printed editions of the sonnet, rendering the ambiguous pronoun in its last line even more ambiguous, further add – intentionally or otherwise – to this doubling. In *Le Cabinet satyrique*, the sonnet ends:

>   Puis de luy doucement
> Lasse et non assouvie en fin je me retire.²⁵

(Then finally, tired and not sated, I gently withdraw from him/it.)

The switch in pronouns, as the poet now withdraws not the instrument from herself but rather herself from the instrument, suggests the interchangeability between them: either can be equated with Messalina, who seeks and then withdraws from sexual pleasure, or with the site of that sexual pleasure; but in each case, agency rests with the poet as the subject of 'withdraw'. The poet's self is thus divided, across these variants, into a subject (*je*, the sexual agent), a direct object or reflexive pronoun (*me*: as direct object, the body that feels and provides sexual pleasure; as reflexive pronoun, the self that apprehends sexual pleasure) and disjunctive object (*de moy*, the site of sexual pleasure and of the self). This division of the self into aspects with distinct sexual roles underlines the entirety of the poet's sexual autonomy: where Juvenal's 'necdum satiata' punishes Messalina for the lust that means she withdraws in reluctance and dissatisfaction, l'Aubespine's 'et non assouvye' acts as a promise that the poet will return to the sexual pleasure that partly defines her whenever she pleases. Thus l'Aubespine lays claim to the sexuality and the control (over herself and others) for which Messalina was vilified, and playfully rewrites Juvenal's condemnation of Messalina's insatiable lust as a celebration of a joyous opportunity for endless delight.

Conclusion

When Dorothy L. Sayers made Aristotle the champion of detective fiction, she laid claim to the (intellectual) authority conferred upon writers by the classical world. That classical world has long granted women, in particular, a degree of sexual licence in their writing. Yet this is perhaps an over-simplification. If Sayers's highly classical near contemporaries, Mary Renault and Marguerite Yourcenar, both draw extensively on the classical world in their novels, they do not rely wholly upon it to represent the sexual taboos of homosexuality and incest. While Renault's *The Charioteer* ([1953] 2013) draws heavily on Plato's *Phaedrus* for its portrait of mid-twentieth-century male homosexuality, heralding her decision to set all her subsequent novels in the classical world, homosexuality features intermittently in her earlier novels, most notably *The Friendly Young Ladies* ([1944] 2014), which has very few of the classical allusions so prevalent in her other works.²⁶ Equally, Yourcenar's representations of homosexuality in her novels are not confined to *Mémoires d'Hadrien* (Memoirs of Hadrian) ([1952] 1974), in which she imagines the emperor's account of his life and love for Antinous, and for which she won the Prix Femina Vacaresco in 1952. Her sympathetic portrait of incest in *Anna, soror* ... (1981) is set in seventeenth-century Naples;²⁷ while its titular quotation of Virgil's Dido (*Aeneid* 4.9) establishes a confidential and confessional relationship between the brother and sister who are its protagonists, she does not rely on classical licence for her subject.

The three poets discussed in this chapter each take licence to re-examine and re-assess a powerful female figure from the classical world. In Marguerite de Navarre's *Fable*, the implacable Diana becomes defined by the generosity that makes her responsive to prayer. This rewritten, conflicted and thoughtful Diana acquires attributes seldom found in the classical gods, so ready to act in instant and unthinking response to raw emotions. In Louise Labé's first elegy, the incestuous Semiramis is portrayed as pitiable, in a staunchly sympathetic representation of the alterations and humiliations of love. The self-estranged poet's identification with Semiramis facilitates the complicity she desires from her readers between women in love. Similarly, Madeleine de l'Aubespine's identification with Messalina reclaims her from ignominy and rewrites satirical condemnation of women's sexual desire as celebration of its erotic pleasure.

These three rewritten classical women each represent a divided self. Diana is divided both from her nymphs and between competing emotions. Semiramis is divided from her former self through the change of character brought about by love and through the exemplarity she thus acquires: her identity is no longer fixed, as she becomes analogous with Labé's female version of Tibullus' ridiculous old lover, with the poet herself, and with any of her readers who may fall in love. Finally, Messalina provides l'Aubespine's poet both with a dual self (as sexual actor and as site of sexual activity) that emphasizes her autonomy, and with an identity – a *moy* – that is accessible through sexuality.

As rewritten by women, all three classical figures thus acquire complex identities and a capacity for internal conflict that rescue them from the simplicity of the sexual qualities – chastity; incest; lust – by which they are so often and so reductively defined. In exchange, they invite their female writers to take advantage of their classical credentials. Marguerite de Navarre draws on the classical world chiefly because it allows her to reflect upon divine thought processes and so to illustrate the relationship between man and God. Just as Marguerite tempers the cruel world of Ovid's *Metamorphoses* by imbuing it with divine generosity and forgiveness, so Labé injects pity into satire; her two monitory figures from the classical world are invoked, as fellow amorous women, to enable a sympathetic complicity between the poet and her readers. Similarly, l'Aubespine draws on and disarms classical satire in her evocation of female sexual desire as something not to be mocked but celebrated. Far from simply relying on the classical world to authorize their subjects or their works, these three writers also reconsider the female figures they encounter within it. The licence that they take from the classical world is thus to rewrite it for their own religious, poetic or erotic ends.

Notes

1. Atwood (2005); Miller (2018); Haynes (2017); Haynes (2022).
2. On sixteenth-century women's strategies to legitimize their writing, see Larsen (1990).
3. On the challenges facing the early modern female intellectual in her engagement with the classical world, see Taylor (2024).

4. References are to Navarre (1547: 3–37). See also Simone de Reyff's critical edition (Navarre 2012); for a bilingual edition, see Navarre (2008: 236–79). Unless otherwise stated, translations from French are mine; translations from Latin and Italian are from the editions indicated.
5. References are to Labé (2004); for a bilingual edition, see Labé (2006).
6. For a bilingual edition of her works, see l'Aubespine (2007).
7. There is little critical work on Marguerite's *Fable*; for a full discussion, see Reyff (2012).
8. On other French retellings of this popular tale, including Maurice Scève's 1547 eclogue *Saussaie* (Willow Plantation) (1971: II, 7–31), and on the other influences on Marguerite's version, see Reyff (2012: 21–3).
9. On the iconography of Diana under François I, echoing the rise to influence of Diane de Poitiers, see Reyff (2012: 24).
10. References are to Navarre (2000); for an English translation, see Navarre (2004). On thematic similarities between the *Fable* and the *Heptameron*, see Stone (1993).
11. The story is told, sympathetically, from the widow's perspective; similarly, Natalie Haynes (2017) retells from Jocasta's (and Ismene's) perspective the Oedipus myth, in which a mother's attempt to avoid incest by sending away her son again leads inexorably to it. On Marguerite's sources for this tale, see Nicole Cazauran's note (Navarre 2000: 677, n. 338).
12. On women writing within these male-authored genres, see Jones (1981).
13. The elegy echoes particularly Ovid, *Heroides* 2.
14. See also Barsby's commentary (Ovid 1995: 41). On the fortunes of the *Amores* in sixteenth-century France, see Moss (1982: 3–7).
15. On Labé's (re-gendered) imitation of Tibullus, see Sterritt (2005).
16. On the reception of Semiramis from Diodorus Siculus to the modern era, see Harty (1987).
17. On the reception history of incest and the rehabilitation of Semiramis, see Archibald (2001).
18. Ovid emphasizes the futility of resistance in order to celebrate his own ready submission to love (*Amores* 1.2.9–22).
19. Similarly, in Sonnet 19, the poet is cast as one of Diana's nymphs, wounded by the arrows – and bow – she had ineffectually directed at her prey (Labé 2004: 131–2).
20. L'Aubespine translates Ovid's *Heroides* 2 and the first canto of Ariosto's *Orlando furioso* (l'Aubespine 2007: 79–107). On her translation of Ovid, see DeVos (2023).
21. On Messalina, see Levick (1990: 53–67), esp. pp. 64–7 on the mock-marriage.
22. On the political expediency of Messalina's sexual liaisons, see Levick (1990: 56).
23. The clarification that the poem is about a lute ('D'un Lut'), as if to correct the sexual reading, is given only at the end in BnF ms. français 1718 (fol. 57^r) and in Kłosowska's modern edition (l'Aubespine 2007: 56–7). In *Le Cabinet satyrique* (1618: 308; see also Fleuret 1924: I, 362–3), the sonnet is given the title 'Le Luth' (The Lute), as if to encourage the musical reading and allow the sexual reading to emerge only incidentally. On the 'instrument' as either a male sex object or a dildo, see Kłosowska (2008: 194–6).
24. Kłosowska here follows (and punctuates) the text given in BnF ms. français 1718, fol. 57^r. The variant 'contemple' (contemplates) for 'contente' (contents) in *Le Cabinet satyrique* (1618: 308) personifies the instrument, bestowing him/it with some agency (without necessarily making 'it' an animate 'him') and suggesting that some of the poet's pleasure comes from being seen. Other variants similarly affect the poem's eroticism: *Le Cabinet satyrique* replaces the manuscript's 'je le touche' (I touch him/it) in the first quatrain with 'je le taste' (*taster* has

the senses of tasting, trying, handling or groping for), and 'sur mon sain' (on my breast) in the second quatrain with 'et sur moy', replacing the reference to the poet's breast with the less suggestive but also more comprehensive evocation of her whole body.

25. *Le Cabinet satyrique* (1618: 308). In a curious lapse that nevertheless extends the ambiguity of the pronouns on which the sonnet's enigma depends, Kłosowska's edition of l'Aubespine follows BnF ms. français 1718 for the translation, but conflates the manuscript and the *Cabinet* readings of the text: 'Puis de moy, doucement, / Lasse et non assouvye, enfin je me retire' (l'Aubespine 2007: 56–7). Although accidental, this lapse makes the poet's sexual autonomy absolute and adds a further aspect to her self-division, suggesting that the poet's identity – her *moy* – resides in the sexual pleasure that she is able to access and withdraw from at will.

26. On Renault's adaptation of Platonism, see Endres (2012). On the classification of Renault's novels as middlebrow, and so as falling between the gendered categories of (masculine) modernism and (feminine) popular fiction, see Stewart (2011).

27. In the 'Postface', Yourcenar describes incest as the last taboo (1981: 150).

CHAPTER 3
LUCREZIA MARINELLA AND ANCIENT RHETORIC: A WOMAN'S APPROACH TO ELOQUENCE, PERSUASION AND METAPHOR IN THE LATE ITALIAN RENAISSANCE
Francesca D'Alessandro Behr

Over the last thirty years, Renaissance writer Lucrezia Marinella (1571–1653) has been mostly studied for her treatise *The Nobility and Excellence of Women and the Defects and Vices of Men* (1601) in which she defends women and their accomplishments. In her own time, however, she was celebrated above all for her hagiographical works. In this contribution I will discuss her approach to a rhetorically ornate style programmatically discussed in the preface titled 'To Readers' ('A' lettori') attached as a foreword to one of her hagiographies, the *Life of the Virgin Mary, Empress of the Universe described in Prose and Ottava Rima* (1602) and featuring the florid style she is defending.[1] This preface reveals Marinella's own ideas about effective speech and knowledge of ancient rhetoricians whose thoughts she selectively employs to defend her rhetorical choices. For Marinella persuasion is connected to symmetry between object and the words employed to depict it. Sublimity is credible if depicted with a sublime style which she uses to describe the life of the Virgin Mary or other saintly persons. This idea of rhetorical symmetry is borrowed from Aristotle's *Rhetoric*, one of the first texts to systematically discuss it.

Ancient rhetoric in the age of Humanism

In 'To Readers', Marinella lists rhetoricians she appreciates, discusses some features typical of their eloquence and explains the reasons behind her mode of composition. She mentions Alcidamas, Plato, Isocrates, Apuleius and, most importantly, Gorgias of Leontini and Aristotle. Several of them wrote, as she did, in a rhetorically florid style which, in her judgement, is the most suitable for describing elevated subjects and convincing the public of their veracity.

Marinella was familiar with rhetorical principles elaborated in antiquity. Like many Cinquecento humanists preoccupied with communication, she grasped the importance of classical rhetoric for persuasion as an activity involving the mind and the heart. During this time, even preachers from the pulpit employed rhetorical devices in their sermons and persisted in their use even after the Tridentine Church recommended simplicity in style.[2]

As Nancy Lee Christiansen suggests, in the Renaissance, rhetoric is not simply the art of public or political speech but the art of all human discourse: 'Rhetoric functions as the umbrella term for the three language arts (grammar, logic, rhetoric/*trivium*) that each name one dimension of language (the linguistic, the cognitive, and the social) and that together compose all acts of human communication, including solitary thinking and self-reflection' (Christiansen 2019: 165). Thus, Renaissance humanists bring to bear rhetorical principles elaborated in antiquity upon a wide variety of writing, literature and speaking.

Scholars like Charles Trinkaus and Mark Fumaroli have demonstrated that Renaissance humanists 'believed in the potency of speech for moving the hearts and minds of men, and in the need for language to be beautiful and pleasing. They were rhetoricians, and this meant that they were committed to persuasion.' (Trinkaus 1970: xviii and Fumaroli 1980). This statement describes well the attitude of Marinella who defends her words for what they can accomplish in her readers. Most of all, she appreciates Gorgias' prose as well as Aristotle's ideas about rhetorical appropriateness (*Rhet.* 3.7.1). Her foray into this debate has broad theoretical implications.

Marinella is one of the first women in the Early Modern Age who used classical texts, philosophy, rhetoric, scientific discourse and contemporary literature to argue and promote her ideas. In *Nobility*, the text that most directly displays her position in the *querelle des femmes* – the debate on the nature and status of women that flourished in Europe between 1350 and 1600 – she employs classical authors normally used to reinforce the inferiority of women to opposite ends, namely, the establishment of women's worth and equal opportunities in her society; in her epic *Henry or Byzantium Conquered* (1635), she summons Ovid's poetry (especially *Heroides* and *Metamorphoses*) as well as Vergil's *Aeneid* to raise doubts about war. In the Preface under study in this chapter, she conceives of persuasive rhetoric with the aid of Aristotle and Gorgias. All her literary production displays a deep interest in the classics, which from the Quattrocento and onward were systematically studied, translated and printed, primarily by men, giving rise to the movement known as Humanism. Humanists were convinced that their methodologies and concerns would foster individual and societal progress. They were eager to communicate this awareness to all audiences. Although Humanism is generally viewed as socially conservative, in Western history it was a ground-breaking movement that fostered critical thinking and the reassessment of traditional assumptions. Through *litterae* (learning and education) the experience of humanists was related to the most significant experiences of the history of humankind (Behr 2018: 3–34).

During this time, women had limited access to public arenas of learning (e.g. universities), but thanks to the advent of the printing press, the availability of translations of classical texts, and an encouraging family environment, Marinella was able to gain access to the same texts that male scholars were accessing. Through them, she gained a contextualized perspective about her society and strove to persuade her contemporaries to see the world in different ways (Behr 2021). Besides her appreciation of women and peace, at the end of the sixteenth century, while many intellectuals in Europe were preoccupied with highlighting differences between religious creeds in the aftermath of Luther's Reformation and the publication of the *Index of Prohibited Books* (1559), Marinella worked to find points in common between an array of modern and ancient traditions and authors. She certainly appreciates Christian writers, but she is also convinced that we have much to learn from ancient sources. She expounds her humanistic ideas and trust in logic and rationality as keys towards true religious devotion and societal flourishing (Prodi 1991; Behr 2022: 144–56). Because of her conviction that the perfecting of humanity is possible, realized through God's grace, the aid of rationality and persuasive writing, she must be considered one of the first female Christian humanists active in Italy (cf. Zimmermann 2017: 1–119).

Gorgias of Leontini's style

In 'To readers,' Marinella defends her style, which, as she puts it, occupies 'the highest peak of eloquence' ('To Readers': f. a3r) while also championing that of Gorgias of Leontini. She begins with a swipe at Aristotle for having tried 'in vain . . . to burn the wings of Gorgias' fame,' ('To Readers': f. a3v) and in fear that many 'moved by the authority of Aristotle . . . would try to destroy the greatness of her own poetic prose' ('To Readers': f. a3r). Despite this gibe against Aristotle, Marinella displays thorough understanding of key principles presented by the Stagirite in his *Rhetoric*.

She discusses Gorgias of Leontini extensively and compiles a sort of micro-history of his reception ('To Readers': f. a3r-v). Among those who followed his style in the fifth and fourth centuries BCE, she includes Critias, Alcibiades, Thucydides, Pericles, Isocrates, Alcidamas and Plato. In describing Gorgias' accomplishments, she draws from Philostratus' *Life of the Sophists* and Aristotle's *Rhetoric*. In Venice, the city where she lived, a concentration of printing initiatives witnessed renewed attention to ancient eloquence and sophistry. Between 1503 and 1513, Aldus Manutius printed *Greek Orators*, the first collection of ancient rhetoricians' texts that was inclusive of sophistic pieces such as Gorgias' *Encomium of Helen*, the *Rhetores Graeci*, containing Aristotle's *Rhetoric* and *Poetics* and finally Philostratus' *Lives of the Sophists*. The Latin translations of the *Lives*, from which Marinella is quoting, were based on the Aldine text (e.g., Bonfini 1516).

Marinella praises Gorgias because 'he brought light to the darkness that obfuscated the reasonings of his times' ('To Readers': f. a3r). For this reason, she explains, Philostratus called him 'father of the art of reasoning' ('To Readers': f. a3r) and in the *Lives*, he details that what Aeschylus did for tragedy by providing basic principles and requirements such as costumes, characters, and conventions necessary for the genre, Gorgias did in the field of eloquence (Philostratus 1921: 29–30). The picture Marinella develops of Gorgias remains dependent on Philostratus' description of Gorgias' style and the kind of people it attracted in the following way:

> he [Gorgias] set an example to the sophists with his virile and energetic style, his daring and unusual expressions, his inspired impressiveness, and his use of the grand style for great themes . . . and he also clothed his style with poetic words for the sake of ornament and dignity . . . and when already advanced in years, he delivered discourses at Athens, there is nothing surprising in the fact that he won

applause from the crowd; but he also . . . enthralled the most illustrious men, not only Critias and Alcibiades who were both young men but also Thucydides and Pericles who were by that time well on in years.

Philostratus 1.9.1=Philostratus 1921: 31

In 'To Readers,' she repeats that the aged Pericles and Thucydides were fans of Gorgias and uses these men's appreciation for Gorgias to assert Aristotle's mistaken judgement:

> not only Critias and Alcibiades followed him [Gorgias] but also Thucydides and Pericles arrived to their old age . . . therefore it is obvious that Aristotle *is mistaken* when in the Third Book of *Rhetoric* in ch. 2, says that only *men lacking of true science* valued that style; *his words are:* 'Hodie eorum plerique qui disciplinis exculti non sunt, tales pulcherrime loqui existimant.' [Today the majority of those who are not educated, think such style of speaking, the most beautiful] ('To Readers': f. a3r, emphasis added)

The passage demonstrates Marinella's familiarity with Aristotle's text (especially *Rhet.* 3.2) whose Latin translation Carlo Sigonio had undertaken with the assistance of her father Giovanni (Sigonius, Maioragius & Marinelli 1584: 482–3).[3] To qualify Gorgias' success and style in public speaking, she also reports Philostratus' account of this orator's ability to spellbind his Athenian audience and adds that Aristotle called Gorgias' speeches, 'poetic elocution because he employed in prose all those ornaments and all those wonderful and extravagant words which are typically used in poetry' ('To Readers': f. a3v).

Aristotle

In his *Rhetoric* Aristotle acknowledges that artistic prose began as an imitation of poetic style and identifies Gorgias' speeches as exemplars of this kind of poetic prose which he does not endorse (*Rhet.* 3.1.8–9) claiming that the style of prose should differ from that of poetry (*Rhet.* 3.1.9 1404a28).

Marinella remembers Aristotle's contention with the rhetorician from Leontini and some of his expressions. She cites Aristotle criticizing Gorgias for the problematic expression 'things pale and bloodless' ('pallida et exanguia negotia,' 'To Readers': f. a3v). While possibly referring to unripe stalks of corn with the sap being still fresh in them, the words were used by Gorgias perhaps to signify 'recent events,' but to these days the expression remains obscure.[4] We can trace it to *Rhetoric* 3.3.4 where Aristotle is listing what he considers the principal causes for frigid – i.e. non-persuasive – lexis and points to the employment of inappropriate metaphors as source of it:

> The fourth cause of frigidity of style is to be found in metaphors; for metaphors also are inappropriate, some because they are ridiculous – for the comic poets also employ them – others because they are too dignified and somewhat tragic; and if

they are farfetched, they are obscure, as when Gorgias says: 'Affairs pale and bloodless,'... for this is too much like poetry... these expressions fail to produce persuasion.

Rhet. 3.3.4[5]

For Aristotle, lack of propriety in the creation of metaphors results in unconvincing discourse because absence of perceptible proportion between analogous elements in a metaphor impairs intelligibility by making the sentence impractical, too elevated, or too obscure. He does not disavow metaphor per se but the poor use of metaphor (Driscoll 2012: 25).

In addition, since metaphor can serve to elevate discourse, Aristotle considers it generally inappropriate for average stories, everyday people, and prosaic topics. In archaic Greece, performance and verse lent memorability and socio-cultural authority to speech. Only in the fifth century with the development of science, philosophy, history, and political discourse, did prose become the medium for authoritative discourse (Goldhill 2006: 3–4). In Aristotle's *Rhetoric* we find the earliest systematic theoretical account of the subject of prose and an attempt (not always successful) to set prose style apart from poetic style. While recommending that prose writing should avoid flatness and banality (*Rhet.* 3.2.1–2), the Stagirite warns against the employment of unusual or frequent metaphors in prose writing. As we will see, Marinella deviates from this principle, employing elaborate metaphors in her prose compositions.

Ultimately, what Aristotle says about a well constructed and properly functioning metaphor follows the larger principle he articulates at *Rhet.* 3.7.1–4:

Propriety (*to prepon*) of style will be obtained by the expression of emotion and character, and *by proportion (analogon) to the subject matter*. Style is proportionate to the subject matter when neither weighty matters are treated offhand, nor trifling matters with dignity, and no embellishment is attached to an ordinary word... Style expresses emotion, when a man speaks with anger of malicious outrage..., with admiration, of things praiseworthy; with meekness, of things pitiable, and so in all other cases. *Appropriate style also makes the fact appear credible.*

Rhet. 3.7.1–4=1408a10–13, emphasis added

By establishing style as completely dependent on the situation and person being described, Aristotle makes propriety and proportion central to his *Rhetoric*.[6] For him, the act of persuasion is intrinsically bound to the proportion between subject matter and style. If the speaker does not engage in this symmetry, she will fail to make a fact or character appear credible and will not stimulate sympathy nor consensus.

Sublime style for divine topics

In the *Rhetoric* Aristotle assumes that prose deals only with ordinary topics requiring the humbler and plainer style appropriate to them. Aristotle's idea is linked to the emergence of prose in Classical Athens in connection with the development of democratic institutions (e.g., the courts) and the rise of genres such as history, political declamation, and philosophy, which were not necessarily bound to public performances and exemplary narrations in verse featuring divinities and heroes. This correlation between prose and ordinary topics is not endorsed in the Renaissance nor endorsed by Marinella, who in the *Life of the Virgin Mary* employs poetry as well as prose to celebrate the mother of Jesus. She considers both forms perfectly suitable for elevated subjects.[7]

Despite her criticism of Aristotle's rejection of poetic amplification in prose, Marinella defends her rhetorically enhanced prose style using the Aristotelian principle of propriety. She writes:

> I chose this fashion of poetic speaking which is more admirable and greater than that used in prose. The matter was described by Aristotle in the cited book in the following way: 'The *elocutio* of prose should be neither low nor high. On the other hand, poetic *elocutio* is not low.' In fact, poetic speech uses words and ornaments which make the argument great and marvelous, as he adds a little after. *And if it is not permitted to me to employ ornaments which make the argument magnificent and grand in the orations and in prose because their subject is low and humble compared with subject and people which are introduced in poetry, as the same philosopher* [i.e. Aristotle] *left written* with the following words: 'But in the writings of poets, ornaments are appropriate; for the things and people about which poets speak are quite distinct from the rest [of the people]; on the other hand, in speech without meter, it is best to employ ornaments to a lesser degree because its topic and protagonists are of a lesser nature' *it follows that without fear of being scolded, I will adorn this narration of mine, with all poetic ornamentation, since I reason about the greatest actions and of people more noble than nobility itself.*
>
> 'To Readers': f. a4r-v, emphasis added

Even though the syntax of the sentence is tenuous, its meaning is quite clear. Marinella is aware that Aristotle is sceptical about poetic ornamentation in prose, yet she introduces Aristotelian 'appropriateness' (*to prepon*) – the necessity to match content and style – to defend her ornate prose style which features elevated topics, none more elevated than the life of the Virgin Mary. By qualifying *prepon* as symmetry, she invites her critics to remember that Aristotle prescribed grandiloquence for grand topics. Therefore, in the end, she can affirm, 'defeated by these reasons and authorities, those who follow the teachings of Aristotle will be able to praise this style of mine' (f. a4v).

Grandiloquence, in her reckoning, is not simply applicable but necessary to discourse related to the depiction of extraordinary characters engaged in astonishing actions: the nature of the subject demands it. Marinella uses here a strategy that she will employ again in her *The Nobility and Excellence of Women* where she criticizes some of Aristotle's cultural biases against women but exposits other ideas of his to prove and bolster women's excellence. In other words, she picks and chooses notions from a chosen authority according to what she wants to demonstrate.

Luca Piantoni observes that in Marinella's 'To Readers' we find an attempt to join the poetics of *decorum* of Aristotle with the theorizations of Demetrius in his *De Elocutione* (Piantoni 2009: 437).[8] Piantoni is correct even if, in the script under examination, Demetrius is never explicitly mentioned. Demetrius' ideas could have reached Marinella directly or through Francesco Panigarola's treatise *The Preacher or Paraphrase, comment and discourses on the book On style of Demetrius Phalaereus* (1609).[9] It was published in Venice by the printer Giovan Battista Ciotti who also printed Marinella's *The Nobility and Excellence of Women*. Panigarola was one of the most famous religious preachers of her time. In his books, he defends the necessity of the ornate style for sermons that entail teaching (*docere*) but above all, moving the soul (*movere*). While Cardinal Carlo Borromeo in his manual about religious preaching (*Instructiones predicationis verbi dei*, 1573) recommends staying away from a contrived style and superfluous rhetorical tropes, Panigarola supports a richly ornate prose *elocutio* (Delcorno 1987: 468; Hankins 2006).

Throughout the Cinquecento, religious speakers, influenced by their Classical training, progressively abandon the so-called scholastic *sermo* that hinged on technical exegesis focused on logic in favour of speeches structured according to the classical *genera dicendi* (grand, middle, plain). Above all they privilege 'epideictic' ('fit for displaying') rhetoric which in ancient manuals was considered particularly versatile for praise and blame (cf. *Rhetorica ad Herennium* 3.6; Worcester 2001: 3-4ff. and O'Malley 1983: 247ff.). John O'Malley has underlined that if during the Middle Ages Scholastic sermons focused on logic and proof, those produced during the Cinquecento celebrate Christian mysteries with the aid of a beautifully adorned discourse, not different from that employed by hagiographers like Marinella (O'Malley 1979: 109-74). Humanists too favoured that style as suited to commend certain individuals, forms of government, or ideas (McManamon 1996).

In her exposition of the life of the Virgin, Marinella adopts the grand style in accord with Renaissance humanistic thinking that associates epideictic discourse, heroic poetry and religious sermons – forms tantamount to speeches celebrating the actions of virtuous people (Vickers 1983: 519). By considering the oratorical habits of our writer, we understand that she considers amplification and figures of speech as the most suitable to produce persuasion in the audience. Marinella wants to help readers *to see* the greatness and exceptional status of the protagonists of her works.

Defamiliarization and 'bringing-before-the-eyes': Metaphor in Aristotle

To better comprehend how amplification aids persuasion and vividness, it is useful to return to Marinella's 'To Readers' where, with the help of Aristotle, she discusses Alcidamas, a pupil of Gorgias and famous Greek orator of the fourth century:

> Alcidamas, great master among orators, was pleased with poetic eloquence and employed in his prose all those ornaments which suit poets, and above all, [he

employed] epithets, hyperbole, and descriptions. Aristotle retold many ways of sayings used by him [Alcidamas] in his third book of the *Rhetoric*, whose words are 'Alcidomas [*sic*] did not say "sweat" but "humid sweat"; not "laws" but "Queens of States,"' all these modes, according to me, contain in themselves the greatness and magnificence of eloquence.

'To Readers': *f. a3v*

Marinella appreciates Alcidamas' prose filled with stylistic devices typically found in poetry. In the passage above, she exemplifies hyperbole ('humid sweat') and metaphor (laws, 'Queen of states'). As we saw earlier, she admires Gorgias for the same reason, his use in prose of 'copious ornaments' and 'magnificent and *distant* [*peregrine*] words' ('To Readers': f. A3v) useful to trigger the admiration of his listeners. The Italian adjective *peregrino* – from Latin *peregrinus*, foreign – and overall argument leave no doubt that she is drawing from Aristotle and his observations on metaphor.

In the *Rhetoric*, Aristotle discusses metaphor, considering it essential for making a speech non-banal. He describes its potential in these terms:

It is metaphor, above all, that gives perspicuity [τὸ σαφὲς/*to safēs*], pleasure and foreign air [ξενικόν/*xenicon*] and it cannot be learnt from anyone else; but we must make use of metaphors and epithets that are appropriate. This will be secured by observing due proportion [ἀνάλογον/*analogon*].

Rhet. *3.2.8-9=1405a*

Aristotle qualifies metaphor as an aid that bestows exoticism or foreignness [*xenicon*] to discourse. Even earlier in his general discussion about effective elocution and a style that strives towards originality, pleasure and admiration, Aristotle features an adjective containing the idea of 'foreign.' He writes:

We should give our language a 'foreign air' [ξένην/*xenēn*) for men admire what is remote, and that which excites admiration is pleasant.'

Rhet. *3.2.3=1406a*

Aristotle is the first person in antiquity who seriously reflects on the power of metaphor. Not only does he think of it in terms of pleasure and defamiliarization, he realizes that in the crafting of metaphors, strangeness must be combined with propriety.[10] Thus, once again, propriety plays a part: in the passage quoted above (*Rhet*. 3.2.8-9), he resorts to the word proportion (*analogon*) to express it. He explains that the difficulty in crafting a good metaphor consists in featuring at once otherness and similarity produced by a special intuition that creatively combines elements that are proportional but not in an obvious way.

Similarly, in *Poetics* 21, Aristotle discusses metaphor under the sign of 'transference' and 'non-pertinence,' as 'the transfer of a name that belongs to something else (ἀλλοτρίου/*allotriou*).[11] He uses the adjective *allotrios*, signifying 'alien', 'belonging to something else,' a term opposed to 'ordinary' or 'current' (κύριος/*kurios*) (*Poet.* 21 1457b3. See Ricoeur 1996: 330). In other words, in the *Poetics*, metaphor is described as a transgression of the proper use of a word which – quite differently from other improper usages – brings clarity. This happens because in metaphor, another kind of propriety is established, based not on what is tautologically obvious but on what is similar (Guastini 2005). Through this other form of proportion or appropriate transgression, the object in question appears in a new light from which the hearer pleasantly and quickly learns something different about it (cf. *Rhet.* 3.10).

For Aristotle, the enlightenment (*sapheneia*) obtained by the grasping of a metaphor is similar to that produced in the solving of a riddle or enigma (*Rhet.* 3.2.12) such as the one given in the *Poetics* 'old age is to life as evening is to a day' (*Poet.* 21 1457b22–23). The process is pedagogically valuable because in the working out of the riddle, we explore the complex analogy that links the way in which an individual's abilities change over the course of a life to the manner in which the sun's radiance waxes and wanes over the course of a day.

In sum, from the excerpts analyzed above, we realize that Aristotle values metaphor in connection with the defamiliarization of the object. In the *Rhetoric* the phenomenon relates to the capacity of 'bringing-before-the-eyes,' a faculty specifically associated with metaphors (Newman 2002: 5). Richard Moran underlines that for Aristotle the primary virtue of metaphor 'is the ability to set something vividly before the eyes of the audience (*pro ommaton poiein*, *Rhet.* 1410b334)' (Moran 1996: 392). Moran also describes what happens in the mind of the listener/reader when a metaphor is employed. The trope is able to bring forth not merely one idea, but a whole bundle of ideas that readers can see evoked rather than rationally articulated; they engage their mind imaginatively with them (Moran 1996: 394–6). Metaphor achieves a kind of underlying understanding by provoking the reader to active discovery:

> it 'requires us to see what is in front of us as different from what it at first seemed to be' (Davis 123). This linguistic diversion makes it so that 'understanding new metaphors often requires an interpretative effort' (Marcos 128), which is a creative act.
>
> *Driscoll 2012: 27*

Similarly, Carlos Iglesias-Crespo makes the case for a cognitive reading of the rhetorical *energeia* (actuality/vividness, cf. *Rhet.* 3.10–11) of metaphor and highlights the central role attributed to mental images by Aristotle in his reflections on rhetoric and the psyche (Iglesias-Crespo 2021).

Marinella's style dissected

After having reviewed the functioning of metaphors according to Aristotle, it is time to look at them in action, in Marinella's prose. Let us examine what her rhetorical style accomplishes by considering a paragraph of her *Life of the Virgin Mary* in which she is describing the Holy Spirit descending on Mary and impregnating her:

> Here the glorious woman surrounded by the rays of the immortal fire: here the uncreated Word which entering (*passando*) with the immensity of His virtue the purity of the virginal cloister [of Mary], rested in it, almost [as] a Dove in the nest. The spirit of God inhabiting her heart and burning with His love penetrated (*penetrava*) delicately through the innermost parts, and bones of the happy maiden. The effects of such love accomplished in her stupendous things . . . Being enclosed in Mary the Divine Goodness with Its inflamed light began to make her shine, as an alabaster vase in which a hidden light shines.
>
> <div align="right">Vita di Maria: <i>f. 26v</i></div>

The passage is phenomenal in its array of tropes through which Marinella describes Mary's miraculous incarnation. The Word of God is depicted as living rays of light reaching into a secluded space and finding repose there. The virginity of Mary is represented as a cloister. Her impregnation is depicted through the verbs of crossing (*passando* . . . *penetrava*). There is, however, no intimation of violence, rather the act is suspended in great serenity highlighted through the image of a dove-like Holy Spirit settling into its nest. The arrival of God into the body of Mary is portrayed as a homecoming but also a loving gift which produce amazing things while making her shine from within like a transparent alabaster in which a light has been placed.

In the description, rhetorical amplification brings divinely endowed, invisible actions 'before the eyes' of the spectator. Through beautiful and unusual metaphors, Marinella fosters a movement which stimulates the mind of the readers to see the Virgin gently impregnated by a supremely docile but powerful God. Thanks to her metaphorically rich language we can participate to the extraordinary moment when Mary becomes the mother of God. We too become part of a revelation in which impossible to combine ideas are juxtaposed, made visible and credible: virginity and impregnation; closure and openness; kindness and omnipotence; light and darkness, human and divine. With the aid of metaphors, Marinella effectively describes a mystery that definitions and abstract statements would have not been able to convey.

At this point, we can fully comprehend what she says at the end of 'To Readers,' when after having talked about her favorite rhetoricians, she details the reasons for her preference for a style rich in tropes:

> Now these are the authorities of those who kept in their bosom the rivers of eloquence; now I plunge into the reasons, among which the first will be this, that the actions *which participate in greatness, magnificence and divinity* [*che hanno del grande, del magnifico e del divino*] and that go beyond human operations require *a mode of talking that is grand and awesome* [*un modo di dire grande e mirabile*], quite different from that employed in recounting those actions which are small, humble and low. And a different style is sought even more when such actions

depend on persons which surpass for the excellence of their nature, men and heroes.

'To Readers': *f. a4r, emphasis added*

The divine activities of people who exceed their human limits demand the adoption of a style made different and majestic by metaphors, epithets, and hyperboles, tropes apt to describe sublime actions and their non-ordinary makers. What is magnificent and miraculous must be expressed with an extra-ordinary diction that inspires awe but at the same time can be understood. Metaphors and tropes grant to the written word the alterity necessary to describe divine phenomena. In adopting such style Marinella shows herself to have been receptive to Aristotle's views of figurative discourse able to elevate and defamiliarize the object of narration so to make it appropriately credible.

Metaphors and beauty in Marinella's *Man's Amorous Turn to Divine Beauty*

The importance of a writing style rich in tropes must also be put in connection with Marinella's way of conceptualizing beauty, wonder, and metaphor in *Man's Amorous Turn to Divine Beauty*, a short treatise which accompanies the *Life of the Seraphic and Glorious St. Francis* (1597).

In this work, she speaks about how to make oneself worthy of the love of God. She explains that although the body hinders the perfect knowledge of God, the presence of a benevolent and loving God wanting to be known is evident when we look at certain objects:

> and if knowing it [Divine providence] perfectly is not allowed because the body is an obstacle . . . nevertheless you must try . . . Various are the means and ways with the help of which you will arrive to this perception/understanding [of God] . . . many created things which fall directly under your eyes show you an obvious and plain path to know Him, *they are not different from clear and terse mirrors and many and loquacious tongues, which, although mute, reveal His semblance and essence*. Therefore, rightly, some called the creatures, wings, which can elevate and bring [us] to the presence of His divine light.

Mongini 1996: 441–42, emphasis added[12]

Sublime matters are hard to grasp for mortal beings. However, there are items on earth, which, thanks to their qualities, are better suited to communicate the existence and nature of God. Marinella amplifies and clarifies the properties of the items in question (sun and men) by calling them 'mirrors' and 'wings', so that it is through metaphors that reveal their nature better than their proper names.

In the treatise sun and man are recognized as the earthly items that best signify the presence of God. The sun is deemed 'beautiful' for its luminosity and ability to generate life (Mongini 1996: 442). The body and soul of human beings are also characterized as 'marvellous' (Mongini 1996: 443). Especially when 'you consider the excellence of the soul,' Marinella elucidates, 'you remain entirely awe-struck and stupefied' (Mongini 1996: 443). The human intellect, she adds, is admirable above all for its capacity to see what is not there, to figure out what is concealed in 'the depth of the sea, and in the most hidden bowels of the earth' (Mongini 1996: 443). That part of the human mind that she calls 'reasonable' (*ragionevole*), 'dares to spy the highest Olympus' and 'depicts as present things already seen many centuries ago' (Mongini 1996: 443): it can contain all things which make the world beautiful and conceive of them as alive. Thanks to the mind, the presence of beautiful objects, and writers able to describe those beautiful objects in a suitable manner, human beings can see what is not visible. For Marinella 'marvellous' is a specific quality that helps the humankind to perceive what is not immediately perceivable. Beauty (on earth and in the text) is connected to what is marvellous and acts as a channel between the visible and the invisible.

Although she admits her inability to describe 'the Sublime excellence of God,' she resolves to metaphors such as 'divine beauty' and 'eternal Wisdom' to try to communicate it:

> what should we say about the clearest and highest Eminence of Intellectual Beauty, called by many eternal Wisdom? And allow me to describe Divine beauty in this way still lacking and imperfect; because it is impossible to find names or terms through which not only we cannot express it, we cannot even adumbrate it; who can narrate the Sublime excellence of God?
>
> *Mongini 1996: 452*

Thus, when the issue is finding a language able to narrate divinity and beauty, metaphor seems to be the best aid, and in point of fact, Marinella adopts a strongly metaphorical language, even if, as she admits, it is impossible to signify the Sublimity of God (Ferrari-Schifer 2002: 191). Not accidentally, she chooses the metaphor 'wings' which Plato used in his *Phaedrus* and in the *Symposium*, suggesting that Nature and Beauty can be employed by the philosophical mind as ladders towards God. The beauty of what we see on earth and that of written metaphors are essential in the perception of God.

Conclusions

In 'To Readers,' Marinella mediates between her allegiance to Gorgias' highly rhetorical prose style and Aristotle's conceptualization of stylistic appropriateness: for our writer lofty topics, especially lofty religious topics, call for rhetorically enhanced eloquence. She employs classical authorities, such as Gorgias and Aristotle, and *not* religious authorities to defend her approach to persuasive religious discourse. Marinella is not afraid to criticize Aristotle while, at the same time, she displays a deep understanding of his *Rhetoric* and expertly uses some of his reflections for her own agenda.

She employs Aristotle's theorization of propriety (*prepon*) to defend the ornate prose she features in the *Life of Mary* because she is convinced that it is the best at teaching and persuading audiences about divine creatures. By reading Aristotle's *Rhetoric* and *Poetics*, she understood that a style vivified by metaphors can engage readers placing 'before their eyes' what is not immediately evident. The crafting of a beautiful style is essential to create memorable and persuasive descriptions through which the object is defamiliarized and made present.

What Marinella writes echoes her conceptions of metaphor in her *Man's Amorous Turn To Divine Beauty*. Here she qualifies metaphor as a device useful to describe beautiful objects and to compensate for human weakness in the description of divine matters. By reading about divinely endowed individuals and actions expressed through metaphors, we can move closer to God because we can understand their nature and feel them present. For Marinella tropes are essential because they give amplification and vividness to the object, but also because they make us realize its instrumental nature. Metaphors assist us in conjuring up an image of divine actors, just like the sun on earth helps people to envision their creator. Marinella's perspective on rhetorical complexity is in accord with what some Seicento preachers recommended for preaching. It was also what humanists employed in their speeches. Ultimately, an attentive analysis of 'To Readers' reveals an author whose mindset and writing style have been profoundly influenced by the study of ancient rhetoric. Without any doubt, Marinella's knowledge of ancient orators shaped her attitude towards rhetoric and persuasion.

Notes

1. The preface 'To readers,' (in Italian 'A' Lettori') is found in Marinella (1602). I use the digital edition from Bayerische Staatsbibliothek (Munich). All English translations of Marinella's Italian are my own.
2. While in England the employment of elaborate *elocutio* for sacred rhetoric is perceived as problematic, in Italy it is widely accepted. Cf. Shuger (1988) and Giunta (2012).
3. The citation can be found at the end of the first chapter of modern editions (*Rhet.* 3.1).
4. For more details on Gorgias' expression 'things pale and bloodless' see commentary by E. M. Cope to Aristotle's *Rhetoric* 3.3.4, in Aristotle (1926), trans. J. H. Freese, whose translation I employ throughout.
5. Ibid.
6. A similar principle is in the *Poetics* where Aristotle divides up genres in relationship to the kind of action they represent, see Vickers (1983: 514).
7. For the importance of religious prose writing and women's writing in Italy, Boillet (2021) and Cox (2011: esp. Chapter 6).
8. In antiquity *De Elocutione* was attributed to Demetrius of Phaleron but is currently assigned to a later writer; cf. Demetrio (2007: 4–16).
9. It is a commentary and translation into Italian of Demetrius' (or pseudo-Demetrius') *De Elocutione* (Περὶ Ἑρμηνείας). The text, first printed in Greek in the Aldine *Rhetores graeci* of 1508 was translated into Latin and became quite popular; see Weinberg (1951).

10. Defamiliarization, a neologism that implies 'making strange' and 'pushing aside', is a central concept in Russian Formalism which tries to describe and define *literaturnost* (literariness) and the techniques writers use to transform ordinary language into poetic language, which for the Russian Formalists, induces a heightened state of perception. cf. Shklovsky (1990). On defamiliarization and Aristotle, see most recently Iglesias-Crespo (2021).
11. 'Metaphor consists in giving the thing a name that belongs to something else; the transference being either from genus to species, or from species to genus, or from species to species, or on grounds of analogy.' *Poetics* 21 (1457b7–15), Aristotle (1921: 71–2).
12. For Italian text and page number of *Rivolgimento amoroso dell' huomo verso la divina bellezza* (*Man's Amorous Turn to Divine Beauty*) I follow Guido Mongini's transcription of Pietro Bertano's edition of *Vita del serafico et glorioso S. Francesco descritta in ottava rima da Lucretia Marinella . . . con un discorso del Rivolgimento Amoroso uerso la Somma* [sic] *Bellezza* (*Life of the seraphic and glorious St. Francis described in octave by Lucretia Marinella . . . with a discourse of the Amorous Turn to the Highest Beauty,* Venice 1597) in Mongini (1996).

MODERN

CHAPTER 4
'ALL THE ALLUREMENTS OF BEAUTY AND ELOQUENCE': ASPASIA OF MILETUS AND THE INTELLECTUAL WOMAN IN THE NINETEENTH CENTURY
Isobel Hurst

The intellectual and social prestige of a classical education connected nineteenth-century women in Britain and America with a tradition of learning in which notable women had excelled for centuries. Their models were drawn from classical mythology (including Minerva and the Muses), ancient history (such as Sappho or Aspasia), or more recent precursors (such as early modern female scholars). Constructing a tradition of admired female predecessors as well as contemporary examples of intellectual achievement helped to combat preconceptions about women's physical and mental unfitness for serious study, or the accusation that such mental exertion would render them unwomanly. Despite the validation of identifying with other female intellectuals, women writers also found reflections of their own anxieties about reputation and entering the public sphere. Questions of intellectual excellence, reputation and equality in marriage recur in nineteenth-century depictions of Aspasia of Miletus, a Greek woman who was famed for her learning and her beauty, the beloved partner and intellectual companion of Pericles. As a woman who gained access to the most exclusive intellectual circles of Athens, who debated with Socrates and advised Pericles on politics, Aspasia was a fascinating and aspirational figure. According to her detractors, she was manipulative and compromised by sexual scandal. It might seem surprising that a woman who was often designated a 'courtesan' or 'mistress' should be celebrated in Romantic and Victorian literary culture. Yet Aspasia attracted the attention of women readers and writers precisely because her disregard for restrictive notions of feminine respectability enabled her to achieve an unparalleled reputation as a thinker and speaker.

In this essay I examine the representation of Aspasia in two historical novels, Lydia Maria Child's *Philothea: A Romance* (1836, republished in 1845 as *Philothea: A Grecian Romance*) and Eliza Lynn's historical novel *Amymone, A Romance of the Days of Pericles* (1848). The historical novel was a popular and critically acclaimed genre in the nineteenth century, and many Victorian novelists attempted the genre at least once. Novels set in the ancient world often took the opportunity to address safely distanced versions of contemporary controversies such as religious conversion, arguments for and against representative democracy, gender roles, marriage and divorce. Lynn and Child were not alone in perceiving similarities between what they read about ancient Athens and what they experienced in nineteenth-century Britain and America, where feminine respectability was defined in terms of domesticity and seclusion, and it was rare for women to be highly educated. They risked accusations of impropriety in writing about a woman who (even in the most sanitized interpretation of her life) left the women's quarters and socialized in predominantly masculine gatherings. Nevertheless, Aspasia, a woman who achieved an unprecedented marker of intellectual distinction as Sophocles' teacher, offered a powerful argument against assumptions of women's intellectual inferiority. Child and Lynn do not give Aspasia a central role in their texts, yet her presence is potent. They juxtapose her with more conventional female characters, allowing for complex discussions of propriety, domesticity and gendered double standards, and dramatize her involvement in the political and intellectual world of one of the most celebrated periods in history.

Who was Aspasia?

Scholars seeking to reconstruct a feminist rhetorical tradition point out the difficulty of finding evidence about Aspasia or any other woman in fifth-century Athens. Madeleine M. Henry finds the 'colourful anecdotes' on which Aspasia's reputation depends to be 'almost completely unverifiable' (1995: 3). Although none of Aspasia's writings survive, Cheryl Glenn argues that 'the historical tradition has readily accepted secondary accounts of Socrates' influence, teaching and beliefs' and the same standard should be applied to Aspasia and her female counterparts (1995: 36). Ancient accounts of Aspasia must be read with caution: 'Although she herself escaped the traditional limitations of her gender, she did not escape those who reinscribed her' (Glenn 1995: 41). In this reading, Aspasia's achievements have been almost entirely erased from history to suit misogynistic notions: she is represented only in relation to men such as Pericles and Socrates, rather than as a noteworthy figure in her own right.

Plutarch's *Life of Pericles* (a text which would have been available to readers in the first half of the nineteenth century in the translation known as Dryden's) conveys the equivocal nature of Aspasia's reputation. A highly educated teacher of rhetoric who debated with Socrates and other Athenian philosophers, Aspasia was celebrated for her intellect and attacked for impiety and sexual impropriety. She was accused of influencing Pericles' foreign policy decisions and acting as 'the Hera to his Zeus, the Helen to his Paris, the woman behind his most tyrannical urges' (Kennedy 2014: 68). He was thought to have begun his 'remorseless and disproportionate assault on Samos' to please Aspasia (d'Angour 2019: 41). She is represented by some authors as Pericles' de facto wife and by others as a courtesan. Plutarch calls Aspasia a *pallakē*, or concubine: Laura McClure observes that this term might describe a 'common law wife without citizen status, since she was typically of slave or foreign origins' (2003: 19). Accusations that she was a prostitute or a madam are to be found in Old Comedy: in *Acharnians*, Aristophanes alludes to 'a couple of Aspasia's whores' (1998: 121). She was prosecuted for impiety by Hermippos the comedian 'who alleged further that she received free-born women at a place of assignation for Pericles' (Plutarch 1916: 93). In Plutarch's account the accusation that she kept a house of courtesans is mediated by an account of her wisdom and the respect shown to her by notable Athenian men and their wives:

> Aspasia, as some say, was held in high favour by Pericles because of her rare political wisdom. Socrates sometimes came to see her with his disciples, and his intimate friends brought their wives to her to hear her discourse, although she presided over a business that was anything but honest or even reputable, since she kept a house of young courtesans.
>
> *Plutarch 1916: 69*

Her relationship with Pericles was affectionate: Plutarch finds it notable that 'Twice a day, as they say, on going out and on coming in from the market-place, he would salute her with a loving kiss' (Plutarch 1916: 71). The story of the trial reinforces the idea of Pericles' extraordinary devotion to Aspasia: Plutarch attributes to Aeschines the story that Pericles, weeping copiously, successfully entreated the jurors to spare Aspasia (Plutarch 1916: 93).

In Plato's *Menexenus*, Socrates claims Aspasia as his rhetoric teacher and recites a funeral oration which he attributes to her: 'she rehearsed to me the speech in the form it should take, extemporizing in part, while other parts of it she had previously prepared, I imagine, at the time when she was composing the funeral oration which Pericles delivered' (Plato 1929: 339). According to this dialogue, Aspasia was the author not only of the speech that Socrates recites to Menexenus but also of Pericles' celebrated funeral oration for the Athenian war dead. After the recitation, Menexenus comments dubiously 'Aspasia, by your account, deserves to be congratulated if she is really capable of composing a speech like that, woman though she is' (381). While the dialogue has traditionally been read as parodic, Jan Maximilian Robitzsch argues that the representation of Aspasia in this text is ambiguous because of the contrasting perspectives of the two interlocutors, Socrates and Menexenus: the treatment of Aspasia in the dialogue is 'neither wholly serious nor wholly ironic' (2017: 288–9). It has also been suggested that Aspasia appears in her role as Socrates' teacher under the name Diotima in another Platonic dialogue, the *Symposium* (d'Angour 2019: 43).

Aspasia is often described by modern scholars as a *hetaira*, a label which has been re-evaluated by feminist critics seeking to challenge what Rebecca Futo Kennedy calls the 'wife–whore dichotomy' in scholarly accounts of Athenian women (2015: 62). Kennedy argues that translating the word *hetaira* with the 'vague and culturally contingent' term 'courtesan' colours Aspasia's reputation in a way that the basic meaning of 'companion' (on the lines of the masculine *hetairos*) would not (2015: 61). Interestingly, the nineteenth-century historian George Grote makes a similar point about the literal meaning of *hetaira* (which he translates as 'female companion'), although he also uses the term 'courtezan' for women 'who lived a free life, managed their own affairs, and supported themselves by their powers of pleasing' (1849: 134). Grote expresses scepticism about the idea that Aspasia kept enslaved girls as courtesans, noting that this scandal was probably invented by Pericles' political enemies. He argues that a 'distinguished and superior' *hetaira* such as Aspasia would have been a better companion than a respectable Athenian wife, since marriageable women lived in 'strict and almost oriental recluseness' and were 'destitute of all mental culture and accomplishments' (133). The underlying assumption, that it would be preferable for a man to marry a woman capable of sharing her husband's intellectual interests, reflects Grote's own partnership with his wife Harriet. His interpretation may also be influenced by the association of equality and intellectual compatibility in marriage with Pericles and Aspasia in poetry and fiction in the period when Grote was writing about Greece.

Aspasia in poetry and fiction

Feminist scholars and nineteenth-century women writers share an interest in the differences in status that enabled Aspasia to evade the limitations of Athenian women's lives. Aspasia was subject to Athenian law but was not 'accountable to the severe strictures of aristocratic Athenian women, whose activity, movement, education, marriage, and rights as citizens and property-holders were extremely circumscribed by male relatives' (Glenn 1994: 182). In Ionian society gender divisions were not as strictly enforced as they were in Athens: elite women 'were more generally integrated with social activities like dining and drinking' (Kennedy 2014: 72–4). Aspasia belonged to a class of women who participated in symposia and luxury culture in their own cities and continued to do so when married to Athenian men (Kennedy 2015: 61). In the nineteenth-century context, the restrictions which applied to Athenian women would have seemed familiar to women of the English middle and upper classes. The more socially free, intellectual and luxurious lifestyle of an Aspasia might be projected onto women of other countries, such as France with its tradition of the salon. Alternatively, poetry and fiction offered opportunities to fantasise about what it would be like to be Aspasia, or to express how it would feel to be an intellectual woman constrained by the demands of propriety and confronted with Aspasia's freedoms.

Aspasia's exceptional position in a prestigious cultural context appealed to nineteenth-century women writers who sought female role models. Her image was enhanced by Romantic periodicals for women: Noah Comet demonstrates that editors praised Aspasia's learning and ambition, while 'exculpating her from the means by which she attained them as symptoms of ancient Greek debauchery' (2013: 37). To avoid associating her with sexual impropriety, she was identified not as a courtesan or as Pericles' mistress but as his wife. In a poem by L.E.L. (Letitia Elizabeth Landon), 'The Banquet of Aspasia and Pericles', she is hailed at the end of each stanza as 'The bright Athenian bride', a beautiful woman with a 'radiant smile'. Reclining on an ivory couch and beaming adoringly at 'the stately Pericles', she wears no jewels but is adorned with a myrtle crown as a symbol of love (Landon 1836). This poem does nothing to connect its heroine with the more cerebral aspects of Aspasia's reputation, a notable contrast with L.E.L.'s Sappho poems.

Some allusions to Aspasia in the later part of the century show an increasing awareness that her exceptional freedom to debate with men came at the expense of other women who were limited by the demands of domestic labour or by notions of proper femininity. Amy Levy's dramatic monologue 'Xantippe' (1881) vividly reimagines the bitterness of Socrates' reputedly bad-tempered wife as anger at being excluded from the life of the mind and forced to focus on the domestic sphere. In the monologue, Xantippe's anger is directed at Socrates, Alcibiades and Plato, who taunt her for her ambition while they admit the foreign woman Aspasia to their philosophical dialogues (Levy 1881: 1–13). In *Work* (1873), Louisa May Alcott imagines a meeting for working women at which a well-intentioned speaker might regale the audience with stories of 'the strong-minded women of antiquity'. The narrator observes that 'it was like telling fairy tales to hungry children to describe Aspasia discussing Greek politics with Pericles and Plato reposing upon ivory couches' (426–7), a self-indulgent motivational speech for educated women which has little resonance for the women for whom better wages are an immediate priority.

Philothea: A Romance

Lydia Maria Child, an anti-slavery campaigner, advocate of Native American rights, champion of women's rights, and a prolific author, published *Philothea: A Romance* in 1836 and a new and corrected edition entitled *Philothea: A Grecian Romance* in 1845. Caroline Winterer points out that Child (née Lydia Maria Francis), the daughter of a baker, did not belong to the elite circles in which eighteenth-century American women had studied the classics. Nevertheless, she gained access to the library of the Boston Athenaeum, where she studied ancient and modern examples of slavery (2007: 169–77). She dedicated *Philothea* to her brother Convers Francis, who was a Unitarian clergyman before his appointment as Professor of Pulpit Eloquence at the Harvard Divinity School in 1842. He was a member of the Transcendental Club in the 1830s, and Robert E. Streeter notes the parallels between the novel's Platonism and Transcendentalist thinking (1943: 648). Child claimed in her preface that it had taken her four or five years to write the text because 'the practical tendencies of the age, and particularly of the country in which I lived, have so continually forced me into the actual, that my mind has seldom obtained freedom to rise into the ideal' (1836: vi). Child represents Periclean Athens at the height of its pre-eminence in art and philosophy, a cosmopolitan society with a lively political scene. She uses the Athenian setting of the text to address concerns in contemporary American society and politics. Matthew E. Duquès argues that '*Philothea* revises ancient history to engage early-nineteenth century discourses about disaster, politics, and the people at the root of each' (2017: 94). Sandra M. Gustafson highlights the significance of the Athenian setting, which allowed Child 'to question the values of her own society without attacking it directly', showing the flaws in 'the democratic practices of participation and persuasion represented by Pericles' and highlighting 'the republican ideals of the common good, which she identifies with Platonic idealism' (2011: 164).

The classical scholar C. C. Felton's discomfort with the text – which he compared unfavourably with J. G. Lockhart's *Valerius: A Roman Story* (1821) and Edward Bulwer Lytton's *The Last Days of Pompeii* (1834) – centred on his sense that while the details might be historically accurate, the spirit of the novel was anachronistic and not sufficiently impersonal: it displayed 'certain ways of thinking, that belong, not merely to modern times, but to Mrs. Child herself'. Disparaging her 'enthusiasm', he argued that 'the copiousness of her imagination, and the ardor of her feelings' made Child's novel 'deficient in *repose*', the solemnizing and soothing quality which Felton considered 'thoroughly Greek' (1837: 79). He commented favourably on the quality of Child's learning but complained that she was 'too laboriously classical in minute details; in her Atticism, she is hyper-Attic, and might be known for a foreigner on classic ground' (1837: 83).

The argument that women were capable of being educated in serious subjects underlies the novel's representation of the principal female characters. Edgar Allan Poe claimed that '*Philothea* might be introduced advantageously into our female academies' (1836: 662). Aspasia is not the only model for a learned woman in the text: Philothea, the granddaughter of the Pre-Socratic philosopher Anaxagoras (formerly Pericles' tutor), receives 'an education seldom bestowed upon daughters' (Child 1836: 14). A shared experience of books and music connects her with Anaxagoras' other pupil, Paralus (the son of Pericles and his former wife), creating a lifelong attachment. In her grandfather's house Philothea has access to intellectual resources most Athenian women could not imagine, including texts by 'Thales, Pythagoras, Hesiod, Homer, Simonides, Ibycus, and Pindar. More than one of these precious volumes were transcribed entirely by her own hand' (77). Her role is not to participate in debates as Aspasia does, but to be a submissive, silent presence: she is 'a most welcome auditor to the philosophers, poets, and artists, who were ever fond of gathering round the good old man' (76). Despite this subordinate role, the narrator stresses that Philothea's intellectual achievements, beauty and purity secure her more respect than is usual for Athenian women.

The novel has two heroines, Philothea and Eudora. As in many nineteenth-century novels, the paired heroines are differentiated by colouring and disposition: 'Totally unlike each other, but both excellent in beauty. One might have been a model for the seraphs of Christian faith, the other an Olympian deity' (10). Philothea is golden-haired, innocent and conventional, and Eudora dark with a more turbulent temperament. At the start of the text they stand on the roof of Philothea's home and discuss the previous night's procession for the Panathenaean festival. Throughout the text, characters or the narrator inform the reader about Athenian culture, philosophy and religious rituals. Here, for example, Eudora describes the procession: 'The virgins all clothed in white; the heifers decorated with garlands; the venerable old men bearing branches of olive; the glittering chariots; . . . the consecrated image of Pallas carried aloft on its bed of flowers' (12). Philothea, who participated in the procession as one of the virgins in white after spending six months in service to the goddess, responds with a description of the ritual inside the Parthenon. While the information these characters exchange is awkward and unconvincing as a conversation, the didacticism evokes the combination of fiction and guidebook in Germaine de Staël's influential text *Corinne, or Italy* (1807).

The conventional heroine Philothea and the more radical Eudora dispute whether Aspasia's freedom and fame are to be envied or deplored in terms which reflect contemporary debates over women's role in public life. Aspasia's aversion to the secluded life of Athenian women makes her a controversial acquaintance for the two heroines. Philothea finds Aspasia a dangerous influence, arguing that she 'invest[s] vice with all the allurements of beauty and eloquence' (Child 1836: 15). Although this sounds ominous, the idea of 'vice' remains undefined to stress Philothea's innocence. Aspasia is seen to be a negative influence on Eudora, who is not a woman of respectable Athenian parentage but a foundling who was kidnapped from Ionia by pirates and bought by the sculptor Phidias. Eudora defends Aspasia by arguing that her house is the only one in Greece where women can socialize with men and prove themselves other than 'mere domestic slaves' (16). The customs of Aspasia's house, as described by Eudora, include women attending entertainments and performing music. There is a crucial disagreement between Philothea and Aspasia about modesty, signified by wearing a veil in the presence of men. Aspasia refuses to accept the 'tyrannical custom' of veiling for herself or her guests: she claims that married women are happy to 'renounce the absurd fashion' at her request (Child 1836: 25). While Eudora complies with Aspasia's request, Philothea emphasizes her status as a maiden and refuses to take off her own veil until they enter the women's quarters. She proclaims that women should not display their beauty or accomplishments anywhere but in their own homes. For Child's contemporaries, this debate intersected with fears about a woman's reputation if she entered the public sphere as a writer or speaker. Kathleen S. Sullivan argues that Child is alluding to Fanny Wright, an advocate of women's right to speak in public, and that Child undermines 'Aspasia/Wright's argument for women's liberation' by making Aspasia's opinion obviously superficial (2007: 62–4).

Descriptions of Aspasia's beauty and accomplishments are undermined by her conflicting emotions – she has a 'radiant and lucid expression which mantled her whole face, and made the very blood seem eloquent', yet 'something of sadness about her beautiful mouth gave indication that the heavenly part of her nature still struggled with earth-born passions' (Child 1836: 23). Despite Aspasia's eloquence, Philothea can easily reduce her to tears by pointing out that the homage she receives is insincere. Aspasia agrees that although ambitious and vain women model themselves on her, she is viewed with contempt by 'the purest and best matrons of Greece'. She acknowledges that for a woman the consequences of fame are not always enviable:

> 'Yes,' she added, the tears again starting to her eyes – 'I know the price at which I purchase celebrity. Poets will sing of me at feasts, and orators describe me at the games; but what will that be to me, when I have gone into the silent tomb?'
>
> *30*

Philothea responds by distinguishing between the kind of immortality Aspasia seeks and her own religious hopes for eternity: 'The public voice is your oracle; I listen to the whisperings of the gods in the stillness of my own heart; and never yet, dear lady, have those two oracles spoken the same language' (32). She exhorts Aspasia to use her influence with Pericles, to inspire him to prize goodness and freedom over the material prosperity of Athens.

Aspasia's power to harm the two heroines is seen in her malicious thwarting of their marriage prospects. Under a law reinstated by Pericles in 451 BCE, men with non-Athenian wives could not pass on Athenian citizenship to their sons. Child represents this law as an example of Aspasia's influence (although it made her son, Pericles the younger, a non-citizen).[1] In the novel, Aspasia spitefully urges Pericles to revive the law in order to punish Eudora's lover Philaemon, who is stripped of his Athenian citizenship, his right to vote in the public assembly and to inherit his father's property because his mother was a Corinthian. The law also makes it impossible for Philothea, the daughter of a Laconian mother, to marry Pericles' citizen son Paralus. Having separated Eudora from Philaemon, Aspasia encourages her flirtation with the politician and military commander Alcibiades, who intends to seduce Eudora by pretending that he will divorce his wife and marry her. When Eudora overhears Alcibiades comparing her with a foreign courtesan, she realizes that Aspasia has endangered her reputation. After the trial of Aspasia, Anaxagoras and Phidias, Philothea and Eudora accompany their guardians into exile and Aspasia is not seen again in the text. Her schemes are ultimately unsuccessful but still do harm: at Pericles' request, Philothea returns to Athens to marry Paralus when he is near death during the plague and then dies of grief. Eudora is more fortunate – she is found to be the daughter of the Persian ambassador and marries Philaemon. Although the Periclean laws which discriminated against foreigners have been repealed to allow Aspasia's son to become Pericles' heir, Eudora and Philaemon choose to remain in Persia rather than returning to Athens. They settle in a location which is 'frequently visited by learned men from Greece, Ethiopia, and Egypt' and offers 'opportunities for literary communication between the East and the West' (283). Philaemon is absorbed in literary pursuits, but Eudora has given up her ambitions. Described as a wife, daughter and mother, she names her daughter after the saintly Philothea rather than the transgressive Aspasia.

Amymone: A Romance of the Days of Pericles

In 1848, Eliza Lynn's historical novel *Amymone: A Romance of the Days of Pericles* was published in London. A contradictory figure, she is best known as the overtly conservative and antifeminist journalist Eliza Lynn Linton, author of 'The Girl of the Period' (1868), who decried the modern English girl as a mercenary, selfish pleasure-seeker. As a young woman Lynn championed free love, challenged the unjustness of patriarchal society and advocated equality between men and women. When she wrote *Amymone* she was living independently in London as an unmarried woman and a writer, against her father's wishes. An autodidact who researched her historical novels at the British Museum, she regretted her lack of formal education, yet she later campaigned against higher education for women (Anderson 1987: 23). The Preface to *Amymone* emphasizes the author's awareness that by celebrating Aspasia she risked censure. She demands justice for Aspasia, rejecting 'the old prejudices and falsehoods against her', and explicitly frames her story as a critique of the treatment of women in the contemporary world: 'The principles which she advocated in Athenian society . . . are the same in character, as those which agitate our present world. I have but clothed in Grecian form the spirit of modern England' (Lynn 1848: i. v-vi). She argues that the 'conservatism' of Athenian society and of 'posterity' alike condemn educated and independent women, a criticism which is expressed by equating independence with sexual availability. Aspasia's real offence against patriarchal society, she argues, was her independence:

> Had she been the Hetaira she was named, notable only for her beauty and her luxuriousness, we should have had odes in her praise and monuments to her honour . . . But being what she was, independent in thought, act and principle, and brave to express and maintain what she felt to be the truth, no calumny was too gross, no slander too malignant, for the foreign woman's reformations.
>
> *i.vi*

This is a powerful reminder that the 'luxuriousness' Victorian novel readers would be expected to condemn might nevertheless be celebrated in poetry or art. Lynn is also attacking a double standard which demanded that unmarried women should be chaste while their future husbands were free to consort with women whose existence was ignored by a hypocritical society. That this was a particularly middle-class ideology is underlined in Elizabeth Barrett Browning's *Aurora Leigh* (1857). Lady Waldemar makes a distinction between women's responses to the Aspasia type of cultured courtesan and the prostitute, when she claims that Romney Leigh

> Ignored the Aspasia we all dare to praise
> For other women, dear, we could not name
> Because we're decent.
>
> *Browning 2010: iv. 73*

With an upper-class disregard for strict morality, Lady Waldemar can acknowledge that a modern *hetaira*, perhaps an actress or a singer, might be an object of admiration, even envy, for a self-consciously audacious woman. Yet the more dominant middle-class code of propriety prescribes that a 'decent' woman must make a display of innocent ignorance.

Despite her combative Preface, in the first volume of *Amymone* Lynn presents Aspasia as a passionately devoted and relatively silent wife. Her novel responds to her mentor Walter Savage Landor's hugely popular *Pericles and Aspasia* (1836), a series of imaginary letters in which the intelligent and well-read Aspasia lives quietly as a wife and mother. Adam Roberts notes that Landor's Aspasia 'is not a *hetaira*. It is not clear what she is' (2015: 373). This idealized representation of the marriage between Pericles and Aspasia was well received. In *Woman in the Nineteenth Century* (1845), Margaret Fuller praises

Landor's depiction of a relationship in which 'grace is the natural garb of strength, and the affections are calm, because deep' (1845: 161). Lynn depicts a similarly harmonious partnership but gives Aspasia a more consequential (though discreet) influence over Pericles. She elevates him above 'the mere legislator, the mere politician'; her 'spirit of beauty' permeates the 'masculine energy, the wide ambition, the bold thought, and daring views, which had placed him at the helm of government' (Lynn 1848: i. 59). There are flattering comparisons with Ares and Aphrodite, Hector and Andromache, and Orpheus and Eurydice (i. 59–60). Lynn intersperses lengthy declarations of love between Pericles and Aspasia with the narrator's praise of the holiness of their 'pure souls', unclouded by 'earthly passion' (i. 64). She does not completely desexualize Aspasia but represents her 'sensuousness' and 'voluptuousness' as being 'refined' by her intellect and by a love which rests on the basis of 'esteem' (i.76).

When Pericles' home is filled with Athenian luminaries such as the tragedians Sophocles (a general in the Samian war), Euripides and Pericles' teacher Anaxagoras, Aspasia does not participate in their debates but presides in dignified silence over the 'court' of the 'republican monarch' (i. 87). Aspasia first speaks only to express her anxiety that the Athenians may turn against Pericles, and again when only a few men remain. Pericles is prophesying a future civilization greater than that of Athens, and her disconcertingly self-centred response is that such an ideal society would understand her to be a virtuous woman. She complains that she, living in 'pure, chaste, wedlock of soul', but despising 'formal customs', has been labelled 'an Hetaira, abandoned, shameless, and undone' because of her education (i.91). This speech receives little attention, as the men are departing for the war, and Aspasia disappears from the text for some time. The narrator takes up the defence of the *hetaira* by contrasting her with 'modest' women who are barely educated and are expected to maintain their purity by staying within the home. The terms in which Lynn presents the limitations on respectable women anticipate Grote's description of Athenian marriage but could also be read as a critique of Victorian middle-class gender ideologies.

> Where the hetaira had all love, liberty, and consideration, where her education was most carefully watched, and her mind and person tenderly trained and adorned with accomplishments, the modest woman, the wife and the sister and the daughter were kept in almost prison seclusion; debarred all exercise of free will; denied from almost all but religious amusements; cut off from every means of improvement and self-culture.
>
> *i. 113*

Although Aspasia is prosecuted on a 'charge of blasphemy and general immorality', the real target is Pericles, whom Hermippos hopes to ostracize or send to his death (ii. 19–20). The danger to Aspasia is enhanced by the enmity of women. While in Child's novel the virtuous heroine Philothea privately undermines Aspasia by telling her that the praise she receives is insincere, in Lynn's novel the outwardly virtuous but secretly dangerous anti-heroine Amymone hates Aspasia and hopes to shame her in public. She loathes the 'spirit of woman's freedom which the beautiful and spirited Milesian had awakened in the city', which the narrator explains as freedom from narrow superstition, bigotry and unequal law. Amymone 'labour[s] ceaselessly to obtain an influence counter to Aspasia's, which should destroy and annul her work' (ii. 68). Amymone is outwardly a virtuous, conventional and exemplary married woman, but the reader is given access to her real character, proud, vengeful, ambitious and filled with hate for Aspasia. She plots to gain citizenship for her foreign husband by murdering his patron and forging a will. Despising her husband and the idea of love, she 'surpassed Clytemnestra in her hatred, while wanting in the passion, guilty though it was, which impelled her to her crime. For this the world called her chaste and virtuous' (ii. 78). Lynn emphasizes the wickedness of this woman who is treated with great respect by Athenian women, contrasting her with 'sweet Aspasia; the wife whose maidenhood bore an hetaira's name' (ii. 78). Amymone confronts Aspasia about her views on marriage and her denial of traditional religion (like Eliza Lynn, Aspasia has rejected the religion of her childhood, seeing it as having only symbolic value). She speaks of marriage as a bond based on love, which does not require a ceremony and ends when the tie is broken. She is aware, however, that her views are premature as far as society is concerned. Amymone reports their conversation to Hermippos, who uses Aspasia's speeches as the basis of his prosecution. She also disputes with a young woman who defends Aspasia and is therefore condemned by the Athenian ladies who 'stamp on Chrysanthe's name the fatal brand they graved on all whose thoughts went beyond the straitened line they drew' (ii. 98). Amymone is outraged that 'contrary to all Athenian modes of modesty, [Aspasia] mingles with her master – I cannot name him husband – and with his guests', and that she claims equality with men (ii. 99).

Lynn repeats and amplifies the claims she made in her Preface, that Aspasia's unmerited reputation was based on prejudice against learned women and has been perpetuated by misogynistic slanders. Lynn emphasizes that the internalised misogyny of 'chaste' women can be just as cruel as the bigotry of the men who wrote the surviving accounts of Aspasia's life:

> And yet she was branded with the name of courtesan, because she had learnt those arts of education which had hitherto been reserved for this class; because she had endeavoured to rescue philosophy, learning, and art, from the purposes of seduction to which alone they were applied; because she strove to establish the truth of an equal law between the sexes; an equal though a diverse; and threw off many of the conventional restraints of her time; because she did all this, the chaste matrons of the violet city shrieked out against her; and men, more narrow, mean, and bigoted, repeated the slanderous lie, till after ages caught the echo, and Aspasia's name lies still deep-stained with a calumnious infamy.
>
> *ii. 79*

Aspasia makes a statement of her principle of equality between men and women, which explicitly makes education the basis of a better kind of marriage:

> Above all I would not have art and learning confined to one class, that class to which an illiberal lie assigns me; but I would endue the modest maiden and the chaste matron with those powers by which to keep their lovers and their husbands faithful... But to these add strength and power, add independence and equality; not the equality of likeness, but of fitness.
>
> *ii. 104*

Amymone's loathing of Aspasia's principles is so intense that it propels her to speak at the trial although 'a woman's testimony was a thing unallowed by law, but in great cases sometimes set aside' (iii. 277). She sets aside her own display of modesty to speak of her private conversations with Aspasia. As the trial proceeds, a verdict against Aspasia seems likely until Pericles tears off his 'orator's garland' and speaks as a husband rather than as a statesman, successfully imploring the people to free Aspasia. The focus of the novel then switches to Amymone, who is tried and imprisoned for 'murder, sacrilege and unlawful assumption of political rights' (iii. 316). The leader of the Athenian matrons is revealed to be illegitimate and a criminal, her supporters desert her and on the final page of the novel she murders her own child. The woman who bitterly opposed Aspasia's hopes for equality between men and women is exposed as cruel, vindictive and amoral despite her pose of respectability.

Child and Lynn both recognise Aspasia as a significant example of a woman who is both beautiful and intellectually distinguished, a radical influence on other women and a partner in a fulfilling relationship with a man. They acknowledge that the use Aspasia makes of the freedom associated with her equivocal position is tantalizing yet emphasize that her freedoms place her not merely in social jeopardy but at risk of exile or death. In these texts she is a contradictory character and is seen by virtuous women as a potential antagonist whose motives are to be suspected. Child's Aspasia is rebuked and silenced by the exemplary Philothea and disappears from the text after the trial. Lynn gives Aspasia a stronger claim on the reader's respect by giving her speeches which sympathetically articulate notions of equality between the sexes and by showing how bitterly some women oppose such arguments. There is no happy ending envisaged for Aspasia in either text: these authors are yet not ready to imagine her as the heroine of her own story. It is left to the intellectual women of a later period, feminist scholars scarcely imaginable in the nineteenth century, to reconstruct Aspasia's extraordinary life from the fragments of her ancient reputation.

Note

1. The son of Pericles and Aspasia, born in 441 BCE, was exempted from the citizenship laws in 430 BCE after the deaths of his citizen half-brothers Xanthippos and Paralos (Bicknell 1982: 243).

CHAPTER 5
A NIGHT IN ANCIENT ROME: RENÉE VIVIEN'S SCHOLARLY AND LITERARY RE-CREATION OF THE CULT OF BONA DEA

Jacqueline Fabre-Serris

Bona Dea is the last story in the collection *La Dame à la louve* (The woman with the wolf),[1] published by Renée Vivien in 1904.[2] Renée Vivien was the pseudonym of a young Englishwoman, Pauline Tarn (1877–1909), who was partly educated in France and lived permanently in Paris from 1889. She wrote in French numerous collections of poems and a collection of novels, *La Dame à la louve*.

The stories of this collection are attributed to male and female narrators, from different cultures, depicted as having lived in different times, mostly in the modern age, some of them in the distant past. Vivien often set her fictions in ancient Greece. *Bona Dea* is the only one set in Rome. Bona Dea is a Roman goddess worshipped only by women. Little is known about her cult, one of the oldest in Rome. The goddess is not often referred to by ancient poets, but some particularities of her cult are reported by Servius, Macrobius and Plutarch.

When I started working on the *Bona Dea* of Vivien, I assumed that Vivien had read a contemporary literary text on the Roman goddess, and I was looking for a poet or a novelist in her literary milieu or among the writers belonging to the so-called decadent movement.[3] In vain. Actually, Vivien's main source appears to have been a scholarly book, the *Dictionary of Greek and Roman Biography and Mythology*, published by the eminent English classicist and lexicographer William Smith, in 1849. Later, trying to clarify the origin of the proper names present in the novel, I came to the conclusion that Vivien had probably used other contemporary scholarly sources. On balance, it is not so surprising that she was interested in classical antiquity – not as a dilettante, but in a more serious way – and that she was familiar with some recent publications, including those of classical philologists. Her friend Pierre Louÿs enjoyed competing with some of them when he wrote his *Songs of Bilitis* (1894) and claimed that his book was a translation from ancient Greek. We know that Vivien herself learned Greek 'to read Homer in the [Greek] text' as she said, in 1898, with a private teacher, Gaetan Baron, who trained her rigorously, using the most-up-date methods and the best reference books (Fabre-Serris 2016: 93–5). In 1903, Vivien published *Sapho, traduction nouvelle avec le texte grec* (*Sapho, a new translation with the Greek text*), from the edition of Henry Thornton Wharton, that her lover, Natalie Barney, had procured for her. Printed in 1885 in London, this English edition was based on the German edition of Theodor Bergk (Leipzig, 1880). In 1904, as the same time as *La Dame à la louve*, Vivien also published a translation of

Greek lyric poetesses, entitled *Les Kitharèdes*. Vivien's *Sapho* was the first book to make available in France almost the complete works of Sappho.[4]

In this chapter I want to explore this unexpected background in order to highlight how, in *La Dame à la louve*, Vivien succeeded in creating such an impressive reconfiguration of the cult of Bona Dea. I will put this compelling reconstitution of 'a night in ancient Rome' in perspective not only with her well-known commitment in celebration of lesbian love but also with a lesser-known aspect of her personality: her progressive involvement in mysticism at the end of her life.

The cult of Bona Dea as described in contemporary dictionaries and in Vivien's fiction

Many details in Vivien's description of the cult can be attributed to Smith's article. In her novel, the festival in honour of the goddess takes place in the house of a Roman citizen on a spring night: 'The day is dying. It is the spring evening devoted to the Good Goddess, Bona Dea . . . Tonight, my father's house will be the temple in which the sacred rites are carried out' (Vivien 2020: 105).[5] According to Smith, 'her festival, which was celebrated every year on the 1st of May, was held in the house of the consul or praetor, as the sacrifices on that occasion were offered on behalf of the whole Roman people'.[6] In reality the worship of Bona Dea was celebrated twice a year, on 1 May in the temple of the goddess at the bottom of the Aventine Hill, and during the night of 3 to 4 December in the house of a magistrate *cum imperio*. What also supports the identification of her source with Smith is that Vivien makes the same mistake as he does, when talking about a spring evening instead of a night of December. Who is Bona Dea? Smith wrote: 'Good Goddess. A Roman divinity, who is described as the sister, wife, or daughter of Faunus.' Vivien refers to the goddess only as the daughter of Faunus: 'How beautiful the statue of the daughter of Faunus is!' (105). Smith added to this phrase some onomastic details by referring to Servius and Macrobius: 'and (she) was herself called Fatua, or Oma (Serv. *Ad Aen.* 8.314; Macrob. 1.12)'. Fauna and Fatua, as well as Ops, are indeed names given by Macrobius to identify the goddess in his *Saturnalia*. Oma is a name found in Servius. It is very interesting that this last name, Oma, is repeated by Vivien but with an addition that reveals the use of another source. She specifies that Oma was the secret name of the goddess: 'But her secret name, which must never be uttered by the profane lips of man, I will quietly reveal to you; it is Oma. Do not divulge this sacred name' (108). In Servius' commentary edited by Georg Thilo and Hermann Hagen, the comment ad hoc is considered to be corrupted regarding the word *Omam*: *hic Faunus habuisse filiam dicitur †omam castita et disciplinis omnibus eruditam, quam quidam, quod nomine dici prohibitum fuerat, Bonam Deam appellatam volunt*. ('This Faunus is said to have had a daughter, instructed in all areas of knowledge, who, according to some people, was called Bona Dea because it was forbidden to call her by her name.')[7] According to Giuseppe Ramirez,[8] who edited a new edition of Servius' commentary on *Aeneid* 8 in the CUF (Collection des Universitaires de France) in 2022, the passage has been handed down from only one manuscript, Parisinus lat. 7929

(F). The reading *Omam* is certainly corrupted, which is why Thilo appends the † symbol. Scholars have tried to find a plausible solution, but there seems to be no certainty. The edition of Thilo and Hagen was published between 1878 and 1902, after the publication of Smith's dictionary, which explains his error. Vivien probably did not know the edition of Thilo and Hagen. Where did she find the idea that Oma was the secret name of Bona Dea? In my opinion she found it in Helena Blavatsky's book (posthumously published in 1892), *The Theosophical Glossary*.[9] I conjecture that the following article was probably consulted and used by Vivien:

> **Bona Oma** or **Bona Dea**. A Roman goddess, the patroness of female Initiates and Occultists. Called also Fauna after her father Faunus. She was worshipped as a prophetic and chaste divinity, and her cult was confined solely to women, men not being allowed even to pronounce her name. She revealed her oracles only to women, and the ceremonies of her Sanctuary (a grotto in the Aventine) were conducted by the Vestals, every 1st May. Her aversion to men was so great that no male person was permitted to approach the house of the consuls where her festival was sometimes held, and even the portraits and the busts of men were carried out for the time from the building. Clodius, who once profaned such a sacred festival by entering the house of Caesar where it was held, in a female disguise, brought grief upon himself. Flowers and foliage decorated her temple, and women made libations from a vessel (mellarium) full of milk. It is not true that the mellarium contained wine, as asserted by some writers, who being men thus tried to revenge themselves.

In this passage Bona Dea is described only as the daughter of Faunus, and characterized as a chaste goddess, whose name (Oma? or Fauna? it is not clear) men are not allowed to pronounce. Blavatsky, who co-founded the Theosophical Society in 1875, was interested in Servius' comment, probably because she gave a mystical meaning to the syllable Om, as we read later in her dictionary:

> **Om** or *Aum* (sk.) A mystic syllable, the most solemn of all words in India. It is 'an invocation, a benediction, an affirmation and a promise'; and it is so sacred, as to be indeed the word at low breath of occult, *primitive* masonry. No one must be near when the syllable is pronounced for a purpose. This word is usually placed at the beginning of sacred Scriptures, and it is prefixed to prayers. It is compound of three letters **a, u, m**, which, in the popular belief, are typical of the three Vedas, also of three gods – **A** (Agni), **V**(Varuna), and **M** (Maruts) or Fire, Water, and Air. In esoteric philosophy these are the three sacred Fires, or the 'triple' Fire in the Universe and Man, besides many other things. Occultly, this 'triple Fire' represents the highest *Tetraktys* also, as it is typified by the Agni named Abhimânin and his transformation into his three sons, Pâvana, Pavamâna and Suchi, 'who drink up water', i.e., destroys material desires. This monosyllable is called Udgîtta, and it is sacred with both Brahmins and Buddhists.

I will return later to the mystical dimension that Vivien has introduced in her novel when referring to Oma as the secret name of the goddess. To continue the comparison with Smith's dictionary, he specified that 'the solemnities were conducted by the Vestals, and only women, usually of the higher orders, were allowed to take part in them (Cic. *Att.* 1,13, *De Harusp. Resp.* l.c.; *D. C.* 37–45). During the solemnity, no male person was allowed to be in the house, and portraits of men were tolerated only when they were covered over.' This last detail is repeated by Vivien at the beginning of her novel: 'Cover the picture of my father with an impenetrable veil, so the gaze of the Immortal Virgin is not offended by the sight of a man' (105). Later in the text, we also find two allusions to the presence of the Vestals: 'No man may sully with his presence the venerable temple in which she delivers her oracles. And only the priestesses have heard the divine sound of her voice' (108), 'With their chaste hands, the Vestal Virgins have garlanded the walls that are perfumed by the foliage' (108). Vivien has also reproduced Smith's description of the ritual. He wrote: 'The women who celebrated the festival of Fauna had to prepare themselves for it by abstaining from various things, especially from intercourse with men.' Vivien states: 'The wives who are coming tonight have purified themselves by refusing the carnal embraces of their husbands' (109). Smith added this description: 'The house of the consul or praetor was decorated by the Vestals as a temple, with flowers and foliage of every kind except myrtle, on account of its symbolic meaning. The head of the goddess' statue was adorned with a garland of vine-leaves, and a serpent surrounded its feet.' Vivien follows Smith's article: 'With their chaste hands, the Vestal Virgins have garlanded the walls that are perfumed by the foliage' (108); 'My fervent hands placed a crown of wine leaves upon her divine head. A serpent is coiled at her delicate feet' (109), but she develops the expression 'flowers and foliage': 'They have chosen the simple flowers and the herbs most beloved of Fauna: balm, thyme, chervil, fennel and parsley. And here are the hyacinths . . . And here are the roses' (108). This appears to be a very insightful amplification of this information found in Smith: 'Fauna was also regarded as a goddess possessed of healing powers, as might be inferred from the serpents being part of her worship; but we know that various kinds of medicinal herbs were sold in her temple, and bought largely by the poorer classes.' All the flowers and herbs listed by Vivien are indeed known as medicinal plants. Smith explained at length that wine was both officially forbidden in the cult but nevertheless consumed by women: 'Although no one was allowed to bring wine with her, a vessel filled with wine, stood in the room, and from it the women made their libations and drank. This wine, however, was called milk, and the vessel containing it *mellarium*, so that the name of wine was avoided altogether.' As we have seen, this detail of the cult was wrongly contested by Blavatsky. Vivien only says: 'Here is the golden vase into which I poured the wine of Lesbos' (105). Smith explained that the solemnity commenced with a sacrifice and that 'after this sacrifice the women began to perform Bacchic dances, and to drink of the wine prepared for them'. Vivien is not interested in this detail, and, more important, has another interpretation of what women were doing at night. According to her, the love relationship between women was performed under the protection of the goddess: 'Fauna smiles upon the love of the intertwined women. That is why the women will kiss at nightfall in front of her lovely statue, moulded so carefully by Theano, the Greek' (109). This is why much of the novel consists of a speech addressed by a Roman elite woman to one of her slaves with whom she is in love and whom she wants to initiate into love: 'I will reveal to you the potency and sweetness of female love' (106).

Vivien's onomastic choices

Who is this woman? The narrator gives her name: 'I, Caia Venantia Paullina, daughter of Caius Venantius Paullinus' (105). Disclosing her identity by stating the name of her father is consistent with the Roman practice for a woman. However, instead to saying: 'Venantia, daughter of Paullinus' on the model of *Julia, Caesaris filia*, the narrator uses a first sequence of three female names that clearly echoes the second sequence of three male names. Three names are highly unusual for a woman.[10] Caia is a very common name, perhaps to be related to the ritual formula of marriage, transmitted by Plutarchus (*Quaest. Rom.* 30): ὅπου σὺ Γάιος, ἐγὼ Γαΐα. (*ubi tu Gaius, ego Gaia*, 'where you are Gaius, I will be Gaia'), in which these names can be written in modern transcripts: *Caius* or *Caïus, Caia* or *Caïa*. What about the two other names? One thing is for certain, that they have been carefully chosen by Vivien. The third can probably be referred to the actual first name of Vivien: Pauline (Tarn), which highlights her personal involvement in this novel. More difficult to understand is the choice of Venantia. It may be resulting from two combined references that both add a Christian and mystical dimension to this very personal recreation of the festival of Bona Dea. The only Roman woman known under the name Venantia is a woman related to the noble family of Decii (PRE 2, 1152) who is the addressee of a letter written by the bishop Fulgence of Ruspe (468–533) on the remission of sins. The remaining work of Fulgence of Ruspe was published by Teubner in 1898 in the same volume as Fulgentius Fabius Planciades the mythographer, with whom he was often confused (but not by Smith). Furthermore, the name Venantia may also be related to the Christian poet Venantius Fortunatus (530–600), who wrote many poems for the royal nun Radegund. Venantus Fortunatus was well known at the end of the nineteenth century.[11] His poems were edited and translated by Charles Nisard in 1887 under the title: Venance Fortunat. *Poésies mêlées*. Two famous painters represented the poet reading his poems to Radegund: Lawrence Alma-Tadema in 1862 (*Venantius Fortunatus reading his poems to Radegonda VI*) and Puvis de Chavannes in 1874 (*Saint Radegund listening to a reading by the poet Fortunat*). Vivien had probably one of these poems especially in mind, the *De uirginate*, composed by this author for the installation of Radegund's spiritual daughter Agnes as Abbess of the Convent of the Holy Cross, which Radegund founded at Poitiers in the 540s after she fled her husband, the Frankish King Lothar. The poem of Venantius Fortunatus and the novel of Vivien indeed have in common descriptions of how a girl was introduced by an older friend in a religious community during a ceremony in which a protector of women, Bona Dea or the Virgin

Mary, was worshipped and invoked as promoter of virginity. Obviously both authors did not have the same idea of what should be understood and valued as female chastity.

The young slave, beloved by Venantia Paullina, is called Amata. I argue that Vivien chose this name because of an onomastic detail she found in Smith's *Dictionary of Greek and Roman Antiquities* published in 1842 and reprinted several times (entry: Vestals). Amata is the name for a young girl elected to become a vestal used by the Pontifex Maximus at the time when he took her by the hand and addressed her in a solemn form, as is attested by Aulus Gellius (1.12.14) on the authority of Fabius Pictor: *Sacerdotem Vestalem, quae sacra faciat, quae ius siet sacerdotem Vestalem facere pro populo Romano Quiritibus, uti quae optima lege fuit, ita te, Amata, capio.* ('I take thee, Amata, as one who has fulfilled all the legal requirements, to be priestess of Vesta, to perform the rites which it is lawful for a Vestal to perform for the Roman people, the Quirites' (entry: Vestals, 1189)).[12] In his dictionary,[13] Smith, after describing this ceremony, adds that he disagrees with Aulus Gellius who explained that the new Vestal was called Amata because there is a tradition that the first young woman chosen bore that name. According to him 'the title Amata seems simply to signify "beloved one"'(1189). In my opinion, Vivien has read Smith's article and has chosen the name Amata to refer to this cultic detail, one that made perfect sense with the situation represented in her novel: the introduction of a young girl, who was the protégée of an older friend, into a female community whose most important function was to observe chastity and celebrate a goddess/a worshipped woman (famous for her involvement in preserving female virginity).

Chastity or secret sexual practices during the festival of Bona Dea?

In *Fasti* 5.157–8, Ovid recalls that the sanctuary of Bona Dea on the Aventine Hill was restored by Livia, the wife of Augustus. He underlines that by so doing the wife of Augustus was following the example of her husband (5.157–8): 'in order to imitate her husband and she has followed her spouse in all things'. As we know from various sources, Livia actively supported the policy of restoring Roman cults and female virtues constituting the backbone of the return to past promoted by Augustus. The cult of Bona Dea, like the other cults performed by women, was supposed to promote female chastity.

In her novel, Vivien had personal reasons for describing the festival of Bona Dea as constituting an initiation session to love between women. It is not surprising that she includes in her description some allusions to Sappho's poetry, which aims at making Bona Dea the Roman counterpart of the goddess called upon by Sappho, Aphrodite. She writes: 'The wine is as luminous as Peitho's locks' (105). The reader acquainted with Vivien's *Sapho* can recognize an allusion the poem she wrote as a personal variation on Sappho's *Ode to Aphrodite*: 'Et quelle *Peithô*, plus *blonde* que le jour / aux cheveux d'argent, te trahit et méprise, / Psappha, ton amour?' (and what Peitho, blonder than the day / with silver hair, betrays you and despises, / Psappha, your love?') (Vivien 2009: 35). In the *Ode to Aphrodite*, Sappho calls Aphrodite for help in obtaining the favors of a girl who was reluctant to answer to her advances. The narrator of Vivien's novel is more or less in the same situation: she is trying to convince her young slave, Amata, to make love with her during the festival of the goddess, which implies benevolence and assistance from Bona Dea. The second reference to Sappho complements the previous one. Venantia describes her beloved as follows: 'You were but a sickly, graceless child' (Vivien 2020: 105), 'When you were but a graceless, sickly girl, I taught you the odes of Psappho of Lesbos, whose beautiful Doric name is Psappha.' (106). Vivien repeats here an expression she had used in her own translation of Sappho's fragment 50: 'Tu me semblais une enfant petite et sans grâce' ('You seemed to me a small and graceless child') (Vivien 2009: 35). Later in the novel, the narrator describes herself as the 'priestess' of Sappho, who, in this passage, somewhat replaces Bona Dea as a more appropriate patroness to be called upon: 'Know, my beautiful slave, that Psappha, reclining among the Lethean lotuses, smiles when I call upon her, and extends her protection over my love affairs, because I am her priestess. She will help me conquer and capture your undecided heart, Amata. I love you just as Psappha once loved the elusive, hesitant Atthis' (Vivien 2020: 106–7).

We find two other references to Greece in 'Never have I seen a virgin ('une Parthène') as desirable as you' (107) and in 'the women will kiss at nightfall in front of her lovely statue, moulded so carefully by Theano, the Greek woman' (109). Parthène is a feminized transliteration of παρθένος ('girl, virgin'). Who is this Theano? We do know any Greek sculptress by this name. The name Theano may have been invented or employed as referring to a real person. In the latter case, one plausible candidate may be the Greek lyric poetess Theano (fifth century BCE), who was compared by the Ancients to Sappho herself. This Theano is referenced as a Locrian poetess in the Suda: Θεανώ: Λοκρίς λυρική· ᾄσματα λυρικὰ ἢ Λοκρικὰ καὶ μέλη ('Theano: Locrian, lyric poetess, [she wrote] lyric or Locrian odes and songs', § th.85), and so described by Clearchos according to Athenaeus (14.4 Kaibel): Κλέαρχος δὲ ἐν δευτέρῳ Ἐρωτικῶν τὰ ἐρωτικά φησιν ᾄισματα καὶ τὰ Λοκρικὰ καλούμενα οὐδὲν τῶν Σαπφοῦς καὶ Ἀνακρέοντος διαφέρειν ('Clearchus, in book II of the *Erotika* says that the love songs and the so-called Locrian songs do not differ in any way from those of Sappho and Anacreon'). So, placed under the double patronage of both Sappho and Theano, the speech addressed by Venantia to her beloved is presented as a form of teaching: 'I will teach you' (used three times, 106), or revelation: 'I will reveal to you' (used twice, 106–7).

The teachings of Venantia

As I said before, men were prohibited from attending the festival of Bona Dea. Apparently, Vivien relies on this cultic detail to attribute a strong rejection of male love (compared to female love) both to her narrator and to Bona Dea herself: 'For the love between women is nothing like the love of men. I love you for you, and not for myself' (107); 'She (Bona Dea) is humble and sweet and forgiving for women. She hates men because they are ferocious and brutal. Men love only their pride or their brutishness. They are neither just not loyal. They are sincere only about their own vanity' (107–8). This judgement on male nature is without any nuance: man is brutal, vain and beastly, while female love is described both as powerful and sweet. The narrator says that at the beginning she was attracted by the weakness of her young slave when she was still a child: 'I immediately cherished you fervently for your languor and your fragility' (105); 'I love you for your trembling, fragile self. My strength was attracted by your weakness' (106). She wanted to protect her: 'I once opened my arms to you, to console you as much as to embrace you ... For I am the one who rules and protects' (106). Now that Amata has become a beautiful girl, her mistress feels love for her, paradoxically compared, for its excessive force, to male love: 'I love you with the frenzy of male desire' (106). However, in no way does Venantia want to force her: 'I love you ... with the languor of female tenderness'; 'I will teach you the manyfold art of pleasure' (106). What does this pleasure consist of? It appears to be relatively chaste. Venantia speaks of delicate kisses and tender caresses: 'I will teach you the deliberate softness of hands that linger over belated contact. I will teach you the tenacity of lips that delicately persists. You will discover the all-consuming power of gentle caress' (106). Dupont (Dupont and Eloi 2001: 243–60) has argued that the Romans had praised and advocated the love kiss (called *basium, osculum or suauium*), as the act of love providing the most refined pleasure that can be achieved between lovers. Vivien may have had in mind some of Catullus' poems on this topic, addressed to women or men, the best known being the *carmen* 5: *Da mi basia mille, deinde centum, / dein mille altera, dein secunda centum/ deinde usque altera mille, deinde centum.* ('give me a thousand kisses, then a hundred, then a thousand more, then a second time a hundred, then a thousand again, then a hundred', 7–9).[14] In Vivien's novel, the quest for kisses, attenuated in the final formula: 'I desire only the smile upon your lips' (Vivien 2020: 107), may seem surprising in a master–slave relationship. In Rome the masters had full power over their slaves, who were sexually submissive to them. Venantia stresses that her slave is now free: 'You are free, my beautiful slave! Here is the linen robe I wove for you ... You are free. You may leave this house which protected you in childhood' (107). Does this mean that this passage is to be taken as a poetical evocation of the *manumissio*, i.e., the act by which a master proclaims that a slave is now free? If so, the abolition of the social status of Amata serves to support the new relationship that Venantia wishes to create between her and her beautiful slave. In this new relation, the use of the words 'master' and 'slave' is perpetuated, but seems to be taken metaphorically. In the Roman elegiac genre, love relations are often described in reference to the relation between master and slave, since the poet presents himself as the *seruus* of his *puella*, assimilated to a *domina*, even if she is of lower social status. Here the relations Venantia now wishes to have with Amata are erotically mutual and interchangeable, and, as a result, she is ready to become the slave of her (former) slave: 'You will obey me, my sweet burden, but you may do with me all that you wish. I will be both your master and your possession' (106); 'You will bend to my wilful embrace. You will abandon yourself to my imploring caress' (109).

Beauty is at the origin of desire. Venantia is in love with Amata, because her slave is beautiful:

'And because you are beautiful, Amata, because you are the most graceful of young women, I will reveal to you the potency and sweetness of female love'

106

To enhance her beauty, Venantia adorns her slave with her own jewels:

'My pearls will shine more lustrously around your neck. My beryls will be clearer upon your arms. Take my necklaces. Take my rings too. Then you will ready for the feast of Bona Dea.'

107

The word *beryllus* is very rare in Latin. The association of beryls and pearls may refer to *De Virginitate* of Venantius Fortunatus, to which I alluded at the beginning of my chapter. Venantius uses indeed these two words when he describes the splendid jewels given to Agnes, when she is received in the Christian community (the Virgin Mary, the prophets, the Saints, the angels …), during a scene supposed to redouble in heaven the enthronement on earth of Agnes as new abbess:

Inseritur capiti radians diadema beryllis
   Ordinibus uariis alba zmaragdus inest.
Alligat et nitidos amethystina uitta capillos
   Margaritato flexilis arte sinu.[15]

On pose sur sa tête une couronne radieuse sertie de béryls entremêlés de blanches émeraudes. Une bandelette couleur d'améthyste lie ses beaux cheveux et retombe flexible sur sa collerette garnie de perles.

(263–6, trans. by Nisard, read by Vivien)

A radiant crown is placed on his head set with beryls interspersed with white emeralds. An amethyst-colored band binds her beautiful hair and falls flexible on her pearl-trimmed collar.

My translation

Some later passages of the novel may be interpreted in the same vein, i.e., as introducing or supporting a philosophical-mystical dimension in the praise of the Roman goddess, who is more or less assimilated to the Virgin Mary or a divine entity resulting from syncretism between pagan, Christian, and Oriental wisdoms:

But the Goddess is all *truth* and *justice*. She is full of pity as the water that refreshes our lips and the sun that warms our limbs. She is the merciful spirit of the universe ['*l'Âme clémente de l'univers*'] … But her secret name, which must never be uttered by the profanes lips of man, I will quietly reveal to you: it is *Oma*. Do not divulge this sacred name … A serpent is coiled at her delicate feet. For she who is Eternal Gentleness is also Eternal Wisdom ['l'*Éternelle Douceur* ... l'*Éternelle Sagesse*'].

108–9

We know that Vivien converted to Catholicism at the end of her life. It is not surprising that her interest in this religion[16] was combined with a penchant for occultism, widespread at the end of the nineteenth century and at the beginning of the twentieth century in France. The word 'occultism' emerged in nineteenth-century France in connection to the success of the theories developed by Eliphas Levi and his numerous disciples, and was introduced into the English language by Blavatsky. From that perspective, the last passages I have quoted furnish instructive testimony to the success of the Theosophical Society, founded by Blavatsky in 1875. Their members were very active in disseminating 'the wisdom in divine things', which implied, among other things, a comparative study of ancient philosophies and religions through keys to allegorical and mystical reading. With the mention of Oma as the secret name of Bona Dea, the novel of Vivien reveals a direct influence from the ideas of Blavatsky,[17] or more exactly shows how she has appropriated these ideas in order to give a mystical and deeper dimension to her praise of Lesbian Love.

Conclusion

The novel 'Bona Dea' is a strange and fascinating text in which the regular repetition of various expressions and phrases, sometimes short ('I love you', 'you are beautiful', 'you are free', 'I will teach you'), sometimes more developed ('I once opened my arms', 'For I am the one who rules and protects', 'I desire only the smile upon your lips'), produces an entrancing rhythm, intended to add solemnity to Venantia's words while revealing what will happen during Bona Dea's festival, reserved only for initiated women. Seen from this perspective, Vivien has conceived a 'recreation' which appears to be an ingenious variation on a secret female ceremony, about which the Romans themselves were wondering when clearly expressing doubts regarding the chastity that women were supposed to celebrate and respect during the cult.[18]

This recreation is a reflection of its time. The starting point was evidently two details in the article on Bona-Oma – Bona Dea, written by Blavatsky: men were excluded from the cult and not even allowed to pronounce the name of the goddess; only women were initiated into this cult, which suggests, since Bona Dea was described as prophesying only for them, that women were the only addressees of its secret revelations. If Vivien was drawn to the idea, developed in the theosophical movement, that there were some hidden messages in ancient religious and philosophical knowledge, she proceeded here much as did the ancient mythographers, who were using various reading keys to interpret the nature and the attributes of gods, as well as all details of religious practices. By referring to Venantius Fortunatus, she introduced a discrete link between the most archaic Roman goddess and the Virgin Mary, which allowed her to associate the ancient philosophical concept of 'soul of the world' with the Christian ideas of benevolence and mercy: 'The Goddess is humble and sweet and forgiving to women;' 'She is full of piety as the water that refreshes our lips and the sun that warms our limbs;' 'she is l'Âme clémente de l'Univers' (Vivien 2020: 107–8). However, in my opinion, the most fascinating aspect of this recreation of the Roman Goddess is that Vivien has added to the series of ancient and modern speculations, a feminist interpretation, one that should not be considered as restrictive because she focuses on the love between women, but appreciated as aiming to reevaluate and correct the traditional point of view on 'l'âme du monde', implicitly identified to a male principle. Obviously, she describes this female principle in a poetic rather than philosophical way: 'It was she who made the first flowers grow. Flowers are an act of love from Bona Dea, a symbol of Her favour for mortal women' (108); 'Bona Dea is contented with the joy of the universe. The pitiful nymphs serve her and honour her, the nymphs who in feverish summers carry in the palms of their hands a water sweeter that honey ... The Goddess has coloured the apple trees crimson. She has made the virginal garden crocus gold. She has turned the nocturnal-blue violets purple' (108–9).

Notes

1. On the novel *The Woman with the Wolf and other stories*, see Boyd (1999).
2. On Renée Vivien, see DeJean (1989), Bartholomot Bessou (2004), Albert (2009), Albert and Rollet (2012).
3. On Decadentism and Sapphism, see Albert (2005).
4. For a detailed examination of Vivien's *Sapho*, see Fabre-Serris (2016: 78–9, 93–102).
5. I have used the translation of *La Dame à la louve* by K. Jay and Y. M. Klein (2020) (Editions Gallic).
6. The *Dictionary of Greek and Roman biography and mythology* (1849, originally published in 1844 under a slightly different title) is available online at the Perseus Digital Library. The edition used here is the Perseus one, without page numbers.
7. My translation.
8. I am very grateful to Giuseppe Ramirez for clarifying this passage for me.
9. The *Theosophical Glossary* is available online on the websites of the University of Pennsylvania and of the Theosophical World. It was published posthumously by G. R. S. Mead.
10. Two names (the names of the *gens* and of the father) are standard in the imperial period. Three names are possible, though very unusual (for example Marcia Gaia Felicitas, CIL 9, 2232).
11. I am indebted to Ida Mastrorosa for these very insightful assumptions about the name Venantia.
12. My translation.
13. The *Dictionary of Greek and Roman antiquities* is online at the LatiusCurtius site (see the entry Vestals).

14. My translation.
15. Nisard explains that he used the Latin text established by Friedrich Leo, who edited Venantius' *Opera poetica* in the *Monumenta Germaniae historica*.
16. See, for example, the poems *Une Chapelle* ('et voici ce que fut la chapelle où l'on prie / celle où pieusement on célèbre Marie', 'and this was the chapel where we pray / the one where we devoutly celebrate Mary', 7–8), and *Chapelle des Marins* ('et la foule s'assemble au fond de la chapelle/ où l'on cherche Marie et n'espère qu'en elle', 'and the crowd gathers at the back of the chape l/ where they seek Mary and hope only in her', 2–3) in the collection *Le vent des vaisseaux* (1910).
17. Blavatsky married but the marriage was not consummated 'because of her aversion to men' (Wikipedia).
18. See Tibullus (1.6.21), Ovid *Ars. Am.* (3, 633; 637–8) and Juvenal (6.314–34).

CHAPTER 6
SOFIIA PARNOK'S SAPPHIC CYCLE *ROSES OF PIERIA*: TRANSLATION AND COMMENTARY
Georgina Barker

Introduction[1]

Russia's first openly lesbian poet Sofiia Parnok (1885–1933) met Sappho in 1914 through the translations of the Symbolist poet and classicist Viacheslav Ivanov, whose literary-artistic salon (in 'The Tower') Parnok attended when she was in Petersburg (Romanova 2005: 57). Ivanov's *Alcaeus and Sappho: Collected songs and lyric fragments translated in the metres of the originals by Viacheslav Ivanov*[2] was the first full translation of Sappho to appear in Russian, in 1914; he released a second edition in 1915, containing fragments newly unearthed from Oxyrhynchus (Ivanov 2019: v). Another full translation, more literal than Ivanov's, by the doctor and classicist Vikentii Veresaev, was published in 1915, but Parnok seems to have ignored it. Though Sappho was still widely considered a heterosexual poet, though Ivanov (and Veresaev) insisted on Sappho's heterosexuality, and though Ivanov filled in the gaps in Sappho's fragments and put his own poetic stamp on her words, the homoeroticism of Sappho's lyrics to and about women shone through for any eyes that were prepared to see it – and Parnok's were. She began writing Sapphic imitations immediately, trying out lyric metres and unrhymed verse (in the classical style). A contemporary description of Parnok at a literary party she attended with her girlfriend Tsvetaeva shows the intensity of her connection with Sappho: 'Elegant-enigmatic Sonia Parnok – with clever, bright eyes, Russian Sappho . . . Sonia enigmatically half-sang Sapphic stanzas – calmly, even thoughtfully, . . . occasionally drawing on her cigarette' (Boris Zaitsev, in Romanova 2005: 107). The epithet 'Russian Sappho' has stuck to Parnok ever since.

Parnok's receptions of Sappho belong to two distinct (but contiguous) periods in Parnok's life, and are inextricably connected with them. The first is her tempestuous love affair with the young, great poet Marina Tsvetaeva, which lasted a year and a half, 1914–16. The relationship was very creatively productive – the two wrote many poems to each other, and Tsvetaeva shared Parnok's interest in classical antiquity. The second is her time in Sudak, Crimea, on the Black Sea, where she spent four years, 1917–21, with her lover Liudmila Erarskaia. Crimea was the epicentre of Russia's Civil War, and Parnok might easily have died there (of starvation, cold, typhoid, cholera, tuberculosis, stray bullets, Bolshevik repressions . . .), but she was surrounded by fellow artists and in a region redolent of antiquity – as the only part of the Russian empire on the classical map – and she immersed herself in Ivanov's *Alcaeus and Sappho* (Parnok 1979: 357).

Out of these two periods came three cycles of classical-inspired poetry: 'Roses of Pieria' (12 poems), 'Penthesileia' (3 poems), and 'Wise Venus' (6 poems). 'Roses of Pieria' centres on Parnok's – intertwined – relationships with Sappho, Tsvetaeva, and her own poetry. 'Penthesileia' dramatizes Parnok's abandonment and re-embracing of Sappho through the epic story of the Amazon queen's fight with Achilles. 'Wise Venus' gives heterosexual erotic advice poetry a lesbian twist via a blend of classical and pseudo-classical influences (Sappho, Asclepiades, Ovid, Pierre Louÿs). Parnok collected these three cycles under the title *Roses of Pieria*.

Roses of Pieria was published in 1922. The future-orientated Soviet Union it came out into was entirely unrecognizable from the antiquity-obsessed Russia of seven years previously, when Parnok had started writing her Sapphic poems. Moreover, the circumscribed tolerance for lesbianism within intellectual circles during the decadent turn-of-the-century was fast disappearing in the new Soviet era (Healey 2001: 60). The book met with indifference (Parnok 1979: 330–1); even Parnok herself had lost her passion for her Sapphic work, calling it 'too aesthetic' (Burgin 1994: 172–3). Parnok never wrote about Sappho again – at least, not explicitly.[3]

Roses of Pieria is aesthetic: it puts her lesbian loves into a form she hoped would be acceptable to a contemporary readership (it wasn't), and it finds temporally distanced ways to talk with elegance and irony about extreme passions (including a painful break-up). And while it embodies fully neither classical antiquity nor Parnok's subjectivity, it establishes Parnok in a 'lesbian continuum' (Adrienne Rich's notion; Burgin 1992: 218) that is relatively well populated: not only Sappho, but also Amazons, Asclepiades' Samiennes, 'Bilitis', and Tsvetaeva. Backed up by so many fellow woman-loving women, Parnok in *Roses of Pieria* wields the power to queer the heterosexual narrative about love.

Parnok is best known now not for *Roses of Pieria*, but for the subsequent poetry collections *Vine* (1922) and *At Half Voice* (1928) (after which a combination of ill health, poverty, and the impossibility of publishing reduced her poetic output drastically). In Parnok's later poems she lowered the Sapphic mask to speak more directly from the heart about herself as a lover of women and to the women she loved – but I think the Sapphic mask helped her to craft her authentic lesbian voice. For more details about Parnok's life and works, see especially: Burgin 1994 (in English); Poliakova 1983 (in Russian); and Romanova 2005 (in Russian). For English translations of selected Parnok poems, see www.dianaburgin.com.

Below are my translations of all 21 poems from *Roses of Pieria* – the first time the entire collection has been published in English. My translations are literal, but aim to convey the poetics of the original Russian, and I have replicated as far as possible the original metres and rhyme schemes (or lack thereof), since these are essential to the poems' classical reception. Each poem is followed by my commentary on its classical reception.

Roses of Pieria
Anthological Poems

by Sofiia Parnok, translated by Georgina Barker

Roses of Pieria

Inspiration's flower

Inspiration's flower! Roses of Pieria!
Sappho, my sister! Souls partner
Across centuries – one faith we share.
Though we gathered in days that differ
Our wicker baskets – they are similar,
Those that seduced us – roses of Pieria!

- Metre: Dactylic tetrameter
- All lines rhymed loosely with 'Pieria' (home of the Muses)
- Source: Sappho 55[4]

The short opening poem is like the epigrams which often opened poem cycles in antiquity (such as those found in the Greek Anthology, which the book's subtitle references). Though no such epigram by Sappho survives, Parnok's reference is to her fragment 55, which in Ivanov's translation (2019: 137) goes as follows:

Time'll be up: in earth
You'll lie,
No fond memory

Leaving in hearts.
In vain you live!
You're too lazy to gather

The roses of Pieria,
with a chorus of girlfriends.
So you'll go down to Hades,

A shade without a face, to a crowd
Of murky shades,
Erased by forgetfulness.

The poem is therefore programmatic and dedicatory: Parnok devotes herself and her cycle to Sapphic inspiration, represented here and throughout by roses.

Despite the millennia between them Parnok insists on her kinship with Sappho, calling her 'sister' and saying they have 'one shared faith', and speaking of herself and Sappho exclusively as 'we' in the second half. It becomes clear in the final words that Parnok believes the basis of their similarity to be the Pierian roses, which symbolize not only beautiful poetry, as in Sappho's fragment 55, but also beautiful girls (this is implied by the feminine gender of the Russian for 'rose' and the sexual connotations of 'seduced' in the final line). This throws the same ambiguity back onto their 'shared faith': is it just poetry, or is it also lesbianism?

Lyre

The first lyre, poet, was created by a god's first whim:
Out of the cradle – into the meadow, and up to the tortoise – hop;
Her transparent shell is plucked off by the mischievous child,
Supple branches are handed down to him by the willow herself;
See, they have bent over the shield in a fluid semicircle,
See, already the sweet strings have been drawn taut by Hermes;
With the first lyre in his hands he slyly makes his way to the grotto,
Hides the toy, while he himself, distracted by the new game,
Aims his whirlwindlike flight towards distant Pieria,
Where in the primordial shade the Muses hold a circle dance –
Into the Pierian garden, where you, as tenth muse, Sappho,
In centuries' time will come to pluck the eternal roses.

- Metre: Elegiacs (Dactylic Hexameter / Pentameter)
- Unrhymed
- Sources: Sappho T 60 (Palatine Anthology 9.506), fr. 55; Homeric Hymn 4 to Hermes

Hermes created the lyre from a tortoiseshell, centuries before Sappho would become famed as its player; her coming is foretold at the end of the poem (the 'tenth muse' was the epithet Plato gave her). The story comes from the Homeric Hymn 4 to Hermes *(lines 20–72), but Parnok adds Sappho to it – as does Osip Mandel'shtam in his own poem alluding to the story, 'Tortoiseshell' (1919).*

Time's up

> *You're too lazy to gather the roses of Pieria!*
> Sappho

Time's up. What'll you take
The threatful gods,
Negligent reaper?

It'll yield an empty wheat head,
Just how poor off
You were for tears.

The roses'll say: for us
He could not spare
A droplet of blood.

Gods, as soon draw breath,
See already – ash
Is all your harvest.

- *Metre: Greater Asclepiad*
- *Unrhymed*
- *Source: Sappho 55*

Parnok riffs on Sappho's fragment 55, attacking a man – in place of the original's woman – who will die having written no poetry. She takes the epigraph directly from Ivanov's translation of fragment 55 (see above; she ignores his line break and ends with an exclamation mark where his translation continues 'with a chorus of girlfriends') (Ivanov 2019: 137). The metre, length and stanzaic form of Parnok's poem mimics Ivanov's poem almost exactly; Ivanov had broken up Sappho's four asclepiadic lines into shorter units to create four stanzas. The effect is of extreme terseness (to an extent that my English translation cannot capture) – it has between 2 and 4 words per line – perhaps reflecting the addressee's lack of poetry. Parnok also adapts the opening phrase 'Time's up' from Ivanov's translation's opening words 'Time'll be up': she thus shifts the temporality of Sappho's threat from future to past, and blurs the distinction between Sappho and herself, such that the poem could easily be read as coming from either poet. The 'negligent reaper' is ironically not death but the addressee, who has not picked enough flowers (written enough poems – or perhaps loved enough girls?). The roses are themselves given a voice, supporting the implication that they are girls as well as poems.

Aeolic lyre – as soon as I hear its song

Aeolic lyre – as soon as I hear its song,
I begin to burn, I don't walk – I dance,
My voice is emulous, my hand is nimble –
Music's in my veins.

It's not the pen I try, but the strings I tune,
Absorbed by an inspirational concern:
To set loose and free, to pour out of my heart
The ringing of strings.

> I have not forgotten, clearly, in this life [5]
> Unforgettable bliss of unforgettable songs
> That in ancient times my girlfriends used to sing
> At school for Sappho.

- Metre: Sapphics
- Unrhymed
- Source: Sappho 31
- Originally published in Severnye Zapiski (May–June 1915)

Parnok describes the effect of encountering Sappho's poetry. She enacts her stated impulse to imitate Sappho, evoking in the first two stanzas Sappho's style from fragment 31 (in Ivanov's translation; 2019: 85):

> ... I glimpse
> Your form – I can't feel my heart in my breast,
> I can't open my lips!
>
> My poor tongue is dumb, while through my veins a fine
> Flame runs with a scorching chill;
> Roaring in my ears; my eyes darken, are extinguished;
> My legs cannot hold ...

She takes Sappho's focus on various body parts (ears, legs, voice, (hand), veins, and heart), her burning and ringing, but she turns Sappho's negatives into positives: whereas Sappho is incapacitated by her emotions, Parnok is invigorated. This puts Parnok in the place of Sappho smitten by fragment 31's beautiful singing laughing woman. By imitating fragment 31 Parnok equates her response to Sappho's poetry with the response of a (female) lover to her (female) beloved.

In the second and third stanzas Parnok demonstrates her familiarity with contemporary scholarship about Sappho: she stresses the musical, rather than written, nature of Sappho's poetry; and she follows the idea of Sappho as a schoolmistress, which Ivanov insists on in his introduction to his Sappho translations (Ivanov 2019: 16–17). However she puts an erotic spin on the girls' school setting, imagining herself there in a past life.

'Aeolic lyre ...' was set to music by Mikhail Gnesin (1927, Op. 26) (Parnok 1979: 328).

All of me was twined in vines of memory

> All of me was twined in vines of memory,
> I say, turning weak from happiness:
> 'Lesbos! Cradle of melody
> On the last harbour of Orpheus!'

My soul was avid with a wondrous avidity,
We never gave the Muses free time to spend.
I was not alone in that country,
O, my magnificent girlfriend!

Under my hand, still not strong as it could be,
You forgave my lyre's imperfect sound,
You, whose languid name is in me,
Like the moon, it draws the waves spellbound.

- *Metre: Trochaic Hexameter (l.1) / Pentameter (ll. 2–4)*
- *Alternate Rhyme*
- *Source: Sappho 96?*

Parnok describes her apprenticeship in Sapphic poetry. There are two possible identifications of Parnok's addressee and companion here (and they may be intended to be interchangeable): Tsvetaeva or Sappho.

Tsvetaeva became Parnok's lover around the time when Parnok discovered Sappho (Burgin 1994: 330 n. 74); Parnok uses a similar phrase to 'weak from happiness' (line 2) about post-orgasmic languor in another poem addressed to Tsvetaeva ('That evening was dull-beige' (January 1915)); 'girlfriend' (line 8) may allude to Tsvetaeva's 'Girlfriend' cycle (addressed to Parnok, written October 1914–July 1915); the name that 'draws the waves' (line 12) may encrypt 'Marina'. If Tsvetaeva is 'you', the final stanza expresses Parnok and Tsvetaeva's unusual power dynamic – Parnok was older and a more experienced lover of women, but Tsvetaeva was the more accomplished poet – casting Tsvetaeva in the implied role of teacher as well as inspirer, while introducing a sexual innuendo through the ambiguity as to whether it is her lyre or her lover that is under Parnok's hand.

The 'vines of memory' (line 1) imply an ancient setting and addressee; the explicit location of Lesbos (lines 3 and 7) likewise suggests Sappho; 'girlfriend' (line 8) may simply mean 'female friend' rather than 'female sexual partner'; 'You, whose languid name is in me' (line 11) may encrypt 'Sappho', as Sappho and Sophia are near-anagrams; the moon and waves (line 12) may allude to fragment 96.8–10, 'she ... pours | A blaze over the salty sea | ... the moon'. If Sappho is 'you', the final stanza puts Sappho in the familiar role of teacher, with an added sexual implication. And the final words, 'draws the waves spellbound', suggest that Parnok's apprenticeship and identification with Sappho makes her attractive to Tsvetaeva (Marina).

Well after her break-up with Parnok, but just before the publication of Roses of Pieria, *Tsvetaeva wrote a poem on this same theme, Orpheus' arrival in Lesbos after his dismemberment: 'So they floated: head and lyre' (1921). Its final lines imply Sappho finding Orpheus' head: 'Perhaps a bareheaded Lesbian | Has pulled in her net?'*

Sappho's Dreams [1]

> *Sappho told her dream to Cypris ...*
> Sappho

1
I dreamt – I call out to my darling girlfriends:
Must I run long? Little scamps, pets, where are you?
And with my futile cry I stir forth only
A sleepy echo.

Then the dawn arises in golden sandals,
But it is not our sea there that shines pinkly,
And a different earth billows in the dew – [6]
Where are you, Sappho?

In the fragrance of herbs is an unknown whiff
Of bitter sweetness. In the meadows of home
Neither anise, nor rose, nor honeysuckle [7]
Ever smelled like this.

I step with difficulty, as if each foot
Is softly fluid – not like me, and the lyre,
The lyre – my faithful shield – wearies my arm with
A new heaviness ...

I bend to a stream – o, wicked miracle! –
In the clear mirror the reflected face
Both enrages me and delights me, in tears –
Who is it, Sappho?

- Metre: Sapphics
- Unrhymed
- Sources: Sappho 134, 96

Parnok implies her privileged insight into the very dream that Sappho told to Aphrodite (Cypris) by taking fragment 134 (in Ivanov's translation)[8] as an epigraph. But in the body of the poem Parnok interacts with another, longer Sapphic fragment, 96, from which she takes the luscious descriptions of Lesbos and the idea of a lesbian Sappho. Here is Ivanov's fragment 96 translation (2019: 93–4) in full:

To Atthis

....
....

From afar, from Sardis of our fathers,
Towards us she directs her thought, in longing of desires.

Why hide it?
In the days when we lived together, you
Were a goddess to her, you alone!
Arignota fell in love with your song.

And now, there,
In the tender host of Lydian women,
Like Selene, she rose –
The evening stars' rosy-fingered empress.

At the hour
When day has guttered out, is not it she alone who pours
A blaze over the salty sea,
Radiance over the flowery steppe – the moon?

All adew,
The aromatic meadow is steaming;
Roses have sumptuously opened; a sweet
Smell streams forth from anise and honeysuckle.

But for her,
Poor thing, there's no peace! All night she
Wanders the house . . . Atthis is not there!
And the captivity of lonely separation wearies her.

Loudly she
Calls us . . . Sensitive, Night catches
And carries from across the sea,
With the splash of waves, the echo of unintelligible laments.

Naturally fragment 96 caught Parnok's attention: Sappho's original poem is very homoerotic, and Ivanov's translation, which fills in the gaps with his own conjectures, makes the poem if anything even more gay, suggesting with the exclamation 'Why hide it?' that the lovers are out and proud, while the domesticity of his setting makes them seem like a modern lesbian couple. Parnok reacts to this by having her Sappho call out endearments to her girlfriends at the beginning. Sappho soon realises she is no longer on Lesbos, which Parnok evokes through Sappho's/Ivanov's imagery: she turns Sappho's dusk to dawn but keeps the goddess personification and her pinkness, and she keeps entirely the image of the meadow steaming with dew and all of Ivanov's flowers (different from Sappho's in the original). With these sweet-smelling flowers she contrasts a 'bitter sweetness' (l. 10) that Sappho does not recognize – wormwood, which Parnok's friends Adelaida and Evgeniia Gertsyk both noted as characteristic of Sudak (Romanova 2005: 38); wormwood was rife on the Black Sea shores in antiquity too, as Ovid attests (Ex Ponto 3.1.23–4).

There is a simple explanation for both Parnok's 'access' to Sappho's dream and for why Sappho finds the landscape different, her lyre suddenly heavy, and her reflection unrecognizable: in her dream Sappho has inhabited Parnok's body in the future. (However, Burgin (1994: 180) concludes that Parnok's Sappho is in the underworld.) A metapoetic reading of the 'fluid foot' and the 'heavy lyre' is Parnok's acknowledgement that Sappho is a greater poet than she. (As in the earlier poem 'Lyre', Parnok again puns on the word 'shield', which can also mean 'shell' and thence 'lyre'.) Typically, in the last stanza Parnok hints that Sappho fancies the face she sees – i.e. Parnok's. This progression from conceding the other's greatness to implying her own sexual attractions/accomplishments is similar to Parnok's approach to Tsvetaeva in the preceding 'All of me was twined in vines of memory'.

Sappho's Dreams [2]

In time someone, believe me, will remember us, too.
Sappho

2
'In time someone, believe me, will remember us, too . . .'
Thus I spake – and sank onto my girlfriend's bosom;
A strange dream – was it? – seized me, but then around
Everything came to life: above my bed, above my lyre
A chirring, a buzzing, as though a swarm of bees
Was tangled in the strings, or cicadas were crackling.
'Sappho!' I hear – all the voices in a hubbub
Were chorusing over and over my name – 'Sappho!'
I see: scurrying busily, back and forth,
From lyre – to bed, and from bed – to lyre: mice.
What do they need with Sappho? And suddenly
Everything lit up (they could not see it!) – You
Are before me, Cypris! Your ineffable face
Smiles upon me. The divine voice: 'Now that's fame, Sappho:
They are arguing about who your eternal –
Mead of gods! – love songs are to – young men or maidens?'

- Metre: Pentameter – Dactylic (first three feet) and Trochaic (final two feet), or trimeter made up of two dactyls then a dodrans
- Unrhymed
- Sources: Sappho 147, 126, 1

Parnok takes fragment 147 (in Ivanov's translation; 2019: 153) as epigraph and first line, and uses Ivanov's metre (the metre of Sappho's original line, which is damaged, is uncertain) for the entire poem (Ivanov 2019: 350). She stages Sappho – the poem's 'I' – speaking the line, followed by an archaic verb for 'I spoke', which (probably coincidentally) gets closer to fragment 147's 'φαιμι', 'I would say', than Ivanov's translation 'believe me'.

The poem's central issue arises naturally from the Sappho fragment: yes, Sappho has indeed been remembered in posterity, but has she been remembered correctly? The trippy dream sequence of insects buzzing, a hubbub of voices, and mice scurrying seems to represent people in modernity discussing Sappho: not only her poetry (represented by the lyre – and perhaps also by the bees and cicadas), but also her sex life (represented by the bed). The vermin suggest Parnok's disapproval of such prurience.

Aphrodite then appears – in a scene drawing on Sappho's poem 1 – to explain to her what all the fuss is about: her sexual orientation. This final question has been answered already by the poem's second line, which depicts Sappho with her female lover, of course. As if pointing out the obvious, Parnok grounds this homoerotic image in Sappho's own poetry, fragment 126: 'Fall asleep on the bosom of your girlfriend. | On her sensual bosom fall asleep.' (Ivanov's translation; 2019: 122.) This unshakeable fact of Sappho's lesbian sexuality renders the modern readers' question ridiculous, and it rightly receives no response from Sappho.

And straight-up beautiful, shapely youth, are you

And straight-up beautiful, shapely youth, are you:
Two blue suns under a fringe of eyelashes,
And curls in a dark-flowing whirlwind,
Gloriouser than laurel, crown your tender face.

A very Adonis, my young forerunner!
You began the cup, now put into my hands –
Pressing up to my beloved's lips,
I cheer myself with this unhappy thought:

'Twas not you, o young one, disenchanted her.
Wondering at the flame of these loving lips,
It's not yours, o first one, that jealously
A lover will recall – but my name.

- Metre: Alcaics
- Unrhymed
- Sources: Sappho 137, 140, 168
- Dated 3 October 1915; originally published in Parnok's first collection, Poems (1916)

Parnok steps into Alcaic stanzas, a metre named for Alcaeus, Sappho's contemporary on Lesbos. She does so to put a modern love triangle – her jealousy of Tsvetaeva's beautiful young husband Sergei Efron (Burgin 1994: 133) – into an ancient framework. Parnok's Alcaics encode Efron as Alcaeus – most probably as Sappho's rival poet (casting herself as Sappho), or perhaps as Sappho's reputed lover (casting Tsvetaeva as Sappho). The fact that Parnok calls him 'Adonis' – a character who often featured in Sappho's poems as Aphrodite's beloved (fragments 140, 168)[9] – suggests that Parnok is thinking of Tsvetaeva as Aphrodite, and herself as Sappho. The 'male' metre (Ivanov called Alcaics 'manly energetic'; 2019: 9) implies that Efron's advantage stems from his masculinity – but so does his sexual inferiority.

Metre aside, the poem is unlike any written by Alcaeus, except in one detail: the comparison of Tsvetaeva to a cup to be drunk (line 6) may refer to Alcaeus' many sympotic (drinking) poems. The poem need not be like Alcaeus' poems, though, since Sappho had her own poem in Alcaics, fragment 137, apparently written in response to a poem by Alcaeus to her (Campbell 1982: 153), which Ivanov translated (2019: 155):

To Alcaeus

But if your secret intent were innocent,
Your tongue would not be hiding a shameful word –
Then directly from free lips would speech
Pour forth about the holy and the right.

It is this lofty reproof which Parnok adapts to put her rival in his place. However, unlike Sappho, she asserts not greater purity of speech, but her superiority as a lover.

Much too tightly clamped shut were those lips

Much too tightly clamped shut were those lips –
How and where could a word have slipped past them?
But I was called in your voice – I can hear it –
By a tender name.

But when we, so close and newly strangers,
Were returning, over a midnight Moscow
From distant coastlines the wind was hurtling –
It smelled of the sea . . .

Wind, wind from the sea, my only avenger,
Will fly here yet again, so that you, pining,
Will remember the hour when I with my lips
Listened to your heart.

- Metre: Sapphics
- Unrhymed
- Source: Sappho 1
- Originally published in Parnok's first collection, Poems (1916)

Sofiia Parnok's Sapphic Cycle *Roses of Pieria*

The scenario seems to be an estrangement between Parnok and her lover in the aftermath of a quarrel. Though the masculine form of 'remember' (line 11) implies a male addressee, Parnok is highly unlikely to have written a poem of this kind to a man. The timing (1915/1916) and scenario both fit with Parnok's – famously tempestuous – relationship with Tsvetaeva. The multiple references to the sea, like in 'All of me was entwined in vines of memory', suggest 'Marina'. (Burgin (1992: 137) likewise believes this poem addresses Tsvetaeva.)

Beyond its form, the poem makes no explicit reference to Sappho. However, parallels with Sappho's poem 1 (the Hymn to Aphrodite) can be discerned, especially in the final stanza, when Parnok calls on the sea wind to 'fly here yet again' to remind her lover of her. The sea wind takes the place of Aphrodite, whom Sappho summons ('yet again') to make her beloved love her. The substitution is apt, since Aphrodite was born from sea foam, and in Ivanov's translation she even flies through the air like 'a whirlwind' (2019: 83). While Sappho calls Aphrodite her 'fellow fighter' or 'ally', Parnok calls the sea wind her 'avenger', repurposing Sappho's military metaphor. Parnok had no way of knowing from the available Russian translations that Sappho's beloved in poem 1 is female: Ivanov's translation casts her as emphatically male ('Who is he, then, your offender?'; 2019: 84), while Veresaev's translation is characteristically vague about her gender ('Who has slighted | You [. . .]?'; 1963: 234). This may be the reason for Parnok's flipping her lover's gender in the penultimate line; she did not feel the need to hide her lovers' gender in the other poems in either Poems *or* Roses of Pieria.

Like a small girl you appeared before me, awkward

Like a small girl you appeared before me, awkward.
                                                                Sappho

'Like a small girl you appeared before me, awkward' –
Ah, Sappho has pierced me through with a one-line dart!
In the night I fell to thinking over the frizzy little head,
Motherly tenderness replacing passion in my frenzied heart –
'Like a small girl you appeared before me, awkward'.

The memory arose of how you dodged a kiss through some fraud,
The memory arose of those eyes with their incredible pupils . . .
Into my home you came, I'd made you happy, as a new outfit would:
A belt, a fistful of beads, or some colourful pantofles –
'Like a small girl you appeared before me, awkward'.

But under the blow of love, you – are as malleable gold!
I bent down over the face, which was pale in passion's shade,
As though death had wiped over there with a snowy puff, powdered . . .
I give thanks even for the way, my sweet, that in those days
'Like a small girl you appeared before me, awkward'.

- Metre: Dactylic Pentameter 'Elegiacs' (in each stanza the odd lines are in Ivanov's metre and the even lines miss out the unstressed syllables at the caesura and the end like in an elegiac couplet's pentameter line)
- Alternate Rhyme: ABABA – ACACA – ADADA
- Source: Sappho 49b
- Dated February 1915 (?); originally published in Parnok's first collection, Poems (1916), where it was 'the poem that raised the most consternation among Parnok's reviewers [. . . probably because] it assumed a lesbian Sappho' (Burgin 1994: 138)

This poem – Parnok's first love poem to Tsvetaeva (Burgin 1994: 118) – arises from Sappho's fragment 49b (in Ivanov's translation),[10] which serves as epigraph, opening line, and refrain closing each stanza. A quarter of a century later (1940) Tsvetaeva noted, proudly, that Sappho's line was 'completed by S. Parnok and addressed – to me' (Poliakova 1983: 70).

Fragment 49b has no evident lesbian subtext – especially within Sapphic poetics, where to be 'ἄχαρις', 'graceless/charmless' (translated by Ivanov as 'awkward') is to be unattractive. (Though 49b has become wrongly paired with fragment 49a (see Parker 2006), which is lesbian (if Sappho is the speaker), Ivanov keeps the two fragments separate, so Parnok would have had no reason to connect them, aside from their being on neighbouring pages.) Nevertheless, Parnok clearly found it apposite to the age difference between herself and Tsvetaeva (seven years), and to Tsvetaeva's lack of experience with lesbian love.

By interweaving the Sappho quotation with scenes from her own love affair Parnok casts herself both as inspired by Sappho, and as Sappho herself. Being inspired and being in love are inextricable concepts here, as the second line shows with its depiction of Sappho's fragment piercing Parnok – like Cupid's arrow.

You are drowsing, my girlfriend

> *Fall asleep on the bosom of your girlfriend.*
> *On her sensual bosom fall asleep.*
> Sappho

You are drowsing, my girlfriend,
– A child on the breast of her mother! –
How sweet: for you – to drift to sleep,
For me – to be unable to wake up,

Since, isn't this a dream, tell me,
As there is this blissful bed,
And twilight all songful, and you,
And you in my quiet arms?

O, gently caressing curls
On a moist temple! O, violets!
Ones like these used to flower
In the meadows of our home.

We would plait garlands, you and I,
And where garlands are, there are songs,
Where songs are – there are delights . . .
Are you asleep, my last, sweet dream?

Float on above me, float on,
My Aeolian sky,
Blaze on, my last sunset,
Sparkle on, my ancient mead!

- Metre: Amphibrachic Trimeter (Ivanov's metre for fragment 126; Sappho's original metre is uncertain)
- Unrhymed
- Sources: Sappho 126, 94

This poem takes its epigraph and scenario from fragment 126, the same one Parnok referenced in 'Sappho's Dreams' 2; here the roles are reversed, and the poet (it is unclear if she is Parnok or Sappho) is not the sleeper but the woman whose breast is being slept on. Parnok's likening of the sleeping girlfriend to a child and the poet to her mother in the first stanza is reminiscent of the preceding poem, 'Like a small girl you appeared before me, awkward'. In stanzas 3–4 Parnok draws on Sappho's most overt moment of lesbian eroticism, from the middle of fragment 94, which Ivanov (2019: 91–2) translates as follows:

Recollect all
The hours of irrevocable pleasures –
How you and I rejoiced in beauty.

We used to sit together, plait
Wreaths from violets and roses,
Weave garlands from colourful firstlings of meadows –

Living attire for a tender neck,
Fragrant jewellery –
I would adorn you entirely, like Spring, in flowers.

Having doused your wave of curls with
Royal myrrh, your breast with perfumes,
You, too, would lie down with us – to sup and sing.

Parnok takes from Sappho, via Ivanov, the details of the 'violets', 'garlands', and 'delights', as well as the general sensuality. Parnok takes from Ivanov alone the details of Lesbos' meadows (which connects with Parnok's quotation of fragment 96 in 'Sappho's Dreams' 1) and the girlfriend's curly hair (which again connects with her description of the sleeping Tsvetaeva in 'Like a small girl you appeared before me, awkward'). Parnok appears to have intuited directly from Sappho the detail of the 'blissful bed', which appears in stanza 2: this is remarkably similar to fragment 94 lines 21–3, where Sappho says (to the woman she's cheering up) 'on a soft/springy bed ... you'd let out longing'. Where does Parnok get the bed from? The other Russian translation – Veresaev's – while more literal, still essentially makes it a sympotic couch: 'And how with your tender hand, | Near me, from the soft bed | You reached for the sweet drink' (1963: 235). No translations of the time, into any language, saw that the woman and Sappho were in a bed (Denys Page would only put the 'bed' question to rest (!) some forty years later, in 1955, writing: 'στρωμνή regularly means not a couch, for reclining, or a seat of any kind, for sitting, but a bed, a place where you lie down for the night'; 1959: 79). It is unlikely that Parnok delved into the Greek herself. So she probably invented the bed based on fragment 126, and ignored Ivanov's sympotic setting (which removes nearly all the homoeroticism from Sappho's scene) to keep the intimacy of fragment 126. Her incidental uncovering of the sexual meaning of fragment 94 is testament to the validity of lesbian readings of Sappho.

The sad parting between the woman and Sappho which begins fragment 94 and prompts their recollection of past joys also seems to have influenced Parnok's poem: not its plot, but the melancholic feeling that the poem's present is simultaneously the distant past. Related to this melancholia is the fact that whereas Sappho builds up in fragment 94 (or what remains of it) to the bed and, perhaps, the orgasm, Parnok sets her poem in the post-orgasmic bed.

The final stanza sets the reader up for the end of the cycle: Parnok/Sappho wishes that the Lesbos of Sappho's poems will continue forever, concluding with an untranslatable pun on 'play/sparkle' and 'mead/poetry' – the Russian for 'play' is used of drinks to mean 'sparkle'; the Russian for 'hops / intoxicating drink' is often used about inspired poetry.

So on different shores

So on different shores, beside a different songful sea,
Millennia later, in a spring as young as ever,
Recollecting her ancient childhood in Aeolia,
A maiden on a pensive day plucked at the strings.

On the wind from across the sea flowed to her the breath of Hellas,
The wind, unperceived by others, ruffles her heart:
The maiden fancies – she'll dream your dreams through, Sappho,
Your songs whose sounds never reached us – she'll sing them through.

- *Metre: Elegiacs*
- *Unrhymed*
- *Originally published in* Kamena *(1919 no. 2) (Parnok 1979: 331)*

The final poem of 'Roses of Pieria' presents Parnok as a modern-day Sappho who remembers a former life in Lesbos. This theme brings the cycle back round to the opening poem, as well as to the very first Sapphic poem Parnok published, 'Aeolic lyre – as soon as I hear its song'. Parnok wrote this in 1918 by the Black Sea, in Sudak (Burgin 1994: 154). As in 'Much too tightly clamped shut were those lips', the sea wind carries a reminder of the (classical) past, and also, probably, of the now ended relationship with Tsvetaeva. Parnok concludes by promising to continue and complete Sappho's lost work.

Penthesileia
A triptych

This 'triptych' tells of the fight between Penthesileia, queen of the Amazons and ally of the Trojans, and Achilles, leader of the Myrmidons and greatest of the Greek warriors.

The third poem, 'Return', was written first, in the year of Parnok and Tsvetaeva's break-up; she later added 'Challenge' and 'Duel' to create a narrative about her turn away from, and return to, Sappho.

'Penthesileia' was set to music by Valentina Ramm (1929, Op. 9) (Parnok 1979: 331).

- *Source: Quintus Smyrnaeus'* Posthomerica *Book 1 (the only extant classical text depicting Penthesileia's battle with Achilles, based on the lost* Aethiopis *from the Epic Cycle)*
- *Originally published in* Zhizn' *(1922 no. 2) (Zuseva-Ozkan 2018: 81)*

Challenge

My heart to the sensual mode I do not tune,
The languid lyre I have smashed to splinters –
It is time I sing of ill-fated Troy,
Of deadly battle's magnificence.

You were and ever will be of another faith
(Your male god is crueller than the cruel Erinyes!),
And destined with bloodied heart to fall
In combat – is Penthesileia.

Before one another we have come again.
Is your spear blunt? Your sword not resonant?

Or is martial steel not honoured by
The untameable blood of the Amazons?

- Metre: Tetrameter – Dactylic, or Dactylic (first two feet) and Trochaic (final two feet)[11]
- Alternate Rhyme

Parnok signals her turn from amorous and lyric to martial and epic themes through a recusatio *(a refusal to write in the expected genre), dramatically breaking her Sapphic lyre. Sappho did include themes from the Trojan war in her poems, most famously fragment 16, where she (like Parnok here) gives a female perspective on epic events. Sappho is even reported as singing about Achilles, in fragment 105b, but as this was not translated by Ivanov, Parnok probably did not know it. So Parnok's* recusatio *is not entirely apt.*

Parnok comments on the gendered aspect of epic vs. lyric and hero vs. Amazon in the middle stanza. She addresses Achilles (who is not named). Calling him 'of another faith' echoes the phrase 'one faith we share' in her dedicatory poem to 'Roses of Pieria', suggesting that Parnok and Penthesileia are still, despite the recusatio, *on the side of Sappho, lyric poetry, and (perhaps) lesbianism. Parnok finds Achilles' 'male god' crueller than the (female) Erinyes. The 'male god' might be Ares or Zeus, representing war or fate – this does not come from the* Posthomerica, *but instead fits Parnok's pacifist version of Penthesileia. The Erinyes reference Penthesileia's motive for coming to Troy to fight: the Furies had pursued her since she accidentally killed her sister Hippolyta when hunting, and war could appease them (Posthomerica 1.21–31). The insistence on Penthesileia being fated to die follows the* Posthomerica *(1.103–4, 200–4, 389–93).*

As with Sappho in 'Roses of Pieria', Parnok slips between her own persona and that of her main character. By the third stanza she speaks as Penthesileia, goading Achilles to fight her. Her aspersions on the capabilities of his weapons bear sexual implications.

Duel

To the challenge bold a single reply – the spear!
He cast it, but his first throw's aim was off:
It sprang away from ringing bronze,
Not breaking through the battle armour.

It flashed again. The wind cut off its flight –
Death flies and again did not fly all the way . . .
For the hero, unexpected unsuccess
Only heats his age-long fury.

And for the third time the madman cast his spear.
From her heart the maiden quietly withdraws her shield –

He sees: the wicked point
Entered the armour as a fateful thorn.

- Metre: Alcaics
- Unrhymed

With epic diction Parnok stages the fight, one spearcast per stanza. This copies the number of spearcasts in the Posthomerica, but Parnok makes all three Achilles' (who is still not named), while Penthesileia notably does not attempt a single blow. This is a major change from the Posthomerica, where Penthesileia is the aggressor, and casts the first two spears, one at Achilles, which is turned aside by his armour (Posthomerica 1.547–9) like Achilles' first spear here, and one at Ajax, which hits his greave but does not harm him (Posthomerica, 1.563–7), the only spearcast scenario Parnok alters completely. The third spearcast in the Posthomerica is Achilles'; it pierces Penthesileia under her right breast (Posthomerica 1.592–6) like in Parnok's version (though there is no mention of her shield), and does not kill her, though this is not immediately obvious, again, like in Parnok's version.

The metre of this poem brings a new meaning to 'Penthesileia' (one established incontrovertibly in the next poem). Parnok has written in Alcaics once before in Roses of Pieria: in 'And straight-up beautiful, shapely young man, you are', where the metre expresses her jealousy of Efron, Tsvetaeva's husband, and stands for his maleness. That earlier Efron-Adonis here becomes Efron-Achilles – still in Alcaics, just as male, but much more dangerous – the fatal foe of Parnok-Penthesileia.

In the last line the spearpoint in Penthesileia's heart turns into a thorn.

Return

Not a deadly spear – an undecaying rose
I took as my weapon out into battle.
Differently of old my foremother went up
Against Achilles.

He is just the same in murderous combat –
Hatemongering at heart, but I am pining:
I did not carry ancient hatred with me
As far as this life . . .

Quietly returning from the field of war
And cursing warrioresses' hard lot,
Pressing her hands to her chest, she starts to cry,
Penthesileia.

- Metre: Sapphics
- Unrhymed

- Originally published separately under the title 'Sapphic Stanzas' in Severnye zapiski (1916 no. 9) (Burgin 1994: 146)

Parnok marks Penthesileia's 'return' from the battlefield in the triptych's multivalently titled final poem by writing in Sapphics. The metre overturns her opening recusatio – she has 'returned' to Sapphic poetry. And perhaps never left it, for she says that she fought not with a spear but a rose. The rose, symbol of Parnok's lesbian poems and loves throughout 'Roses of Pieria', was foreshadowed in the 'thorn' that pierced Penthesileia's heart in 'Duel'. So these lines, along with the final stanza, retroactively recast the 'maiden' of the preceding poem as a victim not of war but of love.

This erotic battle centres on Tsvetaeva – who in 1910 as a teenager had fallen in love with a statue of Penthesileia (Burgin 1995: 64–5), and who depicted Parnok as Amazon-like in her cycle 'Girlfriend' (1914–15), dedicated to Parnok, through repeated references to Parnok's 'helmet' of auburn hair (Burgin 1995: 67). It is for Tsvetaeva that Parnok writes as Penthesileia, using the story of Penthesileia and Achilles (who is finally named) to express her feelings of defeat and heartbreak after she and Tsvetaeva broke up and Tsvetaeva 'returned' to her husband (Burgin 1994: 183).

Many years later Tsvetaeva also used Amazons to talk about lesbianism, in her essay Mon frère féminin: lettre à l'Amazone (1932/1934). She addressed the letter to the lesbian socialite Natalie Clifford Barney, but her true addressee, the basis for her description of lesbian relationships, and the 'Amazon' of the title was Parnok. Evidence supporting this conclusion are the numerous echoes in the letter of her 'Girlfriend' poems (Burgin 1994: 115); and an anonymized reaction to the news of Parnok's death in 1933 which she added in her revision of the letter the following year, ending with 'an implied epitaph to Parnok' (Burgin 1994: 324 n. 52) that reads: 'When I see a willow despairing, I understand Sappho' (Tsvetaeva 1979: 45).

Parnok calls Penthesileia 'foremother' just as she had called Sappho 'sister' at the start of the book, claiming the Amazons too as part of her lesbian ancestry. Perhaps this is why Parnok leaves Penthesileia wounded but alive at the end of the fight, altering the ending of Penthesileia's story in the Posthomerica, where she considers begging Achilles for mercy but is ruthlessly skewered – only to be postumously desired and regretted by him (Posthomerica 1.601–74).

Wise Venus

Parnok takes to the 'erotic advice' genre. This entails a move away from Sappho, whose love lyrics are altogether too direct/candid for Parnok's new style, and towards Ovid, whose Ars Amatoria is the primary example of didactic-elegiac love poetry. But whereas Ovid styles himself 'craftsman of love', appointed by Venus' (1.7), Parnok takes the guise of the goddess of love herself, becoming the 'Wise Venus' of the title. This is reminiscent of Sappho's special relationship with Aphrodite, and ventriloquising of the goddess in poem 1. And despite the turn from Greek love lyric to Latin love elegy, from Aphrodite to Venus, Parnok has not left Sappho behind altogether. Parnok's mix of influences is felt in the mix of metres – three poems in Ovidian elegiacs, but the other two in Sappho's lyric metres; and in the mix of characters – whose names (besides Venus and other mythical figures) are mostly drawn from Sappho's poems.

The reason Parnok cannot abandon Sappho is that her claim to being the Wise Venus is based on her experience as a lover of women – yet Ovid's Ars Amatoria *is entirely heterosexual. So she queers her heterosexual model by bringing in elements from Sappho's Lesbos, drawing as much on Pierre Louÿs's* Les Chansons de Bilitis *(1894 – erotic pseudotranslations of the 'ancient poetess' Bilitis) as on Ivanov's Sappho translations. Louÿs was clearly a useful bridging point for Parnok between Ovid and Sappho: the* Chansons *show the influence of both authors; they contain both heterosexual and homosexual poems; and 'Bilitis' even writes one erotic advice poem.*

'Wise Venus' is a sexually ambivalent cycle: it provides a countercurrent to Ovidian elegy's presumptive heterosexuality, actually presuming women's lesbianism; yet it retains Ovidian elegy's cynicism and pragmatism, so its lesbian characters tend to lose out to straight couplings, their defeat aided by the Wise Venus herself. The title may, then, be an ironic nod to the practicality of lesbianism's capitulation to heteronormativity.

Dedication

If you discover that you've been spurned by a headstrong beloved,
If you discover that Eros' bow was not taut, ever,
That the unkissed lips – so red – for a kiss not yours have parted,
And, intransigent with you, are pliant with another,

If into desert – gardens have been transfigured by this loss,
Still, scrape an inattentive finger the lyre strings along:
In your sorrowing, poet, remember your latin brother's words:
'After all, faster will fly the day deceived by a song'.

- Metre: Elegiacs
- Alternate Rhyme
- Source: Ovid Tristia 4.10.112–14?
- Dated 1912; originally published in Parnok's first collection, Poems (1916), where she also uses the quote in the final line as an epigraph, attributing it to Ovid (Parnok 1979: 326, 123)

Parnok dedicates 'Wise Venus' to those unsuccessful in love. She sets the Ovidian tone for the cycle in the final line by quoting Ovid, calling him 'your latin brother' (line 7) – i.e. a fellow poet and a fellow sufferer in love. His solution to this suffering: dispel it with poetry. The quotation, 'After all, faster will fly the day deceived by a song', does not seem to correspond directly to any line of Ovid, and appears to be Parnok's own formulation,[12] but the sentiment is one commonly expressed by Ovid, especially in his exile poetry. Tristia 4.10.112–14 comes closest to Parnok's line: 'my sad fates with what song I may I lighten. | [...] | thus nevertheless I use up and deceive the day.'[13]

Do not call upon death

Do not call upon death: hopelessness is discourteous to the gods.
My young man! Do buck up. Hearken unto the Wise Venus. –
Dearer than a boyfriend to some intractable maidens – is a girlfriend.
With a woman's hand you'll unlock what has been closed to you.

Constrain your mighty hips – the pride of any man – with a tight girdle,
Twine your muscles' glorious swell in a snaking bracelet.
Long would Achilles have stayed among the Ionian maidens unknown,
Had not the sight of a spear awakened in him the hero.[14]

Let your gaze not light up at the familiar sound of the battle cry –
By one sign only do not fear to give yourself away:
In front of your severe lady do not stifle a languishing sigh –
It's not for men's hearts that her arrows are sharpened by Eros.

- Metre: Elegiacs
- Unrhymed
- Sources: Louÿs 137, 128; Ovid Ars Amatoria 1.681–704

Parnok posits women's lesbian preferences and adapts the (heterosexual) erotic advice accordingly. As the Wise Venus, she counsels a young man in how to win over a lesbian. She advises him, of course, to pretend to be a woman.

With the detail of the adept 'woman's hand' Parnok subverts Bilitis's advice in 'Conseils à un amant', 'her' only erotic advice poem, that 'The hands of a woman in love are trembling and without caresses. Exempt them from being zealous' (Louÿs 2003 no. 137). She may also have reacted to 'Thérapeutique', in which a client of Bilitis (in her courtesan phase) asks what he can do to make her love him; she replies: 'Imagine that you are a woman' (Louÿs 1894 no. 128).

Parnok's example of a cross-dressed man, Achilles, rather mocks the serious Achilles of 'Penthesileia'. Her use of this episode hinges not on his cross-dressing's failure (his self-betrayal, seizing the spear placed among jewellery by Odysseus, entailing his death in the Trojan war), but on its success: his seduction of the Scyrian (not Ionian) girl, Deidamia. Ovid features this episode prominently in Ars Amatoria *(1.681–704).*

This poem in particular gained so much notoriety that it was parodied by an acquaintance of Parnok's, Mikhail Vazlinskii, in a short poem in 1924 (Burgin 1999: ch. 4):[15]

Dearer than a boyfriend to some intractable maidens is a girlfriend.
It's not for men's hearts that my arrows are made sharp by Eros.
So sang in Pieria (on 4th Tverskaia-Iamskaia Street)
Sappho's very own sister, Lesbos's true daughter.
Well, there's no accounting for tastes. Blessed is she who in the 20th century
The feat of the girlfriend of girlfriends could on Iamskaia embody.

He quotes Parnok's poem's most lesbian lines, 3 and 12, as the opening two lines but changing 'her' to 'my' to make Parnok the speaker. Equating Pieria with the street in Moscow where Parnok lived, which was known as a red-light district (Burgin 1994: 165), is somewhat double-edged. The sobriquet he (affectionately? patronisingly?) gives Parnok, 'girlfriend of girlfriends', again references line 3, and possibly also Tsvetaeva's 'Girlfriend' cycle, and/or Martial's 'tribad of tribads' Philaenis (epigram 7.70).

Not always in the wind it blazes up brighter

Not always in the wind it blazes up brighter,
O my friend – sometimes the torch just goes out.
Not always is the wave to ships more conducive
Than the quiet sea.

You hurry delight, impatient boy,
You accuse the maiden of lazy passion –
Have you forgotten that many like lightning
Less than the slow flame?

The lyre does not bestow wondrous song upon
Someone whose hand madly grabs onto the strings –
There are many rules (here's one – remember it!)
In the tender art:

Slipping from smooth shoulders down in a long kiss,
Don't rush to get to where in a drowsy laze
Two white doves, two adorable miracles
Are sweetly breathing.

- *Metre: Sapphics*
- *Unrhymed*
- *Sources: Ovid Ars Amatoria 2.717–18; Louÿs 61, 62, 129*

Parnok advises the lover to take his time – a piece of advice elaborated from Ovid Ars Amatoria 2.717–18: 'Trust me, not to be hurried is sex's pleasure, | But gradually enticed by slow delay'. Her analogy with lyre-playing – especially when combined with the poem's Sapphic metre – reminds the reader that she has inhabited Sappho's persona earlier in the book, and is expert in loving women, in song and in deed. The poem (like, presumably, the patient lover) reaches its destination – a woman's breasts – in the final lines. Calling them 'doves', Parnok deliberately writes like Bilitis, who compares breasts to doves three times ('L'antre des nymphes', 'Les seins de Mnasidika', 'La commande'; Louÿs 1894 nos. 61, 62, 129).

Where his arrows are

'Where his arrows are – ask that archer of yours, o goddess!
Empty is Cupid's quiver: they're all in my heart!
He did not save a single one for my haughty Hermione – [16]
In vain at those darling knees I pour out tears of love.

With his melodies Orpheus tames ferocious predators –
Woman's heart, I swear, is crueller than the heart of a beast:
In vain my cithara sings to her with the most sweet of sounds . . .
How can I conquer the unconquerable girl? Teach me.'

'Remember: as golden rain the Thunderer descended on Danaë . . .
I've told you all. If you're a clever boy, you'll understand.'

- Metre: Elegiacs
- Unrhymed
- Sources: Ovid Ars Amatoria 2.699, 3. 311–48, 2.273–80; Sappho 23, 1

A man complains his love is unrequited; his beloved's heart is not softened even when he plays music to her. (Her name, Hermione (line 3), is from Helen's almost-as-beautiful daughter, who appears in both Sappho (23) and Ovid (2.699).) The man has perhaps taken Ovid's advice from Ars Amatoria *3.311–48 (to women) recommending music and poetry, including the examples of Orpheus (321–2) and Sappho (331), which Parnok also cites (line 5) and alludes to with the cithara (line 7). In a scenario reminiscent of Sappho 1, Parnok/Venus replies to his plea. She gives a different mythical exemplum: Danaë, whose rape by Zeus as a golden shower here symbolises the power of money. Ovid bemoans the fact that poetry will not get the girl and instead 'love is won over by gold' at* Ars Amatoria *2.273–80 (he also puts advice for fleecing a lover into the mouth of a bawd in* Amores *1.8); but nowhere does he deploy Danaë in this way.*[17] *Parnok's cynicism here suggests no real love or desire can be felt by Hermione towards the man.*

Eros holds the mirror

Eros holds the mirror in front of her, and in its fragile glass
Eternal gold of the braids, eternal sky of the eyes.
But on the rug, at her knees – so enticing and strong –
Face buried in her hands, there sits a sorrowful maiden.
'Woe is me! Woe is me! Where, oh where is my nights' proud coolness?'

'What's up with her?' whisper her girlfriends around, slyly smiling.
'All that happened, was once – it was towards evening, by the temple –
As he was walking past, that playboy glanced at me.
That was really all that happened . . . And also at the lyre contest . . .
I hear my girlfriends saying: "It's your turn, Mnasidika."
I went out, and had barely touched my songful hand to the strings,
When they started to burn red hot: he had just then come forward.
Never taking his eyes off me – they were clouded dark with desire, [18]
A rose – why did he bring that swarthy rose right to his lips? [19]
How did I sing? What about? O, competitress – the rose! O, the lips!
Sappho frowned. What do I care if she is angry!
O, how cruel that mouth must be, and how hot and how moist . . .
Muddle up some reason in me! Let me forget him!
The bed burns me at night. Whenever I close my eyes, I see
Lips and rose, and again that rose and those lips of his . . . [20]
What should I do, tell me, so I won't be constantly seeing them?'

The wise goddess answers her with a single word: 'Kiss'.

- Metre: Elegiacs
- Unrhymed
- Sources: Sappho 82; Louÿs 55

Venus looks at her face in a glass mirror (an anachronism; Parnok 1979: 331) while a girl (Mnasidika) kneels before her, lamenting that she is in love with a beautiful boy. While watching her play the lyre in a contest, he meaningfully kisses a rose; Sappho is angered by their flirtation. Now Mnasidika cannot stop thinking about the boy's lips kissing the rose. She asks how to be rid of her obsession: Venus tells her to kiss.

The naming of the main character 'Mnasidika' brings a lesbian subtext to the poem: she may have been a lover of Sappho (fragment 82: 'Gyrinno, for bliss | You are born; | But Mnasidika – is more beautiful'; Ivanov 2019: 149), but is best known as the lover of 'Bilitis' (nos. 52–98, 148, 152, 155). But here she loves a boy . . . However, he indicates his love by kissing a rose – underscored multiple times by Parnok – which alludes to 'Roses of Pieria', in which roses represent Sapphic poems and beloved girls. This suggests the 'playboy' is Parnok herself. The boy with the rose as a masculine-presenting lesbian is supported by the fact that Bilitis takes the male role at her wedding to Mnasidika, wearing 'the virile tunic' and carrying her over the rose-covered threshold ('Les noces'; Louÿs 1894 no. 55). Then, why does Sappho frown over the girl's infatuation? It might simply be because it has made Mnasidika play badly; or, more likely, because it is a personal betrayal of Sappho as a lover. Venus' final instruction to kiss is ambiguous: it could be to bring love about, or it could be to dispel desire by fulfilling it; Venus does not even specify whom or what Mnasidika should kiss.

Atthis, a tender stalk from far-off Sardis

'Atthis, a tender stalk from far-off Sardis,
With swift Hero together don't go to temple –
Disdaining your ritual, goddess,
They tease the men with their futile beauty.

Guest in their haven of unlawful delights:
Archer who has forgot duty and honour.
O goddess, summon Eros away!
Must this be borne long? Punish the traitresses.'

'I smite a frightful smite: falling to the rim
Of a bottomless cup, they'll drink themselves to death
Crying out from thirst. Quenching for them
There was none, is none, and never will be!'

- Metre: Alcaics
- Unrhymed
- Sources: Asclepiades 7 (Anthologia Palatina 5.207); Sappho 96, 49a, 131, 137; i.a. (Sappho/Alcaeus) 11

Venus hears another prayer: to punish two girls who have become lovers, making men jealous. She – at her most anti-lesbian – sentences them to endless thirst.

The starting point for this poem is an epigram from the Greek Anthology by Asclepiades, which was available to Parnok in a fairly close Russian translation (Alekseev 1896: 8):

> Samiennes Bitto and Nanna do not want to go to Aphrodite's temple and fulfil her laws, but now get up to something else, not good. Mistress Aphrodite, punish those who betrayed you and avoid love's enjoyments!

Parnok expands on Asclepiades' epigram and transposes it to a Sapphic milieu. She perhaps draws additionally on Sappho's Alcaic fragment 137 (again – see above: 'And straight-up beautiful, shapely youth, are you'), which has a similarly reproving tone.

Parnok derives details of the girls – 'far-off Sardis', 'swift' (lines 1–2) – from fragments 96 and i.a. (Sappho/Alcaeus) 11 (in Ivanov's translations; Ivanov firmly attributes i.a. 11 to Sappho). Hero appears only in i.a. 11: 'A pupil [f] of mine | was Hero, | in running – swift' (Ivanov 2019: 148). Atthis is Sappho's most famous beloved, mentioned in multiple fragments. The more complete ones, 96, 49a, and 131, are all translated by Ivanov,[21] who does not censor their sexual overtones: for fragment 96 see above ('Sappho's Dreams' 1); fragment 49a reads: 'In years gone by, you, o Atthis, I loved [f]'[22] (Ivanov 2019: 142); fragment 131 reads: 'Yes, Atthis! Towards me you have cooled! | Andromeda alone to Atthis is dear' (Ivanov 2019: 145). Parnok's description of Atthis as a 'stalk' points to a possible real-life archetype for Atthis: her girlfriend Liudmila Erarskaia, whom Parnok compares to a 'stalk' in two love poems.[23]

Parnok's use of Alcaic stanzas (like in 'And straight-up beautiful, shapely youth, are you' and 'Duel') represents the lesbian's male enemy – here, the unidentified man denouncing the girls Atthis/Erarskaia and Hero/Parnok to Venus – and also the choice Parnok's lovers must make between her and a heterosexual life.

Notes

1. Thank you to Maria Wyke and Helena Taylor for constructive criticism on drafts of this commentary.
2. I give all quotations from Russian, Greek, Latin and French in English translation only, and all translations are mine.
3. Parnok has one more poem in Sapphics, in *Vine* (1922): 'A hero does not die to women's wailing'. Two firmly modern love poems from Parnok's last few years show influence from fragment 31: 'You are a young woman, a long-legged woman!' (1929) (see Burgin 1992: 255–6); and 'Gypsy Song' (1932) (see Parnok 1979: 357).
4. I use Lobel-Page numbering for all Sappho fragments; these differ from Ivanov's numbering.
5. Variant: final two words inverted (Parnok 1979: 328).
6. Variant: originally misprinted (clearly unmetrically) 'And a different earth all around billows in the dew'; corrected by Parnok in the copy belonging to Ol'ga Tsuberbiller, her life-partner (Parnok 1979: 331).
7. Literally 'lungwort', here and in Ivanov's 'To Atthis' below.
8. Ivanov wrote four versions of this fragment; Parnok uses the version from the first and second editions (Ivanov 2019: 226).
9. Also fr. 211(b) iii; T 58. Ivanov translated frr. 140 and 168 as one fragment (Ivanov 2019: 107).
10. From the first edition; in the second edition Ivanov changed his translation, taking it further away from the original (Ivanov 2019: 345).
11. Similar to the metre of 'Sappho's Dreams' 2.
12. Tsvetaeva also quotes this line and attributes it to Ovid, probably following Parnok, in two letters: to S. N. Andronikova-Gal'pern (15 July 1926); to A. S. Shteiger (8–18 August 1936). *Tsvetaeva.lit-info.ru*, <http://tsvetaeva.lit-info.ru/tsvetaeva/pisma/index.htm> [accessed 11 March 2022].
13. Thank you to Jennifer Ingleheart, Peta Fowler, and Donncha O'Rourke for helping me track this quotation down.
14. Variant: 'awakened' –> 'gave away' (Parnok 1979: 331).
15. The Russian original was published from the archive of Mariia Shkapskaia in RGALI (РГАЛИ, ф. 1276 С.Я. Парнок, оп. 1 е. х. И). (Burgin 1999: ch. 4 n. 77).
16. Variant: 'Hermione' –> 'Rhodocleia'. A Rhodocleia was the beloved of Rufinus, a poet in the Greek Anthology; at least one of his epigrams to her was translated (in the nineteenth century) by Vladimir Pecherin, who uses the same epithet, 'haughty', for her as Parnok does

here (Golosovker 1935: 163). Poliakova suggests that Parnok changed it because the unusual name sounded 'parodic' (Parnok 1979: 331).
17. Danaë is mentioned at *Ars Amatoria* 3.415–16 for a different reason.
18. Variant: 'Never turning his eyes from me – they were clouded with desire' (Parnok 1979: 331).
19. Variant: different word order of first half line (Parnok 1979: 331).
20. Variant: 'Those dark lips of his, those suffocating lips of his . . .' (Parnok 1979: 331).
21. Atthis is also mentioned in fr. 8, not translated by Ivanov; Atthis was not originally in fr. 49a (see Parker 2006), but appears in Ivanov's translation (and most others).
22. The feminine ending of 'loved' in the Russian makes it clear that the speaker is female.
23. 'Wherefore this for me, o my God?' (February 1916); 'A flower wilts on its delicate stalk' (1917) (Parnok 1979: 192, 188; Burgin 1994: 144, 150–1).

CHAPTER 7
'REBELS AGAINST THE TYRANNY OF MEN': *THE BIRDS, THE BEES* AND AGITATION FOR DEGREES AT GIRTON COLLEGE 1898–1948
Mara Gold

The performance of Greek comedy and parodies of Greek drama by women during the early twentieth century reveal a great deal about their political activism, including criticisms of the lack of opportunity for women to engage with politics and education. As this chapter argues, the potential of comedy to depict contemporary identities and expose gender inequality led to a rise in comic depictions at the beginning of the twentieth century. Comedy made women's activism more palatable and also created a shared bonding experience with other like-minded women. Some attention has been paid to suffrage comedy in scholarship and it is generally agreed that Elizabeth Robins' *Votes for Women* (1907) was the first suffrage play performed and published.[1] Staged at the Court Theatre in London, it led to the birth of the 'first women's theatre movement of the twentieth century' (Hayman and Spender 1985: 36). Oxbridge women's colleges began using comedy in a similarly political way almost a decade earlier, using the traditionally patriarchal subject of Greek drama to reflect their own activism around agitation for degrees, especially in their 1904 production *The Bees* (a parody of Aristophanes' *The Birds*). Numerous scholars have made connections between the women of Greek tragedy and the status of women during the late nineteenth and early twentieth centuries (particularly over the last two decades) but the potential of comedy to perform political activism during this period has only just begun to be examined in scholarship.[2]

This comic potential was not lost on those opposed to women's rights who reinterpreted tragic events as farce through ridicule, just as the concept of the 'New Woman', college woman or even more specifically, the 'Girton girl' was extensively mocked in the media (Clark 2019: 660, 663). Looking back on events leading up to women's enfranchisement, in *The Strange Death of Liberal England*, journalist George Dangerfield stated, 'It is almost impossible to write the story of the Women's Rebellion without admitting certain elements of brutal comedy. An Aristophanes alone could do it justice' (Dangerfield 1936: 148). He later expressed regret that Aristophanes or Plautus were not around to mock the death of Emily Davison at the 1913 Epsom Derby, resituating the tragic as comic (Dangerfield 1936: 191). In some ways he was correct, for it was to Aristophanes that many suffragists and advocates for women's education turned to expose their plight. One obvious figure from antiquity that feminists viewed as either a suffragist or suffragette is Lysistrata from Aristophanes' comedy by the same name, as

Emmeline Pethick-Lawrence noted in an October 1910 edition of *Votes For Women* (Lawrence 1910: 6). Whilst Lysistrata may have been claimed as being a feminist figure, in the play's original performance context, her comedic value was based on the idea of women's autonomy being absurd, much like Dangerfield's interpretation of women's suffrage. With all the ridicule heaped upon them, it was almost inevitable that women struck back by taking comedy into their own hands, often at the expense of men and patriarchal institutions.

Comedy has a long history of making political statements by subverting the status quo, with Aristophanes himself considered the earliest surviving master of that medium. In fact, according to Edith Hall, Aristophanes is seen as the origin of several vital aspects of modern literature, performance, and even communication, including the Western notion of freedom of speech and the tradition of the political cartoon (Hall and Wrigley 2007: 2). It is no surprise that women used this to their advantage during early feminist movements, particularly the fight for women's suffrage. 'Comic irony was used as a tool to convince audiences of the legitimate grievances of women through the use of humour, thereby turning irony into a subversive tool' (Costa 2018: 362). Susan Carlson and Viv Gardner both highlight the popularity of comedy over 'straight' plays and that the Actresses' Franchise League repertoire was predominantly comedic (Carlson 2000: 201; Gardner 1985: 60), which Katharine Cockin describes as a destabilizing force, particularly with regard to the AFL offshoot, The Pioneer Players (Cockin 2017: 91–122). Established in 1908, the AFL produced propaganda plays, organized lectures and meetings and sold plays and sketches by pro-suffrage writers. They often collaborated with other leagues, such as the Women Writers' Suffrage League, but did not promote (nor condemn) militant tactics.

The AFL's 'smash-hit', according to Julie Holledge, was Cicely Hamilton and Christopher St John's 1909 comedy *How The Vote Was Won*, which *The New Age* reviewed as 'the most rippling piece of fun which has been put on the boards for a long time, and the sooner it is put on for a regular run, the better for the public gaiety' (Hamilton and St John 1909: ii; Holledge 1981: 66). The play, which 'cleverly gives Lysistrata an economic edge', follows the story of a women's general strike and critiques as ridiculous the argument that women should not have the vote because, according to English law, they live under the authority (and purse strings) of their closest male relative (Blodgett 1990: 100). Rather than denying their husbands sex, as in Aristophanes' version, this modern Lysistrata calls for women to abandon their professions (including acting) and seek financial support from their male relatives, which results in the retraction of this argument and the granting of votes for women. The original *Lysistrata* was performed soon after, in 1910 (and would not be performed again on a British stage until the 1930s); moreover, as Hall notes, staging this particularly lewd play was not possible until the context of the suffrage movement became evident (Hall and Wrigley 2007: 86). Gertrude Kingston, a prominent member of the AFL, chose the comedy to commemorate her taking over the lease of the Little Theatre and becoming its manager (Hall and Wrigley 2007: 86). Translated by Laurence Housman, who had several plays banned due to censorship laws, this production was largely only approved because it was an adaptation of ancient Greek (Hall and Wrigley 2007: 87). The play spoke directly to the suffrage movement and included several contemporary suffrage jokes. It was subsequently printed by The Woman's Press in 1911, thereby indicating that the play would have been circulated amongst feminists and educated women (Paxton 2018: 56–7).

While there are not too many sources relating to women performing Aristophanes before this point in time, we do have evidence of women using comedy as a subversive tool both within and outside the women's colleges. *The Bees* of Girton College appears to be an early example of a trend that was emerging alongside the creation of the Actresses' Franchise League in 1908: the suffrage play. Despite the name, this group of plays did not exclusively deal with the issue of the vote but covered several women's rights issues, including work and education (Costa 2018: 363). Most suffrage plays had a similar formula and plot development to *The Bees*, however, unlike other suffrage plays, this one is written in verse to closely mimic Aristophanes' style (in translation, at least). Sutherland notes that scholars agree that suffrage plays were more effective at convincing people of their cause than novels. Although most scholarship pertains to 1908–14, *The Bees* of 1904 (and later *The Newmendies* of 1907) indicate that this type of thinking was already being established, at least in formal women's learning environments (Eltis 2013: 164–8; Sutherland 2015: 69). Sos Eltis draws our attention to the fact that 'suffragists were well aware of the propagandist potential of public performance and spectacle' from the movement's earliest days, the cause of which was deeply woven into the fabric of women's colleges (Eltis 2013: 167). Most of the founders, staff and students were suffragists themselves. However, the main political agenda at Girton and other Oxbridge women's colleges was the issue of women's degrees and improving higher education for women, since it affected them most directly.[3] Therefore, although suffragists and women's rights activists outside of the colleges were engaging in propagandist performances before the creation of the Actresses' Franchise League, their efforts were less organized and formalized than they had already become at Girton.

The Oxford University Dramatic Society (OUDS), whose membership was closed to women students until 1963, has received a fair amount of serious academic attention, while scholars often reduce dramatics at the Oxford women's colleges to frivolity.[4] Most attention paid to these productions comes from the individual histories of the Oxford women's colleges; however, these are often treated as fun visual interludes due to the charming photographs archived. Oxford and Cambridge both staged Greek Plays in alternating years, beginning at Oxford in 1880 (and still continuing today). At Cambridge, only men could act in the Greek play until 1950, with the notable exception of Girton College's Janet Case who played Athena in Aeschylus' *Eumenides*, which was performed in 1885 (Alley 1982: 3). In 1883, the students of Girton had staged their own production of *Electra* in Greek, which was well received by the audience and both Yopie Prins and Isobel Hurst argued for its significance (Hurst 2009: 92–5; Prins 2017: 116–51). As highlighted above, while scholarship has taken into account women in the theatre, and specifically women and Greek drama, the dramatic and comedic efforts of women's colleges have largely been ignored, even though they reveal some of the same feminist and political themes found in professional women's theatre, particularly the Actresses'

Franchise League (Dolgin 2015: 197–9). Therefore, women's college dramatics should be considered alongside feminist theatre histories, perhaps not as equals in production value or talent but as both a continuation of and inspiration for themes that were central to feminist ideologies. Peter Swallow's much-needed chapter 'Women's Aristophanes: Old Comedy and the Fight for Gender Equality' provides an excellent comparison between the original text of *The Birds* and the script of *The Bees* in the context of British Aristophanic performance during the long nineteenth century, acknowledging the overtly feminist elements of *The Bees*. This chapter aims to develop his work by examining *The Bees* and other Greek comedies at women's colleges within their specific feminist educational context rather than adopting a comparative approach to the texts themselves.

The 'New Woman' and Greek comedy in Cambridge

In 1899, the first Greek comedy was performed at Girton College in original Greek (although scenes and speeches were recited at the Classical Club) in the form of Aristophanes' *Birds*.[5] This was not their first ever Greek play: that was *Electra* in 1883 (a more high-profile affair) but it does appear to be the first example of a production of Aristophanes at an Oxbridge women's college.[6] Although Jenkyns concludes that Aristophanes was the least influential Greek writer in the nineteenth century, towards the end of the century his potential began to be realized, particularly at Oxbridge (quoted in Hall and Wrigley 2007: 67). The 1883 Cambridge Greek play was *The Birds* (to be performed again twenty years later, in 1903), which made the bold claim to be the first full Greek comedy to be performed since antiquity.[7] Almost a decade later, the first comedy to be performed as the Oxford Greek play was *The Frogs* in 1892, which prompted a reviewer to note that 'it suggested that Greek tragedy, unless the very greatest, is not so well adapted to the appreciation of the modern audience as the comedy of Aristophanes'.[8] Later, *The Bees* (in 1904) and *The Newmenides* (in 1907) were directly inspired by the Cambridge Greek play, which, in both cases, was staged just a few months earlier when they were 'fresh in the minds of the audience, and so better enabled them to appreciate the cleverness of the skit'.[9] According to the review of Girton's *The Birds* in 1899, the novelty of it garnered a great deal of interest from students as well as 'many visitors'.[10] The acting was supposedly well-executed and the costumes praised (particularly the wings of the chorus of birds), but unfortunately the collapse of the stage at the beginning of the performance that almost caused a fire appears to have been the focus of the review.[11] It was a fairly faithful rendition of the original text, using the music from the Cambridge Greek play production of *The Birds* in 1883, which was procured with great difficulty.[12] The president of the Girton Dramatic Society, E. B. L. Watson (later Swetenham) reminisced on the experience thirty years later, recounting the difficulties they encountered in casting the play. She recounts how none of the good actors took Greek as a subject and how none of the good Greek scholars acted.[13] Eventually, she succeeded in breaking 'the aloof dignity of the classical scholars' and persuading the 'stars to commit to memory the lines of Aristophanes', thereby resulting in the cast eventually catching 'the spirit' of the play.[14] While there was initial trepidation at the prospect of performing Greek comedy, 'the spirit' of Greek comedy had already begun to blossom at Girton.[15] According to Watson, the only reason the college agreed to stage a Greek comedy in its original form was due to the success of a classical burlesque of the Agamemnon myth that had been performed earlier that academic year by the dramatic society.[16] In particular, Classics lecturer (and later Girton's mistress) Katharine Jex-Blake 'heartily appreciated the parody' and supported Watson and the Dramatic Society to produce the *Birds*.[17] Because of the success of their burlesque, Swallow suggests that the production of *The Birds* maintained a 'burlesquing style' in opposition to the 'archaeologising style of the Cambridge Greek play'. Such parodies appear to have already become a tradition for at least one women's college in America, with Smith College staging their first documented parody of the Harvard Greek play, *Oedipus Tyrannos*, in 1883.[18]

Before *The Birds*, Girton students had begun experimenting with comedic interpretations of Greek drama for political means. Performed on 3 December 1898, *The Return of Agamemnon* was a tragicomic dramatization of F. Anstey's story by E. B. L. Watson, president of the Girton Dramatic Society, that 'successfully ruined any future appreciation of the original of Aeschylus'.[19] Watson purposely archived the text of the play and it was performed again approximately twenty years later.[20] Like the *Agamemnon*, the play opens with the Watchman's soliloquy, but the bulk of the action revolves around Agamemnon, Clytemnestra (his wife) and Cassandra (his new concubine) as he returns from the Trojan War to find his wife has taken a lover. Much of the plot was the same, albeit exaggerated for comic effect – for example, Clytemnestra boils her husband Agamemnon in his bath (rather than stabbing him). However, rather than dying and causing the series of events that would play out in the rest of Aescylus' *Oresteia* trilogy, Agamemnon not only survives but reconciles with his wife after 'mutual recriminations'.[21] The setting of the story incorporates elements from both the classical world and contemporary Britain as well as the world of contemporary Cambridge, in Girton's version, with Agamemnon and Cassandra returning from the Trojan war on 'dusty bicycles'.[22] Part of the comedy, it would appear, was the combination of these ancient and modern elements, which would subsequently become a tool for performing their inclusion not only in classical and University education but for unpacking their identity as women college students and intellectuals. Although the original story by F. Anstey included a combination of these elements (such as a guide to Corinth, a conversation manual, tourist tickets and a correct card for the Olympian races), the bicycles were a purely Girtonian inclusion.

The use of the bicycles in the play would have alluded to contemporary Cambridge, with which bicycles were synonymous, as Henry Balfour highlighted in a speech on the merits of cycling in 1899, stating that all of the most recent and future vice-chancellors are cyclists.[23] Considering that cycling was a perfectly acceptable activity for gentlemen, the king (although comical within the context of the play) may have been less out of place on his bicycle than his female companion, Cassandra. Eventually becoming a tool of feminism, women on bicycles were ridiculed in the 1890s and considered unladylike and threatening to the status quo, very much part of the 'New Woman' tradition (Wånggren 2017; Chen 2017). Similarly doomed with the gift of prophecy that nobody would listen to or believe, Cassandra shared the plight of the college woman in many ways – they possessed the knowledge to make an impact yet were not taken seriously nor recognized with degrees. Following the vote on women's degrees and the riots surrounding it in 1897, the parallels between Cassandra and the Victorian intellectual woman may have been particularly poignant. During these riots, male students and academics created an effigy of a stereotypical woman's college student in the style of the 'New Woman' in her 'rational dress', consisting of bloomers (see Figure 7.1).[24] They hung the effigy in the market square on the day of the debate along with protest banners that included the slogan 'No Gowns for Girtonites' before violently tearing it to pieces and shoving it through the gates of Newnham.[25] Although they would not debate the issue

Figure 7.1 Effigy of woman undergraduate, 21 May 1897 (UA Phot.174/4), Cambridge University Library.

again until 1921, women were unsuccessful in gaining full membership of the University until 1948.

The Bees and agitation for degrees

The Girtonian comedy that takes up the feminist cause for education most explicitly is the 1904 play *The Bees*, which is a rather loose adaptation of Aristophanes' *The Birds* and will be the main focus of my analysis.[26] Staged by second-year students, it criticizes the fact that whilst they were admitted to Oxbridge, women could not obtain degrees, thereby leading the protagonists to establish their own college.[27] The play not only rejects common opinions against women's education but also pokes fun at fears about the learning of Greek and Latin as radicalizing women and making them unfit for marriage (Evangelista 2009: 10). There are very few sources relating to the staging of this production, but the survival of the text implies that it is in itself a valuable source that sheds light on life at a women's college and women's education activism at the turn of the century. It was performed at Girton for the Girton community. The text itself was printed by Metcalfe & Co., Cambridge, 'for private circulation only', thereby suggesting that it may have been circulated to a limited external audience, particularly within a women's education context.[28] It was unusual for second-year plays to be formally printed, so it was either sufficiently popular to be deemed publishable or its value as a comedic commentary on Oxbridge women's education was recognized. In addition to the printed and handmade copies at Girton College, there are printed copies in the British and Bodleian libraries, with the latter copy including a personal dedication.

Without the need for hidden meanings, the purpose of *The Bees* is patently clear: two heroines, Peitheteira and Euelpide, leave Cambridge where they are not allowed to properly graduate to establish the feminist Beebuzzburough College and refuse to return until they are granted degrees.[29] This creative adaptation of *The Birds* did not primarily seek to justify women's higher education, which was clearly on the rise despite continuing concerns; instead, it actively sought to improve the conditions for women in higher education, specifically in Oxbridge. The fact that Beebuzzburough is the play's version of Cloud Cuckoo Land from Aristophanes' original perhaps says something about the unlikelihood of women receiving degrees at Cambridge, although the forty-four additional years that it did take would undoubtedly have appalled the feminist students responsible for the play. The play begins with the two protagonists who are 'rebels against the tyranny of men' leaving Girton to find a place where 'in unlettered and untutored ease, with dons to wait on them, they may settle down and get degrees'.[30] The usage of 'settle down' here appears to be a conscious play on the term 'settle down' to imply marriage and family, thereby tying into anxieties around women's education ruining their marriage prospects. Many were keen to prove that both were possible, particularly when the public eye was on them, as with Somerville's performance of *Demeter* in 1904. However, it would appear that within their own private college setting, the women of

Girton were not shy in suggesting they might prefer to 'settle down' with degrees rather than with a husband, even if it was for comic effect.

On their mission, they come across a number of characters who are a mixture of modern characters, such as the Chancellor and the Examiner, and stereotypes of various university characters thinly veiled as ancient Greek ones, such as the interfering soothsayer/chaperone who offers 'to her mind indispensable' services to the new institution. The Queen Bee and her chorus of bees (the highlight of the production according to the *The Girton Review*) are the benefactors; when their work is done, the ceremony of inauguration is performed by the priest/senior student with the sacrifice of a college 'tray'.[31] The 'tray' is a reference to a college ritual of drinking hot beverages (particularly cocoa) in your room with your friends at night (Pederson 2002: 162). Instead of jackdaw and crow, Peithetaira and Euelpide hold an owl and a butterfly (the symbol of Athena, associated with women's education and the 'New Woman'). Punctuated with music and dancing that featured hockey sticks, the play concludes with a trembling undergraduate who fears his Gods/proctors detailing how their 'long and chatty papers' are missed. When the university begs for their return, they stubbornly concede, with a promise that they will get their much-coveted degrees.

The choice of *The Bees* to parody *The Birds* was by no means coincidental, as bees had already been established as both a positive symbol for feminism as well as a negative metaphor for feminist aggression. Jane Wright contends that 'by the nineteenth century, the bee had literary and cultural associations with, among other things, classical learning, eloquence, poetry, ideal creativity, chastity, industry, and (increasingly) all-female communities and female leadership', almost all of which could be associated with women's colleges (Wright 2015: 273). Tennyson had elaborated on this idea in his 1847 poem *The Princess*, which heavily relies on bee symbolism as well as the classical tradition, to tell the story of a princess who founded a women's 'university-hive' surrounded by her 'bee-maidens' (Wright 2015: 256, 273). Although now considered by some as anti-feminist due to the 'extent to which violence and anxiety pervade *The Princess*' as well as the ending – which sees the princess choosing love (and presumably marriage) over her university – it was largely received as a positive step towards the tolerance of women's rights at the time of publication (Hall 1991: 49). It subsequently became a popular story for performance, including Gilbert and Sullivan's comic opera *Princess Ida*, as well as being performed at numerous Victorian girls' schools and women's colleges (Norcia 2013: 1–20). A production of *The Princess* takes place in a fictionalized Oxbridge women's college in L.T. Meade's *The Sweet Girl Graduate*, which depicts Greek and Latin as central to the identities and friendships of the two protagonists (Bogen 2014: 51).

Although *The Princess* can be seen as anti-feminist and has been interpreted as warning of the dangers of women's education and, in this case, the violence that might ensue, this story was cleverly used in performance by women for their own purposes, particularly at the end of the nineteenth century (Norcia 2013). Teacher Elsie Fogerty (who went on to found the Central School of Speech and Drama in 1906) directed her own adaptation of *The Princess* in girls' schools around the country in the 1890s before publishing the text, stage directions and other notes (Fogerty 1907). Her version, which only subtracted and never added to the text, cleverly relied on stage direction and performance notes to highlight the power of the patriarchy and the subjugation of women (Norcia 2013: 5). Unlike the original and other adaptations (including Gilbert and Sullivan's), Fogerty styled her *Princess* on Greek tragedy (with costumes to match); rather than making fun of women's failed attempts at creating a university, she promotes women's education through resigning her tragic heroine to her patriarchal fate (Norcia 2013: 8). Norcia notes that 'Fogerty's attention to the visual spectacle of the performance reflects the conscious role-playing of women at institutions like Cheltenham College and Girton' (Norcia 2013: 15). It is this 'conscious role-playing' that performances like *The Bees* were free to explore within the safety of their own women's learning environment, where they did not have to be concerned with playing at least one of their roles, thereby maintaining decorum so as not to corroborate negative stereotypes regarding educated women. Not only were they performing their own identities as women's college students within a women's college space, but they were also performing the type of role-playing they had to undertake in order to navigate their uneasy position not just as educated women but also as women within the traditionally male spaces of Oxbridge. Plays by and for women (and girls) performed in women's learning environments can be considered a platform which they could use to explore feminist ideas and identity without disturbing the status quo outside their community.

Rather than the protagonist abandoning her aspirations for education, particularly her education in a women's learning environment, as does the princess of Tennyson's poem, *The Bees* sees the women conceding their women's university in the sky but committing more strongly to Girton now that they can receive degrees there. With its performance date in 1904, both the height of performances of *Princess* in the 1890s and the publication of Fogerty's adaptation would have certainly had an influence on *The Bees*. Many of the women at Girton would have been at the types of schools that Norcia identifies as those that performed Fogerty's adaptation in the late 1890s and early 1900s. Some would have recognized the tragic nature of the heroine's ultimate subservience, as Fogerty had intended; however, *The Bees* provides the polar opposite – comic rather than tragic, and an ultimately positive outcome that solidified their identities as Girton students who were equal to but separate from their male counterparts. *The Bees* subverts both the all-male comedy of ancient Greece and the opinions of many men (and in this case a male writer), ridiculing them both and giving women a voice. Jenkyns' contention that there existed a Victorian idea of ancient Greece as an Oxford college applies again here: if we consider the chorus' function in Aristophanes as the mouthpiece of popular opinions in Athens, in *The Bees* we can consider the chorus as voicing the popular opinions of Cambridge. In the same manner that women were subverting the status quo of the university by imposing their own spaces on Oxbridge, they were subverting the equally male-dominated realms of theatre and literature, but in their own private spaces. Therefore, is it truly subversive if they were performing opinions and identities that the audience largely shared in a space that protected the outside from itself as much as it protected itself from the outside?

Isobel Hurst notes that the 'prestige' of Classics at Oxbridge and other institutions was declining at the same time as Greek became more accessible to women, thereby allowing the subject to be 'safely left to women' (Hurst 2006: 95). The combination of the safety of the women's college environment and the relatively new idea that classics could be 'safely left to women' allowed college women to push the boundaries of what was considered acceptable. With the authorities at Girton not necessarily approving of, but allowing, theatrics, parodying Greek comedy (and subsequently tragedy with *The Newmenides*) allowed college women to use Classics for their own purposes in ways that were previously inaccessible to them (Pedersen 2002: 163–5; Sutherland 2015: 62), thereby taking ownership of the subject, the college space (by way of turning it into a performance space) and of their own convictions regarding women's education. In particular, with the second-year play being very much under the control of students, they had the freedom to explore 'subversive' themes and make fun of the university (and even their own college) and society as a whole to highlight how unfair their situation was. Therefore, it would appear that these types of plays were a stepping stone between Fogerty's subtly feminist staging of *The Princess* at girls' schools (and undoubtedly other productions which could fall into this category) and the publicly performed suffrage comedies with their Aristophanic background. This not only makes sense chronologically – considering that Fogerty took her interpretation to girls' schools during the 1890s, *The Bees* and *The Newmenides* were staged during the 1900s, and suffrage comedy appeared during the 1910s – but it also suggests that there was a knock-on effect from girls' schools to women's colleges and from women's colleges to the suffrage movement. Even if the same people were not directly involved in all three types of production, the influence of these ideas and trends within their social and educational circles would have been almost unavoidable.

In 1892, the anti-feminist journalist Eliza Lynn Linton stated, 'the whole cohort of Wild Women is like an angry beehive which a rough hand has disturbed', playing into the bee symbolism but using it against the type of feminist Victorian spinster or 'odd woman' who 'preaches the lesson of liberty' that Yopie Prins finds a new metaphor for in the Greek Maenad (Linton 1892: 463; Prins 2017: 48). The bee metaphor is found in other suffrage entertainments, such as suffragist composer Ethel Smyth's 'The Boatswain's Mate' which situates the feisty feminist female protagonist, Mrs Waters (based on Emmeline Pankhurst) as queen bee (or landlady) of 'The Beehive' pub (Wood 1995: 628).[32] Composed in 1913–14, this opera of 'high lesbian camp' ridicules men and asserts women's rights, particularly the 'right to desires' and includes two suffrage songs in the overture – '1910' and 'The March of the Women'; it was the official anthem of the Women's Social and Political Union, with words by Cicely Hamilton.[33] Further, feminist publications, such as Colorado's *Queen Bee*, also adopted bee symbolism.

In *The Bees*, the position of the bees themselves is initially hostile towards Peitheteira and Euelpide, but on the orders of the Queen Bee they begin to support their cause, singing, 'Hurrah, hurrah, sing high/To the gods Girtonian cry!'[34] While the chorus of bees may not be a positive symbol for feminists, as they are aggressive and willing to hurt or kill the protagonists, the Queen of the Bees is portrayed as a kind of feminist icon. In fact, we see the two sides of perceptions of women through bee symbolism – the angry 'Wild Women'

'Rebels Against the Tyranny of Men'

and the strong female leader. Staged six years after the riots that erupted surrounding the debate on women's degrees in Cambridge, the chorus of bees reflects some of the violent attitudes displayed towards women at that time. Male students had maimed and decapitated an effigy of a female student before dumping the remains at Newnham College, a decision and an act which devastated and terrified both the staff and students.[35] While it is unclear whether the chorus depicts female 'worker' bees or male 'drone' bees, they are clearly used as a mouthpiece to reflect attitudes towards women in higher education, just as they were used in Aristophanes to voice common opinions of the general public, which are commonly changed by the characters of the play. Swallow deems the play to not be particularly funny, with its success lying primarily in its effectiveness as a performance of activism (Swallow 2023: 213). However, with all its extremely topical and specific illusions, it would have been more accessible as a comic text within the context of Girton College, particularly as it was intended to make light of a situation they could not control. Furthermore, the success of its activism would largely depend on the success of its humour.

In the case of *The Birds*, a hoopoe bird convinces the chorus to give the protagonists (Peithetairos and Euelpides) a fair hearing on their desire to leave Athens, where they do nothing but argue over laws all day, and find somewhere better.[36] Eventually, due to the number of people flocking to the new city in the sky, a delegation of the gods arrives, consisting of Poseidon, Heracles and a Triballian god (worshipped by barbarians), who are outwitted by Pisthetairos and concede Zeus' sceptre and, most importantly, Basileia or 'Sovereignty' (his consort). *The Bees* follows this plot quite closely, with the Queen of the Bees taking the place of the hoopoe and the delegation of gods consisting of the Chancellor of Cambridge University (as Poseidon), the Examiner (as Heracles) and the Triballian god representing the University of London (the first university in the UK to allow women to read for a degree, in 1878). At the end, Heracles offers to roast the birds for the feast and Pisthetairos bids someone to fetch him a magnificent tunic for the wedding (symbolizing the transfer of ownership of Zeus' estate and his consort) and a large celebration begins. Peithetairos chooses to stay in Cloudcuckooland, but in the final act of *The Bees*, they celebrate their victory in Peithetaira's study and decide to return to Girton, where they finally have everything they wanted.[37] The Examiner offers to boil the milk, which is yet another reference to the ritual of evening cocoa parties or 'tray' at the college and Euelpide bids someone to buy her a cap and gown.[38] By including this tradition, the women of Girton assert their identity as a women's college community even though they will officially become members of the University like their male counterparts. Peithetaira herself exclaims:

Dear Girton! Every day and every hour
My thoughts have turned to thee. And now
we've gained
The *one* thing lacking, no need to linger.[39]

The play then ends with all the performers coming back to join the chorus of bees for a final celebratory song. Paralleling the chorus of birds' singing a wedding march, the chorus of bees sings a paean of victory for Peithetaira and all Girtonians:[40]

Make a way, make a way
Now at last they are nigh,
Merrily round them, merrily round them fly.
See how enchanting the hard won B.A.
Granted to her at last to-day,
Coming like Majesty down
As a crown to the town,
As a glorious prize.[41]

Unfortunately for the women of Cambridge, it would be another forty-four years before they would receive their 'hard won BA'.

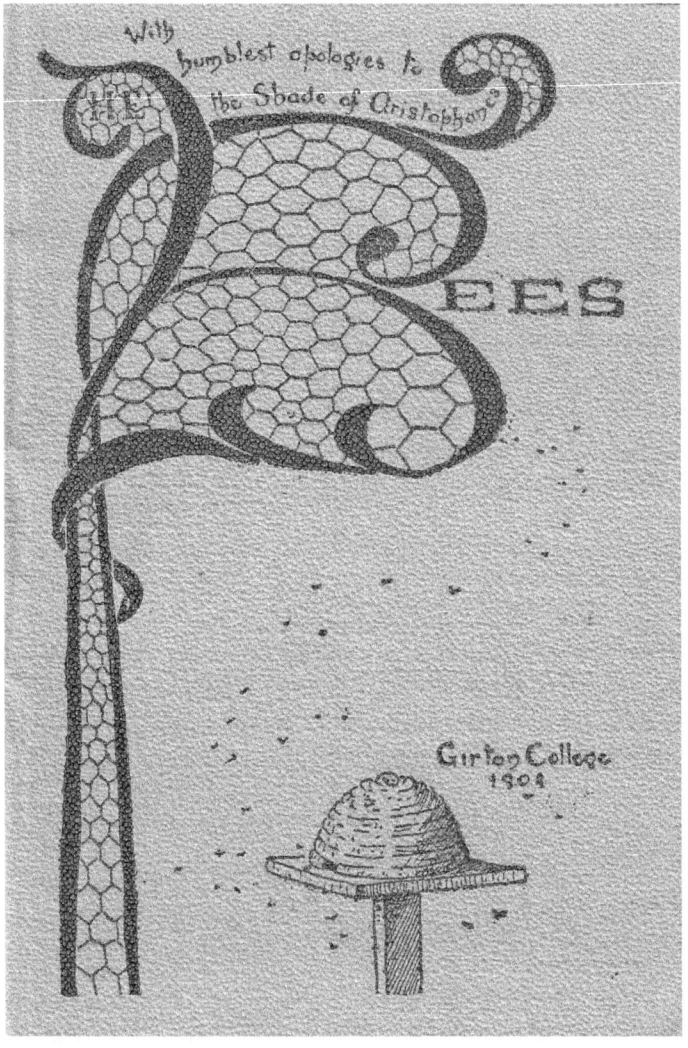

Figure 7.2 Printed version of the play text. GCRF 1/3/5, Girton College Archives.

Dramatis Personae

1. Peithetairo — G. Clayton
2. Euelpide — G. Morlan-Jones
3. Queen of the Bees — W. Skinner
4. Dragon Fly — B. Smythe
5. A Priest — D. E. Brown
6. A Poet — S. Myers
7. A Soothsayer — E. Buckley
8. Heniochos — W. Newman
9. Prometheus — E. Denny
10. Chancellor of Cambridge University — E. Oliphant
11. Examiner — W. Chittick
12. Tribollian God (London University) — J. Paine
13. Iris, Messenger of the Gods — G. Sykes
14. A Slave — D. Zimmern
15. Chorus of Bees. W. J. Wood – Leader
    J. Butler. K. Davies. M. Gough. D. Hewson.
    E. Lewis. H. Scott. R. Sills. T. Williams.
    Queen Bee's Song sung by E. Sandford

Figure 7.3 The original handwritten cast list. GCRF 1/3/5, Girton College Archives.

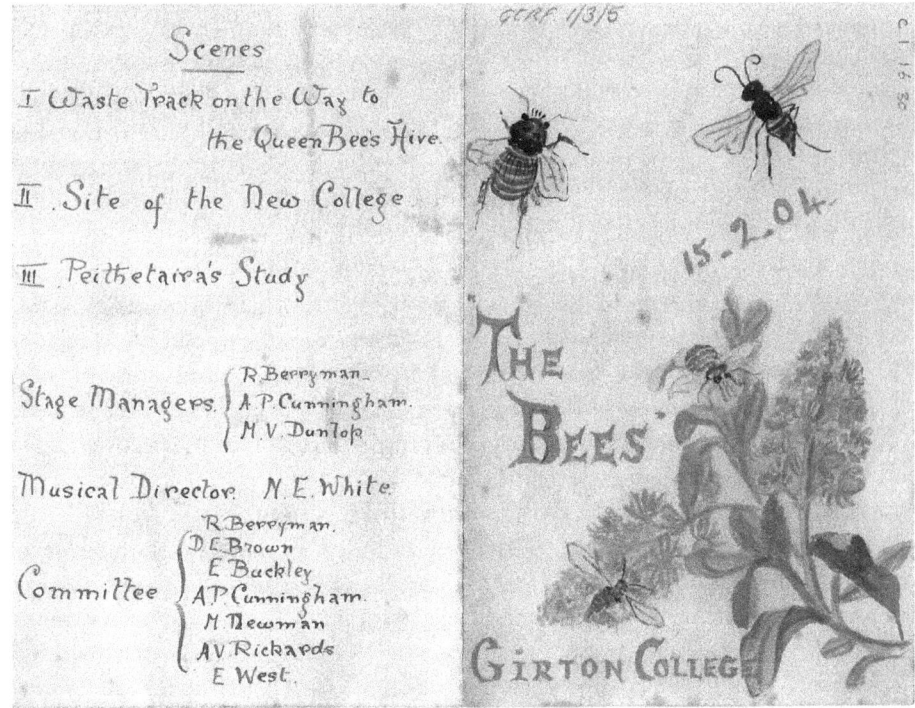

Figure 7.4 Hand-illustrated programme for *The Bees*. GCRF 1/3/5, Girton College Archives.

119

Women Creating Classics

Performance activism at early-twentieth-century Oxbridge women's colleges

In 1907 both Girton and Somerville (an Oxford women's college) performed topical comedies about gender roles. Girton second-years performed their parody, The *Newmenides*, about the recent updates to the study of Mathematics made at Cambridge, making fun of academically lazy but athletically focused male maths students.[42] Final-year students at Somerville performed 'What We Have Come to: or the Higher Education of Women,' a self-proclaimed mash-up of Greek tragedy and pantomine detailing the journey of Princess Suffragina who defies her parents and goes to Somerville, which is located in the underworld and managed by Athena.[43] Both lament women's lack of degrees at their institutions. Aristophanes' *The Frogs* was performed at University House, the women's hall of residence at Birmingham, in 1908, and at Somerville College in 1911, both using Gilbert Murray's translation and taking advantage of the play's topical allusions by putting in some of their own. In University House's programme, they noted that they have substituted modern events and persons for Aristophanes' topical allusions, believing it to be true to the spirit of Aristophanes.[44] By 1911, dramatic entertainments at Somerville College had become a regular feature in the social and academic calendar: for example, it was tradition for the second-year women to put on a comic play at the end of the Michaelmas term. The decision to stage Aristophanes' *The Frogs* in Michaelmas 1911 is likely to have been influenced by the Oxford Greek play just a couple of years earlier; however, that Somervillians did independently look to ancient Greece for dramatic material can, for example, be seen in the performance in 1910 of 'an Athenian trial' by classical students under the direction of their tutor Emily Penrose, the Principal of Somerville (Adams 1996: 133). In 1911, 'numerous topical allusions' were introduced into Murray's translation of *The Frogs*: for example, 'mention was made of the Registration Fee, which had penetrated to Hades under the guidance of Miss Rogers'.[45] These topical allusions must have been introduced in collaboration with Gilbert Murray, the translator, who is said to have 'allowed himself to be smuggled secretly into college to direct and stage-manage the second-year play . . . which had, traditionally, to be kept as a surprise for the rest of the college. As an official guest on the night of the actual performance, he rose from his seat beside the Principal to express his thanks with the words "It was so good that we all felt we really *were* in Hell," one of the play's settings' (Adams 1996: 118–19). The women of Oxford were able to receive degrees by 1920, marking a decline in the performance of Greek comedy at the women's colleges, highlighting its effectiveness as a medium for performing women's politics within the University.

On 20 October 1921 (Michaelmas Term), a funeral procession engulfed King's Parade, mourning an effigy of the Last Male Undergraduate, to protest about the vote for women's degrees occurring in the Cambridge Senate House that day.[46] Although the vote had been won in Oxford the previous year, Cambridge voted against degrees for women yet again and this caused yet another, more terrifying riot. Not content with merely harassing women on bicycles, the crowd headed to Newnham (as Girton was too far out of town), where they attempted a violent break-in and caused a huge amount of damage. In the following term (Lent Term 1922), the Girton Classical Club produced Aristophanes' *Frogs*, which 'came as a pleasing surprise' to the students whose 'knowledge of Greek drama was confined to "Kelly's Keys" [to the classics]', according to the *Girton Review*.[47] Performed in English, the play remained faithful to the original cast of characters, but inserted their own verses for a 'touch of topical humour' to reflect the situation regarding women's degrees as well as women's college life more generally.[48] With lines such as, 'Why, then this most particularly high-browed maid deserves a real degree!', it appears that the play was largely focused on the central issue of the Girton community at the time: their defeat in the vote for granting women's degrees. Unfortunately, it is unclear how much of the play they altered (as the entire script does not survive), but the chorus' songs, at least, were Girtonian parodies of the topical references that Aristophanes' choruses are known for. Classical tutor Janet Ruth Bacon co-wrote the contemporary verses and acted the part of Aeschylus alongside the students, thereby highlighting a sense of camaraderie and shared sense of humour between the academic staff and students.[49] The chorus' first song suggests that all the political references have been changed to Girtonian ones, as they state, 'But in our play we don't intend to mix Greek politics . . . We only mean to give you our opinions of certain types of you – not the Athenians.' The effect of this was twofold: using an Aristophanic framework allowed them to explore their own social and political issues within a legitimate and established format and brought Greek drama alive for those disconnected from it, those who 'had never realised before how humorous and intensely human a Greek play could be'.[50] Women at Cambridge did not achieve degrees until 1948 and the use of Greek comedy as a performance genre and as a method of private communication continued much later than at Oxford.[51]

*

This chapter highlights the significance of women's use of Greek comedy and reclaiming Classics for feminist purposes, particularly for the advancement of women's education. Plays performed by and for women in women's colleges served as a platform for exploring identity, women's rights and community. Girton College's production of *The Bees* demonstrated how women adapted Aristophanic frameworks to criticize the limitations imposed on women's education and to address social and political issues. These performances allowed college women to reclaim Classics for their own purposes and take ownership of their identities. By subverting the male-dominated realms of the Classics and higher education within their own private spaces, women shaped suffrage plays and brought Greek comedy to life for those disconnected from it. Overall, these comedic efforts contributed to the empowerment of women in college during the fight for the awarding of college degrees to women and full membership of the University.

Notes

1. Suffragists were, however, one of the earliest subjects of mockery in narrative cinema, with suffrage parodies dating back to as early as 1898, just three years after the first narrative film (Sloan 1981: 412).

2. The most important contribution on the topic of feminism and tragedy is Yopie Prins' *Ladies Greek: Victorian Translations of Tragedy* (2017), which provides an unparalleled overview of how women translated, engaged with, and performed Greek tragedy, but Edith Hall (Hall and Macintosh 2005), Isobel Hurst (2006) and Ann Heilmann (2005) have also produced extremely valuable scholarship. The main contributions on feminism and Greek comedy during this period consist of Murphy and Porcheddu (2017) and Swallow (2023).
3. https://www.girton.cam.ac.uk/news/girton-college-and-the-campaign-for-womens-suffrage/, accessed 28/02/20.
4. On occasion, the Oxford Greek Play brought in women who were not students to take on the female roles – these included semi-professional actresses, wives of Oxford academics, and even female academics like Jane Harrison, who in 1887 played Alcestis in the Euripides play by the same name, to mixed reviews (Wrigley 2011: 215); http://www.apgrd.ox.ac.uk/digital-resources/blog/2018-03-14; last accessed 05/02/24.
5. Cambridge, Girton College Archives, *Girton Review* (July 1899, 5–6).
6. The small write-up of the production in the 'Girton College' section of the Notting Hill High School Magazine specifically mentions that the play was performed in costume, thereby indicating that perhaps they had held informal readings of Aristophanes at the college prior to this.
7. https://www.cambridgegreekplay.com/plays/1883/birds, accessed 01/03/20
8. 'OUDS. The Frogs', *Oxford Magazine* (2 March 1892: 206–7).
9. *The Bees* parodied Aristophanes' *The Birds* performed in 1903 and *Newmenides* pariodied Aeschylus' *Eumenides* performed in 1906. *The Girton Review* Lent Term, 1904.
10. *Girton Review* (July 1899: 5–6).
11. *Girton Review* (July 1899: 6).
12. *Girton Review* (July 1899: 5–6).
13. 'Greek Drama at Girton 1898–1921', in *Girton Review* (Michaelmas Term 1928: 8–9).
14. 'Greek Drama at Girton 1898–1921', in *Girton Review* (Michaelmas Term 1928: 9).
15. 'Greek Drama at Girton 1898–1921', in *Girton Review* (Michaelmas Term 1928: 8–11).
16. 'Greek Drama at Girton 1898–1921', in *Girton Review* (Michaelmas Term 1928: 8–11).
17. 'Greek Drama at Girton 1898–1921', in *Girton Review* (Michaelmas Term 1928: 8).
18. Elizabeth C. Lawrence, 80. Cla, folder 48, Smith College Special Collections.
19. *Girton Review* (April 1899: 13).
20. Watson says the performance happened 'about ten years ago' in her 1928 reminiscence, Girton College Archives.
21. *Girton Review* (April 1899: 13).
22. *Girton Review* (April 1899: 13).
23. Henry Balfour's speech to the National Cyclists' Union (1899).
24. According to the Rational Dress Society, the concept of rational dress consisted of (1) freedom of movement; (2) absence of pressure over any part of the body; (3) not more weight than is necessary for warmth, and both weight and warmth evenly distributed; (4) grace and beauty combined with comfort and convenience; (5) not departing too conspicuously from the ordinary dress of the time (Levitt).
25. https://cudl.lib.cam.ac.uk/view/PH-UA-PHOT-00174-00004/1
26. Or at least the most feminist script that has been archived in its entirety.

27. Women were not able to receive degrees in Oxford until 1920 and in Cambridge until 1948.
28. Although I cannot be sure, the name inscribed in the Bodleian library's copy (along with 'May Term 1904') suggests that this was a personal copy of a women's college student.
29. *The Bees: With humblest apologies to the shade of Aristophanes*, Girton College Archives, C.1.16 30 (a)
30. *The Bees*, 6.
31. *Girton Review* (Lent Term 1904: 4).
32. Smyth's overtly feminist 'March of the Women' with lyrics by Cicely Hamilton (1910) is now performed at Girton's College Feast commemorating the anniversary of women's degrees at Cambridge.
33. Elizabeth Wood characterizes this opera as overtly lesbian, based on the (occasionally coded) content and its dissection of gender as well as Smyth's own life (Wood 1995: 628–9). Mary Benson, who Elizabeth believes is referenced in the opera by her nickname 'Ben', was Smyth's mentor (and possible lover or at least 'intimate friends', as Martha Vicinus categorizes it in her book of the same name), called her numerous female partnerships 'swarmings', which is perhaps also a reference to bees (Vicinus 2004: 131).
34. *The Bees*, 14.
35. https://www.cam.ac.uk/TheRisingTide; last accessed 04/01/24.
36. Aristophanes, *The Birds*.
37. *The Bees*, 21–3.
38. *The Bees*, 22–3.
39. *The Bees*, 23.
40. 'College Notes' (Lent Term 1904), *Girton Review*: 3. For more on the original song, see Straus (2018: 135).
41. *The Bees*, 23.
42. Girton College Archives, *Newmenides*, 1907.
43. Oxford, Somerville College Archives, Going Down Plays, 'What We Have Come to: or the Higher Education of Women, 1907.
44. Birmingham, University of Birmingham Special Collections, UB/HUH/A/10/1/5, Programme for *The Frogs*, 1908.
45. Hilda Walton, 'Oxford Letter', Somerville Students' Association: 25th Annual Report and Oxford Letter', October 1912, 28.
46. Sarah Watling, 'The Gender Riots that Rocked Cambridge in the 1920s', https://blog.oup.com/2019/07/gender-riots-rocked-cambridge-university-1920s/, retrieved 01/06/20.
47. *Girton Review* (April 1922: 8).
48. *Girton Review* (April 1922: 8).
49. *Girton Review* (April 1922: 7).
50. *Girton Review* (April 1922: 8).
51. An ideal example of this can be found in Classics tutor Norah Jolliffe's papers at Girton. Jolliffe, who had been in 1922's *The Frogs* as a student and then returned as tutor, wrote her own parodies of Greek drama and also used hellenic humour in her private communications well into the 1940s (Girton College Archive, GB 271 GCPP JOLLIFFE, The Personal Papers of Norah Christina Jolliffe).

CHAPTER 8
'SAVED WITH ABLATIVES AND DECLENSIONS IN THE TOILET STALL': CLASSICAL LEARNING AND THE POETRY OF MAXINE KUMIN (1925–2014)

Judith P. Hallett

In memory of David Konstan (1940–2024)

Appreciations and assessments of the American, Jewish, feminist, pastoral-agrarian and Pulitzer-Prize winning writer Maxine Winokur Kumin, who died in 2014 at the age of eighty-eight, rarely acknowledge the references to classical antiquity permeating her work.[1] Nor do they explore the significance imparted by Kumin to her own engagement, as an American Jewish feminist country dweller, with classical learning.[2] Instead, critics quite rightly focus on the literary products of her unusual 'residential trajectory' from abundantly peopled, privileged urban and suburban surroundings during the first half of her life to a rural, isolated 'derelict one-time dairy farm' during the second.[3] Such a focus helps to illuminate her evolving artistic vision – which she herself describes as 'metamorphosis from composing light verse to creating the poetry of witness' – a vision that vividly reflects these changes in her day-to-day environment.[4] Some details about Kumin's 'residential trajectory' warrant immediate attention, since they also help illuminate how and why her writings engage with the classical world and its serious study. They, and the group of her poems that I have chosen to highlight, also point up why Kumin's own engagement with the classical world deserves further and closer scrutiny.[5]

As she relates in her posthumously published memoir, *The Pawnbroker's Daughter*, Kumin was born in 1925, a few months after her parents, pawnbroker Edward Elias aka 'Pete' Winokur, a descendant of Russian Jews, and classically trained pianist Belle aka 'Doll' Simon Winokur, of 'proud German Jewish origins', had moved with her three older brothers into a 'spacious Georgian colonial house,' adjoining the convent of the Sisters of St Joseph in an affluent quarter of northwest Philadelphia's Germantown. Although the family strongly identified as Jews, her mother entrusted her earliest education to the Roman Catholic nuns next door. But from the age of twelve onward, again at her socially ambitious mother's behest, Kumin commuted as a tuition-paying student to the Cheltenham Township public schools in nearby Elkins Park, a more affluent Philadelphia suburb. There, she remembered, 'dutifully I plodded through algebra and plane geometry, but in Latin and English classes my soul leapt up'. We will return to those Latin classes later. In September 1942, ten months after the start of the Second World War, she entered

Radcliffe, the women's undergraduate college of Harvard University in Cambridge, Massachusetts. On 5 June 1946 she graduated *cum laude* (with a thesis on the novels of Stendhal and Dostoevsky); on 6 June, her twenty-first birthday, her fiancé Victor Kumin, a Boston Latin School and Harvard graduate, was discharged from the military; on 29 June they were married in Philadelphia.[6]

For the better part of the next three decades the couple occupied a 'snug little Cape Cod colonial' in the affluent Boston suburb of Newton. There, after receiving an MA in Comparative Literature from Radcliffe in 1948, directed by her undergraduate professor Harry Levin, the first Jew tenured in the Harvard English Department, Kumin brought up three offspring and put down roots as a writer. In 1957 she 'stumbled upon' a poetry workshop at the Boston Center for Adult Education conducted by John Holmes, a Tufts University professor. Her classmates included another young Newton mother three years her junior, Anne Harvey Sexton, who lacked Kumin's academic credentials but displayed similar literary promise. The two women forged a 'deep personal and professional relationship' lasting for seventeen years until Sexton, whose confessional, deeply personal poetry had earned her a Pulitzer Prize in 1967, took her own life.[7]

Thanks to Holmes, whom she called her 'Christian academic daddy', Kumin obtained both an adjunct post teaching composition – as the first woman hired – in the Tufts University English Department, and membership in the New England Poetry Club. In 1961, the same year that she published her first book of poems, *Halfway*, both she and Sexton were selected to join the first cohort of women to receive grants from the Radcliffe Institute for Independent Study. Kumin viewed this form of recognition as a 'validation' that 'freed [her] to see [herself] as a writer', not only in poetry but also in other genres. Indeed, her literary oeuvre encompasses twenty-five children's books, five novels, two memoirs, a collection of short stories and four essay collections.[8]

At the time Kumin wrote her memoir, only a handful of the children's books and her essay collections remained in print. Her stellar literary reputation rests exclusively on her poetry, in particular her fourth poetry book *Up Country: Poems of New England*, winner of the 1973 Pulitzer Prize. Three years later, she and Victor sold their Newton colonial and moved full time to remote Warner, New Hampshire. A decade previously, they had invested inheritances from her grandmother and his mother in a property at the end of a dirt road, its house overgrown with brambles and trees, its barn on the brink of disintegrating. To herald that she had been 'launched in the poetry business,' they named, 'half in jest', their new digs 'PoBiz Farm', 'for whatever ventures poets undertake to make money', and set about restoring the premises and raising horses.[9]

Once permanently ensconced at PoBiz Farm, Kumin published a new book of poetry every three or four years along with performing a host of outdoor toils – reclaiming cow pastures from the second growth forest, digging potholes, putting up wooden fences, repairing ancient clapboards – labours that she calls 'the sprucing up'.[10] This roster of backbreaking tasks required for farm upkeep instantly summons to my mind the elder Cato's litany of 'upkeep responsibilities' he demands that his slave *vilicus* ('steward') oversee in chapters 5 and 142 of his *De Agri Cultura* ('On Farming').[11] Cato, however, has yet to rate mention by those investigating the classical antecedents of Kumin's agrarian writing. Rather, critics prefer to situate it in the traditions of two other ancient Roman writers, Horace and Vergil: by comparing her georgic and pastoral poems to those of Robert Frost for their keen attention to the rhythms of nature in rural New England. As Helen Bacon has documented, Frost evokes both of these Latin poets, as well as their Augustan contemporary Tibullus.[12]

While refusing to disavow the humorous 'epithet' 'Roberta Frost' that she thereby acquired, Kumin felt that this name marginalized her work, protesting that she started confronting ethical issues in her own poetry as early as 1971, with 'Heaven as Anus'. Attacked as pornographic, it 'seized on the US government's use of animals for experimentation', unforgettably concluding: 'It all ends at the hole. No words may enter / the house of excrement. We will meet there / as the sphincter of the good Lord opens wide / and He takes us all inside.'[13] Righting ethical wrongs affecting women and minorities topped her agenda when she worked for the US government itself from 1981 through 1982, as Poetry Consultant to the Library of Congress (a position renamed Poet Laureate four years later). In that capacity she was able to select several women poets to read in a monthly series, most notably Adrienne Rich. Kumin also persisted in championing diversity and inclusivity when appointed a chancellor of the Academy of American Poets, in the late nineties. After twice 'lobb[ying] for the appointment of the Black poet Lucille Clifton to fill a vacant post' and 'watching the vacancies go to white males', she and fellow chancellor Carolyn Kizer resigned in protest, which ultimately led to restructuring of the board, and representation of women and minorities.[14]

Kumin imbues her natural surroundings with classical touches: naming her outermost pasture at PoBiz Farm the 'Elysian Field'; calling a beloved hound dog, rescued from a kill shelter, Virgil; entitling a poem which likens her struggles with writing verse to an encounter with a horse '*Ars Poetica*: A Found Poem'.[15] A poem she published in 2007, 'Still We Take Joy', decries the ruinous impact of the US military involvement in Iraq by invoking Virgil's *Georgics* and Greek mythology, observing:

> It's civil war as it was in Virgil's time,
> brother Roman against brother Roman,
> warrior farmers far from their barren fields,
> I am reading *that pastoral of hard work* . . .
> On January 12th, an ice-locked day,
> I dig three carrots, just as the poet instructs us
> to take joy in the very life of things
> so that, when Zeus comes down in spring
> *to the joyful bridal body of the earth*
> and the animals all agree it is time,
> I can believe the wheel will turn
> once more, taking me with it or not.[16]

Kumin evoked classical antiquity and partook of classical learning in confronting other ethical issues a full decade before she published 'Heaven as Anus': in her very first volume of poetry, *Halfway*, with 'To Anne at Passover', described by her as 'the first poem in which [she] addressed the issue of living as a Jew in the Christian world.' Its words explicitly draw on her teaching of Plato as part of the Tufts core curriculum, by noting that she and her students now

> mind the syllabus which juxtaposes
> Socrates, inviting the poison cup,
> saying *there is no fear that it will stop*
> *with me*, and Jesus, apportioning His week,
> however accidentally, with our Greek.

She terms the chronology of the poem 'simple', based on her Tufts classroom experience: 'During the final class before Easter recess, students discuss their reading assignment, the scene in which Socrates calmly drinks the cup of poison hemlock. It is an execution that invites sharp contrast with the crucifixion of Jesus; the Greek philosopher is "bathed and bedded according to the fashion, / friends who see you out your only Passion" (see commentary below).'

The Anne of this poem is Anne Sexton. 'To Anne at that time,' Kumin disclosed, 'Judaism was a curiosity, faintly tinged with disrepute . . . What Sexton knew about Jews was stereotypical anti-Semitic doctrine . . . Jews were a token and somehow alien presence in the schools she attended. It was remarkable that we were able to break through all the barriers of prejudice and received opinions on both sides.' What Kumin herself knew about Plato was minimal, but 'the syllabus required [her] to read closely texts [she] had bare acquaintance with from [her] own educational experience, and to stay one step ahead of the freshmen.' She recalled: '[The course] was hard work and I am happy to reflect back on its rigors. *The unexamined life is not worth living*, the philosopher taught us. Without the noble example of Socrates, without the many-times-told-tale of the New Testament and its central tragedy, without the Jewish notion of divine election from which derives the much-abused epithet "the Chosen People," my life would have been, if not unexamined, at least underexamined.'[17]

Kumin movingly revisits, and examines, a painful and consequential moment in both her own life and her classical learning in 'The Snarl,' published in 2005. It seeks to distil her complex reaction to a phone call she received in her New Hampshire home from a man then residing in Castine, Maine, who said he had seen her on television. From his almost instantly recognizable voice, she realized that both he and his wife, apparently estranged from him or at least still in Philadelphia, had been in her senior Latin class at Cheltenham High School, taught by Miss Juanita Downes, during the 1941–2 academic year (an emotionally-fraught period of time during which, although Kumin does not mention the fact in this poem, the Japanese attacked the US Navy base at Pearl Harbor, and the US consequently entered the Second World War). After describing the wife as 'one of the clique that had snubbed me down to the bone / so that I ate my dry sandwich daily in the john after Latin class,' she invokes Vergil's *Aeneid*, 'Aeneas, loitering in Carthage, must not forget / his destiny: he is to found Italy. / Dido must burn on her pyre.'

'Saved with Ablatives and Declensions in the Toilet Stall'

Figure 8.1 1942 *El Delator*, Cheltenham High School yearbook photo and personal description of Maxine Winokur.

She then links the couple with Dido and Aeneas, as she recalls seeing their wedding notice, thinking them

> an unlikely pair:
> she in her pageboy bob, queen of the front row,
> chewing forbidden gum, passing notes, swiveling
> to aim her triggered breasts to the multitude,
> he the louche bad boy in the back row of the class
> quick with the smartass right answer spoken out
> of turn, shirttail untucked, sardonic lip curled even then . . .
> He wants to . . . what is it he wants to tell her?

Invoking the *Aeneid* a second time, she answers 'That the curse of the Harpies is upon them, / that fortune will force them to chew on the very tables / once spread for feasting?,' then – returning to her narrative – asks,

> Weren't both of them
> in my class when Miss Downes brought on the doves
> That led Aeneas to the golden bough he needed

> to get into the kingdom of the dead?
> Juanita Mae Downes who never married.
> Juanita Mae Downes, a graduate of Bryn Mawr
> in the impoverished thirties, who saved my life with ablatives
> and declensions there in the toilet stall,
> my feet pulled up
> so no one entering the bathroom would notice.
> He now in Castine, Maine, the wife still in Philadelphia.
> All these sixty years fled. Miss Downes, be with me,
> I am suffering from acute miserere, but who among us
> would use it to call down mercy? Only your A+ students
> and he was one of them, were allowed to read about
> Dido and Aeneas making their illicit marriage bed
> in the cave in Book IV.

Then a third invocation of the *Aeneid*:

> *Excess of love, to what lengths*
> *you drive our human hearts.*

Then back to her narrative.

> And so he loves her
> and leaves her. No mercy for Dido. None, we learn, has Dido
> for herself.

Then a final invocation of the *Aeneid*: 'I have lived. I have run to the finish the course / that fortune gave me. I go to the dark, go gladly.' Then her epilogue, to Miss Downes: 'How I treasured my translation with your well done! printed / across the top page in tidy red letters. / Let him yearn, in Castine, Maine. No mercy on his head.'[18]

In *The Pawnbroker's Daughter*, Kumin explicates the web of personal and literary associations in this poem: initially by praising Downes and her English teacher Dorothy Lambert as 'two heroic figures who made a profound difference in my life'; and by relating that, 'With Miss Downes I studied Latin year by year, moving from Caesar's Gallic Wars through Cicero to Virgil (including the forbidden Book IV set in Dido's cave; Miss Downes was a purist and omitted nothing).' She next relates:

> I started school in Elkins Park as an outsider, respected yet friendless in a social structure that yawned above me. The fathers of my classmates were doctors, lawyers, academicians, the owners of department stores or drugstore chains. I was a pawnbroker's daughter . . . I had lunch alone in the locker room or in the girls' toilet, sitting in a locked cubicle with my legs pulled up out of sight . . . I took refuge in my scholarship; getting all A's was my only balm . . . Now college loomed.

'Saved with Ablatives and Declensions in the Toilet Stall'

> Although I had applied to Wellesley ... I was not accepted. For while they did not openly practice the quota system, virtually all the top colleges and universities at that time – 1942 – sharply limited the number of Jews and other minorities they accepted. Instead, I attended Radcliffe, which I confess I had never even considered until being rejected by Wellesley.[19]

In the interest of full disclosure, while I am powerfully drawn to Kumin's poetry as an American Jewish feminist classicist, although I am by no means a fan of farming, I must confess that the appeal that Kumin's writings hold for me is not purely academic. I myself attended Cheltenham public schools, as a Township resident, from 1949 onward, and graduated from its high school exactly twenty years after she did. Juanita Downes – who, for the record, lived from 1892 through 1976, held degrees from Swarthmore and the University of Pennsylvania and is not to be numbered among the [Bryn] Mawrters – retired the year before I entered high school.[20] But I studied with Albert Weston, one of Kumin's English teachers, benefited from the same guidance counselor's wisdom, and followed the identical Latin IV syllabus. I did not encounter the emotionally devastating social exclusion that she did, and had the good fortune to be one of three Jewish girls from the Philadelphia area accepted by Wellesley in 1962 (one of whom chose to attend Radcliffe instead). Still, while I experienced different adolescent agonies, and did minimal time in the school's toilet stalls, I, like Kumin, owe an incalculable debt to my own Latin teacher, Marie Hildebrand, for saving my life, or at least fostering the academic passions I pursued.[21]

Let me offer two parting points about this powerful poem. Downes' other students do not recall her fondly. To account for dwindling numbers in her Latin classes (sixty in Latin 2, four in Latin 3, three in Latin 4), the Renaissance historian Werner Gundersheimer claims that few of her students 'were masochistic enough to submit to her rigorous inquisition' and she was too trapped by 'her own rigid and dogmatic training' 'to break away from the rugged constraints of literalness and philological exactitude to capture moods and feelings' in Latin poetry. Another distinguished historian, Ellen Wolf Schrecker, got so exasperated with Downes' rightwing political views that she bit her on the finger, sending her to the hospital with a wound requiring stitches. In Gundersheimer's words, 'few people could stand her ... even fewer liked her ... she taught [Latin] and you learned it. Or else.'[22]

But Kumin viewed her reverentially. I read Kumin's invocation of Miss Downes, asking Downes 'to be with me' and characterizing herself as suffering from acute 'miserere', as an allusion to lines 17–20 of poem 76, by Catullus: here begging the plural gods, if it is in their power, to *miserere*, 'show pity', on him as he tries to recover from a painful love affair.

> *O di, si vestrumst miserere, aut si quibus umquam*
>   *Extremam iam ipsa in morte tulistis opem.*
> *Me miserum aspicite et, si vitam puriter egi,*
>   *Eripite hanc pestem perniciemque mihi.*

O gods, if it is in your power, to show pity, or if you have ever brought final aid to any at the very moment of death, look upon me in my wretched condition and, if I have lived my life without blame, take away this disease and destruction from me (translation my own).

There is no evidence that Miss Downes exposed her Latin students to Catullus, although Virgil frequently echoes him. Or that Kumin studied Latin at Radcliffe. But the novelist Mary McCarthy ends her 1942 novel, *The Company She Keeps*, by quoting from this very Catullan poem:

'Oh my God,' she said, pausing to stare at a drugstore window that was full of hot water bottles, 'do not let them take this away from me. If the flesh must be blind, let the spirit see. Preserve me in disunity. '*O di*,' she said aloud, '*reddite me hoc pro pietate mea*.'

It was certainly a very small favor she was asking, but, like Catullus, she could not be too demanding, for, unfortunately, she did not believe in God.[23]

Kumin presumably was acquainted with the work of McCarthy, like Anne Sexton's mentor Robert Lowell, a resident of Castine, Maine.[24] And whatever Kumin's reasons for the 'miserere', which Catullan scholar Michael Putnam would merely trace to the Latin mass, and its plea to a single Christian god, words the young Maxine Winokur imbibed at her Catholic school next door, her attribution of divine powers to Miss Downes, whose 'well-done' Kumin deeply treasured, was rich recompense for the life saved by a Latin teacher.[25]

Notes

1. See, for example, the obituaries by Fox (2014), Marquard (2014) and in the [Kumin's 'hometown'] *Philadelphia Inquirer* (2014) as well as the interview by Shomer (1996) and the essay by Dubrow (2021). To be sure, Dubrow does acknowledge that Kumin's 'Sisyphus' 'takes its title from Greek mythology'. But she asserts that 'the poem seems more inspired by Albert Camus's famous essay, which interprets the myth through the lens of existentialism,' since the 'speaker condemns inaction – her own inability to admit her identity as a Jew – viewing this failure to act as a choice.' While Shomer's interview says nothing about Kumin's engagement with classical languages and texts, she concludes with Kumin's statement that she had two important secondary teachers: 'One was a Latin teacher, Juanita May Downes, with whom I studied for five years, so that I was translating Ovid's *Metamorphoses* into matching hexameters my senior year in high school' (555). For more on Downes, see below.
2. Indeed, Wilner (2015) emphasizes Kumin's avoidance of Latinate vocabulary, observing: '[her] choice of words is a diction decidedly Anglo-Saxon – the Germanic-descended language of peasants and pig farmers in England, not the Latin of Church and university . . . the Latinate words in English, more elevated, more distanced from the sweat of bodily life, are seldom found in her poems, whose diction, over time, grew ever more plain.' Hurley (2014) quotes Kumin's neighbor, poet and University of New Hampshire English professor Deborah Brown, as saying Kumin's work is unfairly pigeonholed as 'pastoral': 'That's a very

limiting term . . . I think she wanted to be remembered as a poet who had a broader range than that.' He then quotes from Kumin's pastoral poem 'Come, Aristotle', which observes, in regard to growing parsnips: 'Aristotle says, *to suck up whatever sustenance may flow to them wherever they are stuck* . . . We ate them in groups of fours . . . inverted fleshly angels pried from the black gold of ancient horse manure. Pure, Aristotle.' But he does not view these evocations of classical writings as evidence of her 'broader range.'

3. See, for example, Klein (2015) as well as Shomer (1996) and Wilner (2015).
4. See Kumin (2012) and the subsequent discussions by Burroway (2014) for a detailed explication of this phrase.
5. Kumin's poetry abounds in what I am calling 'classical engagements', far greater in number than I can possibly discuss in this essay. Indeed, assessments and appreciations of what is distinctive and powerful in Kumin's writings often single out poems featuring classical allusions, even titles, but then fail to examine and analyze these references in any detail. The discussion by Hurley (2014) of 'Come Aristotle', quoted in note 2, serves as a case in point. Similarly, to argue that Kumin 'trafficked in none of the sentimental effusions of traditional pastoral poetry', Fox (2014) quotes Kumin's 'Highway Hypothesis', which coins a Graeco-Latin neologism to repudiate the affective stance of the genre: 'Bucophilia, I call it_/ nostalgia over a pastoral vista.' But she does not explore the classical resonances of the coinage. Wilner (2015) does much the same thing with Kumin's quotation of Socrates' words in 'Either Or', although she does elucidate Kumin's reference in 'Path, Chair' to 'the farthest field saluting the Greek gods and goddesses' by noting that Kumin and her husband named a pasture on their farm 'the Elysian field.'
6. Kumin (2015: 15–68, especially 17, 22 and 26). See also Shomer (1996).
7. Kumin (2015: 71–83), especially 75, 76 and 83; Shomer (1996); Doherty (2020: xi–xiv, xvi–xvii and *passim*), especially 34–8 and 295–303. For Levin (1912–94), see Galperin (2011).
8. Kumin (2015: 75–81), especially 76, 79 and 81; Shomer (1996); Doherty (2020: *passim*), especially 33, 37, 75, 84–5, and 125.
9. Kumin (2014) and (2015: 81–4, 96–100), Pride (2005); Doherty (2020: 205–7, 281–6).
10. Kumin (2015: 84, 120–4, see also Kumin (2014).
11. Dalby (2010: 64–71 and 198–9); see also 198–9 on the duties of the *vilica*, female partner of the *vilicus*, set out in chapter 143.
12. Bacon (1974). See also Talbot (2003) on Frost's use of a classical Latin metre favored by Catullus, phalaecean hendecasyllabics, to rebut his critics. Kumin's affinities with Frost also include her strong interest in metre. See, for example, Kumin (2015: 91), one of many reflections on her poetic priorities, that center on metre: 'Although metrics serve as a way of giving shape to my anger and enabling my poetry to voice moral outrage, some of my rants are in free verse.' See also her recollections of her secondary school training in translating Ovid's *Metamorphoses*, composed in Latin dactylic hexameters, into English dactylic hexameters, shared with Shomer (1996: 555), quoted earlier in note 2.
13. Kumin (2015: 86–7); the full text of the poem is quoted in Appendix 1.
14. Kumin (2015: 85–6).
15. Kumin (2015: 125) and above, n. 5, for the pasture named 'Elysian Field'; 153–5 for the dog named Virgil – and 108 for an earlier dog named Caesar. .
16. See Moscaliuc (2008: 166), who observes, 'Even a poem like "Still We Take Joy," in which the poet celebrates the timelessness of the *Georgics* of Virgil, whose gardening advice is as sound today as ever, is injected with worry and grief. As the speaker tries to take joy in the three

carrots she digs out, "just as the poet instructs us," she cannot shake off the acute awareness that "in Baghdad sewage infiltrates/the drinking water and no one dares go out/to market."'

17. See the the detailed commentary provided by Kumin herself in Barron and Selinger (2000: 91–9).

18. I do not agree with the negative assessment of this poem by Schneider (2010), who claims, 'The ideas in this poem do not really snap into place. They rattle around and knock against each other. The juxtaposition of the historical and literary archetypes beside the one-time high school sweethearts is fanciful but not really convincing . . . it's not clear how the old classmates should be regarded—are they tragic figures . . . or just ordinary people who never understood themselves? Do Virgil's words really have any relevance here or are they merely an association triggered by recollection of she shared Latin class?'

    Kumin, however, does not represent these two classmates as high school sweethearts, merely as having married, 'an unlikely pair', not altogether happily, after high school. Kumin, moreover, portrays herself as tragically persecuted by her female classmates, as thus identifying with Dido, suffering and seeking mercy in vain, and as painfully oblivious to the eruption of the Second World War, and its consequences for her generation, her fellow Jews in Europe, and her nation.

19. Kumin's memoir provides more information about her Cheltenham High School Latin teacher, Juanita Downes, quoting from Kumin (2015: 25–37).

20. For Downes, see the article in *Beaver News* (1953) announcing her appointment as a part-time assistant professor in the department of classical languages, to the Beaver (now Arcadia) College faculty. It states: 'Miss Downes has been connected with the college on a part-time basis for many years, having taught a methods course in the department of education. At present, Miss Downes is a teacher of Latin in Cheltenham Township High School. Miss Downes was graduated from Swarthmore College, received her master's degree from the University of Pennsylvania, and studied at the American Academy in Rome.'

21. For Latin and English teacher Marie Shaeffer Hildebrand Bintner (1931–2016), see 'History with Chuck' (2024): her English students included Israeli prime minister Benjamin Netanyahu, Cheltenham class of 1967.

22. Gundersheimer (1985). My conversations on February 20, 2018, with both Gundersheimer, Cheltenham High School Class of 1955, and Robert Bronstein, Cheltenham, Class of 1959, also merit fuller quotation. In addition to sharing his 1985 essay from the University of Pennsylvania *Gazette*, which compares his experiences studying Latin with Downes in high school and with Rolfe Humphries at Amherst College, and relating the anecdote with Ellen Wolf Schrecker, Gundersheimer recalled that Downes sent former students Quaker calendars each Christmas. For Schrecker, a distinguished American historian known for her work on McCarthyism in the US, see her *Prabook* entry (2024).

    Bronstein reported that "She wore black on the Ides of March, celebrated the Saturnalia, and always sat on the arm of her desk chair. Cheltonian students [staffers of the school newspaper] waited in vain for that chair to break.

23. McCarthy (1939: 222–3).

24. For the summer sojourns of Lowell and McCarthy in Castine, where Kumin claims that her snarling-voiced male high school Latin classmate who phones her now dwells, 'in his assisted living', see Corbett (1993); for Lowell's mentoring and support of Sexton, see Doherty (2020: 23–30, 32–3 and 203–4).

25. Many thanks to Jane Ashcom, Robert Bronstein, Werner Gundersheimer, the late Ellen Jaffe, Ann Kuttner, Robert Levine, Michael Putnam, Ellen Wolf Schrecker, and Elaine Showalter for their helpful comments and criticisms on this paper. My deepest gratitude to Paul Cartledge, the late David Konstan, Mary Lefkowitz and Hanna Roisman, who have supported me in my ethical conviction that there is no justification for criticizing the words employed and ideas expressed by Jewish scholars and writers simply because they are, like Kumin and myself, Jewish.

CHAPTER 9
'TO READ, TO SEE, TO SPIN, AND TO TURN': REINTRODUCING BARBARA KÖHLER'S ELEKTRAS

Lena Grimm

I

As I am writing this, in the summer of 2023, the German Literary Archive is undergoing the process of cataloguing Barbara Köhler's (1959–2021) personal library.[1] It is a substantial one – currently, her books take up thirteen metres of the archive's bookshelves – with an accordingly extensive cataloguing process. Köhler's books are well-loved and thoroughly studied, often brimming with postcards, photographs, torn scraps of paper, and handwritten notes, reflecting on a particularly interesting word, drawing connections between different parts of a text, or jotting out the first versions of a translation project. Were you to walk along these bookshelves, you would see books in German, English, French, Ancient Greek, Hungarian, and Portuguese; you might notice texts by authors including Samuel Beckett, Homer, Paul Celan, Josephine Balmer, Rosmarie Waldrop, Sigmund Freud, and Gertrude Stein, among many, many others. Each of these books will be carefully examined, described, and catalogued – and there are still more books that have not yet arrived at the archive.

For those familiar with Köhler's work, the volume and breadth of her collection is unsurprising. From her literary emergence as a member of the East German underground poetry scene in the 1980s to the time of her death in 2021, Köhler authored over a dozen books, three volumes of translation, and a wide number of text-installations, poetry readings and lectures (Knott 2024: 240–4). Moving between written texts, visual art and performance, Köhler worked in an intergeneric and deeply collaborative manner, often developing years-long partnerships with artists of many different media. This was true of Köhler's work even in her early career: as she said of her time at the Leipzig Literature Institute, 'The interesting thing about the literature institute was the possibility of working with fifteen other people who also write. It was similar with the unofficial [underground] magazines. You didn't just send off your text but came into contact with other people, the magazine existed as an "artistic synthesis" [*Gesamtkunstwerk*].' (Dahlke 1997: 286)[2]

Köhler described her monographs as accumulations of multiple influences, conversations and languages as well. *Niemands Frau* (Nobody's Wife, 2007), her response to the *Odyssey* and its reception, includes over thirty pages of notes and reflections on her experience learning ancient Greek, examining other authors' translations and interpretations of the epic and thanking the collaborators with whom she translated, performed and discussed her text in the decade she was writing it (Köhler 2007: 109). In many ways, her library is a reflection of this practice of poetic creation, layer upon layer of texts, languages, exchanges and genres in material form.

We cannot, however, walk the length of these shelves together. Instead, we can find another route to Köhler: through translation, which itself joins in and extends the forms of poetic creation, collaboration, and artistic mediation that are visible in Köhler's works and library. As Köhler herself wrote, translation has the capacity 'to release the material over and over, to read, to see, to spin and to turn it ... between languages, sides, times, images, symbols and gestures and words and names' (2009: 151–2).[3] Understood in this sense, translation is fundamentally pluralistic, an ongoing endeavour that allows multiple translations of the same text to coexist or come into dialogue with one another, rather than compete for status as a singular 'authoritative' translation. The poetic cycle translated here — 'Elektra. Mirrorings' (1991) — has in fact been translated before, by Georgina Paul (1999), and translated, for that matter, beautifully. My own translation is not an attempt to supplant Paul's work, but rather to find my own way to open new possibilities of reading and interpreting alongside both Paul and Köhler's works – and in so doing, to reintroduce this early work from Barbara Köhler to an Anglophone audience.

II

Elektra is a figure particularly well suited to a pluralistic approach to translation: she was already multiple in Classical Athens (fifth to third centuries BCE), an era in which each of the three major tragedians wrote their own versions of the Elektra myth. Köhler's personal library reflects this plurality: among her books is a 1983 Reclam edition of *Elektra*, which compiles Aeschylus, Sophocles, Euripides and Hugo von Hofmannsthal's versions of the Elektra myth, each of which draws from and diverges slightly from the ones before it.[4] In some versions, for instance, Elektra helps her brother Orestes murder their mother; in other versions, she doesn't. Regardless of her culpability, Elektra's own future disappears with her mother's: what happens to her after the murder is left unclear in each tragedy. Even in Aeschylus' *Oresteia*, the only complete trilogy of Greek tragic plays to survive to this day, Elektra appears in the second play just to disappear altogether in the third instalment, in which Orestes is both tried and acquitted for his matricide and goes on to help establish the Athenian court system. Elektra, always plural, is also always disappearing.

Though these poems were not officially published until 1991, as part of her debut collection, *Deutsches Roulette* (German Roulette), Köhler began writing her own version of the myth just a year after the publication of the Reclam edition (Paul 2004: 21). Köhler's poetic cycle seeks to offer Elektra precisely what the tragedies do not: a language and a future beyond Orestes'. As she writes in the second poem of the cycle: 'a new piece begins / and no role foreseen for elektra and no / language other than orestes' who will align himself with the new gods / and rule'.

This movement beyond tragedy plays out across and through the structure of the poetic cycle. Over the course of these eight poems, many different versions of Elektra emerge, some explicitly called Elektra, some called Ophelia and Ulrike, some appearing only as an unnamed 'i.' (I translate 'ich' into 'i' to reflect Köhler's tendency to avoid capitalization in these poems.) Though these Elektras begin on stage, the majority of the cycle takes place off the stage – at the vanity where she removes her tragic mask and smashes the mirror, in the unnamed spaces in which the reader encounters different versions of Elektra, in a flat landscape with an open horizon. Together, these Elektras do not form a unified figure, nor do they uncover an 'original' forgotten Elektra or directly extend her role in tragedy (i.e., imagine 'what happens next' for Elektra within the plot of the play). Reading Elektra through a series of other authors, Köhler 'resists closure' (Paul 2004: 31) between these various Elektras, instead proliferating an already plural figure without giving any one version precedence over another.

Translating Köhler's Elektra carries on this proliferation. These two different translations of an excerpt from the cycle's fifth poem, for instance, produce different possibilities for Köhler's Elektras:

another woman	an other
on the morning of her Latest Judgement	on the morning of her doomsday
... elektra am I the end	... elektra am i the end
of the prayers the damnation	of the prayers the damnation
and the salvation I am	and the release i'm
leaving the stage ...	going off the stage ...
(Paul 1999)	

The very first words of these translations diverge from one another. Paul translates 'eine andere' as 'another woman,' reflecting the feminine gendering of the German word. My own translation opts for 'an other,' relying on the 'her' later in the sentence to indicate to the reader that the figure in question is female. What this formulation keeps, however, is the gap between 'eine' and 'andere' – a space that is unremarkable in German but jarring to an English speaker, forcing the reader, I hope, to pause and consider this phrase more carefully than a word as commonplace as 'another.' This pause when reading one's own language, however temporary or minor, gestures towards a sense of alienation and difference that is crucial to the project of the poetic cycle as a whole: alienation permeates both Köhler's sense of authorship generally and the position of the poem's subject(s) specifically. For Köhler as an author, writing from a place of difference provided the possibility of 'formulating an ex-centric position' that might lead to a structure of 'equal worth rather than hierarchy' (Dahlke 1997: 293); the 'an other' in Poem V also parallels the 'an other' that appears in Poem III, so framing this speaker as both 'another' in a series of multiple Elektras and 'an other,' an Elektra that is strange and estranging in a manner distinct from the rest.

Secondly, there is the word 'erlösung,' which Paul translates as 'the salvation' and I translate as 'the release'. Paul's translation retains the specifically religious dimension of the word 'erlösung', while my translation does not have a particularly religious connotation, instead conveying these religious overtones more clearly elsewhere in the poem. 'Release', however, places particular emphasis on the sense of entrapment that pervades Elektra's experience and from which she seeks to escape ('i'm going off the stage . . .'). For those who choose to read this introduction before reading these accompanying translations, translating 'erlösung' as 'release' may also serve as a tangible example of how translation directly extends Köhler's own poetic project. Just as translations, in Köhler's terminology, 'release' a material over and over again, Köhler's poetic cycle 'releases' Elektra herself again and again. So, too, does the work of retranslation: multiple translations can open up new possibilities of interpretation, emphasizing the range of meanings encompassed by Köhler's text in a way that a single translation might not. To be 'another woman,' in the context of Elektra's myth, means at the same time to always be 'an other' vis-à-vis her male counterparts; Elektra's 'release' from the tragic stage is at the same time her 'salvation' from a fate in which she, as 'an other', disappears.

III

What language, then, is there for Elektra? How can it be brought outside of the space of tragedy, and how might it be translated?

Elektra's language, both in tragedy and in Köhler's poetry, is lament. Lament is both a language that Orestes does not practise in the way Elektra does – the public performance of grief was considered, in ancient tragedy, to be part of a woman's duty to her family members, and not the typical purview of a male hero like Orestes – and a language that binds each version of Elektra to the others. In Sophocles, Elektra grieves to the point of excess, beyond socially accepted parameters even in a society that expected women to lament. Anne Carson translates: 'Women, I am ashamed before you: I know / you find me extreme / in my grief' (Sophocles 2001: lines 338–40). Carson's own preface to her translation focuses specifically on this extremity, transliterating and enumerating each of Elektra's lamentations over the course of the play; Virginia Woolf, in 'On Not Knowing Greek,' writes that Elektra 'stands before us like a figure so tightly bound that she can only move an inch this way, an inch that . . . Her words in crisis are, as a matter of fact, bare; mere cries of despair, joy, hate' (1925: 43); Ezra Pound's Elektra combined transliterated Greek alongside contemporary English to produce lines like this: 'DEIN EN DEINOIS ENENGASTHEN / It's too horrible, I can't keep it in' (1990: 11).

The Elektras of Köhler's poems often perform similarly interruptive expressions of grief: see, for instance, Poem I, 'I WANT TO BE GUILTY', Poem II, 'LOVE ME MY CHILD', Poem IV, 'my noose is already tied / ACH DEAR MANIA', or Poem V, 'I HAVE STOPPED / BEING LOVED'. In these moments, Köhler's Elektra can be read as performing, though not a direct translation of the highly formalized laments of classical tragedy, a loose recreation of this tradition.

There is another way that Köhler reckons with the lament of tragedy: as a language of self-mourning that does not just place her in contrast to most of the male heroes of

Greek tragedy, but also opens up other (female) lines of connection. In Aeschylus, for example, Clytemnestra speaks the following line in the moment that she understands she will not be able to dissuade Orestes from killing her. Anticipating her own death while she is still alive, Clytemnestra mourns herself:

Living, I sing a gravesong for myself before a deaf stone.[5]

Köhler underlined this sentence in her edition of *Elektra*. Her own Elektras seem to 'inherit' her mother's self-lament, as we might see in Poems V and VII – 'as i said to him this evening / i can't move i am / dead dead dead', 'look at me while dying hear / my breath' – among others. Elektra and Clytemnestra remain in sharp contrast to one another, but share this mode of self-mourning: they both must lament themselves when no one else will, constituting a form of mourning that traces disrupted lines of genealogy between mother and daughter as well as father and son. Elektra's lament, in Köhler's hands, so becomes a language which expands vertically, on both sides of Elektra's family tree, and horizontally, encompassing her many different selves.

While Köhler extends the possibilities of Elektra's lament in some instances, her poems diverge from the sphere of ancient tragedy more dramatically in others, staging the emergence of lament in Elektra's mind in addition to the act of speaking itself. This is not to say that lament in twentieth-century Germany and fourth-century BCE Athens share no fundamental features. Then and now, lament is an expression of mourning that at once produces meaning and yet can never fully convey the enormity of grief. Insofar as lament can consist of screams and cries, it has the capacity of making meaning outside of typical syntactic structures and of transcending language barriers. (We all understand the visceral nature of the scream, even if we speak different languages and hail from cultures with different mourning practices). Lament disrupts language's flow in order to convey the force of grief and yet, in attempting to do so, reveals the limits of what language can represent or communicate.

Playwriters in ancient Greece largely emphasized the act of performing lament, rather than the internal life of the speaker themselves. When Clytemnestra speaks her line above – 'Living, I sing a gravesong for myself' – we might note that she references herself, but does so by gesturing towards the linguistic and performative act of mourning, not her emotional or mental state. Köhler, on the other hand, writes with an attention towards both the external performance of grief and the mind's inner workings. We might see this, for instance, here, in the lines partially quoted above:

she invented unthinkable sentences:
I HAVE STOPPED
BEING LOVED
as i said to him this evening
i can't move i am
dead dead dead the dying stops words
come to mind like mister hitchcock's birds

The woman in this poem speaks on the beginning of her last day, that is, the day of her death – an event language cannot fully express, even internally ('unthinkable sentences'), as expressing the speaker's death completely would mean to annihilate language. Instead, words 'come to mind like mister hitchcock's birds', an excess of language that nevertheless cannot communicate the central void of the poem, and points again to the limits of language. Suspended in the time before her death, yet also already 'dead dead dead', this version of Elektra hovers between life and death. She is a spectre that mourns herself even before pronouncing a word out loud, inventing laments for herself inside her own head. Köhler's lament moves beyond the space of ancient tragedy not just because it does not precisely reproduce ancient Greek ritual forms, not just because she alludes to Alfred Hitchcock, but also because she emphasizes lament's emergence in the mourning subject's mind.

Translating Elektra's laments, then, meant not only retaining her interruptive all-caps cries, but also learning to pay attention to the moments when Elektra falls silent. The first stanza of Poem VII is one good example:

no longer do i want to be / the image of his notbeing
(to be what he is not, notwhite = black) i want to find
an end and begin from there / since we are finite
we finally become

Lament is a language that begins at an end: this 'i' uses lament to locate her own death, from which a new beginning arises. She mourns herself and opens the possibility of her beginning again on the other side of tragedy. But because lament inevitably comes up against the brink of life and language, Elektra will never arrive at a stable mode of being or expression through lament; it is a mode of survival that operates at the cost of unmaking her. This is particularly clear in the last two lines of the stanza. In German, these lines read: 'denn endlich sind wir / daß wir endlich werden' (Köhler 1991: 30). Paul's translation reproduces the repetition of 'endlich' through the English word 'last': 'for that we do not last means that we may become at last' (1999: 227). Rather than prioritize this repetition, I aimed to recreate the somewhat paradoxical functions of lament in this cycle – a sustaining and destabilizing force, a language that begins at an end – through the pairing between 'finite' and 'finally'.

Translation, like lament, runs up against the limits of language. In the stanza above, for instance, Köhler's German includes a play on words I could not recreate in English: 'nichtweiß = schwarz,' which I translated as 'notwhite = black.' In German, 'weiß' is both an adjective meaning 'white,' the colour, and the first and third person singular conjugations of the verb 'to know.' Placed back into the context of the lines above, 'nichtweiß = schwarz' can be read at least two ways: firstly, as 'notwhite = black,' suggesting that the speaker no longer wants to be defined via negation – 'what he is not' – but instead seeks a mode of being in which she can exist on her own terms. Secondly, as 'notknowing = black,' suggesting that the speakers seeks not only a way of being in the world alternative to this 'he', which might be read as Orestes specifically or as the male hero more generally, but an alternative mode of knowing the world as well. To not know any alternative to 'the image of his notbeing' means, after all, the end of Elektra, her disappearance in a future in which 'orestes rules'. This layering of meanings and negations, however, does not function in English: instead, translating this phrase requires selecting only one of these possibilities.

All of these tensions – between life and death, the finite and the infinite, one mode of being and knowing and another – carry through to the end of the poetic cycle. In the cycle's final poem, an 'i' emerges onto a landscape that is empty, save one vague figure in the distance. This place, says the poem, is a place 'to win without needing to triumph'. We might read this line as a critique of the dynamics played out in tragedy and its receptions – Orestes' 'triumph' over Clytemnestra most of all. Seen in this light, 'to win without needing to triumph' is to find a way out of this cyclical violence. When reading with an eye towards Elektra's lamenting language, however, we might also see this: in this empty landscape, her lamentations sprawl endlessly, winning herself an escape from tragedy, but never reaching an existence that affirms a triumphant, living, Elektra. Instead, she is always already dead and quite wholly alive, alive in many different iterations and forms, moving forever towards and around her selves but never uniting.

If the Elektras of tragedy are elusive figures, present for a moment, absent the next, Köhler's Elektras are just as evasive as ever. They remain fleeting, at the edge of our sight, and Köhler does not offer us a way of seeing all of them at once. Yet in reconfiguring Elektra's lament as a language through which she is both here (and not), alive (and not), herself (and not), Köhler perhaps gives us the ability to listen to Elektra's language after so many others did not. We need not be deaf stones when Elektra sings her own gravesongs – but instead, as careful readers (and listeners) of her language, may learn to 'release' Elektra again in our own ways.

Women Creating Classics

Elektra. Mirrorings

I

    out of some forgotten beginning out of the firewall
    where the stage ends out of the mirror's background
    steps a form just visible through layers of images
    accumulations of history and memory But
    this woundred mouth shameless lips they speak
    I WANT TO BE GUILTY

    the form nears becomes body doubled multi-
    plied one in all images incline towards herself and demands
    stands for herself in front of all the black could something begin
    dance kiss live RED IS THE COLOR in extinguished light

    yet (and why) i bear the play of hero and
    happy end the drama in which all roles are victims

    but death exists and
    there exists a time before

II
Opening Act in the Theater

Homage to Heiner Müller

elektra king's daughter and slave in mycenae grew up
in the tradition of bloodshed murder and war in a lineage
of slaughterers since tantalus every act is called re-
tribution demand the blindborn EYE FOR EYE elektras home the hate her hope orestes my brother
my prince my vengeance will come my beloved
put an end to the killing we will live in light and
clarity i want to see myself in your eyes
why are you looking at me like that am i not elektra prettiest
among the women once i was young when i delivered you
into safety out of fear of the queen – they are truly
pretty the girls from phokis the well-bred-soft-
firm-in-flesh what do you want here with your sister
the barbarian with your mother the murderess with the
bones of your father who slaughtered his daughter and
in front of Troy a thousand men before he fell under his wife's axe
what do you want if you don't want to know me

orestes turned back after years of exile in a foreign
city that should be called home received by the merci-
less love of a sister the strangest of all recognizes
him orestes flees from her in the bloodpath of his forefathers in
the family's heroes-gallery in the bedroom of the mother
the queen of fear who offers her naked breasts to her son and
murderer LOVE ME MY CHILD yeahyeah i'm coming to
kill you HAVE YOU A HEART MAMA i want to see it
clump of muscleflesh that beats and is warm
will become cold mama like the knife in your
breast in my head can you still hear me a new piece
begins and no role foreseen for elektra and no
language other than orestes' who will align himself
with the new gods and rule

at the vanity elektra sits sets the mask aside

III

    i sit in the mirror my image smiles
    puts on makeup tries a gesture out
    its mouth speaks of love it means you
    in your eyes the image

    i sit in the mirror before an other
    lays a hand on the image it is smooth
    her mouth remains mute she means me
    in her eyes the image

    i sit in the mirror am i a reflex
    it is nothing behind the image it is
    a mirror and if i hit then i strike
    your face and my face

    fragmented have you seen
    the shards of your gaze

IV

for Ulrike Meinhof

alone with this voice ulrike on the far side of dayand-
night the torment WHITE AS SNOW fluid neon in the
veins black butterflies before eyes germany
blonde wall on which my noose is already tied
ACH DEAR MANIA outside it is may the blue lies
of sky promise shadows AS BLACK AS EBONY
which hold themselves to the fairytale of GOODANDEVIL
so as not to fall like me so as not to fly in this
abyss of voice in this murderish light
ULRIKE! who even knows what she's seen recently the
truth maybe AS RED AS BLOOD did she leave
the mirrors

V

an other on the morning of her doomsday
she invents unthinkable sentences:
I HAVE STOPPED
BEING LOVED
as i said to him this evening
i can't move i am
dead dead dead the dying stops words
come to mind like mister hitchcock's birds
i lay there and counted the sweetnesses
of this hopelessly secretless being
like fivemarkbills what does sex
even cost – make it quick or should i reveal
to you what chirps behind my brow
so that for you this frenzy of ecstasy
passes like for me the playing along
with so much emptywished childhood
MAMAANDPAPAETC the mistake
in the genetic calculation
elektra am i the end
of the prayers the damnation
and the release i'm
going off of the stage
in a possible
Nothing outside of love
hope carries my name

VI

THE AGED OPHELIA with a pokerface
spells in the crossword puzzle the initials of the sphinx
between seven down and twentytwo across
the scream of the godabandoned forgive them for they
do not know – ophelia knows and paints giggling the
last greek letters in the five spaces between
hand and hand and if you ask her an image that conjures
the devil (she still remembers who that is) as well.
forgotten across the centuries this oracle
drinks malt coffee and vermouth from the rest of the pension
refuses to die takes again and again an empty
page a pencil and makes crosses an entire
hero's graveyard for
         hamlet & consorts

VII

no longer do i want to be / the image of his notbeing
(to be what he is not, notwhite = black) i want to find
an end and begin from there / since we are finite
we finally become

comfort evades like the One, like god / three wishes
pass by your open eyes / look at me while dying hear
my breath / which counts down to death in the shadow of your
face

VIII

dream behind the labyrinth begins a landscape a
plain empty like the sky above it. no housing
no hiding spot only the possibility
                            of going. under the
feet no sand; loose earth that looks fertile but
does not yield any growing things. windstill, cool air
rises from the earth. i turn around without the feeling of
being followed of which this landscape reminds me.
no other image, an empty horizon. i look to the
sky, a clear blue without depth, from which neither threat
nor promise emerges. there is no fear. there
is no hope except to go foot before foot there is
no ground
        for staying still. at some point i
perceive a form. it is not clear if it is female
or male, nearing or withdrawing. the form of
a human spreads its arms an unsettled
gesture between crucifixion and flight i know this is
the place
        to win without needing to triumph

Notes

1. Special thanks to Jan Bürger, Janet Dilger, and Lorenz Wesemann at the DLA.
2. "Interessant am Literaturinstitut war ja die Möglichkeit, mit fünfzehn Leuten zusammenzusein, die auch schreiben. Bei den inoffiziellen Zeitschriften war es ähnlich. Du hast nicht einfach deine Texte hingeschickt, sondern bist mit Leuten in Kontakt gekommen, es gab die Zeitschrift als „Gesamtkunstwerk" Feste usw." („Gespräch mit Barbara Köhler")
3. I've translated this quote from an essay titled 'Penelopes Gewebe' [Penelope's Weaving], a reflection on Köhler's engagement with the language of the *Odyssey*. The quote in German is: „den Stoff immer wieder und immer wieder anders zu lösen, zu lesen, zu sehen, ihn zu drehn und zu wenden . . . zwischen den Sprache, den Seiten, den Zeiten, Bildern, Zeichen und Gesten und Wörtern und Namen" (2009: 152). The word „lösen" has multiple meanings – it can mean to resolve a problem, to solve a math problem, or to dissolve something in a liquid. Köhler provides this description of translation following a reflection on the ancient Greek word λύω, which encompasses the meanings 'to solve' and 'dissolve' but can also mean 'to loosen, unbind, release' (a ship or a hostage, for instance). Köhler reads λύω as a sort of metaphor for translation that she represents in German through 'lösen'; I have translated it further as 'release' not to draw a direct equivalence between 'lösen' and 'release' but rather to take Köhler's movement between Greek and German in this essay into account when translating.
4. Aischylos, et al. *Elektra: Aischylos, Sophokles, Euripides, Hugh von Hofmannsthal*. Edited by Rudolf Schottlaender. Translated by Ulrich von Wilamowitz-Moellendorff, Reclam, 1983.
5. Initially translated from Greek by Ulrich von Wilamowitz-Moellendorff and later edited by Rudolf Schottlaender; translation into English from German by myself. The German reads: 'Lebend sing ich mir Grabgesung vor taubem Stein'.

CONTEMPORARY

CHAPTER 10
HOW TO BE THE BEST: MADELINE MILLER'S PATROCLUS
Jessica Lawrence

There is a moment, fleeting and to the casual eye insignificant, in book 17 of the *Iliad* where Menelaus stands astride the corpse of Patroclus and exhorts his fellow Greeks to protect the body from Trojan desecration. His reasoning? The man was kind (Hom. *Il.* 17.670–2). From this still point in the heat of battle the author Madeline Miller created *The Song of Achilles*, a work that offers the chance of a revelatory re-evaluation of the epic and what it means to be *aristos*, the best.

In the Homeric poems, being the best of the Greeks, *aristos Achaiōn*, has a relatively narrow definition as the apex of warriorhood, and, within the confines of the *Iliad*, that definition is the character of Achilles himself. Achilles' renown rests upon his almost superhuman ability to kill and conquer in battle and the figure of Patroclus was originally also cut to that Homeric cloth. Homer's Patroclus certainly does his fair share of gruesomely violent acts in the name of war. His rampage in book 16 attests to his 'heroic' qualities as he skewers a Trojan through his jawbone and flips him out of the chariot on the end of his spear 'as a man sitting on a jutting rock drags to land a sacred fish' (Hom. *Il.* 16.406–7) and immediately proceeds to smash a rock so hard into a man's face that his skull splits in two (Hom. *Il.* 16.411–12). That Patroclus was a Homeric hero in the widely understood sense is, therefore, not in question. What Miller has succeeded in doing, though, is seizing upon what makes him different, realigning his story to set one of his distinctive character traits as definitive and in the process triggering a reappraisal of Homeric heroism. *The Song of Achilles* argues that Patroclus' kindness and empathy to all, while not faultless in its execution, makes him truly the best of the Achaeans and hence more deserving of the centuries of focus and fame that Achilles has received. What I will argue is that Madeline Miller decentres Achilles as the traditional 'best Greek' by examining instances of Patroclus' Homerically attested kindness to draw her readers to a radical reunderstanding of the value system of the Homeric world and what it means to be the best.

*

νῦν τις ἐνηείης Πατροκλῆος δειλοῖο
μνησάσθω· πᾶσιν γὰρ ἐπίστατο μείλιχος εἶναι
ζωὸς ἐών·

now let everyone remember the kindliness of poor Patroclus. For he was kind to all while he lived.[1]

Hom. Il. 17.670–2

We begin with those two lines which are the catalyst for Madeline Miller's radical act of reorienting our perception of what it is to have *kleos* in Homer. *Kleos* is a person's fame or glory, achieved by the performance of great deeds, and etymologically signifying that it is about external perception: it refers to what is *heard* about the person in the medium of poetry. Particulary in the *Iliad*, a hero's glory is only practicably achievable through martial prowess, and the attainment of *kleos* in epic song is directly linked to being *aristos*.[2] These lines, however, turn kindness into the most salient character-trait of Patroclus, setting him apart from the Homeric ranks: 'kindness' does not feature prominently, if at all, in the value system of other Homeric heroes; but coded into these verses and their diction is how *uniquely* kind Patroclus was – or that his very disposition towards kindness *is* unique. 'Kindliness' (ἐνηείη) is a so-called *hapax legomenon*, occurring only once in the entirety of Homer, and it comes after a significant interval of lines devoid of *hapax legomena*, compounding its singularity (van Emde Boas, 2004: xxvi). The word (and hence the phenomenon) are so rare in Homer's world (and for Homer's audience) that the *hapax* requires a gloss: Menelaus follows ἐνηείη with an explanation ('for', γὰρ): 'Patroclus knew *how* to be kind' (ἐπίστατο μείλιχος εἶναι) – 'to all' (πᾶσιν). In his kindness therefore he is also unique in his comprehensive compassion. Amidst the war and the valorisation of violence, Patroclus is marked out as extraordinarily empathetic, capable of universal kindness that reaches beyond the bonds of male friendship: it is not just Achilles who receives his compassion but it is available and offered to everyone (hence Menelaus' use of the indefinite pronoun (τις, 'each person' or 'any person') and third person imperative (μνησάσθω, 'remember')). Commentaries allow the significance of these lines to slip away; Edwards dismisses their thematic import by designating the use of the hapax legomenon ἐνηείης for Patroclus as motivated by 'artistic reasons' (Edwards 1991: 127). This vague concession entirely misses the force with which Homer trumpets the singularity of Patroclus and his distinctive quality. After all, kindness and its acts are of marginal importance within Homer's world, animated as it is by the pursuit of personal distinction on the battlefield and (agonistic) honour.

In her focus on Patroclus' singular kindness and her attempt to turn this easily overlooked and, in Homer, marginal quality into a central criterion of excellence, Miller joins other recent creative endeavours that subject Homeric values and martial ethos to a searching critique; but she does so on terms that are as rare and unique as Patroclus' hallmark in Homer. Other attempts at revisiting the ethics of the *Iliad* and providing an updated understanding of its characters have largely been concerned with the violence of Achilles and the validation of his victims. Both of these approaches have worth; but neither allows genuinely new understandings of the *Iliad* or its characters to emerge: it is an approach to the epic that dates back to antiquity, in particular Greek tragedy.[3] Christa Wolf's 1983 novel *Cassandra*, for instance, is relentless in its portrayal of Achilles as a man with nothing but dehumanizing violence on his mind. Wolf's characterization is so focused on Achilles' depravity that he becomes sub-human and animalistic. Wolf repeatedly calls him a 'beast' or a 'brute', mimicking (and mocking?) Homer's compositional techniques with what we might call dishonourable epithets. The figure of Cassandra reduces him to something so universally reviled that even the very dirt should reject him ('Let the earth vomit out his ashes', Wolf, 1984: 122). Likewise, Jonathan's Shay's 1994 book, *Achilles in Vietnam,* sees war veterans as comprehending themselves and their reactions to the violence surrounding them through the prism of Achilles' bestial battle lust (Shay 2003: 82). And even Pat Barker's *The Silence of the Girls* (2018) gives centre-stage to Achilles and his brutality, starting with the programmatic opening lines:

> Great Achilles. Brilliant Achilles, shining Achilles, godlike Achilles . . . How the epithets pile up. We never called him any of those things; we called him 'the butcher.'
>
> Barker 2019: 1

For a narrative that has the stated purpose to centre the victims of the war, and therefore the victims of Achilles, the girls of the novel's title are already subordinated to that single facet of Achilles' characterization. Barker's novel is driven by the violent aftershocks of war. Miller's work, in opposition to these briefly mentioned examples, has rejected the easy path of focusing on a dehumanized Achilles, nor is he made redundant. But he is displaced from the centre, making space for a fresh reading of his and Patroclus' character and their relationship, which allows a strikingly original re-evaluation of the Homeric system, while finding the cue for it in Homer's own text. Miller's alternate vision embraces not only original narrative aspects of the *Iliad,* and ancient works meditating on the Iliadic narratives, but also specific lexical choices on Homer's part to reframe the entire poem and our received understanding of its story. She allows the reader to see just how much Patroclus, and his *ability* to succeed as a man by being kind, matters to us all.

*

In Miller, Patroclus has a proud father, an impaired mother, and he explicitly lacks Achilles' most famous physical virtues, the virtues which Achilles needs to maintain his position as *aristos Achaiōn*:

> When I was delivered, a boy, he plucked me from her arms . . . In pity, the midwife gave my mother a pillow to hold instead of me. My mother hugged it . . . I became a disappointment: small, slight. I was not fast. I was not strong. I could not sing. The best that could be said of me was that I was not sickly . . . This only made my father suspicious.
>
> Miller 2011: 1–2

So, what does Miller allow Patroclus? She allows him gentleness. The final paragraph of the short first chapter is taken up with Patroclus' only memory of time with his mother. It is marked with his care and consideration for her: she enjoys the ripples from skipped stones so he chooses rocks from around her feet 'careful not to disturb them' and appreciates that he is 'good at this' (3). Although literally he is referring to the ability to skip stones, what he is really good at is finding what brings his mother joy and providing it, despite his father's disapproval. This disapproval is focused on the mercy that Miller has Patroclus show at a young age, mercy that would be shunned in these martial dynasties.

*

In book 23 of the *Iliad*, Patroclus' ghost appears to Achilles in his grief and reminds him of their shared history. Part of this history is the reason why they spent their childhood together: Patroclus' accidental murder of a peer, the 'son of Amphidamas' (Hom. *Il.* 23.87), an act that brought such shame that he was exiled to Peleus' court to be raised. The incident is a fleeting handful of words in the *Iliad*; even Homer's Patroclus' regret amounts to little more than 'but I didn't mean it' (he describes his flash of violence as οὐκ ἐθέλων, 'unwilling' (Hom. *Il.* 23.88)). In Miller, the account of the death of the named Clysonymus takes two full pages, with the moment itself described with horror:

> I planted my hands on his chest and shoved, as hard as I could. Our land was one of grass, and wheat. Tumbles should not hurt. I am making excuses. It was also a land of rocks. His head thudded dully against stone, and I saw the surprised pop of his eyes . . . I stared, my throat closing in horror at what I had done.
>
> *Miller 2011: 16*

The effects of the incident on Patroclus' character are resounding: the accidental homicide traumatises the boy, but also endows him with a strong sense of personal responsibility. The sequence of events that leads up to the death deserves close attention as it is such a watershed moment in the biography of Miller's Patroclus. First, Miller highlights Patroclus' resentment at his powerlessness despite his royal status, 'He didn't bother to threaten me . . . I should be worth threatening' (16). This resentment, a lack of charity to another, fuels the frustrated push that he gives the boy which unluckily causes his death; the emotional effect on the young Patroclus is violent and immediate ('Sometime later, they found me . . . I was limp and pale, surrounded by my own vomit', 17). And the event continues to haunt him for the rest of his life. Miller goes out of her way to highlight the lasting impact that this moment of resentment has on Patroclus' already strong empathetic tendencies. He suffers from nightmares about it ('That night I dreamed of the dead boy, his skull cracked like an egg . . . When my eyes dragged closed again, he was waiting for me still, covered in blood', 22; 'The boy came, night after night, with his staring eyes and splintered skull', 24), which alienate him from his fellow exiles and foster sons, and enhance his solitude ('No one spoke to me. I was easy to ignore', 23).

*

Madeline Miller has herself acknowledged that *The Song of Achilles* takes its lead from many sources beyond the *Iliad* and can be viewed as a patchwork of myth, allowing her to draw on many mythic threads to achieve her narrative goal.[4] Achilles' time on Skryos is not mentioned in the *Iliad* but it was a known part of his myth and found its most striking Roman articulation in Statius' *Achilleid*. Miller includes the episode in *The Song of Achilles* to explore both the positive and negative limits of extreme, or all-encompassing, empathy. In Statius, Deidamia's rape is a key narrative moment, and he paints her as quickly complicit in the 'relationship' that Achilles has imposed upon her (Stat. *Achil.* 1.662–74). It is described as 'the crime that both now shared' (669). After all, for the Romans, 'rape is a problem of male self-fashioning, not female victimization' (Heslin 2005: 275). Miller rejects Deidamia's passivity in favour of exploring the emotional nuances of sexual advances in complicated power dynamics:

> Almost, I fled. But I could not bear to see her face broken open with more sorrow, more disappointment – another boy who could not give her what she wanted. So I allowed her hands, fumbling a little, to draw me to the bed . . . I will not say I was not aroused. A slow climbing tension moved through me. It was a strange, drowsy feeling, so different from my sharp, sure desire for Achilles. She seemed hurt by this, my heavy-lidded response. More indifference. And so I let myself move, made sounds of pleasure, pressed my chest against hers as if in passion . . . Afterwards we lay breathless, side by side but not touching. Her face was shadowed and distant, her posture strangely stiff. My mind was still muddied from climax, but I reached to hold her. I could offer her this, at least. But she drew away from me, and stood, her eyes wary . . . I did not understand what she had wanted; I only knew I had not given it.
>
> *Miller 2011: 139–40*

Miller's Deidamia operates within the same power dynamic as mythic Deidamia – she is the daughter of a king and therefore has a certain amount of limited agency. The agency she does possess plays itself out in the sphere of marriage and childbearing. When Miller's Achilles is deposited at Deidamia's father's court by his mother, Thetis, disguised as a woman (just as in the *Achilleid*, Stat. *Achil.* 1.338–62), only Deidamia knows initially. She proceeds to fall in love with Achilles and they have sex, with Achilles consenting only owing to his mother's insistence. Deidamia conceives Pyrrhus, but Achilles shows a distinct lack of interest throughout their relationship, which frustrates and confuses Deidamia, who is unable to explain to herself why Achilles is not attracted to her. Deidamia's desperation increases with Patroclus' arrival: in his disguise as 'Pyrrha', Achilles claims Patroclus as his husband, thereby forcing Deidamia out of their false relationship (2011: 122).

Deidamia's sense of self-worth, and her social status, reside in her need to be desired by men. She intuits that Achilles, despite the sex, does not desire her (he says of the encounters 'I did not want it . . . I did not like it', 127) and turns to Patroclus in pursuit of self-validation. What Patroclus is demonstrating with his kindness is how, at its limit, that same kindness equates to emotional blindness. Miller makes the 'invented' sexual encounter between Deidamia and Patroclus (it has no precedent in our ancient sources) an episode of co-violation. Both actors in the scene are catastrophically in the wrong with regards to the other: Miller has Deidamia place Patroclus in a situation in which if he refuses sex she will accuse him of rape (137) and Patroclus is so enmeshed in his attempts to be understanding and kind to everyone that he causes Deidamia fresh harm whilst recognising and yet embedding further the trauma she has suffered in her relationship with Achilles. He completely fails to anticipate (and, afterwards, to fully understand) the damage he inflicts on Deidamia, just as he fails to see how she has violated him. Miller is careful to hide the extent of Patroclus' blunder from his own narratorial voice but not from the reader. His ignorance of the unequal power dynamic between them – that as a man he automatically wields more power than Deidamia – and his blindness towards the abuse he suffers perpetrated by Deidamia – coming as it does as a result of his enormous emotional miscalculation – leaves his actions understandable, if not completely blameless.[5] Miller doesn't assign guilt or question intentions but allows her Patroclus the space to be more than a paragon of virtue, showing her readers that being the best is not the same as being perfect. In Miller, this episode illustrates an extreme example of how kindness can bring both triumphs and tragedies.

*

One of the true triumphs of Patroclus' kindness, from Homer on, is his relationship with Briseis. In spite of being the catalyst for the tension of the *Iliad,* Homer only allows a brief insight into her thoughts on her situation once Patroclus has died. In her lament she affords him the honour of implying that her grief at his loss is comparable to the grief she felt at the loss of her husband and brothers (Hom. *Il.* 19.291-4), suggesting Patroclus had a significant impact on her sense of safety when enslaved among the Greeks (Dué 2002). However, it is her final two lines that summarise the root of her particular grief for this dead man among the many dead men she has known: he was 'always kind' (μείλιχον αἰεί, Hom. *Il.* 19.300).[6] In this, Miller has a foil to the tragedy of Patroclus' kindness to Deidamia, which allows her to expand upon the Homeric precedent and explore how the extreme sensitivity built into Patroclus' characterization can positively impact a different kind of woman. In the world of the *Iliad,* Briseis' worth was confined to her body at the moment of her enslavement. Her relevance as a woman with noble status by either birth or marriage is completely erased. She is no longer reliant on an internalized patriarchal need to prove sexual desirability; in an oxymoronic fashion her enslavement frees her to benefit from Patroclus' kindness. The two find release in still moments together:

> There was a peace in sitting beside her, the waves rolling companionably over our feet. Almost, it reminded me of my mother, but Briseis' eyes were bright with observation.
>
> *Miller 2011: 218*

Briseis and Patroclus' first meeting in *The Song of Achilles* is an emblematic moment for Patroclus' willingness to recognize the full humanity of anyone he meets. According to the conventions of Homeric society, there is no requirement for him to recognize the enslaved Briseis as a fellow person with a distinct identity above and beyond her status of 'property' of her master. But he introduces himself in respectful terms and is rewarded with her saying her name in return (217). The early stages of their friendship are sketched in terms of Patroclus' patience with her unfamiliarity and inability to communicate: he makes time for them to just be silent in each other's company (and explicitly likens these moments to the peaceful memory of his mother), and puts effort into helping her learn Greek (218). Patroclus' time with Briseis affords him positives too. In her presence he feels he can escape from the reality of the looming danger of their situation: 'It was easy, in those moments, to forget that the war had not yet really begun' (220). As we have already seen, Miller's Patroclus' commitment to empathy for all does have its pitfalls. In the instance of Briseis, it leads him to make the mistake that everyone, including those he most loves and admires, will operate in a similarly humane fashion. He assumes that because Achilles remembers parts of the tales that Briseis tells around the fire this somehow equates to Achilles acknowledging her humanity as Patroclus had done ('I was pleased, I felt that he had seen her, had understood why I spent my days with her when he was gone', 238). However, he thereby wilfully ignores what ought to have been blatantly obvious to him, namely that the only other person Achilles is interested in recognizing the worth of is himself, Patroclus. This sets the scene for him showing Achilles what it truly means to be the best.

*

Miller's version of Agamemnon's claiming of Briseis illustrates both how poorly the pride of Achilles serves him and how willing Patroclus is to sacrifice *his* pride in the service of another's wellbeing.[7] In the *Iliad,* Briseis is at the centre of the contest of honour between Agamemnon and Achilles. Agamemnon is the leader of the entire Greek army and heroic in his own Homeric right but, still, Achilles is the best in terms of sheer physical prowess. Agamemnon's desire to impose his power upon Achilles in order to dim his light is baldly stated in his intention to take Briseis, Achilles' chosen prize. The words Homer gives Agamemnon are simple, conveying the violation of honour Agamemnon intends: 'I myself will go to your tent and take fair cheeked Briseis, your gift of honour' (Hom. *Il.* 1.184–5).

Miller orchestrates an extra element to Agamemnon's snatching of Achilles' 'prize' in order to highlight the empathy Patroclus feels for Briseis. In the process she sets up Patroclus to undermine the power of the Homeric conception of *kleos*. Patroclus is aware that Agamemnon's intention will be to rape Briseis and that Achilles will take that as justification to kill Agamemnon. So, he 'betrays' Achilles by going to Agamemnon and warning him, with a blood oath, that that will be the outcome (275–8). He can't retrieve Briseis because of Achilles' pride but he can shield her with the threat of Achilles' violence. The question that hangs between Achilles and Patroclus is why, between the two of them, only Patroclus is capable of the humanity and care for his fellow man that requires that personal honour be superseded:

> 'Her safety for my honour. Are you happy with your trade?'
> 'There is no honour in betraying your friends.'
> 'It is strange,' he says, 'that you would speak against betrayal.'

There is more pain in those words, almost, than I can bear. I force myself to think of Briseis. 'It was the only way.'
'You chose her,' he says. 'Over me.'
'Over your pride.' The word I use is hubris. Our word for arrogance that scrapes the stars, for violence and towering rage as ugly as the gods.

Miller 2011: 280

Miller's Patroclus explicitly separates friendship and honour, devaluing the latter by placing them in hierarchy, and implicitly links honour and pride together as less noble attributes. This exchange leads Miller's Achilles to voice that central question of both the *Iliad* and the purpose behind *The Song of Achilles*' Patroclean kindness: what makes a man the best of the Achaeans? Achilles tells Patroclus that this disregard for both his own and Achilles' honour in favour of friendship makes Patroclus 'a better man than I' (281). Miller does not give Briseis the uninterrupted lines of speech over Patroclus' corpse that are all that the *Iliad* allows her character, but she does use the moment to have another voice oppose the idea that Achilles is *aristos Achaiōn*. When Achilles finds Briseis performing funeral rites he orders her away and Briseis challenges Achilles' selfishness:

'Do you think you are the only one who loved him?'. . . 'He was worth ten of you. Ten! And you sent him to his death!' . . .
'You have never deserved him. I do not know why he ever loved you. You care only for yourself!'

323–4

As Patroclus and Briseis' relationship was not hampered by gendered societal expectations (Briseis did not require Patroclus' sexual desire and Patroclus applied his extraordinary empathy to a willing recipient), Miller uses their friendship as a vehicle to redefine for the reader what a broader understanding of *aristos* might, and should, be.

*

Patroclus, in both the *Iliad* and *The Song of Achilles*, has a special skill that allows for an uncomplicated exploration of one facet of his kindness: his aptitude for healing. Learned directly from Chiron in Miller and from Achilles who learned it from Chiron in Homer (cf. Hom. *Il.* 11.831-2), it affords Homer and Miller an easy win in Patroclus' gentle, selfless characterization (Hainsworth 1993: 311). At the conclusion of *Iliad* book 11, Patroclus is on an important, if marginally servile, errand. As he sprints through the camp to Achilles he bumps into a limping Eurypylus, an arrow sticking out of his thigh (Hom. *Il.* 11.810), and Eurypylus explicitly begs his help. Patroclus allows that he is in a rush and in the same breath, almost as though he is talking to himself to confirm his own value system, declaring 'I will not abandon you in your distress' (11.841), *even* when acting at Achilles' behest. What follows is a specific list of actions that Patroclus takes to leave Eurypylus in a stable and safe condition on his way to recovery (the medical validity of this A&E to-do list has been evaluated and ratified by contemporary trauma care experts: Koutserimpas, Alpantaki and Samonis 2017). He leads him to Eurypylus' hut and lays him down (11.843), cuts out the arrow (11.844–5), washes the wound (11.845–6), applies a herb with implied coagulant and painkilling benefits (11.846–7), and the scene closes on an overly optimistic note, 'the blood stopped flowing' (11.848), the looming threat of the Trojans momentarily forgotten in the triumph of Patroclus' care.

Miller translates this episode conspicuously faithfully in *The Song of Achilles*:

Ahead of me, a young man struggles to stand on an arrow-pierced leg. Eurypylus, Prince of Thessaly. I do not stop to think . . . and carry him to his tent.

Miller 2011: 303

At the sight of Eurypylus struggling, Miller's Patroclus also feels no hesitation in where his immediate duty lies: 'I wind my arm under his shoulder'. Even the physical specifics come straight from Homer: 'and grasping below the chest' (καὶ ὑπὸ στέρνοιο λαβὼν, Hom. *Il.* 11.842). Miller's Patroclus also takes up a knife, uses it to remove the arrow, and binds the wound (2011: 303). The difference between the Homeric and Miller episode is that Patroclus' skill in Miller is more realistic: 'He will live, or not, by the will of the gods. I have done all I can' (304), and her chapter ends with fresh blood spouting, rather than ceasing (305). Miller faithfully reconstructs the Eurypylus episode as another example of how Patroclus' kindness – his attitude of care for his fellow man coming so naturally to him – is already an acknowledged, if hitherto underappreciated trait, in the epic.

*

An overarching theme of *The Song of Achilles*, then, is a quiet renegotiation and at some level also refutation of orthodox Homeric ideology: Miller has an agenda to prove that a value system centred in the pursuit of *kleos* through supreme prowess in warfare is outmoded. The ways in which Patroclus demonstrates his kindness clarify her purpose: to show that *kleos*, and its accompanying benefits, have been misapplied to Achilles. Her novel critiques the lack of appreciation down the millennia for the Patroclean man. At the close of *The Song of Achilles,* Miller crystallizes her argument by focussing on how very replaceable the traditional heroic pursuit of *kleos* can make a man.

It is Thetis who communicates the redundancy of holding Homeric *kleos* in *The Song of Achilles,* when she confronts the grief-stricken Achilles, paralysed by his mourning over Patroclus' body:

'This is not my son.'
His chest heaves. 'Then who is it, Mother? Am I not famous enough? I killed Hector. And who else? Send them before me. I will kill them all!'
Her face twists. 'You act like a child. At twelve Pyrrhus is more of a man than you.'
'Pyrrhus.' The word is a gasp.

'He will come, and Troy will fall. The city cannot be taken without him, the Fates say.' Her face glows.
Achilles stares. 'You would bring him here?'
'He is the next Aristos Achaion.'
'I am not dead yet.'
'You may as well be.'

Miller 2011: 330

Thetis, as a goddess, makes perfect sense to deliver the brutality of the meaninglessness of Homeric *kleos*. In *The Song of Achilles* she is repeatedly set up in opposition to Patroclus as the two represent the warring sides of who Achilles can be. Patroclus consistently appeals to Achilles' human emotions and his empathy, and Thetis consistently requests he rejects them as signs of weakness and hindrances to his advancement as the greatest of the Greeks. Thetis is now emblematic of how narrow the Homeric honour system and lineage can be at its extreme. Achilles' son by Deidamia, Pyrrhus, has been raised by Thetis and is literally waiting to step into his father's shoes; he can do so with almost no narrative break, because the characteristics that Achilles has been taught to prize, and by extension the audience of the epics have also been indoctrinated in, are transferrable in their entirety. What makes Achilles so apparently great in the *Iliad* is that he is a little bit better at doing what every other hero does. He is fast*er*, strong*er*, *more* efficient. His abilities do not sit in contrast to other heroes, who are fast and strong and kill efficiently; he is the pinnacle of a pile of similar men and by that logic he can be replaced as soon as someone just a little fast*er*, just a little strong*er*, just that bit *more* efficient in war comes along. Patroclus, however, was explicitly designated as unique in the *Iliad*, and retained that individual honour. The epics are not full of heroes designated kind. No other hero has all of the qualities that Patroclus has; he remains distinguished for a characteristic that is not particularly valued and so is not sought by those seeking Homeric honour and notoriety. It is Patroclus' ability to empathise, singled out by Menelaus in Homer, that affords him true fame in Miller's novel.

*

Miller designates Odysseus as the mouthpiece of her novel's message:

'Patroclus was no commoner . . . He killed Sarpedon, second only to Hector.'
'In my father's armour. With my father's fame. He has none of his own.'
Odysseus inclines his head. 'True. But fame is a strange thing. Some men gain glory after they die, while others fade. What is admired in one generation is abhorred in another.' He spread his broad hands. 'We cannot say who will survive the holocaust of memory . . . We are men only, a brief flare of the torch. Those to come may raise us or lower us as they please. Patroclus may be such as will rise in the future.'

Miller 2011: 347

In *The Song of Achilles*, Odysseus goes to Pyrrhus to ask that Patroclus' name be included on Achilles' memorial as a reflection of the wishes of both men; Pyrrhus refuses on the grounds that his father's reputation should not be lowered by such direct acknowledgement of his relationship with one he conceives of as a servant. Miller's presentation of *kleos* here anticipates recent scholarly investigations into Homeric fame: '[*kleos*] breaks the present into a 'now' of action and 'another time' for the meaning of that action . . . every present loses its self-identity' (Li 2022: 71). Pyrrhus, as the embodiment of Homeric *kleos* taken *ad absurdum*, cannot perceive the value of a man beyond the suffocating bounds of the epic honour system. Miller needs to ensure that her argument, that it is Patroclus' unique kindness that makes him the best of the Achaeans and the rightful heir of the level of fame bestowed on Achilles for millennia, cannot be misconstrued or mislaid amidst the narrative device of telling the tale of Patroclus and Achilles' love. Miller pre-empts and embeds the future into Odysseus' voice. She has rectified the wrong done to the oft overlooked figure of Patroclus and restored his fame as understood in a contemporary key. For Miller, and so for her resurrected and re-valued Patroclus, kindness ensures the true *kleos*.

Notes

1. Translations are my own unless otherwise indicated.
2. For a thorough and succinct examination of both *kleos* and what it means to be *aristos Achaiōn* and the interplay between the two concepts see Nagy (1999), particularly pp. 26–41.
3. Callen King argues that the 'Achilles ode' in Euripides' *Electra* 'transforms Achilles' career from an example of human achievement to a paradigm of inhuman destruction' (King 1980: 212).
4. 'In . . . *Achilles* I drew on many traditions, cross-referencing and interweaving multiple sources' (Miller 2022: 51).
5. With echoes of Lucretia's story: see Glendinning (2013: 64–8) for the trope of the unavoidable stain of rape.
6. Butler argues that there need be no relationship definition in Homer, for the depth of the emotion conveyed meets the audience's needs for understanding (Butler 2016: 28).
7. For the negative connection between *biē*, 'violence', and *hubris*, 'pride', in Homeric heroes see Nagy (1999: 318–19).

CHAPTER 11
VOICES OF RECOVERY IN JOSEPHINE BALMER'S *THE PATHS OF SURVIVAL*
Sheila Murnaghan

Josephine Balmer's *The Paths of Survival* is a sequence of poems about a text that survives from antiquity only in fragments: *Myrmidons*, the first play in Aeschylus' lost trilogy based on the *Iliad*. Brief one-to-two-line snippets from the ten surviving fragments of *Myrmidons* are interspersed with twenty-eight longer poems that give voice to an array of figures who played some role in the generation, preservation, or destruction of the play as a written text. The sequence moves backwards in time from the librarians who rescued ancient texts from the bombed national library in Baghdad in 2003 to Aeschylus himself revising the play just before his death in 456 BCE. These figures – some real historical people, some imagined – encompass scribes, monks, lexicographers, translators, archaeologists, anthologists, book collectors, book discarders, various military conquerors of Alexandria, crusaders, modern fighter pilots, all of them male, with just one exception, the twentieth-century Italian papyrologist Medea Norsa. As in a tragic plot, accidents of fortune play a large role in the story of this play's survival. A papyrus is destroyed when Norsa's house in Florence is hit by an allied bomb in 1944, but after her death a transcription of it shows up unexpectedly among her papers. A complete copy of the *Lexicon* attributed to the ninth-century BCE Byzantine patriarch Photius, found in a Macedonian monastery in 1959, is the only source for a particular line that identifies both the author and the play and so reveals that the line belongs to *Myrmidons*.

Like the history of its survival, *Myrmidons* itself was notably male-dominated.[1] From what we can tell, it was one of the relatively few classical Athenian tragedies with no female characters. The play dramatized Achilles' stubborn withdrawal from battle and ended with him learning the news of Patroclus' death and grieving over it. *Myrmidons* has been an object of particular interest ever since antiquity for two reasons: the first, which was made fun of by the comic playwright Aristophanes (*Frogs* 911–15), is that Achilles spent a large portion of the beginning of the play in silence, only breaking into speech when the action was well under way; the other is that Achilles' relationship with Patroclus, presented in the *Iliad* simply as close comradeship, was overtly erotic; this is clear from the few lines of his impassioned lament that survive. In the context of the fifth-century Athenian culture in which the play was composed and first received, the erotic bond between comrades-in-arms was represented positively, as a precipitating factor in the hero's return to battle and so to his recovery of his proper role as a member of his community.

Superficially then, this collection tells a story that is very much about men: it offers a history lesson about the fortunes of the written word in multiple arenas from which women have traditionally been excluded, including not only war and politics but also authorship and scholarship. Over a long span of time, diverse male agents engage in forms of action that are variously destructive, productive, or protective as the struggles of an epic warrior are succeeded by the creative expression of an Athenian playwright, which in turn gives way to the random gestures and acts of self-assertion, selfless devotion, and casual indifference that impede or advance the play's survival. In a shift of focus reminiscent of the progression from the *Iliad* to the *Odyssey*, survival in the face of hostile external forces emerges as a new arena of male heroism.

This focus on male actors sets *The Paths of Survival* apart from the most familiar traditions of women's rewriting of the classics. A point of comparison, or even counterpoint, to Balmer's project, can be found in a key programmatic statement for women's revisionary myth-making that also foregrounds survival, that of Adrienne Rich in her seminal essay 'When We Dead Awaken.'

> Re-vision – the act of looking back, of seeing with fresh eyes, of entering an old text from a new critical direction – is for us more than a chapter in cultural history: it is an act of survival. Until we understand the assumptions in which we are drenched we cannot know ourselves. And this drive to self-knowledge, for women, is more than a search for identity: it is part of our refusal of the self-destructiveness of male-dominated society.
>
> *1979: 35*

For Rich, women's remaking of classical works involves self-assertion and identity formation, and the trauma that it overcomes is that of the persistent sexism enshrined in and perpetuated by old texts. Her vision is realized in the extensive and growing body of literature in which women writers have reimagined the female characters of mythology. Prime examples include the pioneering works of the American modernist poet H.D., the many poems by twentieth-century women poets centred on Penelope, or the recent surge of novels retelling classical myths from the perspective of female characters who play minor roles in canonical texts, including Madeline Miller's *Circe* and Pat Barker's two recreations of the experience of Briseis, *The Silence of the Girls* and *The Women of Troy* (to choose just a few that are prompted by the Homeric epics).[2] In those works, as Alicia Ostriker puts it in her similarly foundational essay 'Thieves of Language,' 'the old stories are changed, changed utterly, by female knowledge of female experience, so that they can no longer stand as foundations of collective male fantasy' (1982: 73).

Balmer's focus on the preservation of an old text through a series of chapters in cultural history rather than its re-vision, is at first glance a very different endeavor: the trauma whose survival she is concerned with is the loss of something precious, rather than the damage done by toxic values, and so her concern would seem to be not with the re-vision of an ancient work but with its recovery. But in fact *The Paths of Survival* actually has many more points of contact with that body of women's writing, and especially women's revisionist poetry, than might at first appear. These shared features are by no means exclusive to women's rewriting or to women's poetry in general, but they are such notable and persistent constituents of that revisionary tradition that they constitute a kind of feminist poetics.

One such feature is the displacement of the personal onto the classical. While the manifestos of Rich and Ostriker emphasize the refreshing conversion of ancient stories into accounts of real modern women's real experiences, classical content has also served women writers as a cover for accounts of personal experiences and feelings, or what Elizabeth Dodd (1992) has called a 'veiled mirror' in her study of this phenomenon in the works of H.D., Elizabeth Bishop, Louise Bogan and Louise Glück. Balmer, who has often written and spoken about the connections between her work as a translator and adapter of classical texts and her own life, has identified *The Paths of Survival* as the work she wrote between the unexpected death of her mother and *Letting Go* (2017b), an explicit sequence of mourning sonnets about that death (2020: 79). Exploring the double loss reflected in the near disappearance of a classical masterpiece, and in that text's account of a warrior mourning his dead lover, was for Balmer then an indirect path towards a more direct expression of her own loss. And this is not the first time she has made such use of expressions of grief by male classical poets, as she discusses in her self-reflective study of the relationship between translation and creative writing, *Piecing Together the Fragments* (2013: 183–9), especially in relation to her collection *Chasing Catullus* (2004). The bypassing of gender, and with it a far-too-simplistic model of identification, in order to draw on male-authored expressions of grief by classical poets is something that Balmer shares with, among others, Anne Carson, who in *Nox* approaches the loss of her brother by drawing on Catullus' poem about his own dead brother, and Alice Oswald, who in *Memorial*, extracts from the *Iliad*'s busy plot an extended lament for fallen warriors. When being a survivor is understood in relation to the loss of a beloved person rather than, in Rich's terms, in relation to the annihilating force of patriarchy, the voice through which it is conveyed no longer needs to be female.

Beyond that point of autobiography, *The Paths of Survival* itself has the displacement of personal feelings onto ancient texts, whether thought of as accounts of particular mythic scenarios or as material objects, as a persistent theme. Throughout the sequence, Balmer records both the protective role of such forms of distancing and, even more pointedly, their unreliability, documenting the unexpected ways in which old texts can unlock intimate and immediate feelings.

In the final poem of the sequence, tellingly entitled 'Aeschylus' Revision', Balmer reimagines *Myrmidons* itself as a veiled expression of Aeschylus' own grief for Cynaegirus, the exceptionally brave fighter at Marathon who is generally remembered as Aeschylus' brother, but whom Balmer makes into a lover instead (so that she herself echoes Aeschylus by intoducing homoerotic desire into literary history much as he introduced it into the epic tradition). Remembering Cynaegirus' death at his side on the battlefield, Balmer's Aeschylus recalls:

Afterwards, numb, I wrote *Myrmidons*,
never able to admit it was for him
struggling to give my Achilles words.

Balmer 2017a: 76

Now, years later, close to the point of death, he reworks the play as an open admission of his feelings:

> I take out my stylus and begin to strike;
> now I must emend, I must speak out,
> acknowledge to myself, to the living
> and to the dead, if they still care or listen:
> *my love, remember all the nights we shared.*
>
> 77

In the centuries that follow, the scholar's diversion of emotion into attachment to old texts is no protection when those texts become themselves the victims of warfare, as we see with Medea Norsa, the papyrologist. For Norsa the bombing of her house summons up an 'ascending scale of affection' (Kakridis 1949: 58) reminiscent of Andromache describing to Hector in *Iliad* 6 (411–30) why he is the only person left in her life or Antigone in Sophocles' *Antigone* explaining why her brother is the only person for whom she would have taken the risky action that she did (904–15).

> I didn't think of the house I had
> just lost, not even a prayer – God
> forbid – for the beloved sister
> who's shared it all these years,
> (no need to panic for the husband
> and children that were never there,
> the family sacrificed for Greek
> that hadn't filled it, never would)
> this fear was for a thin glass case,
> scrap of papyrus pressed between,
> marbled, translucent, bled at the edge
> like collector's rare butterfly wing.
>
> 19

That same scrap of papyrus acquires an even more urgent significance because of what it has meant the man who excavated it twelve years earlier, a gay student gladly escaping the homophobia of Florence for the backwater of Oxyrhynchus, the Egyptian town where a large trove of ancient papyri was found:

> I was only too happy to keep
> my head down, hands in muck
> and silt.
>
> 22

But this provides is no escape, as one of his finds unexpectedly calls him to action.

> And then, like the first flicker
> of smoking fire, slow to take,
> I found a tattered word: *Antelexa*:
> My heart turned over, I knew it:
> **speak out. oppose. dissent.**
>
> 22–3

Antelexa, the word that directs this student to speak out, comes from a fragment in which Achilles acknowledges to Phoenix, an envoy sent by the Achaean leaders to persuade him to return to battle, that he himself has said nothing. In the Loeb edition by Alan Sommerstein, the fragment reads 'I have [lo]ng been silent and [made] no [reply nor (?)] spoken in opposition' where 'spoken in opposition' translates *antelexa* (Sommerstein 2008: 139). Through a twentieth-century student's personal dilemma, Achilles' admission of silence on the topic of his return to battle is transformed into a summons to forthright speech in the face of bias and oppression; answering this summons ultimately proves fatal for him, since back in Italy he is killed by a homophobic mob.

In a twenty-first century context, the animating power of even the inert materials that carry dead languages is acknowledged by the librarians of Baghdad who need to explain why they are saving texts when people are dying. The poem in which they do so was inspired by a remarkable photograph of the salvaged texts from that library (Figure 11.1). To those librarians, the folded leaves of text themselves appear as new lifeforms.

> They seemed like something living:
> fungus on an oak, the pleated folds
> of open mushroom cup, organisms
> that were once books, manuscripts,
> now debris of 'precision' incendiary.
>
> 14

As the passages quoted so far make clear, the collection is a series of dramatic monologues. A number of critics including Isobel Hurst (2019: 182–3) and Balmer herself (2020: 78) have noted that the dramatic monologue is a form that is, again, by no means exclusive to women poets, but that has proven especially conducive to revisionary mythmaking by such writers as Augusta Webster, Amy Levy, H.D., Judith Kazantzis and Carol Ann Duffy, offering an apt medium for the voicing of silenced and marginalized women. While Balmer is not re-imagining the stories of ancient women through the perspectives of a modern woman, her poems do work in a similar way. Each of her disparate voices testifies to a particular time and place and set of circumstances, but all speak in the same idiom; all are filtered through the sensibility of the collection's modern author. As Balmer herself points out, this means that all are expressions of a woman's perspective: 'I was … writing a feminised text, viewed through the lens of a woman's consciousness, that of its writer. And so, rather than trying to present a crude impersonation of each character, each voice became merged with my own, transforming male history' (2020: 90). The self-consoling words that she ascribes to a

Figure 11.1 Ashes of books in the Iraqi National Library, Baghdad, April, 2003, photo © R. Lemoyne.

Byzantine scribe who watches with horror the looting of his city by the Latin invaders of the fourth crusade, 'Where they had greed, we had Greek', take on a new contrapuntal poignancy as they 'echo not only my own longing to learn Greek as a woman, but the long, long struggle of all women to gain access to the language (see Prins [2017])'.

Even the crudest destroyers of texts are to some extent transformed and recruited into Balmer's project of humane witness and preservation. In 'Amr's Last Words', Amr ibnal-Asi, the seventh-century BCE Arab conqueror of Alexandria, believed to have destroyed the last remaining secular Greek works in the library there, recalls the Ptolemies' assiduous book-collecting, and summons up his own book-burning in words that resonate with the Baghdad librarian's account of the effects of 'precision incendiary'.

> The tragedies of the Greeks were first.
> I can hear the crack of curled papyrus,
> still smell that acrid, smouldering ash.
>
> 39

The allied airman who drops the bomb on Medea Norsa's house is given the same poet's eye for metaphor we see in the comparison of damaged texts to a butterfly's wing or a mushroom cup. As he looks down at where his stray bomb has fallen,

> I saw it fall, a grey speck on a single house.
> For a moment I thought of my baby son

as smoke spiralled up like umbilical cord.
For his sake there had been no time to fuss,
our mission had been achieved without loss.
*Targets: both destroyed. Stray objects hit: one.
Ground casualties: not known. Job: well done.*

21

Not only is this entire sequence of mostly male voices bound together by Balmer's own sensibility, but the collection also documents her identity as a poet who works at the boundary between literary translation and creative writing. This too is not an exclusively female position, but nonetheless has a distinct place in the tradition of women creating classics, with H.D. and Anne Carson as especially distinguished examples. And Balmer herself has been eloquent in championing informed and creative translation as a feminist practice alongside the more prevalent reimagining of archetypal women from classical mythology (Balmer 2013: 48–9). The sequence of dramatic monologues that make up *The Paths of Survival* represent not only a history of the play's fragmentary preservation but also an autobiography of its contemporary reconstitution in the form of a translation. This is anticipated and fulfilled in the 'Proem' and 'Epilogue' that frame the sequence – nominally paratextual material that should not be underrated, especially given that Balmer herself has devoted considerable critical attention to the genre of the 'translator's statement' as a form in which 'translators become characters in their own narrative' (2013: 1–56, 229).

The proem, which is entitled 'Final Sentence' and set in 'the present day' in the Sackler Library in Oxford (since renamed the Bodleian Art, Archaeology and Ancient World Library), records the author's own inspiration, in particular the connection she makes between the loss of ancient texts and the deaths of human beings, and her impulse to reconstruct the process of transmission:

Still I am drawn to it like breath to glass.
That ache of absence, wrench of nothingness,
stark lacunae we all must someday face.

I imagine its letters freshly seared;
a scribe sighing over ebbing taper . . .

11

The 'Epilogue' is Balmer's own translation of all the surviving fragments of *Myrmidons*. Despite its title, this is hardly an afterthought or a straightforward scholarly appendix. Rather it represents the culmination of the whole collection, in which the scattered fragments are brought together and given new life by that particular author in a work of the present day. Ostensibly the oldest poem in a sequence that moves back in time, and the one with an identifiable ancient author, it is also the newest and the most original, a work of reception that takes note both of the fragmentary play's long history of transmission and interpretation and of its contemporary context. It fulfils Balmer's stated claim that the classical translator should draw on both scholarship and the intervening legacy of an ancient text 'to pull that text apart and put it back together in an entirely different way' (2013: 232); in fact it represents a literal fulfillment of the vision announced in the title of the metapoetic study/manifesto in which she makes that claim, *Piecing Together the Fragments*. At the same time, it also fulfils Alicia Ostriker's vision of 'the old stories ... changed ... by female knowledge of female experience' (1982: 73). Aeschylus' play may remain a work about male characters, but in Balmer's version it is infused with a woman's perspective as mourner, as helpless witness to the destructiveness of war, as struggler against silence, and as empathetic observer of the traumatic silence imposed on gay men at certain times in history.[3] She incorporates modern responses to the *Iliad*'s account of male heroism and repositions *Myrmidons* as a more pointed and more necessarily courageous breaking of silence about same-sex desire than it was in its own day.

The translation opens with the first surviving fragment, which happens to preserve the opening lines of the play. These are chanted by the chorus of Myrmidons, Achilles' followers, who complain to him about the toll on them of his absence from battle. Here Aeschylus uses a distinctive element of his dramatic medium, the chorus, to introduce explicit friction between Achilles and the ordinary Achaeans who are the principal victims of his withdrawal but who do not have a voice in the *Iliad*. This is how these lines read in Sommerstein's Loeb translation:

> Do you see this, glorious Achilles –
> the toils of the spear-ravaged Danaans,
> whom you are betraying by sitting idle within
> your hut ... ?
>
> *Sommerstein 2008: 137*

Balmer's version of the chorus' reproach is inflected by even more critical modern perspectives on the Achilles story and on the effects of important men's wars on ordinary soldiers:

> ... Do you see, Achilles –
> This is the sweat of war, the way it is;
> We all pay the price of your politics.
> Think of the men betrayed, spear fodder,
> Sacrificed while their own commander
> Sulks, safe in his tent ...
>
> 78

Balmer chooses not to translate the epithet Aeschylus applied to Achilles, *phaidimos*, which Sommerstein renders as 'glorious'; for the 'spear-ravaged' soldiers, she uses the resonant phrase 'spear fodder', with its connotation of ordinary soldiers sacrificed to the interests of the powerful; and she introduces the conventional, pejorative English term of art for what Achilles does in his tent: 'sulks'.

The new resonances acquired by these fragments in the final translation have developed throughout the preceding sequence. In one poem Balmer projects in her own English words the thrilled reaction of the poet and librarian Callimachus when the text of *Myrmidons* is delivered to the Alexandrian library, 'here were the Greek prows at Troy, torched/ as Achilles sulked', and so slyly retrojects that conventional characterization of Achilles onto a privileged moment of ancient reception. Because she repurposes fragments from the play to introduce groups of poems within the sequence, those fragments have acquired additional new associations by the end of the volume. Following on the passage just quoted, the chorus continues to reproach Achilles with words that the reader has already encountered at the beginning of a section labelled 'Victors'.

> When you hear
> The clash of battle, of slaughter,
> When you hear of men suffering
> Why do you not come to their aid . . .
>
> 37

In that two-poem section, 'Amr's Last Words' is preceded by a poem entitled 'Gloss' in the voice of the ninth-century BCE Byzantine patriarch Photius. Photius glosses the rare word from *Myrmidons* preserved in his *Lexicon*, *abdelukta* – defined by the Liddell, Scott, Jones Greek lexicon as 'not to be abominated' – as '*Above blame*' and '*Absent of guilt*' and applies it to the bloody religious schism of his day: 'Any heretics tortured/ maimed' and 'All Jews slaughtered' (38). When those words reappear as the chorus' reproach to Achilles, the implications of his self-seeking failure to act have deepened and extended into subsequent historical eras.

The voice of Balmer's gay Italian excavator makes itself heard in the fragment that he supposedly discovered. In the Loeb translation, Achilles' response to Phoenix remains simply an acknowledgement of failure to answer his fellow Achaeans' pleas for his return to battle, 'I have [lo]ng been silent and [made] no [reply nor (?)] spoken in opposition,' but Balmer gives it an entirely new valence.

> But enough is enough. I have stayed
> Silent [for too lo]ng. No more [slurs
> to crush the tongue. No more slander].
> Time now to protest, to dissent.
>
> 80

The play's potential as a defence, rather than simply a portrayal, of same-sex desire is also seen in Balmer's translation of the line that is ascribed to the play in Photius' lexicon, in a citation for the rare word *abdelukta*, 'not to be abominated'. In that line from

Myrmidons, Achilles, while touching or even kissing the corpse of Patroclus declares, in the Loeb translation, 'And yet to me, because I love him, this is not loathsome (*abdelukt' emoi tade*).' In her version, Balmer transfers that rare word from whatever action was being performed to the identity of the speaker, Achilles, and expands upon it:

> Yet for me there is no stain, no sin –
> I am absolved because I loved him . . .
>
> 82

The refusal of 'sin' here is particularly notable, since an important strand in the story of the play's transmission concerns Christian censorship or sometimes simply Christian indifference to pagan culture. Balmer conjures up such an act of censorship in connection with the curious accident of literary history that the line containing *abdelukt'* is attributed to *Myrmidons* only when cited by Photius. She imagines the compiler of the one other text in which the line is preserved, a nineteenth-century Oxford scholar and cleric, John Anthony Cramer, deliberately suppressing such a scandalous blot on Aeschylus' reputation.

> *I am absolved because I loved him* –
> a reference if I was not much mistaken,
> to the unspeakable vice of the Greeks.
> In Aeschylus! I copied author and play
> then scratched them out. Better not to say!
>
> 26

Balmer's simultaneously learned and imaginative response to a lost work of ancient drama is ultimately a dramatization of her own activity as a translator – an activity that is itself a form of revision, in a role that cannot be disentangled from those of scholar and original poet. By playing all of these roles, in a sequence of poems supposedly about men, she performs her own acts of survival within an ongoing tradition of women re-making the classics.

Notes

1. For the surviving fragments of *Myrmidons*, see Sommerstein (2008: 134–49); for an overview and analysis of the play, see Michelakis (2002: 22–57).
2. On H.D. and the classics, see Gregory (1997), Murnaghan (2008); for the rich tradition of Penelope poems by twentieth-century British and American women writers, see Murnaghan and Roberts (2002), Doherty (2008), Hurst (2009).
3. As she describes in *Piecing Together the Fragments* (2013: 177–83), Balmer made similar use of the wrenching deaths of Homeric warriors to address the toll on gay men of the AIDS crisis in 'Fresh Meat', an adaptation of the *Iliad*'s account of the death of Hector and foretelling of the death of Achilles that was included in *Chasing Catullus*.

CHAPTER 12
WRONGFUL CONVICTION: ODYSSEAN POSSIBILITIES IN TAYARI JONES' *AN AMERICAN MARRIAGE*

Justine McConnell

Tayari Jones' 2018 novel, *An American Marriage*, winner of the Women's Prize for Fiction, both is and is not an *Odyssey*. While the Homeric epic is an intricate intertext for the narrative, as Jones has highlighted in interviews,[1] the primary context of the novel concerns a debilitating aspect of contemporary society in the United States: what Michelle Alexander has termed 'the New Jim Crow'. The statistics around the imprisonment of Black men in the United States are staggering, and as Alexander has compellingly argued, analysis of that nation's criminal justice system reveals that mass incarceration is 'a stunningly comprehensive and well-disguised system of racialized social control that functions in a manner strikingly similar to Jim Crow' (Alexander 2012: 4). Jones' novel tells the tale of a young African American couple ripped apart by his wrongful conviction for a rape he did not commit. It is a story that, in its proximity to a pattern of real-life events that has devastated so many communities, could seem to be trivialized by a focus on its connection to ancient myth. Yet such a perspective would reveal more about long-standing dismissals of the value of myth than about the power of dialogues between contemporary issues and ancient myth, as Jones herself, and writers such as Ralph Ellison, Toni Morrison and Fran Ross before her knew all too well.[2]

Those interested in Graeco-Roman antiquity tend to valorize myth, but the word itself has, since Herodotus at least, denoted a story that can be contrasted with a more 'true' or 'knowable' one, a *logos* (Puhvel 1987: 1).[3] Yet as the persistence of myths over time and space indicates, they narrate tales that are 'true' at a level more fundamental than that of fact: the power of myth comes from its ability to tap into and embody truths in a way that allows them to travel and transform while retaining the capacity to illuminate contexts far beyond those in which they were developed.[4] Indeed, one of the primary facets of myth is its malleability. Myths shift and change to meet the needs of new contexts. This, of course, is part of why the array of artistic works responding to myth has always thrived and why that generative output is the subject of so much scholarly work on classical reception.

Tayari Jones' novel is in dialogue with Homer's *Odyssey*. However, rather than deciding to rewrite a mythic tale for the modern era, the connection Jones develops seems to spring from her recognition of kernels at the heart of the myths of Odysseus and Penelope which, when dislocated from ancient Greece, still resonate powerfully with the twenty-first-century separation of a husband and wife for reasons beyond their control. It is a point worth stressing, I think, because it simultaneously reminds us that what is at stake in the narrative of this novel is more urgent than myths of supernatural encounters and divine manipulators, but also that the Homeric myths offer a way to confront and comprehend the realities of contemporary inequities that may be otherwise almost too hard to gaze upon.

Through its dialogue with the *Odyssey*, *An American Marriage* offers a corrective to the ancient epic's narrative and focus. As Adrienne Rich declared in her renowned 1972 essay, 'When We Dead Awaken: Writing as Re-Vision', 're-visioning' is 'the act of looking back, of seeing with fresh eyes, of entering an old text from a new critical direction' (Rich 1972: 18). That 're-visioning' is, Rich asserted, 'an act of survival' (Rich 1972: 18). In Jones' hands, the re-visioning of the *Odyssey* takes the narrative of Odysseus' absence and adventures from one that pivots almost exclusively around the male hero to one that recognises and exposes the impact that such an absence has on an entire community. Jones' story is not just that of her Odyssean protagonist, Roy; nor even does it extend that outlook only to encompass his wife, Celestial, alongside his viewpoint. Rather, *An American Marriage* creates space for the story of the husband and wife, a suitor-figure (Andre), and the families of Roy and Celestial. If the novel is an *Odyssey*, it is one that contests the idea of an eponymous protagonist and instead, as Jones' title indicates, focuses on the relationship between him and his wife (the 'marriage' of the title), and on wider society ('American' of the title).

This does not mark a radical break with its Homeric precedent, of course: the *Odyssey*, too, is concerned with the effects of Odysseus' absence on Penelope, Telemachus, Laertes and Anticlea, as well as on Eumaeus and Eurycleia, and wider Ithacan society embodied by the suitors in his palace. But where the *Odyssey* highlights the exceptionalism of its hero and his experiences, *An American Marriage* lays bare the prevalence of wrongfully incarcerated African American men in a criminal justice system underpinned by racist ideology (Alexander 2012). Where Penelope's reaction to Odysseus' return is famously hard to discern, Jones gives equal space to Roy's and Celestial's perspectives through the sections they narrate and their letters to each other as well as granting the 'suitor' Andre a role as narrator, too. Tayari Jones thereby contributes to the ever-expanding afterlife of the *Odyssey* by homing in on the stories and characters that the epic gives only fleeting glances of.[5]

While the overarching trajectory of Roy and Celestial's relationship in *An American Marriage* might suggest a radical diversion from the Homeric precedent, given that – ultimately – they do not end up together, it could also be seen as amplifying the quiet suggestions of the *Odyssey*'s 'reverse similes' (to draw on Helene Foley's work, 1978). As their relationship deteriorates while Roy is in prison, Celestial finds herself not only expected to remain faithful to him but also to maintain their household. In a twenty-first-century context, she does not have the luxury of quietly weeping for her husband and preserving their home passively by refusing the advances of suitors; instead, she must make a living, to support both herself and Roy (since she continues to put money into his prison account to enable him to buy basics such as underwear (2018: 45)), while also being expected to reject the advances of potential lovers.

When Odysseus and Penelope are finally reunited in Homer's epic, the moment is marked by a striking 'reverse simile' in which Penelope is identified with the kind of trials from which Odysseus has just emerged:

ὡς δ' ὅτ' ἂν ἀσπάσιος γῆ νηχομένοισι φανήῃ,
ὧν τε Ποσειδάων εὐεργέα νῆ' ἐνὶ πόντῳ
ῥαίσῃ, ἐπειγομένην ἀνέμῳ καὶ κύματι πηγῷ·
παῦροι δ' ἐξέφυγον πολιῆς ἁλὸς ἤπειρόνδε
νηχόμενοι, πολλὴ δὲ περὶ χροΐ τέτροφεν ἅλμη,
ἀσπάσιοι δ' ἐπέβαν γαίης, κακότητα φυγόντες·
ὣς ἄρα τῇ ἀσπαστὸς ἔην πόσις εἰσοροώσῃ,
δειρῆς δ' οὔ πω πάμπαν ἀφίετο πήχεε λευκώ.

23.233-40

           As welcome as
the land to swimmers, when Poseidon wrecks
their ship at sea and breaks it with great waves
and driving winds; a few escape the sea
and reach the shore, their skin all caked with brine.
Grateful to be alive, they crawl to land.
So glad she was to see her own dear husband,
and her white arms would not let go his neck.

Wilson 2018: 502[6]

This identification of Penelope with Odysseus' experiences highlights their *homophrosyne* ('like-mindedness') in Homer.[7] Yet, it can also be seen as planting the seeds that take root in Jones' novel, in which it is the husband who is immobile (as a result of his imprisonment) and the wife who has remarkable experiences (Celestial's dolls become very successful, with her being awarded a National Portrait Museum prize for one of them (2018: 62-7)). Neither Homer's nor Jones' narratives overlook the fact that both partners endure trials over the course of their separation, but Jones' grants equal space to both, and extrapolates from the *homophrosyne* of Homer to an equality between Roy and Celestial. This equality is not only at the intellectual level but also at the level of action: there may be an expectation that Celestial remains faithful to Roy, but her developing romantic relationship with her childhood friend Andre is judged scarcely more critically in the novel than Odysseus' relationships with Circe and Calypso. This is, in both ancient and modern cases, partly because those extramarital relationships are narrated primarily through the voice of the unfaithful spouse, who garners their audience's sympathies; it is also because the novel confronts the double standard that allows Roy to cheat on Celestial before he is incarcerated,[8] but expects her to remain faithful over the course of a prison sentence that is initially set at twelve years. Where Homer's 'reverse similes' give the audience fleeting glimpses of an imagined gender equality, Jones' novel actualizes that equality in Celestial's work and her relationship with Andre.[9]

Although Roy, adopting an attitude he acknowledges as old fashioned (2018: 12), had wanted to support Celestial financially, his incarceration compels her to take on the bread-winning role that Roy had cast as male. She does so in a way that, again, aligns her with Penelope, but as with the enlargement of the female role throughout Tayari Jones' novel, so too does Celestial's work take Penelope's to a new level. For while Penelope spends her day weaving a shroud for her father-in-law (unpicking it at night to delay the moment when she must choose a suitor once the shroud is complete), Celestial makes a living sewing dolls. As Jones has remarked, 'My heroine, Celestial, is Penelope, only modern, independent, and famous for her art' (2019). Both characters employ traditionally female handiwork with culturally specific resonances, as Penelope and Celestial take their place in the traditions of ancient Greek weaving and African American quilting, respectively.[10] The two female characters create art replete with storytelling potential (in the narrative stitched into the shroud, and in the dolls who, as imagined little people, are bursting with potential stories), but while Penelope's art looks backwards to the past by creating a shroud for the older generation, Celestial's is forwards-looking, both in the idea of dolls being played with by children, and of the dolls themselves being figured as little children.

Yet in both, too, there is an aspect of obstruction and unfulfilled potential: Penelope keeps unpicking the shroud and Laertes is, anyway, not yet dead; Celestial's dolls are intricate, expensive creations made to be looked at not played with, and their physicality and proliferation come to serve as a tragic reminder of the children Roy and Celestial have not had and the pregnancy that Celestial terminated soon after his arrest. In one of her letters to Roy while he is in prison, Celestial recounts making a doll for his mother, Olive, based on a baby photo of him:

> She [Roy's mother] even provided your original outfit. It was surreal, dressing the doll in the clothes your mother had intended for her grandson to wear.
>
> *Jones 2018: 61–2*

Since, even before Olive's commission, Celestial's dolls are modelled on her image of Roy, they initially seem to figure as forerunners of the children the couple hope to have.

However, when Celestial and Roy show his mother one of the dolls near the start of the novel, she instantly recognises him in it and asks if she can buy it. Eager to please, Celestial offers to give it to her despite the fact that it is a special commission for the mayor of Atlanta and is worth $10,000. It is an episode that stages a familiar tussle between in-laws as each repositions themselves in relation to the other following the marriage. When Roy explains that the doll is far too expensive for Olive to buy, she scoffs at herself and relinquishes it, but the imagery of her actions is unwittingly foreboding:

> 'Of course,' she said, folding the blanket over the doll like a shroud. 'What do I need a doll for? Old lady like me?'
>
> *2018: 17*

Given the Odyssean allusions of the novel, the doll's blanket-shroud takes on a new significance. Not only does it mark Olive's acknowledgement that Roy is grown up (with the blanket-shroud a symbolic reference to the end of a relationship in which he is primarily dependent upon her), it also proffers a tentative connection between the shroud the Homeric Penelope weaves and the dolls Celestial makes. In keeping with this sense that it is Celestial who will make Roy (as she makes the dolls that look like him), there is a disruption of generations and familial relationships that will be magnified by Roy's incarceration. The doll's shroud points to an inversion of the generations and the absence of children for Roy and Celestial. And while Celestial's business flourishes during the time that Roy is in jail and she even creates a doll dressed in prison uniform (2018: 64), she does not mention him publicly. Read as a counterpart to the *Odyssey*'s husband-wife dynamic, Roy is silenced while Celestial speaks; read as a contestation of the historical silencing of Black women, Celestial becomes – to echo the words of Patricia Hill Collins – 'one voice in a dialogue among people who have been silenced' (Collins 2000: ix). Contesting too neat a parallel with Homer, however, Tayari Jones gives the reader Roy's voice in the sections he narrates and the letters he writes, unlike Homer who keeps Penelope's thoughts camouflaged.[11] Knowing the oppressive nature of silencing, Jones does not merely invert the Homeric dynamics of speech and silence, but rather creates space and voices for both wife and husband, as Celestial and Roy carve out their stories even in the face of a despotic and prejudiced criminal justice system, their narratives standing as acts of resistance.

Another striking way in which Celestial becomes an embodiment of the hints offered in the *Odyssey*'s 'reverse similes' is in her relationship with Andre. Very little negative judgement seems to attach to Odysseus' infidelities with Circe and Calypso in the Homeric epic. In Celestial's relationship with Andre, the reader encounters the moral judgements of both Celestial's father and of Roy himself, but neither are unalloyed moral stances: Celestial's father believes she should remain married and faithful to Roy primarily because, by his imprisonment, he has become a figure of resistance against white supremacy (2018: 192);[12] Roy has already admitted to his own extramarital flirtations at the start of the novel, so his expectations of Celestial approximate towards a double standard. The novel, meanwhile, particularly by its multi-perspectival structure, refuses to direct the reader towards any simple moral judgement: we are compelled not only to see the individuals within the story, but to see the world through their eyes and voices, and that focalisation mitigates against moral censure.

While Odysseus' relationships with Circe and Calypso are exceptionalized by their immortal status and their presence in the fantastical world of the adventures he narrates in books 9–12,[13] it is primarily Odysseus' male gender that allows him to behave in a way that would be deemed unacceptable for Penelope within the constraints of Homeric society.[14] In keeping with the imaginative elaboration of the lives gestured towards in the *Odyssey*'s 'reverse similes', Celestial's relationship with Andre might be regarded as a gender-switched echo of those between Odysseus and Circe and Calypso. If Jones' novel is read with the *Odyssey*'s 'reverse similes' in mind, Andre and Celestial's relationship becomes a continuation of the mapping of Penelope/Celestial onto the figure of the wandering and absent husband. The effect is not only a feminist re-vision of the *Odyssey*'s dynamics of gender roles but also highlights that, while Roy is absent as a result of his incarceration, it is Celestial who is moving (both literally and figuratively). Like the ancient Penelope, Roy can only watch time pass and strive to keep things as unchanged as possible while Celestial has freedom of movement and the possibility to forge her own path, which the novel depicts her doing.

Part of that new path is the divergence of Celestial's trajectory from the model of the questing hero set by Odysseus. Jones has not merely flipped the gender roles, placing Celestial in the position of the Homeric Odysseus and giving her a narrative of adventure that ultimately leads homewards, instead she grants to Celestial the possibility to forge her own path, both professionally and within her personal life. This is developed throughout and exemplified by the novel's conclusion, where it is Celestial and Andre, not Roy and Celestial, who are a couple.

Carolyn Heilbrun's influential essay 'What was Penelope Unweaving?' suggested that, as well as a delaying tactic, Penelope unweaves the shroud each night because she does not have a pattern of a female narrative to follow:

> During the years between the end of the Trojan War and the suitors' discovery of her unweaving, Penelope has been trying out stories on her loom. She unravels each night what she has woven that day, not only for delay, but also, metaphorically, because unlike other weavers, she is not writing a story of male violence, but the story of woman's free choice, and there is no narrative to guide her.[15]

In one sense, Celestial replicates this pattern: each doll she makes is an altered version of the last and so contains and emanates a different story. Yet, unlike Penelope's unweaving, each of the 'stories' Celestial tries out are seen through to the end and remain as completed narratives, embodied in the finished figures of the dolls. While, following Heilbrun's reading, Penelope struggles to find the 'right' story for a female hero because there have been no models for her to follow, Celestial's dolls articulate that there are a multitude of stories and paths that women can pursue in the modern era.[16] It is an ethos that Andre echoes for men when he reflects on his experience of going to Morehouse College, a leading men-only HBCU (Historically Black College and University) in Atlanta:

> Morehouse was a good fit, teaching me that there were dozens of ways to be a black man. I only had to choose which one was right for me.
>
> *2018: 98*

Celestial's mode of storytelling via the dolls takes poignant shape when she transforms the doll she has been making for Olive.[17] From one modelled on Roy's baby photos, Celestial creates a prisoner-doll:

> I stripped the doll out of the john-johns and used wax cotton to make a diminutive pair of prison blues. Dressing the dolls in these clothes was just as difficult, but it felt more purposeful. In the baby clothes, it was only a toy. In the new way, it was art.
>
> *2018: 64*

This account is penned by Celestial in a letter to Roy; his horrified reaction is exacerbated by the fact that she does not reveal to anyone that her husband is imprisoned and is the inspiration for the doll. He has become, he fears, emblematic for her, rather than an individual. In dialogue with the *Odyssey*, one could see here another instance of Roy occupying a position most similar to Penelope's: the latter as the 'patient wife' and the former as a wrongfully imprisoned man whose experience has come to serve as art. In both cases, the ancient Penelope's and the modern Roy's, the emblematization of each highlights the centrality of the figures of Odysseus and Celestial. This is notwithstanding the fact that it is Roy who opens the novel, and who shares fairly equal space with Celestial in terms of narrative voice (with only smaller sections being voiced by Andre). Yet, as Tayari Jones has revealed, she originally wrote the novel only from Celestial's perspective and only brought in the voices of Roy and Andre at a later stage (Adewunmi 2018). A trace of this persists productively in the published version, not least because – even taking into account the plethora of recent rewritings of Greek myth and epic from a female perspective[18] – it remains a less familiar narrative.

One other key trope within Tayari Jones' novel that consolidates its elaboration of the potential of the 'reverse similes' in Homer is the hickory tree that stands between Celestial's and Andre's childhood homes. It brings to mind Laertes' orchard and the way he shows Odysseus around it in the final book of the *Odyssey*, not least because when Celestial's father gives her and Roy the house in which she had grown up, 'the only string attached was that Old Hickey couldn't be cut down' (2018: 233). Again, Celestial occupies the traditional place of Odysseus, thereby rejecting patriarchal lineages that prioritise father-son relationships over all others, and in doing so, paving the way for a re-visioning of the Homeric epic that has thrown off the restrictions of long-established gender roles.

That same tree, affectionately known as Old Hickey, simultaneously and even more sustainedly, evokes the other prominent tree in the *Odyssey*: the one that Odysseus used as a bedpost when he constructed his and Penelope's marital bed. Throughout the novel, trees serve as allegories for relationships:[19]

> Marriage is like grafting a limb onto a tree trunk. You have the limb, freshly sliced, dripping sap, and smelling of springtime, and then you have the mother tree stripped of her protective bark, gouged and ready to receive this new addition . . .
>
> In my marriage, I never determined which of us was rootstock and which the grafted branch.
>
> *2018: 110, narrated by Celestial*

But with Old Hickey, the Homeric resonance simultaneously alerts the reader to the fact that their Odyssean expectations will not be fulfilled because it is something that Celestial and Andre, not Roy, share. Celestial, mistakenly, believes that she can leave Old Hickey behind when she contemplates moving elsewhere with Andre (2018: 226). Yet, at the novel's close, she and Andre are still there, and Roy confesses, 'I was even jealous of that tree' (2018: 303), acknowledging the way in which the tree stands in for the relationship between Celestial and Andre, its roots deep.[20]

It is this living symbolism of Celestial and Andre's relationship that drives Roy to attack the tree with an axe (2018: 269–70). The specification that he uses a double-sided axe again has a double resonance with the *Odyssey*, recalling both the contest in which Odysseus shoots an arrow through the twelve axe-heads to beat all the suitors in the competition for Penelope's hand in marriage,[21] and his horror when he believes that someone may have moved his bed by cutting the tree trunk that forms one of the bedposts.[22] In *An American Marriage*, as Roy attacks the tree, he is in the position of Odysseus' imagined usurper, a man cutting at the trunk of the olive-tree bed while the rightful husband is away. At this moment, the repositioning of the novel's opening seems complete: Roy has become the outsider in the marriage, making the more binding relationship that between Andre and Celestial. As Roy recounts the episode, the anthropomorphization of the tree serves to emphasize even further its identity as a figuration of Andre and Celestial's relationship:

> Six long strides put me at the base of the massive tree. I touched the rough bark, an instant of reflection, to give Old Hickey the benefit of the doubt. But in reality, a hickory true was a useless hunk of wood. Tall, and that's all . . . Nobody would ever mourn a hickory tree except Celestial, and maybe Andre.
>
> *2018: 269–70*

One more moment remains, again troubling the mythic template by resonances that can mislead the reader's expectations. Despite Roy's attack on Old Hickey, despite the ways in which the Homeric intertext at that moment cast him as the interloper, it is Andre who retires from the scene and Celestial and Roy return indoors to the home they had once shared. That first night, like Penelope and Odysseus reunited,[23] they pass the night awake, sharing stories of their time spent apart (2018: 286, 290–1); but unlike the Homeric couple, they do not make love and, though they spend one more night together, they are never reunited.

The realignment of relationships that is confirmed by those two nights spent together had, in fact, been signalled earlier in the novel by another pair of oblique allusions to the myth of Odysseus and Penelope. After Roy is released from prison, Andre drives to Louisiana to tell him that he and Celestial are now together. As Celestial says goodbye to Andre, she reflects that she does so 'like [she] was sending him off to war' (2018: 211). This is echoed a little later by Roy as he ruminates on his relationship with Davina, a high-school friend who he meets on his release from prison and spends a passionate few days with before driving to Atlanta to see Celestial. As he meets Celestial once more, Roy recalls Davina as a woman 'who welcomed me with accepting arms and a feast fit for a man home from the war' (2018: 239). In both cases, the woman is figured as Penelope; but Celestial's Odysseus-figure is Andre while Roy's Penelope turns out to be Davina.[24] Roy takes some time to realise that, but it is a recognition that all four characters have reached by the end of the novel.

The novel's epilogue serves as a kind of postscript to the story, skipping ahead in time a little while reverting to a narrative mode told via letters between Celestial and Roy, just as they had corresponded while he was in prison. Celestial and Andre are together, as are Roy and Davina. In what reads as a nod to epic's ring composition, the novel closes with Roy reflecting that he is home, providing a kind of response to his declaration in the opening lines that,

> There are two kinds of people in the world, those who leave home, and those who don't. I'm a proud member of the first category . . .
>
> Celestial thinks of herself as this cosmopolitan person, and she's not wrong. However, she sleeps each night in the very house she grew up in. I, on the other hand, departed on the first thing smoking, exactly seventy-one hours after high school graduation.
>
> *2018: 3–4*

In these opening lines, with their consideration of what it means to be home, one comes to recognize that the refusal of pre-established gender roles has underpinned the novel from the start, alongside a rejection of the tropes of canonical retellings of myth. This is a novel that troubles Joseph Campbell's too-rigid notion of the monomyth (2008), even while it conforms to that most characteristic of mythic traits: the malleability to be remade constantly to meet the demands of new contexts.

Tayari Jones' re-envisioning of the *Odyssey* is scattered through *An American Marriage* but does not predominate. When Adrienne Rich declared re-envisioning of old stories to be an 'act of survival' for women (1972: 18), it was as a mode of resistance:

> We need to know the writing of the past, and know it differently than we have ever known it; not to pass on a tradition but to break its hold over us.
>
> *1979: 19*

In Celestial, Tayari Jones presents a Penelope-figure who embodies the Penelope that is indicated by the 'reverse simile' in book 23 of the *Odyssey*, and realises her potential. This is a version of 'know[ing] the writing of the past, and know[ing] it differently', but the context of 'the new Jim Crow' against which Jones' novel is set makes that 'survival' even more potent and urgent. Jones' re-envisioning is both itself 'an act of survival' (in Rich's terms) and depicts characters doing all they can to survive, breaking against the bounds of literary and societal expectations. Audre Lorde spoke of 'the transformation of silence into language and action' (1984: 40–4); in Celestial, Jones has taken the Homeric

Penelope and done exactly that, creating a new Odyssean narrative for twenty-first-century America.

Notes

1. See, among others, Abigail Bereola (2018) and Tayari Jones (2019), in which Jones also observes that 'Every book I have written harks back to the Greeks'.
2. I have in mind here the Odyssean intertext of Ellison's *Invisible Man* (1952), Toni Morrison's engagement with Graeco-Roman antiquity throughout her oeuvre, and Fran Ross's rewriting of the myth of Theseus in *Oreo* (1974). On Ellison, see Rankine (2006) and McConnell (2013); on Morrison, see Roynon (2013), and McConnell (2016); on Ross, see Mullen (2002).
3. For an outline of this debate and the importance of recognizing that Herodotus' distinction is not so much between true and false stories as between ones that he can verify ('know') or not, see Fowler (2011).
4. See, for example, Lévi-Strauss (1955: 430) – 'Whatever our ignorance of the culture and the people where it originated, a myth is still felt as a myth by any reader throughout the world. Its substance does not lie in its style, its original music, or its syntax, but in the *story* which it tells.'
5. This aspect of classical reception is a prominent one, with modern rewritings often telling the stories that remain tantalizingly undeveloped in the ancient material. See Murnaghan (2011: x) on the ways in which the *Odyssey* invites such dialogues by its panoply of characters who must (in all senses) 'recognize' Odysseus: 'hints of other stories and other viewpoints have, in turn, helped to foster the poem's vigorous afterlife'. In the context of reimagining the figure of Penelope, see Hall (2008: 120).
6. Incidentally, Tayari Jones (2019) lauded Emily Wilson's translation of the *Odyssey* as 'breathtaking'.
7. See, for example, Podlecki (1971: 90) and Murnaghan (2011: 103–4).
8. Jones (2018: 10): 'The truth was straightforward: I liked the ladies. I enjoyed a little flirtation, what they call *frisson*. Sometimes I collected phone numbers like I was still in college, but 99.997 percent of the time it ended there. I just liked to know that I still had it. Harmless, right?'
9. For discussion of other modern works that also play with the *Odyssey*'s gender roles, see Gardner and Murnaghan eds (2014: 4–5), and Pache (2014).
10. See, for example, Bergren (2008) on ancient Greek weaving and Callahan (1987) on African American quilting.
11. On Penelope, see (for example) Winkler (1990: 129–61), Katz (1991: 77–113) and Felson-Rubin (1994).
12. As Andre muses, 'Now Mr Davenport [Celestial's father] was loyal to Roy above his own daughter. In a way, the whole black race was loyal to Roy, a man just down from the cross.'
13. See, for example, Segal (1994: 37–64).
14. On the way in which 'masculine identity [is] intertwined with feminine fidelity' and the 'unequal symmetry between identity and fidelity that dictates to each sex its defining terms', see Zeitlin (1995: 121).
15. Heilbrun (1990: 107).

16. Again, this brings to mind Patricia Hill Collins (2000: 275) on the importance of both individuality and collectivity in resisting oppression, particularly for Black women. Celestial's dolls may be seen as symbolic both of individuality (each one being hand-made and unique) and collectivity (together being recognizably her brand).
17. See above p. 180.
18. To name only a few that have engaged with Homer specifically, one may think of Margaret Atwood's *Penelopiad* (2005), Barbara Köhler's *Niemands Frau* (2007), Madeleine Miller's *The Song of Achilles* (2011) and *Circe* (2018), Emily Hauser's *For the Most Beautiful* (2016), and Pat Barker's *The Silence of the Girls* (2018), and further back, Christa Wolf's *Cassandra* (1983) and Atwood's 'Circe/Mud' poems in her collection *You Are Happy* (1974). See also, Cox and Theodorakopoulos eds (2019).
19. Another striking entanglement of trees with the relationship between Roy and Celestial is found in the name of the hotel at which they are staying when he is accused of rape: Piney Woods Inn. The name not only contributes to the novel's arboreal theme, but also intriguingly evokes the renowned Piney Woods School, founded by Laurence C. Jones in 1909 for African American students, during a period in which the South was still segregated.
20. This figuring of Old Hickey as symbolic of Celestial and Andre's relationship features in a number of pivotal moments, such as when Roy returns and Celestial feels she is duty-bound to sleep with him; she recalls 'looking out the window at Old Hickey, ancestral and silent', as Roy begins to understand that she is no longer in love with him (Jones 2018: 247).
21. Homer, *Odyssey*, book 21.
22. Homer, *Odyssey* 23.202–4.
23. Homer, *Odyssey* 23.300–43.
24. This realignment may also be seen to be prefigured in the names of the central characters, each with their Greek and Latin roots (via French, in the case of Roy), not least since Andre's name recalls the opening of the *Odyssey*: ἄνδρα μοι ἔννεπε, μοῦσα (*andra moi ennepe, mousa*) ('Tell me about the man, Muse'), and thereby positions him as the Odyssean figure.

CHAPTER 13
ANIMATING DISABILITY ARTS AND OVIDIAN METAMORPHOSIS IN KINETIC LIGHT'S *DESCENT*
Amanda Kubic

Introduction

Disability arts ensemble Kinetic Light's evening-length danced duet *DESCENT* made its world premiere in September 2017 at the BRITT Festival in Oregon; in March 2018, the work saw its East Coast premiere at New York Live Arts.[1] Kinetic Light is a gender-diverse team of disabled artists working at the 'nexus of access, queerness, disability, dance, and race', whose founding members include Alice Sheppard (she/her), the ensemble's Founder and Artistic Director and a multiracial Black woman; Laurel Lawson (flexible pronouns), Kinetic Light's choreographic collaborator, engineer, designer and dancer and a white person; and Michael Maag (he/him), Kinetic Light's scenographer and lighting designer and a white man (Kinetic Light 2024). *DESCENT*, a multimedia dance piece that takes Auguste Rodin's bronze sculpture the *Toilette of Venus and Andromeda* (1890) as its conceptual anchor, features Sheppard in the role of Andromeda and Lawson in the role of Venus. Since its premiere, the piece has been performed several times in front of live audiences and screened online for virtual audiences.[2] Choreographed with the two dancers in wheelchairs on a large custom ramp installation originally designed by Sara Hendren, Yevgeniya Zastavker and students at Olin College and further enlivened by Maag's light and video projections (Kinetic Light 2023c), *DESCENT* is a celebration of disability arts and disabled artists and, as Sheppard claims, a demonstration of how 'disability is an artistic and creative force' (Hulbert, Niedermeyer and Sheppard 2018).[3] The duet is also a celebration of 'queer, interracial' love (Kinetic Light 2023c), as we see Venus and Andromeda flee and chase, pursue and embrace, ascend and descend, and express their intimate feelings for one another through a complex choreography of desire.

DESCENT is at its heart a story about pleasure – that is, the 'pleasures of wheeled movement and reckless abandon' (Hulbert, Niedermeyer and Sheppard 2018) made possible by the transformative technologies of light, sound, ramps and wheelchairs and the innovative movement vocabularies employed by the artists. At the same time, the piece interrogates the presence of white supremacy, ableism and heterosexism in Graeco-Roman mythology and its reception. By having Sheppard embody the part of Andromeda, the artists of Kinetic Light claim to 'visually restor[e] the racial heritage' of the Aithiopian princess that 'Rodin himself erased' (Kinetic Light 2023c).[4] This heritage is evoked in classical texts like Ovid's first-century BCE hybrid epic poem *Metamorphoses* as well as his epistolary collection *Heroides* and the *Ars Amatoria*, but obscured in many post-classical visual representations of Andromeda's myth.[5] Through this process of racial reclamation and through their re-imagining of Venus and Andromeda as visibly disabled queer lovers, Lawson, Sheppard and Maag *descend* into the histories and mythologies of the classical past and bring to the surface discourses and visual portrayals of Blackness, queer desire and disability. I argue, moreover, that Kinetic Light's performance, although without explicit reference to Ovid's *Metamorphoses* in the virtual versions I have had access to, experiments like Ovid with re-imagining the aesthetics, animating powers and potentials of the body as well as the multiplicity and relationality of its composition.

In this chapter, I argue that *DESCENT* challenges notions of an idealized, normative and bounded classical body and opens up new possibilities for dance choreography and access by drawing on key principles and practices of disability arts and aesthetics as well as the complex logics of bodily metamorphosis, sculptural form and the animacy/animation of female figures that wind their way through Ovid's *Metamorphoses*.[6] In this way, the artists of Kinetic Light participate in a longer tradition of writers and artists, from Isadora Duncan and H.D. to Rita Dove, jay dodd, Fiona Benson and Nina MacLaughlin, who turn to Ovid to transform Ovid – to change his bodies into new forms.[7] I demonstrate that Ovidian figures like Venus, Andromeda, Pygmalion and his sculptural creation serve as important touchstones for analysing how *DESCENT* navigates the gendering and racialization of the body and represents simultaneously animating, animated and disabled bodies. In *DESCENT*, Kinetic Light choreographs mythic bodies in motion and in metamorphosis both as classical statues lit up and brought to life and as subjects endlessly and pleasurably in the process of becoming – becoming enlivened, becoming intimate and connected, and becoming entangled 'trans-corporeal' agents that intermesh 'embodied beings' and the material world that 'crosses through them, transforms them, and is transformed by them' (Alaimo 2018: 435). Choreography becomes an avenue through which artists like Sheppard and Lawson are moved to (re)create the classics – be it iconic classical figures, or more entrenched classical ideals of form, being and embodiment.

Venus and Andromeda: Ovidian intertexts

There is no extant myth from Graeco-Roman antiquity that portrays Venus and Andromeda together, as they are in Rodin's *Toilette of Venus and Andromeda* and in *DESCENT*. Yet it is true that both figures appear in the world of Ovid's *Metamorphoses* as women renowned for their beauty. In addition to their exceptional physical forms, Venus and Andromeda are linked in Ovid's poem via their associations with stone and the sculptural – associations that allow us to consider how artists like Ovid, Rodin and Kinetic Light render these women (in)animate through language, form and movement, and how they perceive the body as something always becoming (becoming otherwise, coming into being, becoming (im)mobile). In this section, I consider how Ovid's depiction of Andromeda in Book 4 of the *Metamorphoses* and his portrayal of Venus, Pygmalion and the artist's statue in Book 10 raise questions about women's animacy and animating power, fetishized beauty and the male gaze's potential to immobilize and reduce female bodies to aesthetic objects. In the subsequent sections, I keep following this chain of receptions and turn to Rodin's late nineteenth-century sculpture, the *Toilette of Venus and Andromeda*, which was likely inspired by Rodin's own engagement with Ovid, before then moving to examine Kinetic Light's critical and innovative engagement with Rodin in DESCENT.

In Book 4 of the *Metamorphoses*, Ovid's depiction of Andromeda, the daughter of the boastful Queen Cassiopeia and King Cepheus of Aithiopia, who is saved from the jaws of a sea monster by the hero Perseus, emphasizes her likeness to stone as she is caught in an immobilizing moment of immense trauma:

> There, Jupiter Ammon had unjustly commanded undeserving
> Andromeda to suffer the penalty of her mother's tongue;
> she whom, when Perseus, the descendant of Abas, saw her bound by her arms
> to the jagged rocks, except for the fact that a light breeze
> moved her hair and her eyes flowed with warm weeping,
> he would have thought to be a work of marble; unknowingly, he is inflamed
> and stunned and, seized by the image of the beautiful form behled,
> he almost forgets to flap his wings in the air.
>
> *Ovid,* Metamorphoses *4.670–7*[8]

On Jupiter's command, Andromeda has been chained up as a sacrifice to the sea beast, looking just like a marble statue (*marmoreum opus, Metamorphoses* 4.675) in her fearful stillness. She exists, in the words of Stephanie McCarter, on the 'brink of disempowerment' (2022: xxiii), a location familiar to many women in Ovid's cosmos caught in the male gaze. Andromeda's marmoreal appearance is inextricably linked to her physical beauty and her appeal to Perseus, who is struck by the quiet and unmoving 'image of [her] beautiful form' (*Metamorphoses* 4.676).

Indeed, Andromeda's living body is here presented as what Salzman-Mitchell describes as a 'fixed, immobile statue-like beauty that the male gaze freezes for his pleasure and delights in at the prospect of making her mobile' (2005: 79). The adjective *marmoreum* may also suggest that Andromeda's beauty is racialized in the *Metamorphoses*, coded as a kind of fetishized marble whiteness (in contrast with Ovid's depictions of Andromeda as dark-skinned in his previous works), although scholars like Bond (2017) challenge us to remember the polychromy of ancient statuary and modern constructions of race and white-supremacy that influence how we read ancient marble statues.[9] Ovid's Andromeda is thus made into a static spectacle, an inanimate and frozen female object of Perseus' desiring and potentially enlivening gaze.

And yet, Andromeda's animacy, her qualities of 'agency, awareness, mobility, and liveliness' (Chen 2012: 2) and her ability to enliven, are more complex than her statuesque qualities may first seem to imply. Indeed, she herself is not wholly inanimate, not totally stuck like stone, as her hair moves in the breeze and her eyes flow with tears. But as Chen (2012: 4) argues, animacy is 'much more than the state of being animate' – it is also the potentiality of being animated, or of animating others. It is a critical concept that allows us to think about how inanimate objects, like the wind stirring Andromeda's hair, and nonhuman animals, like the sea monster, 'participate in regimes of life (making live) and coerced death (killing)' (Chen 2012: 6). As we see in Ovid's text, even in her temporarily statuesque state when she cannot mobilize her own body because of her restraints, Andromeda does have the power to animate others. She participates in such regimes of making live and killing, as her beauty animates Perseus and causes him to become inflamed with love, falter in his flight (stunned and almost statue-like himself for a moment) and eventually rescue her from her plight by killing the sea monster. Perseus is described as *correptus* (*Metamorphoses* 4.676), 'seized' or 'swept away' by Andromeda's beauty, carried off to the point of near distraction. It is only a few lines later, when Andromeda's rescue is at hand and Perseus compels her to speak and tell him why she has been sacrificed, that Andromeda begins to break the sculptural illusion and speak, albeit indirectly, marking her first step in metaphorically metamorphosing into human flesh once again. Andromeda only moves after the sea monster is killed, her mobility and liberation from her chains contingent upon the death of the non-human animal.

Venus, too, participates in such regimes of life and death in Ovid's text and in narratives of metamorphosis that centre the concepts of beauty, subjectivity and the sculptural. While unparalleled physical beauty is one of Venus' own most memorable traits and is remarked on frequently in the *Metamorphoses*,[10] Ovid's Venus is not merely a beautiful statuesque object like the Venus de Milo, meant to be looked at passively and admired. She is a formidable goddess who exercises divine agency and animating power. One illustrative episode comes in Book 10 of the *Metamorphoses*, when Venus brings to life the beautiful sculpture of the artist Pygmalion, with which he has fallen in love. Pygmalion's desire for his statue notably appears animated by his own misogynistic disgust at the real women of Cyprus and his fetishization of the statue's virginity and shyness or modesty (*reverentia*, *Metamorphoses* 10.251), her immobility and her 'white ivory' complexion (*niveum . . . ebur*, *Metamorphoses* 10.247–8). On the goddess's festival day, Pygmalion prays to Venus that his bride be 'just like my ivory girl' (*similis mea . . . eburnae*, *Metamorphoses* 10.276), not daring to pray for the very same 'ivory virgin girl' (*eburnea virgo*, *Metamorphoses* 10.275) that he himself sculpted. Venus grants Pygmalion the favour and in fact brings the statue itself to life, pouring softness and warmth and vitality into its ivory limbs.

The scene of Pygmalion's statue's transformation from sculpted ivory to living woman shows both Venus' animating power and the statue's own complex (in)animacy at the various stages of her metamorphosis. Ovid's verses repeatedly suggest that Pygmalion's unnamed statue, while objectified by his gaze, is more than an assemblage of inanimate ivory pieces, even before she is transformed into a breathing human woman. The fact that Pygmalion's statue is made of ivory, a material that, unlike stone, comes from a living creature, imbues it with a sense of vitality from its very conception. The statue also animates Pygmalion, drawing him into her embrace and enlivening him with desire. Even before Venus brings his statue to life, Pygmalion thinks that his creation returns his desiring kisses, and he worries about bruising her soft body as if it were flesh. Ovid writes that Pygmalion tests the statue with his hands to see 'whether it be a live body or ivory' (*Metamorphoses* 10.254–5) and that he 'gives her kisses and thinks they are returned, and speaks to and holds her, / and believes that his fingers sink into the limbs he touches, / and he fears lest a bruise come upon those pressed limbs' (*Metamorphoses* 10.256–8). To Pygmalion, the ivory sculpture is always already a lively thing. And indeed, Ovid's poem is ambiguous as to when exactly the sculpture definitively comes alive. Near the conclusion of the episode, Ovid writes:

> When he [Pygmalion] returned, he sought the likeness of his girl
> and lying on the couch he kissed her: she seemed to be warm;
> his lips moved again, and he also touched her breast with his hands:
> the ivory, as it was touched, grew soft and, with its hardness set aside,
> yielded and gave way to his fingers
>
> <div align="right">Metamorphoses <i>10.280–4</i></div>

Do the figure's first signs of life occur when she is still in her ivory form, or as she begins to change into a flesh-and-blood human woman? Is it the sculptural material itself that seems warm to Pygmalion's touch, or is the statue already in the process of becoming human when Pygmalion first kisses her? When does the 'it' of immobile ivory become the 'she' of a mobile human woman, eventually able to conceive a daughter with Pygmalion? The exact point of her metamorphosis is unclear, and in fact remain unconfirmed until five lines later when the narrator exclaims 'She was a live body! Her veins, filled with a pulse, leapt beneath his thumb' (*Metamorphoses* 10.289). Her ensuing silent reactions to being kissed – blushing (*erubuit*) and raising her 'fearful eyes' (*timidum ... lumen*, *Metamorphoses* 10.293) – further confirm her transformation into a fully animate human woman, as well as her self-consciousness and alarmed awareness at being touched. As McCarter argues, such transformations in Ovid wherein there is always 'something left of the original form', something superficial or sentient that remains in the new re-shaped body, invite us to consider the relationship between the 'body, its shape, and the identity it contains' (2022: xxii). Here, Ovid blurs the line between inanimate ivory and animate flesh, and as with the myth of Andromeda presents a complex picture of the statuesque (im)mobility and idealized beauty of these women's bodies. These human-to-sculpture and sculpture-to-human transformations and the questions that Ovid's text presents about the mobility, agency and animacy of the female body in metamorphosis are reworked and complicated in Kinetic Light's *DESCENT*, as the artists reject the objectifying heteronormative patriarchal gaze in their re-animation of the work of the nineteenth-century sculptor Rodin.

Animating Rodin's *Toilette of Venus and Andromeda*

Inspired by a visit to the Cantor Arts Center at Stanford University, Kinetic Light's Alice Sheppard created *DESCENT* in collaboration with Laurel Lawson and Michael Maag as a way to think through Rodin's portrayals of beauty and 'incompleteness' and interrogate how the concept of incompleteness might inform disability arts and aesthetics.[11] As Siebers argues, disability aesthetics 'seeks to emphasize the presence of different bodies and minds in the tradition of aesthetic representation' (2005: 542) – not only healthy, beautiful, harmonious bodies of individual genius and integrity (2005: 543). While discourses of disability aesthetics may then frame incompleteness as a valuable quality worthy of representation – and indeed a quality already long present in the artistic tradition, as is clear from Rodin's corpus – works like *DESCENT* also ask us to problematize the concept, to interrogate whether incompleteness means lack or simply becoming, and to consider which bodies are perceived as incomplete and why.

DESCENT incorporates forms from over fifty Rodin sculptures into its movement vocabulary and stage design, including *The Clenched Hand* (*c.* 1885), *The Cathedral* (*c.* 1908), *The Gates of Hell* (*c.* 1880–1917), *Ugolino and His Children* (*c.* 1881–2), *The Helmet Maker's Once Beautiful Wife* (*c.* 1884–7), and *Torso of Adèle* (before 1884), with the latter two serving as 'guide spirit[s]' and movement models for Sheppard/Andromeda and Lawson/Venus, respectively, throughout the dance (Kinetic Light 2023d: 6–11). These spirit guides, or 'fetches' as Maag calls them, often exist in the form of Maag's own line drawings of the sculptures projected on an upstage screen, where they overlook, judge, mirror and even animate the actions of Venus and Andromeda (Kinetic Light 2023e: 11). Yet one sculpture in particular informs the story of transformative love at the centre of the dance: the *Toilette of Venus and Andromeda* (Hickman 2020). While it's not evident that Rodin had Ovid's *Metamorphoses* specifically in mind while crafting this piece, the artist was certainly familiar with Ovid's poetry, as is evidenced in his other works like *Pygmalion and Galatea* (*c.* 1889), *Orpheus and Eurydice* (*c.* 1887), *The Metamorphosis of Ovid* (*c.* 1886, also known as *The Satyrs*), his earlier white marble sculpture *Andromeda* (*c.* 1886, and reminiscent of Ovid's description of Andromeda as a work of 'white marble' in *Metamorphoses* 4.675) and his volume *L'Art* (1912). In this treatise, Rodin declares that he will explain how he approaches 'animating bronze' (Rodin and Gsell 1971: 68) and goes on to cite the transformations of the Naiad-nymph Daphne into a laurel tree and the woman Procne into a swallow in Books 1 and 6 of Ovid's *Metamorphoses*. He notes that while one takes on a 'covering of leaves and bark' and the other clothes herself with feathers, in these moments of transformation 'one still sees the woman which will cease to be and the tree or bird which she will become' (Rodin and Gsell 1971: 68). Rodin argues that painters and sculptors effect a similar kind of Ovidian metamorphosis when giving movement to their pieces: 'He [the artist] represents the transition from one pose to another – he indicates how insensibly the first glides into the second. In his work we still see a part of what was and we discover a part of what is to be' (1971: 69). While Rodin's use of the verb 'glide' obscures much of the violence and trauma involved in these two particular metamorphoses, his invocation of Daphne and Procne illustrates his

Animating Disability Arts and Ovidian Metamorphosis in Kinetic Light's *DESCENT*

Figure 13.1 Rodin, *Toilette of Venus and Andromeda*, modelled after 1890, Musée Rodin cast 1987, Bronze, 20 × 14 1/2 × 23 1/2 in. (50.8 × 36.8 × 59.7 cm). North Carolina Museum of Art, Raleigh, Gift of the Iris and B. Gerald Cantor Foundation, 2009.1.14. https://ncartmuseum.org/object/toilette-of-venus-and-andromeda/.

Image Description: Two female figures emerge out of a rocky base. The figure on the left crouches over the jagged rock while the figure on the right rises up and clasps her arms behind her neck. Both women are cast in dark, shining bronze.

fascination with the point of transition that we see in Ovid when the remainder of the human is still visible in the changed plant or animal form.

Rodin's *Toilette of Venus and Andromeda* likewise illustrates such a point of transition – this time from bronze to flesh, at the very moment that Rodin, as in Ovid's myth of Pygmalion, animates his sculpture. Like many of his mythic sculptures, the *Toilette of Venus and Andromeda* depicts bodies still in the process of materialization rather than as perfectly proportioned, fully formed figures like Pygmalion's ivory statue. The piece represents the instant when 'what was' and 'what is to be' (Rodin and Gsell 1971: 69) exist together, when the mineral of the past and the flesh of the future co-exist. The two female figures, Venus and Andromeda, look as if they are being pulled from the textured, roughly hewn rocky base of the sculpture, their bodies still merged with and emerging from the bronze below. The lower legs and feet of Venus – the raised figure with her hands clasped behind her neck – are still unformed, as are the legs, feet and arms of the second figure – Andromeda – who hunches over with her arm bent above her head. One could even read Rodin's sculpture of these two mythic women washing not as a metamorphosis of

195

bronze to flesh, but in reverse, much like the imagined transformation of Andromeda from woman to marble in Book 4 of the *Metamorphoses*. Venus and Andromeda, rather than labouring to separate themselves from the rocks they rest on, may very well be sinking back into those rocks and hardening back into bronze. As one can see in Figure 13.1, one figure (Andromeda, bound to the rocks as in Ovid's text) wraps one of her arms and one of her legs possessively around the rock, pressing her arms, torso, and face into it as if she were trying to reunite her body with the stone and force herself back into mineral form. Rodin's sculpture thus becomes a study in ambiguity, in that indeterminate moment of transformation. The other figure (Venus) could be rising up to embrace her metamorphosis from bronze to flesh, but it could also be that her metamorphosis and Andromeda's are flowing in the opposite direction – from living woman to alloy.

As noted by the artists of Kinetic Light, there is a tension in Rodin's piece between wholeness and incompleteness. The smooth lines of Andromeda's back and Venus' torso, face, and hair resemble the more idealized forms of beauty in classical sculpture, and yet contrast with the fact that the women are rendered imperfectly, still in a process of endless becoming, located at 'neither beginning or end, but always a middle' (Deleuze and Guattari 1987: 21).[12] Rodin's piece suggests that the incomplete, the unfinished, and the fragmentary carry their own kind of aesthetic value. His sculpture also centres the non-human material out of which these women are formed, thus reminding viewers that these are *made* figures and complicating any distinction between artificially constructed sculpture and natural human body. In this way, Rodin, as we will see with Kinetic Light, makes visible the concept of trans-corporeality articulated by Alaimo, wherein 'the human is always intermeshed with the more-than-human world' and 'the substance of the human is ultimately inseparable from "the environment"' (2010: 2). Rodin's sculpture suggests that the more-than human bronze base may be an environment endowed with its own animacy as it supports and gives life to Venus and Andromeda.[13] Bronze, unlike marble or ivory, is cast and moulded rather than chiselled, and so it can be recast. It can change and shift, giving its figures plasticity but also imbuing them with a vulnerability to erasure over time. And indeed, in *DESCENT* we see Kinetic Light conceptually recast Rodin's bronze, not to erase its form but to breathe new life into it and change its sculptural bodies into new lively forms on stage.

DESCENT: Choreographing a queer love story

Through Sheppard and Lawson's choreography and Maag's lighting and video designs, in *DESCENT* Kinetic Light enlivens Rodin's sculpture and composes a queer, interracial love story for Venus and Andromeda. As in Ovid, here too Andromeda transforms from sculptural, stony beginnings into a dynamic flesh and blood woman. By casting herself in the role of Andromeda, Sheppard, a multiracial Black woman, challenges the possible racialized implications of the term *marmoreum* (marble sculpture, *Metamorphoses* 4.675) that Ovid uses to describe Andromeda in the *Metamorphoses*, and enlivens her beyond the confines of an idealized, whitewashed and inanimate sculptural aesthetic. Sheppard's performance and her restoration of the Aithiopian Andromeda's 'racial heritage' (Kinetic Light 2023c) remind us of the complex racialized histories of mythic figures like Venus and Andromeda – whether it be the historical whitewashing of Andromeda that McGrath (1992) and Derbew (2022) interrogate or the ways that her counterpart in *DESCENT*, Venus, has been rendered throughout the centuries as both an emblematic symbol of white feminine beauty and an 'emblematic figure of the enslaved woman in the Atlantic world' (Hartman 2008: 1).[14] Yet by embodying the figure of Venus, Lawson – a genderqueer artist – also opens up the possibility of reading Venus as a genderqueer character, complicating normative and binary understandings of gender identity and representation. Kinetic Light thus explores queer, gendered and disabled embodiment at the same time that they surface hidden or erased Blackness in the myths of antiquity and interrogate historical processes of bodily racialization and in/exclusion.

Lawson and Sheppard spend over half of *DESCENT* in wheelchairs. This visual representation of physical disability itself disrupts preconceived ableist notions of aesthetic beauty, wholeness, and the physical and creative capabilities of disabled bodies. In a December 2020 after-show interview, Lawson and Sheppard emphasized that *DESCENT* was intended to craft a different image of the dancer – one who might not have the 'theoretically perfect body', but whose body is also not made decisively and tragically 'incomplete' by her disability.[15] The artists make a claim not just for disability arts, led by disabled artists and informed by practices of equity and accessibility, and but also for disability aesthetics, wherein wholeness and perfection are not the only viable standards of value. At the same time, they remind audiences that disability itself should not framed as inherently and inevitably 'lacking' these qualities. As Sheppard noted in an October 2023 artist conversation about *DESCENT*, in the dance Kinetic Light is not engaging with these kinds of 'nondisabled understandings of disability' (2023e: 16). She made clear that their work is not a justification of disabled existence to a nondisabled audience (a category in which I include myself, as a nondisabled person viewing and writing about this piece), but rather a way of speaking to people primarily in the disability community and showing 'revolutionary and vulnerable' moments of intimacy and embodiment, such as the moment of 'strapping and unstrapping' from one's wheelchair, which is brought out of the wings of the stage or dressing room and onto the stage itself (2023e: 16–17). Coco Romack (Romack and Malka 2024: 88) describes this moment of Venus unstrapping from her wheelchair as 'a seemingly mundane yet deeply intimate action known to many wheelchair users' and playfully asks, 'has the sound of crunching Velcro teeth ever sounded so hot?'

In these moments of intimacy, *DESCENT* also challenges the gaze or 'stare' typically directed at statue bodies, women's bodies (one might think here of Perseus staring at Andromeda, or Pygmalion gazing upon his creation), queer bodies, and especially the bodies of people with visible disabilities.[16] The artists of Kinetic Light use their innovative choreography to dismantle the othering, fetishizing, or voyeuristic gaze that simultaneously over-sexualizes women and queer and racialized subjects and de-sexualizes and alienates people with disabilities. As we can see in Figure 13.2, throughout the dance Venus and Andromeda direct their gaze inward toward each other, rather than out at the audience. Their loving gaze is animating, propelling them across the

Figure 13.2 Laurel Lawson and Alice Sheppard in Kinetic Light's performance of *DESCENT*. New Brunswick Performing Arts Center, New Brunswick, New Jersey. Presented by the Dance Department, Mason Gross School of the Arts, Rutgers University-New Brunswick, 2022. Photo by Jaqlin Medlock. https://www.instagram.com/p/Ct_ry9JOiYH/.

Image Description: Laurel Lawson and Alice Sheppard hold each other's forearms, chins lifted as they extend the other curved arm to the side in a counterbalance turn. Alice is a Black multiracial woman with blonde curly hair and coffee colored skin; Laurel is a white person with cropped teal hair. They both wear gray leggings and leatherlike sleeveless tops that resemble armor or petals. Projected illustrated figures dance across the purple stage as a mountain range appears, silhouetted in the sunset, in the background. Image Description courtesy of Kinetic Light.

stage and into each other's arms, much as the sight of Andromeda propels Perseus to her rescue in the *Metamorphoses*. Yet unlike Perseus, Venus and Andromeda look upon each other not as sculptural, immobile objects, but as expressive, dynamic subjects. In a way, it is the love, desire, and intimacy between Venus and Andromeda that animates *DESCENT* and that gives the dance its animating power, pulling audiences into the narrative crafted on stage, which moves through high and low points as the dance progresses.

The movement vocabulary of *DESCENT* captures moments of flight and pursuit, sexual intimacy, physical vulnerability, trust, and union between these two mythic figures. Like the figures in Rodin's sculpture, the dancers of *DESCENT* are not bound by one linear logic of metamorphosis, moving only from bronze to flesh. They, too, flow back and forth between changing material forms as they strike sculptural poses, hold them for a beat, and then shift into the next movement phrase. These moments of metamorphosis in *DESCENT* are moments of pleasure, love and liberation. For example, in one moment of the performance, we see the dancers move with the 'unapologetic abandon' promised by the dance's description (Hickman 2020), together gliding down the stage in their wheelchairs and executing a spin, curved in to face each other with their arms interlocked and turning in slow circles across the stage (Kinetic Light 2021). Here, the romantic arc of the dance reaches a turning point, as Venus and Andromeda at last come together after spending the first few movements of the dance pursuing and fleeing one another. At the very end of the dance, the last image we are left with is Venus careening down the ramp before grasping on to its edge, followed by Andromeda, who races after and launches herself onto Venus' back, her wheelchair positioned directly on top of Venus'. This final pose is the near inverse of an earlier movement phrase, which has Venus balancing on the knees of Andromeda, representing the evolving power dynamic between the lovers and the trust and vulnerability that they come to place in each other as the story progresses. The dance thus ends with a Rodin-esque tableaux: Venus and Andromeda together again, poised on a precipice.

In the same 2020 after-show interview, the artists of Kinetic Light shared that *DESCENT*, a work emerging from disability culture, tells many truths about disability that would normally be concealed, such as one's movement from the floor to the wheelchair or one's experiences of sexual intimacy. For example, in a clip of *DESCENT* 'In Process', we see an intimate moment between Venus and Andromeda as they dance without their wheelchairs. Andromeda pulls a struggling, exhausted Venus up on to the ramp by her hair, lifting Venus by the arms before moving away, which then prompts Venus to roll and grab Andromeda's ankle in a desperate attempt to hang on to her (Kinetic Light 2017: 4:39–4:56). Additionally, in the film version of the performance from 3 December 2020, Venus and Andromeda have an implied erotic encounter at about the halfway mark of the dance, which is represented largely through the dancers' shadow limbs reaching up from behind the ramp against a bright sunset backdrop, entangling, and then falling again. With such scenes of intimacy incorporated into the dance, Sheppard and Lawson remind audiences of the importance of 'disability pleasure and movement joy' (Hickman 2020), of the wholeness and fullness of disabled lives. They contradict narratives that frame disability and disabled people as inherently incomplete or lacking and with their performance show an array of 'new movement possibilities' as well as an 'an entire spectrum of beauty', eroticism and desire (Hulbert, Niedermeyer and Sheppard 2018).

Trans-corporeality and animate environments in *DESCENT*

In the staging and choreography of *DESCENT*, Sheppard and Lawson present themselves as creative disabled subjects in the continual and pleasurable process of becoming: becoming sculptural, mythical, mobile and multiple in their embodiments. I argue that in making wheelchair and ramp technology an integral part of their movements and embodiments of Venus and Andromeda, Sheppard and Lawson enact Alaimo's (2010, 2018) idea of trans-corporeality. That is to say, as part of their process of Ovidian metamorphosis, they blend their embodied human selves with the non-human objects and environments around them, including the sweeping ramp on which the performance is set, Sheppard and Lawson's two wheelchairs, the multicolored lights and female-figure line drawings Maag projects on the stage, their costumes, and the cello music composed and played by Joan Jeanrenaud that swells around them, so as to become an ever-shifting assemblage of 'people, places, and substances' (Alaimo 2010: 22), of flesh, metal, light particles, fabrics, wood panels and sound vibrations. As Lawson claims in the original Instagram caption to Figure 13.2, it's not that Kinetic Light is 'crossing' boundaries of ability, sexuality, race, matter and form, 'It's that we don't even let you know where the boundaries are – we've thrown them out the window' (kineticlightdance 2023).

In framing the performance this way, I do not mean that Kinetic Light stages a narrative of transcendence or liberation from disability and disabled embodiment. Indeed, in response to a question I had submitted in advance to the October 2023 artist Q&A before the online screening of *DESCENT* as to whether Kinetic Light was inspired by myths of metamorphosis from Graeco-Roman antiquity, Lawson and Sheppard acknowledged Ovid as a relevant intertext but pointed to the limitations of metamorphosis as a metaphor for disabled embodiment, as opposed to what Lawson described as 'the concept of the liminal' (Kinetic Light 2023e: 2017). Lawson noted that metamorphosis could negatively imply 'a story about being liberated from one's disability' (2023e: 16), a narrative of transformation or change beyond disability, while Sheppard highlighted how the notion of metamorphosis is often used to transform disability 'from something intolerable into something more pleasing' (2023e: 17). I am mindful that such framings harmfully imply that disability is a state of embodiment to be overcome, and can even be related to the marginalizing 'supercrip trope', wherein disabled individuals are represented as more than human or are said to possess 'some kind of superhuman ability given in recompense' for their disability (Silverblank and Ward 2020: 516). Although some communities, artists and scholars of disability have argued for concepts like the cyborg or the more-than-human hybrid as a way of moving beyond anthropocentric and ableist views of the world and a means for marginalized groups to claim creative agency, visibility and belonging, framing all people who use accessibility technology as superhuman cyborgs can also have the consequence of further exaggerating disability 'for the benefit of the nondisabled audience' (Siebers 2011: 111) and adding to the historical dehumanization of disabled individuals.[17]

Just as Kinetic Light has rejected understandings of metamorphosis that suggest transcending or being 'liberated' from the disabled human body, with Sheppard stating that while many things transform in their performance, 'disability does not transform or change' and 'the disabilities of Andromeda and Venus are the same' (Kinetic Light 2023e: 17), I aim to make an argument for metamorphosis and trans-corporeal being in *DESCENT* that keeps experiences of disability and disabled embodiments as the central anchor, while also recognizing how the environment of the performance shapes those embodiments and how these entangled environments as well as the piece's affects, choreographies and relationships shift throughout *DESCENT*. Like Chen's (2012) concept of animacy, Alaimo's notion of trans-corporeality recognizes the agentive role of non-human objects and environments in the world and destabilizes hierarchies between the human and non-human in ways that open up possibilities for fluidity, instability and multiplicity in our embodiments.[18] As Alaimo argues, quoting Fromm (1997: 2), trans-corporeality can help us see how the environment "'runs right through us in endless waves'" (2010: 11), entering and exiting our bodies, shaping our embodiment and forming the fabric of our being as we continually metamorphose.

One of the most central elements of the environment of *DESCENT* is the ramp on stage, custom built for *DESCENT* and originally designed by Sarah Hendren, Yevgeniya Zastavker and a team of engineering students at Olin College. The ramp installation, which contains curves, peaks, edges and an underbelly, is almost 2 metres tall and covers 7.5 by 4.5 metres of the stage (Hulbert, Niedermeyer and Sheppard 2018). The creators note that the ramp is itself 'a work of art', built for 'beauty and wheeled movement potential' and not for ADA (Americans with Disabilities Act) compliance (Hulbert, Niedermeyer and Sheppard 2018). In fact, the slope of *DESCENT*'s ramp significantly exceeds ADA compliance, a fact that points to Kinetic Light's own transformative vision of disability arts, and their desire to go beyond the basic (and often limiting) legal minimums of accessibility. The ramp is aesthetic and agentive, animating the dancers and interacting with them. Like the dancers' wheelchairs, the ramp shapes and is part of Sheppard and Lawson's embodiment, creating for them a unique choreography and directing how they will move and inhabit their bodies: turning, wheeling, rolling, careening forward and being dragged backward, rising and *descending*. In fact, the dramatic shapes and steep incline of the ramp give rise to movements that an ADA-compliant ramp could not. As Sheppard recalls, 'the dance of *DESCENT* emerged from the structure of the ramp itself' and enabled her and Lawson to 'create a new technique of movement, new movement vocabulary' (Kinetic Light 2017: 1:13–1:25).[19] The curves, peaks, and edges of the ramp, its unique gravitational push and pull, become part of how *DESCENT*'s bodies are changed and formed. Lawson and Sheppard's wheelchairs, too, are integral in developing this expanded movement vocabulary, and like the ramp they become enmeshed with the dancers' bodies and embodiments as they metamorphose in and out of their sculptural forms, as they continuously come into being. Even when Lawson and Sheppard temporarily leave their wheelchairs aside, they remain part of the fabric of this performance, part of the multiple and relational being of Venus and of Andromeda.

DESCENT's creative costume choices and lighting technologies are additional elements that contribute to the dancers' Ovidian metamorphosis and that participate in the shifting nature of their being and becoming. In many iterations of the performance, the dancers wear leafy gold, purple and reddish-bronze costumes sculpted from leather and fabric, reminiscent of the human-plant hybrid form of Daphne detailed in Book 1 of Ovid's *Metamorphoses* and remarked on by Rodin in *L'Art*. Lawson, the designer of *DESCENT*'s costumes, remarked in the 2023 artist conversation that they wanted the costumes to evoke Rodin's bronze sculptures as well as the 'classical armor' of Grecian women and warriors, and to unify the metal wheelchairs and metallic leggings of the dancers' lower halves with their upper halves (2023e: 15). These leaf or petal-like costumes 'invoke the transformation of bronze into flesh and myth into human' (Kinetic Light 2023d: 13) while also blurring the boundaries between human and nature.

Just as *DESCENT*'s costumes bring nature out of the background of the performance, so too do the images of the natural world that are overlaid on the stage throughout the piece. At various moments in the dance, the artists, ramp and stage have projected onto them images like the night sky (and the Andromeda constellation), grass, water and cloud. There are moments in the performance when Venus seems to become immersed in water, or Andromeda seems to *descend* from the heavens and become enmeshed with her own constellation of stars. The dancers' trans-corporeal embodiments change as they ask via their choreography, 'How do you live in water? How do you live in grass?' (quoted from Sheppard; Kinetic Light 2023e: 15). As we can see in Figure 13.3, these images of nature are sometimes accompanied by bright illuminations and dark shadows, or with Maag's own line-drawings of a multitude of Rodin's sculptures. In his illustrations of these sculptures and spirit guides, who themselves animate and mirror the dancers' movements, Maag enacts another kind of animation, which helps us envision these two mythic figures continually becoming otherwise – stone or sea, forest or figure drawing. The fluidity of Venus and Andromeda's metamorphoses, facilitated by these technologies of light and image and color, makes space for bodies that blend the human, divine and material/environmental worlds, while keeping disability at the centre of their embodied experience.

The environment of *DESCENT* also extends beyond the space of the stage to incorporate live audiences or audiences at home experiencing recordings of the

Figure 13.3 Laurel Lawson in Kinetic Light's performance of *DESCENT*. New Brunswick Performing Arts Center, New Brunswick, New Jersey. Presented by the Dance Department, Mason Gross School of the Arts, Rutgers University-New Brunswick, 2022. Photo by Jaqlin Medlock. https://www.instagram.com/p/CnAIqvWL7mN/?img_index=2.

Image Description: Kneeling, Laurel Lawson leans back into the underside of her chair, arms outstretched and open in a wide V. Laurel is a white person with teal cropped hair. She appears small among the expanse of ramp, sky, and a large projection of a reclining spirit figure in the sky; another wheelchair balances at the ramp's peak. Image Description courtesy of Kinetic Light.

performance. As part of their commitment to access and, I argue, as part of their artistic ethos of transformation, Kinetic Light has incorporated elements like audio description, haptic interpretation, visual augmentation, and sensory modulation into their in-person and virtual performances (Kinetic Light 2023a). For in-person performances of *DESCENT*, some venues contained tactile 3D exhibits of dance's ramp installation (Hulbert, Niedermeyer and Sheppard 2018). These technologies allow the dance itself to metamorphose, to change itself into new forms for new audiences – particularly audiences who may be nonvisual, Deaf, or low sensory. As Romack argues (Romack and Yalka 2024: 82), Kinetic Light's artistic practice 'challenges limited ableist understandings of dance performance as a primarily visual output' and expands dance's potential as a kinaesthetic medium by providing aural and tactile points of access.

As with their ramp installation, in *DESCENT* Kinetic Light goes beyond ADA compliance in their audio description practice, a medium which normally provides concise commentary on the movement on stage and 'objective descriptions of choreography, projections, and costumes' (Hulbert, Niedermeyer and Sheppard 2018). Kinetic Light has developed its own app *Audimance* – for which Lawson is the product designer and lead engineer – to offer audiences a more creative choice between different styles of description, including poetic, screenplay, soundscape and 'sounds of the dancers' bodies and the dancers in space' (Kinetic Light 2023b). Similar options are available to audience members like myself who access the performance online, via links to different versions of the piece that incorporate each kind of available audio. For the October 2023 online screening of *DESCENT*, four different versions of the performance were available for audiences to screen: one with ASL and open captions; one with 'spacious emotion & plot focused' audio description and open captions (the version which I chose to experience as a sighted audience member); one with 'layered poetry, lights, and movement focused' audio description; and one with closed captions and no audio description or ASL (Kinetic Light 2023f: 2). Each option provides audiences with a different experience of the dance, with some highlighting the narrative core of the performance as Venus and Andromeda choose each other and embrace their desire and connection, and others focused on the stage environment and choreography. As Kinetic Light claim on their website, 'access is not a retroactive accommodation. We want you to experience the art, not a description of it' (Kinetic Light 2023a). These innovative technologies of access again point to the relational, shifting, multiple embodiments evoked in *DESCENT*, not only in the performers but also in the audience, who are invited to take the journey of metamorphosis along with Venus and Andromeda and enmesh themselves in the dance via their own interactive visual, haptic and auditory environments.

Conclusion

DESCENT shows us the ongoing relevance and resonance of Ovidian choreographies of metamorphosis in an increasingly global, multimodal world of dance and disability arts. As we know from Ovid's *Tristia*,[20] portions of the poet's *Metamorphoses* and *Heroides* may have been danced in Augustan Rome, used as the basis of pantomime performances. The logic of forms changed into new bodies, or bodies changed into new forms, has continued since then to impact the choreography of artists separated from Ovid by vast swaths of time and space, as it allows us to rethink what is means to move, to transform, to exist in a world replete with nature and technology, and to inhabit a body that is shaped by materials and environments, always relational and shifting, always becoming.

In this chapter, I have argued that Kinetic Light draws on such logics in their danced duet *DESCENT*, a piece which makes a claim for the artistic, creative capacity of disability by (re)creating and recasting the famous mythic figures Venus and Andromeda, seen in Ovid's *Metamorphoses* and Rodin's sculpture, through innovative choreography, lighting, stage and sound design. With this chapter, I hope to have responded to Disability Studies scholar Carrie Sandahl's call for dance criticism that pays specific attention to the bodies of disabled individuals on stage and that reads representations of disability as more than 'metaphors for nondisabled audience members' concerns' (a category in which I include myself), like 'the nature of disability' (2018: 129) or 'the nature of dance, the nature of human, and failures of meaning' (2018: 142).[21] While *DESCENT* does open up new possibilities for dance choreography and access, and while its Ovidian resonances do allow us to consider the various ways that bodies may be shaped and formed, *DESCENT* is a dance that elevates disability arts and that showcases the importance of bringing disabled artists and disability – and its intersections with gender, race and sexuality – into conversations about artistic representation, innovation, aesthetics and meaning making.

Notes

1. Versions of my research on Kinetic Light's *DESCENT* have been presented at the Society for Classical Studies Annual Meeting, on the panel 'Ovid in the Global Village: Interconnectivity and Alienation in Ovidian Studies' organized by International Ovidian Society and Del A. Maticic, Nandini Pandey and Jinyu Liu (2023); and at the 'Agency Through the Ancients: Reception as Empowerment' Classics Graduate Conference at Boston University organized by Maya Chakravorty, Peter Kotiuga, Alicia Matz, Joshua Paul and Amanda Rivera (2019). I would like to thank the conference organizers and attendees for their questions and suggestions, especially Erica Krause for pointing me to Alaimo's (2010) work. I would also like to thank Professors Yopie Prins, Artemis Leontis, Peggy McCracken, Valerie Traub, Andrea Zemgulys, Ian Fielding and Christi Merrill for their feedback on this project at various stages, as well as Lena Grimm and Ciara Barrick for their support during the writing process, and Kinetic Light's Mariclare Hulbert, Alice Sheppard, Laurel Lawson and Rachel Hickman for their collaborative fact-checking and feedback. I am grateful for Peggy McCracken and Valerie Traub's 2020 graduate course on 'Ovid's Metamorphoses in Medieval and Early Modern Europe' for pointing me to Chen (2012) and questions of Ovid and animacy; their co-edited volume with Patricia Badir, *Ovidian Transversions: 'Iphis and Ianthe', 1300–1650* (2019) has also been instrumental in my thinking, particularly Traub's Introduction on the 'transversion' as a model of reception (2019: 1–24) and McCracken's chapter on 'metamorphosis as supplement' (2019: 43–59). I would also like to acknowledge how my positionality as a nondisabled, queer, white woman shapes the parameters of my

2. My experience with *DESCENT* has been through two virtual screenings, rather than a live performance: the first on 3 December 2020, which marked the online premiere of the *DESCENT* film, and the second on 28 October 2023. Both screenings used footage from *DESCENT* filmed in 2018 at the Curtis R. Priem Experimental Media and Performing Arts Center at Rensselaer in New York; Shaina Ghuraya worked as the editor and Andy Slater as the audio description sound designer and mixer for the 2020 film (Kinetic Light 2020). The 2023 screening featured two 'never-before experienced' accessible options, including one 'fresh take on the musical interpretation for *DESCENT*' by a Deaf interpreter/hearing interpreter ASL team (Joey Antonio and Nicole Cartagna, artistically directed by Alexandria Wailes) and one audio description track focused on the 'plot and the internal world of Andromeda and Venus' delivered by Cheryl Green; Kinetic Light also offered a 'blended, layered AD track with poetry and emphasis on lights and movement' (TicketTailor 2023). My thanks to Kinetic Light for granting permission to cite from the October 2023 *DESCENT* Artist Conversation Guide, *DESCENT* Artist Conversation Transcript, and *DESCENT* Online & In-Depth Audience Guide.

3. Disability arts is a term often used to define an artistic movement, community and/or aesthetic that takes disability as an explicit theme and/or centre work produced by disabled artists (Brehme 2020).

4. Ancient Aithiopia should be distinguished from the modern country of Ethiopia, as the former is thought to roughly correspond with the southern region of modern Egypt and the northern region of modern Sudan (Derbew 2022: 12). As Derbew (2022: xiii) argues, Aithiopia often also refers to 'an ancient ethereal land that Greek sources sometimes conflate with a historical region'.

5. For more on historical readings of Andromeda's race and ethnicity in literature and visual art, see McGrath (1992). McGrath (1992: 1–3) and Derbew (2022: 163) both discuss Heliodorus' fourth-century CE novel *Aithiopika*, which features a description of a painting with a white-skinned Andromeda. McGrath (1992: 3) also points to Pompeian mosaics that depict Perseus' rescue of Andromeda, wherein Andromeda is portrayed as a 'white Ethiopian'. Yet in support of her argument for Andromeda's Blackness, McGrath (1992: 9) references Ovid's *Heroides* 15 which characterizes Andromeda's skin as 'dark' (*fusca*), as well as Ovid *Ars Amatoria* 1.53 which claims that Perseus took Andromeda 'from the black Indians' (*nigris . . . ab Indis,* trans. McGrath), and *Ars Amatoria* 2.643–4 which refers explicitly to 'Andromeda's colour' (*Andromedae color,* trans. McGrath). It is worth noting, however, that these references in Ovid appear to fetishize Andromeda's Blackness, making her dark skin a point of erotic intrigue and novelty. Kinetic Light challenges this exoticizing racialized gaze in their re-animation of the character.

6. For more definitions and examples of disability aesthetics, see Siebers (2005, 2010). In my discussion of animacy, I work from Chen, who argues for bringing nonhuman animals and inanimate objects into the fold of biopolitics (2012: 6) and draws on the Latin terms *anima* ('air, breath, life soul, mind'), *animare* ('to breathe, to quicken') and *animus* ('(1) soul, (2) mind, (3) mental impulse, disposition, passion') to claim that animacy is more than the state of being animate (2012: 3).

7. See Preston's (2011: 306 n. 45) discussion of Isadora Duncan's performance in Augustin Daly's 1895 production of *Miss Pygmalion*. H.D. (Hilda Doolittle) has several poems seemingly inspired by Ovid's *Metamorphoses*, including 'Eurydice' (1925: 51) and 'Pygmalion' (1925: 48). For more contemporary examples, see Dove's poems in *Mother Love* (1995), dodd's poetry collection *The Black Condition ft. Narcissus* (2019), MacLaughlin's short story collection *Wake, Siren: Ovid Resung* (2019) and Benson's lyric poetry collection *Vertigo & Ghost* (2019).

8. Translations of Ovid's *Metamorphoses*, unless otherwise noted, are my own.
9. The same adjective, *marmoreum,* is used to describe Narcissus in Book 3 of the *Metamorphoses*, when he, 'unmoving' (*inmotus, Metamorphoses* 3.418), is likened to a 'figure made from Parian marble' (*e Pario formatum marmore signum, Metamorphoses* 3.419), a stone known for its white hue. While an in-depth analysis of Ovid's racialization of Andromeda in the *Metamorphoses* and other works is beyond the scope of this chapter, I suggest that Ovid's likening of Andromeda to a 'marble statue' in the *Metamorphoses* could point to a potential whitewashing power in Perseus' gaze, alongside the de-animating power that renders Andromeda into an aestheticized object. The description also opens up questions about why and how we assume marble to be associated with an idealized aesthetic of whiteness. Bond (2017) argues that ancient Greeks and Romans did not necessarily consider marble a 'finished product', and notes that many statues from antiquity were painted with vibrant colors, gilded and decorated. Marble itself also comes in many colors, not only the bright white associated with Parian marble.
10. See, for example, Ovid's *Metamorphoses* 10.533–4.
11. The post show interview where the artists of Kinetic Light discussed their interest in Rodin and 'incompleteness' is no longer available for viewing but occurred on Zoom after an online screening of *DESCENT* on 3 December 2020 through the Northrop Performing Arts Center at the University of Minnesota.
12. Deleuze and Guattari's (1987) concepts of rhizome and assemblage inform my language here. I also have in mind Lanier's invocation of Deleuze and Guattari and his argument that the assemblage obliterates 'conventional notions of "being"' in favor of 'non-unitary multiplicity' and entails an acknowledgement of the subject's fluidity, of 'ceaseless change' and a 'process of endless "becoming"' (2014: 27).
13. I draw here on Werth's (2012: 181) distinction between human and stone, 'vibrant' and 'dull' matter. Chen's (2012) 'Introduction' discusses the potential animacy of stone, while their final two chapters refer to the animacy of different metals (lead and mercury). Bennett (2009) is the landmark text for the concept of 'vibrant matter'. See also Funke (2019) on Pater, H.D. and Freud's conceptions of sculptural materials like bronze and marble in relation to questions of animacy, vibrancy and temporality.
14. See note 5 for McGrath (1992) and Derbew (2002). The Western cultural idolization of the white marble Venus de Milo sculpture is but one example among many of how the figure of Venus has come to symbolize a kind of idealized aesthetic of white female beauty. In contrast, Hartman (2008: 1) examines the 'ubiquitous presence of Venus in the archive of Atlantic slavery' and points to the ways that Venus is both a recorded name and a cultural signifier for enslaved Black women whose voices have been silenced and whose stories have been untold and who suffered extreme violence and death in captivity during the Middle Passage.
15. See note 11.
16. See Garland-Thomson (2005) on the Disability Studies concept of the 'stare' as a way of 'strongly reacting to the other', as 'the human response to novelty, to the unexpected' and as an 'embodied and relational visual exchange' that seeks to 'craft a narrative of recognition from incoherence.'
17. Haraway's (1991: 149) theorization of the cyborg dismantles human/non-human, nature/culture binaries, and claims that we are all 'a hybrid of machine and organism'. For the language of hybridity as 'crisscrossing' the divide between nature and culture, see Latour ([1991] 1993: 3). Reeve (2012: 91) remarks on the absence of 'disabled cyborgs' in current scholarship, partly due to technology's association with medicalized models of disability and partly because the concept often relies on unquestioned assumptions of unimpaired human

subjects. Reeve notes that opinions on the cyborg in Disability Studies are divided, with some arguing that 'cyborg theory cannot offer solutions for the material disadvantage faced by disabled people in society' while 'others see the cyborg as providing a way of understanding the lack of a fixed boundary between disabled and non-disabled people' (2012: 91).

18. Alaimo (2010: 10) discusses how trans-corporeality can bridge the areas of environmentalism and disability activism by turning our attention to the 'deviant agencies' that cut across bodies and places; she uses the example of chemical sensitivity to show how toxins in the environment may 'exacerbate or cause chronic illness'. Alaimo cites Disability Studies scholar Rosemarie Garland-Thomson, who likewise argues for the 'material/social interchanges between body and place', to argue that Disability Studies might use trans-corporeality to think not only about how built environments 'constitute or exacerbate' disability, but also how pollution and chemical and pharmaceutical materialities affect 'human health and ability' (2010: 12).

19. For more on the design and construction of the ramp, see 'Ramp/Kinetic Light' (2016).

20. In *Tristia* V.VII.25–6, Ovid writes of his songs 'being danced [*saltari*] in a full theater' and claims his 'written verses are applauded' there. In *Tristia* II.519–20, he reminds his addressee, the emperor Augustus, that his poems have 'often been danced [*sunt . . . saltata*] in public' and have 'often arrested your eyes'. Pantomime's choreography would have likely informed Ovid's own keen attention to bodily movement and change in his poems. For more on the relationship between Ovid's poetry and pantomime, see Galinsky (1975, 1999), Richlin (1992), Ingleheart (2008) and Lada-Richards (2013, 2016).

21. Sandahl (2018: 129) notes that she collaborated with Kinetic Light and disabled dancer Jerron Hermon in September 2017 in a writing residency at Florida State University to address 'frustrations' with how critics write about disability and disability arts in reductive ways. Sandahl (2018: 130) recounts that Alice Sheppard asked them to 'develop language and ways of writing about dance and disability that also took intersectional issues of race, gender, and sexuality into consideration'.

CHAPTER 14
PASSIM CLOUDS: *HELEN*, MARILYN AND *NORMA JEANE BAKER OF TROY*
Eugenia Nicolaci

> Fame has lavished you with great praises, and every land knows your beauty; none among the most beautiful women is famous like you.[1]
>
> Paris to Helen, Ovid, *Heroides* XVI

In his 2015 study on philosophy of media, *The Marvelous Clouds*, John Durham Peters recalls how, until the 1920s, one of the biggest challenges for photographers was shooting clouds (Peters 2015: 259). Early photographic emulsions were primarily sensitive to light on the blue end and daguerreotype's long exposure times could not capture a subject in motion. This task became an obsession for Alfred Stieglitz, who explained his interest in atmospherics and natural effects as follows: 'Every time I developed [a cloud negative] I was so wrought up, always believing I had nearly gotten what I was after – but had failed' (Greenough and Greenburg 1995: 76). Steglitz's numerous attempts to capture clouds eventually resulted in the project *Equivalents*, a collection of 220 shots taken between 1925 and 1934. Along with the fascination with clouds, the very name 'Equivalent' expresses Stieglitz's view of photography as a medium to reproduce reality. This idea comes from the art of painting, where an attempt to transcribe a subject into an image reveals the human desire to secure a long-lasting copy of an ephemeral experience (Andrews 2003). Yet Stieglitz's account demonstrates that clouds elude any attempt to possess them, be it through the lens of a camera or on the page of a book. With their impalpable essence, clouds become emblematic of the impossibility of immortalizing the true essence of a subject.

In what follows, I explore the symbology of clouds in Anne Carson's *Norma Jeane Baker of Troy: a version of Euripides' Helen* (2019). The play echoes the figure of Marilyn Monroe and interweaves it with the story of Helen of Troy. In a one-actor performance, Carson's Norma Jeane Baker – this was one of the names attributed to the actor before she turned her identity into Marilyn Monroe – reveals to her public how a cloud in her likeness went to Troy while she was locked in a suite in Los Angeles to learn the lines for Fritz Lang's 1952 film *Clash By Night*. Even more striking than the comparison with Marilyn Monroe's mystified life and tragic apotheosis, the most significant element in *Norma Jeane Baker of Troy* is Carson's reference to the alternative story of Helen in Egypt, told most famously in Euripides' tragedy *Helen* (412 BCE). Carson selects from Euripides the word εἴδωλον, meaning 'shape, phantom, vision' but also 'portrait, image in the mind,' and then translates it as 'cloud'.[2] This celestial element comes to symbolize Helen's

Figure 14.1 Marylin Monroe in *The Misfits*, 1960. Photo by Eve Arnold. Courtesy Magnum Photo.

phantom, for whom the Greeks fought at Troy, and for Marilyn Monroe's public image. The cloud guides my reading of *Norma Jeane Baker of Troy*, as it defines the interplay between self and image, truth and legend, reality and illusion, life and death, substance and ephemerality. Here, clouds act as a vessel for the dislocation of a classical myth into a modern pop icon, which becomes possible only through an actor's performance.

The chapter follows three different strands, which unfold as an analysis of Euripides' *Helen*; the second then explores the historical Norma Jeane Baker along with her icon Marilyn Monroe. My reading, making up the third strand, is situated around the similarities and contrasts that allow Helen and Norma Jeane Baker to challenge their identity, while nonetheless preventing them from completely rehabilitating themselves. In conclusion, I show the ways that Carson's version of Euripides provides a refreshing insight into ancient and modern myths of female beauty, along with an exploration of the tension between illusion and reality that goes hand in hand with fame.

'If this tale is true' (Helen, ll. 21)

In 2018 The Shed's Griffin Theater in New York commissioned from Carson the script for a spoken and sung stage performance about Marilyn Monroe and Helen of Troy.[3] The play was eventually performed in 2019 under the title *Norma Jeane Baker of Troy*. This rearrangement of Carson's original script is a staging of the translation process, which takes place during one night in 1964, when an officer manager dictates to a stenographer his version of Euripides' tragedy *Helen*. Suddenly the spectre of a recently-dead Marilyn Monroe starts to haunt the man and insert itself into his work. The haunted translation of Euripides, which constitutes Carson's original contribution to the performance, was published in the form of a libretto, with the reproduction of a grey cloud against a blue sky on the centre of the cover (Carson 2019a). All the paratextual elements in this postproduction script are kept to a minimum, and Norma Jeane Baker's forty-six-page monologue makes up the body of the work, which is accompanied by entries from an imaginary ancient Greek dictionary, and numbered lessons called 'History of War'. The script superimposes episodes from Marilyn Monroe's public life and career on Euripides' subtext, with the names of Fritz Lang, Arthur Miller, Pearl Bailey, Truman Capote and the Chateau Marmont in Los Angeles taking over *Helen*'s plot. The paratextual interludes in the form of fictive lexicographic entries from ancient Greek to English separate each episode and offer a space for reflections on language and its most tangible effects. Here, the author – writing for book publication, not play performance, and afforded the space on the page for criticism and reflection – observes and dissects each word as an object for the purpose of providing an instruction manual. Only in these interstitial spaces is the fictional character of Norma Jeane Baker addressed as Marilyn Monroe. The comparison between the twentieth-century Hollywood actor and sex symbol and the ancient Greek heroine is already presented in the play's title, with the juxtaposition between Marilyn's previous identity and Helen's gained epithet. In the character of *Norma Jeane Baker of Troy* two legends inhabit the same title, as an identity on the edges of ancient myth and Hollywood glamour.

'And who exactly can bring to completion living bodies?' (Helen, ll. 583)

While the name Norma Jeane Baker refers to Marilyn Monroe, Troy was the city attributed to Helen after she eloped with Paris. According to Homer's *Iliad* and *Odyssey*, Helen's husband Menelaus and the other Achaean kings initiated the war against Troy specifically to bring Helen back home. Yet Carson does not align her play with the most famous Homeric tale, but with Euripides' tragedy *Helen*. Euripides himself allocated two different destinies to Helen in his plays *The Trojan Women* (415 BCE) and *Helen* (412 BCE). This last has been considered by many scholars a failed tragedy, mainly because of its happy ending and melodramatic style (Allan 2008: 1–85). The story dwells upon the legend of the so-called phantom that went to Troy, an alternative tradition that exonerates Helen from bringing woe to both the Achaeans and Trojans, claiming that she stayed in Egypt as a guest of King Proteus for the whole duration of the war of Troy (Suzuki 1989: 13). The motif of Helen in Egypt has always occupied a parallel space within the ancient Greek literary tradition. According to Plato (*Phaedrus* 243a), the poet Stesichorus was blinded for having insulted Helen with his verses; to regain her favour along with his sight, in his second work, the *Palinode*, he firmly denies that she ever went to Troy. In his *Encomium of Helen*, the fifth-century sophist Gorgias experiments with the story of

Helen's elopement to showcase the potential of a persuasive discourse to manipulate facts and create paradoxes. If anyone was to blame for the Trojan War, says Gorgias, it would be fate, the gods, or *eros* but certainly not Helen (Gorgias 1982). The multiple faces of Helen and the malleability of her identity are a consequence of her remarkable status as one of the few women within Greek mythology who manages to live to tell her story (Blondell 2013: 204). To survive a tragic fate, Helen's figure changes and adapts to a new context while still maintaining the essence of the most beautiful and canny woman in the world.

Euripides embraces the challenge of engaging with the alternative version of this myth. He imagines Helen pointing at the Nile while sitting at the tomb of the late Proteus, in front of the palace of the new king Theoclymenus. The tragedy presents a vulnerable Helen, who is unexpectedly uprooted from her original context. The unusual location in Egypt, far from Greece and Troy, creates a sense of dislocation. In the imagination of fifth-century Athenians, Egypt was indeed 'an outpost of Greek mythology, an imaginative space of weird possibility in which Greeks could scrutinize, construct, and reconstruct their own identity' (Blondell 2013: 203). The chronicle of Helen's misadventures represents a detailed act of dismantling her official, infamous image, and an opportunity to tell another version of the story. According to Helen's account, the Trojan hoax was arranged by three gods: Hera, who formed an εἴδωλον, a breathing phantom for Paris, to take with him to Troy; Hermes, who wrapped the real Helen in a cloud and took her to Proteus' house; and Zeus, who planned this ruse to unleash the war between the Greeks and Trojans as a solution to Earth's overpopulation, as well as for the purpose of giving Achilles the glory that he deserved. Helen continues her monologue in which she wishes for her body to be wiped clean and repainted in a less attractive form, so that the Greeks would forget all the negative aspects about her. This desire anticipates the ultimate sense of the tragedy, which emerges in Helen's encounters with Teucer, Menelaus and Theoclymenus. Each of these three men expresses the desire to undo, transform, or replicate her body, in the attempt to convert their ideal into a reality. Teucer, a Greek soldier banished from home after the Trojan war, curses Helen for resembling her Trojan phantom, with the language of pictorial reproduction (Eur. *Helen* ll. 70–157):

> Ah! O gods, what sight is this I see?
> The deadly image of a woman most hateful, her who ruined me
> and all the Greeks! The gods' hatred be yours for
> being Helen's double!

The expression 'Helen's double' translates the Greek word μίμημα, meaning 'imitation, copy'. Teucer refuses to recognize Helen in that woman all alone in Egypt, as both place and circumstances differ from his image of her. Nevertheless, Helen is determined to rehabilitate her reputation. When Menelaus makes his entry on stage to beg hospitality after a shipwreck on his way back from Troy, he has just left the εἴδωλον, whom he believes to be his wife, under guard in a cave. The announcement of her sudden vanishment into thin air leaves him alone with the mysterious woman claiming to be the real Helen. Crucially, he decides to trust her. After being reunited with her husband, Helen manages to deceive King Theoclymenus by stealing a ship and some goods from him and sailing out towards Greece. This final trickery brings a comic tone to this apocryphal tale, while at the same time darkly mirroring the canonical version of a seductive Helen who rescues herself on the merit of her beauty and persuasive language skills. The transformation into a virtuous woman does not deny or replace the standard attitude toward Helen, which appears to haunt the play like a mysterious presence. Euripides' *Helen* 'is like a movie star cast against type, whose performance we enjoy in part because of its dissonance with her previous roles' (Blondell 2013: 204).

Perhaps this sense of distance and proximity between Helen and her Trojan phantom inspired Carson when deciding to adapt Euripides' tragedy to the figure of Marilyn Monroe. Norma Jeane Baker – although according to some biographers, her birth certificate reads Norma Jeane Mortenson (Churchwell 2019: 147) – and the disconnect with her stage persona occupies the first lexicographic interlude in *Norma Jeane Baker of Troy*. Here Carson reflects on the Greek term 'εἴδωλον "image, likeness, simulacrum, replica, proxy, idol"' (Carson 2019: 5):

> To make people believe that a replica is the real thing, manipulate 'the optic' of the situation. Managing optics cleverly will generate an alternative version of the facts, which then stands alongside the facts like a cloud in the shape of a woman, or a golden Hollywood idol in place of a mousyhaired pin-up girl from Los Angeles.

Manipulation is the ultimate theme of this play. The term εἴδωλον addresses Marilyn Monroe, 'a cloud in the shape of a woman, or a golden Hollywood idol,' an image standing alongside the facts, yet not in their place. Beyond the obvious allusion to the English *idol*, εἴδωλον expresses the sense of inconsistency and ephemerality which is typical of fame. It suggests that the different destinies attributed to a mythical figure do not automatically exclude the other; rather, they complicate and prolong the story. The apparent contrast between Helen in Egypt and her phantom in Troy is the lens through which to read Carson's relocation of the Greek tragedy into Hollywood stardom system between the fifties and sixties. This was the time when a pin-up girl called Norma Jeane changed her given name(s) and transformed into Marilyn Monroe.

'Who are you? What face I am looking at, lady?' (Helen, ll. 557)

Following Carson's comparison, both Helen's and Norma Jeane Baker's existence blurred under the image the world made of them: Helen's reputation was destroyed by the story of her elopement with Paris at Troy; Norma Jeane became famous by making of her own life a film. Somehow the two women both faced the problem of assimilating with a new identity. Yet, while Helen's destiny was shaped by the works of poets and writers, Norma Jeane herself contributed to create the image of Marilyn Monroe, which circulated mainly through her still photographs and film performances. Not only did she pose for the most famous photographers of the time; she also constructed her public image by way of dramatizing the most obscure and controversial aspects of her biography to the point of embodying the cliché of feminine desire (Churchwell 2019: 5–15).

The visual dimension inherent in the idol Marilyn Monroe is captured in the cover image of *Norma Jeane Baker de Troya*, the Spanish edition of Carson's original play *Norma Jeane Baker of Troy* (Carson 2021b). The book design conflates the two figures of Marilyn's face and Helen's bust in an imitation of 1950s film posters. The posture and facial expression of this collage of Marilyn as Helen of Troy alludes to the iconography of Christian saints, while Marilyn's pose as a pagan Madonna recalls Andy Warhol's series of canvases *The Shot Marilyns*. Warhol's repetitive screen prints were produced from one single shot of Marilyn from the 1953 film *Niagara* in which the actor played her most famous role of the *femme fatale*. Marilyn's transfigured image as shown by Warhol encloses the essence of her cinematic character: an objectified woman whose strong sexual appeal made her both desirable and available. Warhol's use of Day-Glo colours and metallic paints expressed the artificiality of the composition and created an aura of death around Marilyn's provocative smile. A few tiny details on the actor's face slightly mutate or even disappear when observing the four *Shots*. The Red Shot gives a heavy nuance to Marilyn's mouth and eyes; the Turquoise reveals her neck; and the Blue's soft and warm tones highlight the sensuality of the smile. The different gradations of colours make the lines around the face elusive to the point that they lack edges. Contrary to any expectation, Marilyn – or, indeed, Norma Jeane Baker – is not there, as the perishable image of Warhol's paintings only conveys to the observers an aura of death. Despite the illusion to possess the most beautiful woman on earth, the endless repetition of Marilyn's provocative smile reminds how each version of her is never quite the same. The ones who would try to excavate the different strata of her image to catch the true Norma Jeane will end up confusing the many different versions of her face. For Warhol, Marilyn is ultimately ungraspable. She is 'in the composite' of all the different canvases, which Norma Jeane industriously made up all along her life, first by adapting her body to the camera, and then learning to direct and manipulate her own image (Churchwell 2019: 14).

Carson is aware of Marilyn's alluring fugacity in Andy Warhol's artificial *Shots*. Her perspective on Norma Jeane Baker lies at the edges of Marilyn Monroe's official image, within the 'gaps and contradictions' of her stories, in a place which is both Troy and Los Angeles, like in a film set (Churchwell 2019: 9). Here reality and fiction coexist, as seen in another shot of Marilyn, realized by Eve Arnold during the set of *The Misfits* (Figure 14.1). John Huston's 1960 adaptation of Arthur Miller's play *The Misfits* is the story of Roslyn Tabor, a newly divorced woman, and her aging, out-of-time cowboy friends, played by Clark Gable, Montgomery Clift and Eli Wallach. The film is a portrait of life on the margins of American society, in the dry areas around the Nevada desert, which at the end of the fifties was still populated by small groups of people who could not find their place anywhere else. This independent production lies on the fringes of Hollywood movies industry, with a very unusual setting away from film studios. The shooting took place in a particular time in Marilyn's life and career; one when she was trying to turn her image from that of a blond starlet into a serious actor. For this purpose, Arthur Miller, her husband at the time, fits Marilyn with the role of Roslyn, an uneducated, divorced women, with charming sad eyes and a fatigued, extremely sensual body. Despite Miller's declared intention to support Marilyn in her desire to be seen as a real artist, *The Misfits* openly engages with her persona and problematic relationship with stardom (Miller and Toubiana 2011: 6–48). One scene of the film in particular encapsulates this unresolved conflict between self and image. While Roslyn is showing her renewed bedroom to her friend, Guido, the man's eyes fall on some pictures on the inside of a wardrobe door: they feature Roslyn alias Marylin Monroe as a pin-up girl. Despite Roslyn's repeated attempts to close the door, Guido continues to gaze at the pictures. Marilyn's attempt to get away from her image and finally redeem herself seems to vanish once again. Marilyn Monroe is not simply acting in *The Misfits*; she is the film. Along with her frustration, in the same period her marriage with Miller was falling apart, and the abuse of prescription drugs was making her physical and mental health conditions very precarious. Norma Jeane was exhausted with keeping Marilyn Monroe alive. Instead of being a turning point in her life and career, *The Misfits* represented Marilyn's swansong, her last film before her premature death in 1962. Tragically, this last attempt to transform failed and Marilyn gained immortality by fixing her image into the static portrait of eternal beauty and youth.

Eve Arnold was part of the group of Magnum photographers who documented the making of the film. Arnold tried hard to grasp the actors' most intimate, although rarely completely genuine moments (Smith 2002: 228). The specific conditions governing the set of *The Misfits* generated a unique opportunity for the photographer to explore her subjects from different angles. The distant and exotic set, almost entirely outdoors, along with the overabundance of unproductive time, allowed Arnold a certain freedom of movement: although she was closely watching the actor, her presence was not perceived as extraneous. For the first time in the history of photographing Hollywood icons, a studio picture did not show the star's persona in the classic self-celebrating posture. Rather, the shot of Marilyn crystallizes Monroe's body in the alienation process leading to the creation of the scene (Kouvaros 2002: 30). Kouvaros calls this state of alienation 'the residues of moments when nothing seems to be happening' (Kouvaros 2002: 31). These fragments of time represent a glimpse into the intimate transformation of Norma Jeane in her character. Arnold's look at the downtime between one scene and the other, grasps this perfect suspension between life and fiction. Norma Jeane stands under a cloudy sky, while rehearsing lines for a scene, with the Nevada desert mountains in the background and a big boom microphone behind her back. Landscape and machinery actively participate in the composition, creating a moment of suspension between reality and fiction. Marilyn looks down, her fists clenched to her mouth. Far from Andy Warhol's pornographic smile, here she does not direct her attention toward the camera. Instead, her eyes retain the intensity for themselves in that unique moment. An unexpected agency comes from her apparent fragility. Yet the presence of the machinery insinuates doubt that that woman is the real Norma Jeane Baker; or is she already playing Marilyn Monroe? Nature and machinery, reality and fiction, acting and truth are all mixed and confused throughout this photo. The presence of film set equipment offers a key to the scene. The boom microphone on the left side marks the distance between the dense and opaque net of clouds on the horizons and the actor's body at the centre. The saturation of the white and grey colours highlights the focus on Marilyn, despite her ignoring the camera. While the clouds fade into the background, Norma Jeane's body is there, at the centre of the scene.

One of the lexicographic entries in Anne Carson's *Norma Jeane Baker of Troy* offers an interesting clue to read this photo: the definition the term καιρός in ancient Greek, meaning 'opportunity' unfolds in this way (Carson 2019a: 39):

> NOT YET IRONY: Notice καιρός has its accent on the final syllable. This same word with accent moved to the initial syllable, καῖρος, was a technical term from the art of weaving to indicate the thrums of the web or, more specifically, that critical point in space and time when the weaver must thrust her thread through a gap that momentarily opens in the warp of the cloth.

Eve Arnold, in her snapshot of *The Misfits*, succeeds in the difficult task of catching the gap of the καιρός, that suspended moment where Marilyn and Norma Jeane are separated before reconnecting. This 'critical point in space and time' gives the observer the opportunity to look at Marilyn from a new, alternative optic, which results from the interaction between nature and technology. While the lunar horizon marks the dislocation for the actor who finds herself out of her natural place, the black and white colours balance the composition and suggest a general harmony between human and natural elements. Although every detail actively participates in the composition, the centripetal force of the scene is Marilyn's physical presence: her body does not search the camera but shows her vulnerability to the action of nature around. For a moment Marilyn ceases to be an impalpable image and gains a tangible visibility. The boom microphone measures the duration of this fragment of time and reminds us of the difficulty of separating life from fiction, material from aethereal representation, the persona from the woman. Arnold's view of Marilyn constitutes an interesting point of contact with Carson's *Norma Jeane Baker of Troy*. Carson observes Marilyn without separating Norma Jeane from her cloud/εἴδωλον but acknowledging in her the mix of truth and lies. The visual dimension inherent in the idol Marilyn Monroe suggests that there is no hidden truth behind, as her multiple identities coexist on the same level within her. Yet, if the observers can manipulate 'the optics' of the situation, they will see in her either Norma Jeane or Marilyn, Helen of Troy, or Helen in Egypt.

'I did not go to the land of Troy, but a cloud did.' (Helen, ll. 582)

In a phone call interview, which is now part of 2022 Netflix documentary *The Mystery of Marilyn Monroe: The Unheard Tapes*, Marilyn says to the journalist:

Oh, uh, I'd like to ask you how do you go about writing a life story? Because . . . the true things rarely get into circulation. It's usually the false things. If you ever get any of those things you want to ask, I'll tell you. All of those things come from the truth, you know? Because otherwise it's hard to know where to start, if you don't start with the truth.

Marilyn's anxiety to control the circulation of the stories about her life makes her incredibly similar to Euripides' *Helen*. Carson captures the common essence of the two women in the opening of *Norma Jeane Baker of Troy*, which both paraphrases Euripides' text and links it with Norma Jeane's most brilliant performances as Marilyn Monroe. The repetition of the stage directions 'Enter Norma Jeane Baker. / Prologue,' along with the contradictive statement 'This is the Nile and I'm a liar' give a sense of unreality to the storytelling (Carson 2019a: 1). Several stage directions inform the audience that '*NORMA JEANE sits, takes out her knitting.*' This action links Norma Jeane to the Homeric Helen who weaves scenes from the battles of Troy in her chamber. The knitting has a double function of marking the continuity between the canonical Helen and her unorthodox story of captivation in Egypt, while at the same time highlighting the creative power of weaving a story. As with Euripides' *Helen*, Carson's Norma Jeane Baker dismantles the fictionality of the scene whilst asserting her own ability to manipulate and confuse facts. Norma Jeane Baker's tireless knitting on stage reflects Marilyn Monroe's playing with her stereotypical image of 'pathological femininity' (Churchwell 2019: 7) on the edge between *eros* and self-destruction. Details are central in Carson's play, which is not a reframing of the Greek tragedy into a modern context. Rather, Helen's alternative version becomes a malleable material through which one delves into the fictional character of Norma Jeane Baker of Troy. This is made clear in the encounter with Arthur (Miller), Monroe's last husband, who impersonates Menelaus (Carson 2019a: 19):

> I explain to Arthur about the cloud.
> A cloud went to Troy, I say. It wasn't me.
> MGM had the rights to a war movie, big investors
> involved, you know
> how things work.
> That Norma Jeane at Troy, *that wasn't me* (I repeat).
> It was a cloud.

In this instance, the 'breathing image' that Hera 'fashioned from the heavens' (Eur. *Helen* ll. 34–5) becomes emblematic of Hollywood celebrity. The gods are Metro-Goldwyn-Mayer Pictures, whose investment in the production of a movie on the Trojan war, in Carson's imagining, caused Norma Jeane Baker's disgrace. Helen's suitor Theoclymenus, in Euripides, becomes Fritz Lang, the director of *Clash By Night* (1952). The historical production of *Clash by Night* forms an intertext and background here: at the time of film shooting, Marilyn was at the centre of a scandal related to the infamous Golden Dreams Calendar, a series of nude photographs that she posed for in 1949, under the name of

Mona Monroe. Some years later, when a journalist recognized her hiding face in the calendar, the Twentieth Century Fox studio asked her to deny everything. Yet Marilyn persuaded the studio to handle the scandal through a public confession in an exclusive interview: 'I was broke and needed the money' was her apparently naïve reply to her public's highly moralized and perverse curiosity. The calendar episode represents the background for Carson's reframing of Helen's dialogue with Teucer in Norma Jeane Baker's exchange with the Greek sailor (Carson 2019a: 6). Despite the sailor noticing the incredible resemblance between Norma Jeane and her icon, a sense of confusion and disorientation leads him to run from her. Similarly, Arthur, King of Troy, a mix of Menelaus and Arthur Miller, literally bursts into flames at the news that 'That Norma Jeane at Troy ... / It was a cloud' (Carson 2019a: 19). Neither the sailor nor Arthur recognize Norma Jeane since her body cannot be identified in any place away from the camera. Their attitude toward her is the one of Warhol's observers in *The Shot Marilyns*. The public wants to see the exact copy of Marilyn, something that the artist can endlessly manipulate and replicate each time. Yet, once coming closer to her stereotypical image, this desire will confront the destabilising uniqueness of Marilyn's complex, nuanced faces. Desire is about vanishing, claims Carson's Norma Jeane Baker, and acting has nothing to do with it. Indeed, Norma Jeane Baker of Troy is now acting in Carson's script in much the same way as she did all her life. Her role was the same as Helen's, the personification of female beauty and natural sexuality which men want to control. Carson's Norma Jeane Baker fails to rehabilitate her reputation since the audience has no interest in knowing her truth; rather, they prefer to believe in the myths about her life, where she is forever problematic and beautiful. This is stated towards the end of the play by Norma Jeane Baker playing Truman Capote: 'There's nothing mythic here. / She's just a bit of grit caught in the world's need for / Transcendence.' (Carson 2019a: 29).

The obsession with separating Marilyn from her supposed real identity represents the way her myth has survived her death. Her fixed smiling face embodies the most literal translation of an idol/εἴδωλον, that is a statue, a fixed symbol of beauty, desire, and availability. On the other side of this is the real person, an innocent young woman with tragic past, somehow unable to contrast the system of stardom that ultimately destroyed her. Carson seems to align herself with this reading, by putting together in her script two famous stories of maligned female injustice. Yet the ambiguity and contradiction of her far too pretentious Norma Jeane Baker of Troy leave space for doubts: ironically, the simple name Marilyn Monroe is less artificial and more consistent than any allegedly real identities, from Norma Jeane Baker, Norma Jeane Mortenson, to this last Norma Jeane Baker of Troy.

'That was a cloud' (Helen, ll. 582)

In 2021 a translation of Carson's *Norma Jeane Baker of Troy* appeared in Italian with the new title *Era una Nuvola, Una versione dell'Elena di Euripide* ('It was a Cloud, A version of Euripides' *Helen*'). The introduction accompanying this new edition does not clearly state the reasoning behind this change, but it suggests an intention to move away from Marilyn back towards Euripides and his rehabilitation of Helen. Most interestingly, we read that Carson personally selected the new title (Carson 2021c: 7–17). In its new life in another language, the tragicomic ambiguity of *Norma Jeane Baker of Troy* is only apparently eclipsed by Euripides and the attempt to rehabilitate Helen from her traditional story. In fact, the text quotation 'Era una nuvola / It was a cloud' brings us back to Carson's initial 2019 libretto alongside the cover image of a cloud.

The movement and change of this paratextual detail from a visual to a textual symbol sums up what we might call the final act in Carson's intention of making Marilyn a trope for her concept of translation. According to this, an idol/εἴδωλον is not the empty symbol of an absent subject, but rather a dynamic entity which moves and changes like a cloud in the sky. Similarly, translation needs to avoid the temptation of idols, or reproductions of the literal meaning which force a concept to remain static. Carson's adaptation of Euripides' *Helen* manifests the desire to grant new life to an otherwise dead myth of beauty by way of completely changing its form.

Helen and Marilyn both became myths because of the human need for transcendence; yet their juxtaposition highlights the impossibility of crystallizing an identity without doing away with many of its many nuances. Carson reminds us of the power of myths to mix reality with imagination and create stories, which keep changing and transforming according to the point of observation. In the end, Norma Jeane Baker of Troy's multiple, artificial layers form a meditation on how acting is an act of preservation against the prospect of vanishing into thin air.

Notes

1. Ovid, *Heroides* XVI, 141–4. The translation into English is mine.
2. See s.v. εἴδωλον in Liddell and Scott's *A Greek-English Lexicon*.
3. The titles of each paragraph are my translations from Euripides' *Helen*. All the quotations from the tragedy in the text are from Euripides (2017), translated by J. Morwood.

CHAPTER 15
EATING THE CLASSICS: CULINARY REWRITINGS OF CLASSICAL MYTHS IN POEMS BY LENA YAU
Katie Brown

Food structures Lena Yau's narrative universe. Born in Caracas, Venezuela, in 1968 to a Spanish-German family, Yau has lived in Madrid for over twenty years, as one of the nearly eight million Venezuelans who have left the country during the 'Bolivarian Revolution'.[1] From an early age, Yau learned to relate to her family's diverse cultures through food, and she now sees it at the centre of relationships, diasporic identity and memory. Yau served as literary advisor for *El sabor de la eñe*, a glossary of literature and gastronomy produced by Instituto Cervantes in 2011. She has published three poetry collections (2015, 2016, 2018), a novel (2015b) and a short story collection (2021).

Yau, who previously taught Latin and ancient Greek, explains that her earliest experiences of reading were entangled with an interest in ingestion, stating, 'If I was reading children's stories and found a passage with food, I would stop, immerse myself in it, ask myself questions' (Hernández Arias 2020). As she began to write, this way of seeing the world stuck with her and formed the pillar of her writing, extending to her reinterpretations of classical literature, in which cultures of food and hospitality often play a key role. The poetry collection, *Trae tu espada para hacer mi mesa* (Bring Your Back to Make My Table), includes a section titled 'Relecturas', or re-readings, which features culinary reimaginings of classical and mythological characters. This chapter presents these poems in the original Spanish and in English translation.

Veinte años no es nada

Regresó a casa.
Su mujer lo recibió.
Sobre un plato de melanina astillado
el fósil de un escalope de ternera
su comida favorita.
A Ulises los ojos se le llenaron de lágrimas.
Buscó en su bolsillo una hoja de loto que robó en aquella isla.
La engulló.
Dos segundos después su memoria estaba vacía.
De aquellos banquetes con Calipso y con Circe no quedó ni el aroma.

Besó a Penélope con amor y se sentó a comer.
Disfrutó.
Su lengua había olvidado otras patrias.

Twenty Years is Nothing[2]

He returned home.
His wife welcomed him.
On a splintered melamine plate,
the fossil of a veal escalope,
his favourite meal.
Ulysses' eyes filled with tears.
He reached into his pocket for a lotus leaf stolen on that island.
He devoured it.
Two seconds later his memory had emptied.
Of those banquets with Calypso and Circe not even the scent remained.
He lovingly kissed Penelope and sat down to dine,
taking pleasure.
His tongue had forgotten other homelands.

The poem takes its title from the tango 'Volver' (To Return) by Argentine singer Carlos Gardel; the story of a weary traveller who returns in nervous hope to his first love after twenty years away. The lyrics maintain that every fleeing traveller eventually ceases his peregrination. Both Gardel's traveller and the Odysseus reimagined in Yau's poem capture the mixed emotions towards a lost home of the Venezuelan diaspora, and a longing for a return that will dispel the pain of the intervening years. The final line of the poem demonstrates Yau's concern with food as a marker of national identity. Throughout her work, especially in her fiction, she considers how migrants use food as a link with the home they left behind, surrounding themselves with familiar tastes where possible, and feeling the loss of ingredients that can only be procured locally.

Yau maintains that 'Food is one of the forms that love takes, a declaration written on a plate, a different kind of kiss' (Pérez Yebaile, 2015). Consequently, keeping her husband's favourite meal waiting for his return is a sign of Penelope's love and fidelity. In turn, Odysseus' infidelity is symbolized through his sharing food with Calypso and Circe. He makes amends through a further act of ingestion, consuming the lotus leaf, thereby losing his memories of their time apart, as proof of his emotional commitment to his wife.

Yau continues, 'Food is an exercise that encompasses every side of love. Hate too (another side of love). Food is a channel for all feelings' (Pérez Yebaile 2015). Love and hate come together in Yau's darkly comic modern-day Narcissus.

Narciso in the kitchen

Asomó el rostro
lanzando fríos besos
al reflejo.

Encendió el fuego
y rompió la imagen
con un hervor.

Odiaba la sopa.

No quería morir
ahogado en ella.

Narcissus in the Kitchen[3]

He leaned forward
blowing cold kisses
to his reflection.

He lit the flame
and the boiling
broke the image.

He hated soup.

He didn't want to die
drowning in it.

In the modern day, Narcissus' pool of water becomes a pan of soup, which can provide easy sustenance and nourishment for the body but is often considered mundane. Humberto Valdivieso (2015) argues that beyond the 'seductive surface' of Yau's sensuous detailing of – often culturally specific – foods and culinary rituals, and the erotic links between consumption of food and bodies, we find 'the most basic, fragile and authentic elements of our humanity and they show us the beauty of our limits'. Valdivieso adds that reading the poems with a focus on the core impulse of hunger demonstrates that 'we are not made to transcend but to desire'. This denial of transcendence is particularly noteworthy when considering rewritings of canonical texts. In forgoing accounts of their heroism or beauty and instead placing Odysseus, Penelope and Narcissus in the kitchen, Yau strips these figures back to their central humanity.

Yau often says her interest is in 'ingestion', which encompasses not only food itself but how the language of eating permeates our way of understanding the world. The final classical rewriting in *Trae tu espalda para hacer mi mesa,* and the most enigmatic, is 'No decir' [To not say]. In the poem, Yau plays with how, in Spanish, one does not 'hold' one's tongue, but 'swallow' it.

No decir

Lo que Idea no contó
fue que la sirena
se tragó la lengua
para no nombrarlo.

To Not Say

What Idaea did not tell
was that the nymph
swallowed her tongue
to not have to name it.

Though there are various Idaeas in Greek mythology, Yau's reference to her as a 'sirena' [siren or mermaid] suggests the water nymph Idaea, mother to King Teucer by the river-god Scamander. The 'it' that is so horrific Idaea chooses perpetual silence over naming is left open to interpretation. In the light of other stories of nymphs and water gods, one can easily imagine sexual violence here, which fits with recurring themes in Yau's work of machismo and harmful relationships. Yau participated, for example, in the collection *Cien mujeres contra la violencia de género* [One Hundred Women Against Gender Violence] (Kariakin et al., 2015). Swallowing one's tongue alludes to both continued pressures on women to stay silent about abuses against them and an urge to protect oneself from reliving trauma through recounting it.

Explaining her creative process, Yau says, 'I translate everything through the dining table: speech, thought, interpersonal relationships, behaviours, reactions, habits, power, trends, ideologies, the human condition' (Pulido 2020). In these three poems, Yau uses food and ingestion as a lens through which to reimagine the stories of Odysseus, Narcissus and the nymph Idaea and, through them, to address fundamentally human themes of love, frustration and gender violence.

Notes

1. See the Interagency Coordination Platform for Refugees and Migrants for more information about this mass displacement: https://www.r4v.info/.
2. Translated by Colaboratorio Ávila (Katie Brown, Claudia Cavallin, María Gracía Pardo and Raquel Rivas Rojas). First published in *Modern Poetry in Translation* in 2023.
3. The translations of 'Narcissus in the Kitchen' and 'To Not Say' are my own and previously unpublished.

CHAPTER 16
THE OVIDIAN INFLUENCE ON ZADIE SMITH
Tracey Walters

Throughout her career, Smith has succumbed to the temptation to 'play' with the past by rewriting the works of her literary heroes. Her homage to major figures from the British literary tradition is most evident in *On Beauty* (2005), an update of E. M. Forster's *Howards End*; *NW* (2012), a loose reimagining of Virginia Woolf's *Mrs Dalloway*; and *The Wife of Willesden* (2021), an adaptation of Geoffrey Chaucer's *The Wife of Bath*. These writers aid Smith with her perennial experimentation with narrative form and technique. In addition, each writer provides a foundation for Smith's twenty-first-century interrogation of the British experience – focusing on themes of class, gender and identity politics – often from the perspective of the immigrant communities who have reshaped the British cultural and political landscape. While Smith's writing has been shaped by the aforementioned writers, one can reach back even further to the ancient Greeks and Romans to determine how classical texts from antiquity, specifically those by Ovid, also inform her writing. Working within a tradition of Black classicism, Smith brings a contemporized perspective to Graeco-Roman myth. As a Black woman of Caribbean heritage her racialized and postcolonial perspective plays uniquely into her employment of the classics as a tool to reflect on the history of the past and its relevance to current issues of the day. Few writers have associated Smith's oeuvre with Graeco-Roman classical literature: notably, there is an abundance of scholarship dissecting her writings about postmodernism, class, and multiculturalism, but seldom mention of interconnections with the Western classical tradition.

Smith's training at the University of Cambridge exposed her to Graeco-Roman myth, but she also inherits the tales second hand from the writers she emulates who are engaged in their own classical revisionism moulded by the perspectives of their antecedents. Take Ovid, for example, who will be discussed at length; any contemporary writers' allusions to his work are:

> complexly intertwined with our reception of Milton, Shakespeare and many others who form part of the Ovidian line. A modern assessment of the *Metamorphoses* will be infected by our conscious and unconscious knowledge of what earlier writers valued in Ovid, as well as by the particular preoccupations of our own era.
>
> Brown 2002: 3

The question for consideration is: how do Smith's conscious or unconscious renditions of Ovid's writings reproduce a new version of the many versions which came before? Reworkings of classical literature run throughout Smith's oeuvre. *The Autograph Man* and *Swing Time*, for example, borrow from the epic traditions of Homer and Virgil to tell the hero's tale, not necessarily because Smith intends to emulate her Greek and Roman predecessors, but rather because their construction of the hero's tale provides a model for her own stories. Smith's reverence for philosophy often means the occasional Graeco-Roman philosopher will appear in both her fictional and non-fiction work. Take for example, Smith's essay, 'Some Notes on Attunement', where she meditates on the 'tension between taste and time' (Smith 2018: 107). To elucidate her thesis, Smith engages in a lengthy exposition of *On the Shortness of Life*, the Roman philosopher Seneca's treatise on how to live a fulfilled life. Smith writes (2018: 107):

> In a lengthy riposte, the philosopher informs Paulinus that 'learning how to live takes a whole life,' and the sense most of us have that our lives are cruelly brief is a specious one . . . If you want a life that feels long, he advises, fill it with philosophy.

While this engagement with Seneca offers an explicit classical reference, other works draw more on thematic resonances picked up from another ancient text, Ovid's *Heroides*. Novels examining sexual politics, specifically marriage in *On Beauty*, *NW*, and *The Wife of Willesden* feature characters who are reminiscent of the women in Ovid's *Heroides*. Ovid is of particular importance in regard to Smith's characterization of women, especially those who are discontented in their relationships. Ovid's appeal for Smith, when conscious of her intertextual references, might be the same as it is for other writers of colour who revise the Western canon. As Moraru argues, multicultural rewritings 'polemically "update" a "familiar story"' and 'take on the representation of race, gender, or class in the 'model' story and alter it' (2001: 9), thereby 'provid[ing] a theoretical tool for narrating cultural and epistemological change that breaks its way through "forms" without remaining limited to certain literary genres and subgenres – to intertextuality, more to the point, to intertextuality narrowly understood' (2001: 12). *The Wife of Willesden* and selected passages from *On Beauty* and *White Teeth* serve as a few examples of how Smith reconfigures Ovid's stories for the contemporary moment and from a Black, Caribbean woman's perspective.

Ovid's predilection for writing tales about turbulent romances and passionate affairs resonates with Smith's own writings about the volatility of marriage. While the *Metamorphoses* portrays stories of infidelity, mariticide and betrayal – revealing the darker side of marriage – the *Ars Amatoria* ('The Art of Love') and *Heroides* ('Heroines') appear to be more – on the surface at least – romantic and delve into the subjectivity of Ovid's characters. The *Heroides* includes fifteen elegies written by some of the most powerful mythical women, and is credited for a number of approaches that are unusual for male authors of Ovid's period. First, Ovid employs the epistle to tell these women's stories. Next, in addition to granting women control over their own narratives, his portrayals of female protagonists are no longer secondary characters in stories about male heroes. The main theme in the *Heroides* is abandonment and the lamentation of the women left by husbands and partners who went to war and never returned. The women in the *Heroides* are raw and honest about being left in the domestic sphere to ward off future suitors and to tame their own desires. Women such as Penelope and Oenone write heartfelt notes mourning their husbands' absence and admitting their heartbreak. Others, such as Hypsipyle and Deianira, write scathing diatribes accusing their husbands of infidelity and threaten to take their own lives. Ovid's ability to capture the interiority of women's lives with such authenticity has raised suspicion by scholars such as Jacqueline Fabre-Serris, who contends (2009: 149):

> it is legitimate to ask whether other voices may be behind these letters, female voices, which Ovid may have chosen to evoke so as to accord his heroines a more authentic sounder manner of speaking.

Fabre-Serris' statement calls to mind Sappho, who wrote many poems and songs expressing women's passion and vulnerability, as a likely influence on Ovid. In fact, Sappho appears in the *Heroides* with a letter to Phaon. In *White Teeth* and *On Beauty*, Smith also features women who have been abandoned by their husbands either physically or emotionally. The comparison is consistent with the characters in the *Heroides*. Unlike Ovid, however, Smith's characters do not need to utilize the epistolary form to vent their grievances, for characters have the opportunity to confront their men in person.

Heroides

There is a long tradition of women writing in response to bearing the burden of life while their husbands departed for new adventures. In the opening passage of the essay 'Revision,' Levins Morales endeavours to revise history from a woman's point of view (2003: 15):

> LET'S GET ONE THING STRAIGHT ... Female head of household is not a new thing with us. The men left for Mexico and Venezuela and Peru. They left every which way they could, and they left us behind.

Levins Morales condemns male-centred versions of history, which conveniently ignore the contributions of women who washed, cooked, cleaned, raised children and worked the land when the men left their islands, but returned as heroes. Ovid's *Heroides* is one of the texts often cited in regard to this experience of forsaken women left to continue lives without their partners. Of course, Ovid draws from Homer's *Odyssey* and his depictions of the grief-stricken Clytemenestra, wife of Agamemnon; and Penelope, wife of Odysseus. Smith updates the central theme of abandonment pre-Trojan War and Post-Trojan War and redirects the setting to twentieth-century England, Jamaica and America to shed light on the women who were equally frustrated with partners who migrated overseas and failed to return. In *White Teeth* Smith portrays a woman who channels the same kind of anger exposed in the *Heroides*, but she offers a different scenario for the deserted wife. She considers what would happen if the wives initiated a reunion and accosted their husbands face-to-face.

Hortense Bowden is a minor character in Smith's debut novel *White Teeth*, but her story of abandonment is no less important. Hortense is not a long-suffering wife left to attend to children while her husband is fighting an epic war in some distant land. Rather, her betrayal is connected to a history of British colonialism and migration. For fourteen years, Hortense and her daughter wait for Darcus Bowden to arrange the airfare to travel from Jamaica to England, but the promise is unfulfilled. Darcus' desertion is a familiar story for Jamaican women (and other Caribbean women) of the twentieth century and Smith uses this episode to reflect on this history. Smith also offers no historical framing to explain Darcus' journey to England, but his sojourn is part of a significant cultural and historical pattern of migration known to those of Caribbean descent. Between the years 1940 to 1980, there was a mass migration of Jamaicans and other West Indians to England and North America. The first wave departed in the late 1940s and 1950s during the period known as the Windrush era, and later a second wave left the Caribbean from the 1960s through to the 1980s. The second migration wave was a result of Jamaica's 1962 emancipation from Britain, which brought Jamaicans sovereignty but also economic insecurity, political instability and threat of civil war. England, the mother country, offered opportunities for both men and women. Moreover, while this movement to England may have granted social mobility, it also accounted for the splintering of families. Those who were able sent remittances home to support relatives, others created new lives in England and forgot whom they left behind, and men like Darcus gave up. Darcus fails to send passage for his wife and daughter not because of infidelity, as in the *Heroides*. His broken promise to his wife and daughter is reduced to something more arcane, the unknown disease of 'lethargy' (Smith 2000: 26).

Any number of characters from the *Heroides* might be read in association with Hortense, but Phyllis' letter to Demophoon makes for a fitting selection. Phyllis was also impatient for her husband's return and began to question his promise to reunite: 'It might be you are already won by another bride, and feel for her the love that favoured me but ill; and since I have fallen from out your life, I feel you know Phyllis no more' (Ov. *Her.* 2. 29, trans. G. Showerman). Phyllis' anguish is carried throughout the letter as she describes all the ways she arranges for Demophoon's return, such as overseeing the maintenance of his ships. Her anguish is so deep she contemplates ending her life and blaming him for her downfall. Phyllis' epistle betrays her defeat. She considers many scenarios to justify Demophoon's silence and absence. We can imagine Hortense too may have created scenarios to explain Darcus' disappearance, but we have no evidence because readers are not privy to any correspondence between Hortense and Darcus. Actually, we never hear Hortense's speaking voice. While there is no written word, Hortense's story survives in the African tradition of the oral narrative. The narrator asserts that when she finally reunited with Darcus, her verbal assault on Darcas was so powerful it became folklore: 'so the legend went back in St. Elizabeth – [Hortense] gave Darcus Bowden the tongue-lashing of his life' (Smith 2000: 26). Readers must rely on their imaginations to conjure what she might have uttered.

The narrator's description of Hortense's arrival conveys the same anger and tone as any of the heroines in the *Heroides*:

Enraged by a fourteen-year wait, Hortense decided finally to make the journey under her own steam. Steam was something Hortense had in abundance. She arrived on the doorstep with the sixteen-year-old Clara, broke down the door in a fury.

Smith 2000: 26

This description aptly indicates the extent of Hortense's fourteen years of stored anger. Hortense's tongue-lashing renders Darcus speechless. For the rest of their days, Darcus, already not a particularly talkative man, 'slumped deeper into the recesses of his chair, ... HMPH was all Darcus said or ever was to say after' (Smith 2000). Darcus' failure to defend his actions and Hortense's prolonged verbal assault leaves Darcus as mute as the men in the *Heroides* (at least the single letters – in the double letters the men respond). By the end, Hortense positions herself as the authority – the dominant voice in the Bowden household.

Hortense's separation from Darcus is physical, but for Kiki Belsey, in *On Beauty*, the emotional detachment from her husband is equally devastating. Kiki Belsey, devoted wife and mother, experiences a separation that is grounded in ideological differences, vocation and race. In the novel, her husband, Howard, a mid-career professor, is an undermined, yet dominant presence in their academic community. Howard finds some purpose and identity in his Rembrandt scholarship, although he struggles to complete his monograph. His fear of failure, jealousy of a rival colleague, and typical downslide into a mid-life crisis leads to two short-lived affairs with women acquainted with Kiki. After spiralling into an existential crisis of her own, Kiki recognizes that Howard has abandoned her for his research, for sexual dalliances with other women, and petty squabbles with colleagues. She is forced to admit that Howard is no longer the man she met years prior. She feels abandoned by Howard and alienated in their predominantly white town. Kiki's story can be read in tandem with Ovid's *Heroides* 10, from Ariadne to Theseus. Ariadne is left on Naxos island in isolation by Theseus who accompanies her there after she helps him slay her half-brother and then escape through a labyrinth. Once Theseus completes his task, he cunningly returns to Athens leaving Ariadne with only the animals as company. Ariadne is shocked by the abrupt exit and distraught to see Theseus' ship at a distance, a stinging reminder of his deliberate abandonment (Ov. *Her.* 10.123):

I beheld your sails stretched full by the headlong southern gale. As I looked on a sight methought I had not deserved to see, I grew colder than ice, and life half left my body. Nor does anguish allow me long to lie thus quiet; it rouses me, it stirs me up to call on Theseus with all my voice's might. 'Whither doest fly?' I cry aloud. 'Come back, O wicked Theseus! Turn about thy ship! She hath not all her crew!'

Ovid 1971

Kiki does not inhabit an island, but she feels every bit as trapped and alienated in Howard's world of academia in their small college town. Surrounded by his friends, she is as lost as Ariadne. She doesn't speak their language, and what little she knows she defers to Howard who made all decisions about music, art and politics. Just as Theseus used Ariadne to get what he desired, Kiki acknowledges Howard took her for granted through the years she invested in making a home, raising their children and soothing his bruised ego, just so he could be immersed in his work.

After meeting another Black woman in the community and sharing her feelings, Kiki acknowledges her culpability for her current predicament – pushing aside her own goals for Howard's and allowing him to control the narrative for them both. She thinks, 'Why did she always concede what was left of the past to Howard's edited versions of it . . . She let Howard reinvent, retouch' (Smith 2005: 174). As Kiki's story progresses she finds her voice, and demands what she wants. Not only does she confront Howard, she rejects his controlling, dogmatic way of life and begins defining her own narrative and explores her intellectual interests as well as her sexuality. Eventually, she makes the choice to leave and starts life without Howard.

Women Telling Tales

Controlling one's own narrative is central to most of the women in *Heroides*. The same is true for Alvita, the protagonist in Smith's dramatic modernization of Chaucer's 'The Wife of Bath's Tale'. Alvita is, as Smith once wrote, 'the sole author of the dictionary that defines [her]' (Smith [2012] 2018a), a free thinking, sexually independent woman, who refuses to submit to man or societal mores trying to dictate how she lives her life. 'The Wife of Bath's Tale' is one of many stories in Chaucer's medieval *The Canterbury Tales*. It is the longest section in the collection of stories which make up the Tales. *The Canterbury Tales* is in part inspired by Ovid's *Metamorphoses* and *Ars Amatoria*: scholars such as John M. Flyer, Richard Hoffman and Sarah Annes Brown have examined Chaucer's penchant for Ovid's work, which is also detected in his *The Legend of Good Women*. Chaucer's bawdy Tale of the 'Wife of Bath', featuring Alisoun – a woman married five times and looking for a sixth – is a meditation on sexual politics, female sexual autonomy and voice. Throughout the three-part story, 'The Wife's Prologue,' 'Wife's Tale,' and 'Retraction', the Wife of Bath gives a masterclass on fulfilling a woman's sexual appetite and she advises men to submit to their wives' control.

In the year 2018 Smith was unexpectedly commissioned to write a piece to spotlight the cultural achievements of her hometown borough of Brent in north-west London. The idea to rewrite a section of the *Canterbury Tales* was born out of her recognition of the city's medieval past and its likely connection to the pilgrim's journeys fictionalized in Chaucer's *Canterbury Tales*. Initially, Smith intended to rewrite a short monologue from 'The Wife of Bath's Tale', one of the stories in *The Canterbury Tales*, but her enthusiasm for translating Chaucer's medieval English to twenty-first century vernacular was so invigorating that she abandoned the original concept and wrote a play, *The Wife of Willesden* (2021). Smith explains she was struck by the language and relatability of the protagonist, Alisoun, who was created in the fourteenth century and felt so contemporary. Smith is among a number of women who have been inspired to retell the Wife of Bath's story. Two years after the publication of the *Wife of Willesden*, Marion Turner published a fictional biography *The Wife of Bath: A Biography* (2023). Ten years earlier, Julie Walters paid homage to *The Wife of Bath* in the television series *The Wife of Bath* (2003), and in 2010, the dub poet Jean 'Binta' Breeze brought *The Wife of Bath* to south London, in her short recitation of 'The Wife's Prologue,' shot while walking through the famed Brixton market. Breeze's delivery of Chaucer's poetry in Jamaican patois may have also affected Smith's creation of Alvita. Taking into account Roland Barthes' poststructuralist argument, that no one person can lay claim to the originality of a story because every story is a retelling of a former narrative, we can read Smith's rendition of 'The Wife of Bath's Tale' as an amalgamation of intertexts. *The Wife of Willesden* remains remarkably close to Chaucer's plot, but Smith makes it her own with rhymed couplets in contemporary vernacular. She recasts the setting, race, and ethnicity of the characters, and inserts herself into the text to comment on Chaucer's appropriation of Ovid.

The Wife of Bath is propelled 600 years later into multicultural London. Set in Willesden (the site of almost all of Smith's novels) instead of Bath, Smith ensures the characters reflect the ethnic and racial diversity of the city. Alisoun is recast as Alvita, a Black woman of Caribbean heritage. Her culture is presented in her dress, language and mannerisms. Alvita's braids, covered by an isicholo hat, worn by Zulu women to indicate their married status, underscores her African roots. Alvita's diction brings another noticeable change. Smith judiciously brings authenticity to the vernacular of the region and time period. Thus, the language switches from Middle English to the slang of north-west London, Jamaican patois and standard English. Again, to represent the diversity of the community, Nigerian and South Asian characters speak in accented English. Alvita's stories are rooted in history and Black culture and she fully commits to bringing humour to her rendition of Chaucer's classic tale. She replaces biblical characters like Jesus of Nazareth with Black Jesus, and trades Sampson and his tribe of children with pop culture icons Bob Marley and Stevie Wonder (who also fathered many children).

Consistent with Chaucer's text, Alvita makes unapologetic demands for sexual pleasure. During Chaucer's time, the Wife of Bath's brazen talk about her insatiable sexual desires might have been shocking, but at a time of post third-wave feminism, social media and reality television, Alvita's talk is tame. Alvita's treatise on marriage and sexual politics between the sexes is also consistent with modern discourse. Social media, magazines and music continue to pose the question: what do women want out of relationships? Alvita's story does not just question relationships, it also confronts misogyny, respectability politics and authorship.

The Wife of Willesden is Alvita's story, but it is clearly self-referential. On countless occasions, Smith has warned against conflating herself with her character, but here, she literally writes herself into the play as a character who plays an author, with an uncanny likeness to herself – including her trademark headwrap and glasses. Furthermore, there is a slippage between Smith's authorial control and Alvita's authority, perhaps mimicking Chaucer's own presence in 'The Wife of Bath's Tale'. Slade (1969: 16) notes:

> [t]he wife is telling the story on one level whilst Chaucer is telling it on another, so that the usual ironic situation of a statement being made which one audience takes at its face value, and another (more sophisticated) audience at its ironic level, is considerably complicated here by the fact that at times Dame Alison is commenting ironically on the story she is telling ... while at other times Chaucer himself is commenting ironically on her views and reactions.

Similarly, in *The Wife of Willesden* the authorial voice of the obtrusive narrator interjects throughout giving insight, critiquing Chaucer, and guiding the reader.

Here the author is present in the beginning, but moves out of the spotlight allowing Alvita to command her story, but remaining on stage typing as the story unfolds. While the author relinquishes control to Alvita, her presence suggests the need to be present to oversee and protect the story, but also share in real time with the audience/reader. In fact, Smith once wrote (2018b: 337):

> I think to appreciate fiction fully it helps to conceive of a space that allows for the writer's experience and the reader's simultaneously ... That sounds like an impossible identity, but literature, for me, is precisely the ambivalent space in which impossible identities are made possible, both for authors and their characters.

The Wife of Willesden allows for this experience as Smith is an author, character and viewer all at once. Alvita has a lot in common with Smith. Like Alvita, she spins her tales to eager listeners, she is from the same neighbourhood, speaks the dialect of north-west London and patois, she is of Jamaican heritage, and writes on the same topic: women searching for autonomy.

The Wife of Willesden is set in a pub during an open mic night competition. The narrator remarks on the number of men who take the microphone without hesitation, confident their stories should be shared. Conversely, most of the women hold back, and those who share, lack the courage to speak candidly. Alvita has no reservations. She knows hers is a story worth telling. When it is Alvita's turn, she is invited to take the stage, but she elects to share her story from the middle of the pub. Her bold move to orate from the centre of the room is reminiscent of Janie, the Black woman protagonist of Zora Neale Hurston's *Their Eyes Were Watching God* (1937), who consequently also married several times, and shares stories of her many lovers to an audience – albeit an audience of one – and who understands the power of her voice as a Black woman commanding the attention of an audience. As the author of her story, Alvita professes her truth. Even though she regales the audience with stories that rely on a fair amount of hyperbole, the audience listens with amusement. Alvita uses her thirty years of experience as a married woman to give her some authority. As a master of her subject, she draws from a feminist epistemic body of knowledge that gives her authority to speak on the subject.

Alvita's story combines all the passion and resoluteness of the women in the *Heroides*. Alvita has a lot to share about her various relationships: her faithfulness, and infidelity. Her stories are not letters, but they are recounted in a public forum as monologues about her five husbands, some who are cast as characters. Alvita is the dominant speaker, sure of her voice, even as a Black woman in a society that marginalizes Black voices. While Alvita is the dominant speaker, there are a few exceptions when she is joined by characters who help tell her story. Of this group there are voices of women who reaffirm Alvita's treatise on surviving marriage and resisting misogyny. These women (South Asian and Black British) are also reminiscent of the women in the *Heroides*. They bring to the fore voices of women often unheard.

In 'The Prologue', Alvita discusses her marriages. After the prologue, she moves to 'The Wife's Tale', and the story evolves from the personal to the fantastical and draws on Arthurian legend and Ovid's *Metamorphoses*.

The Wife's Tale

Alvita's treatise on feminine desire and male submission transitions from her personal narrative to a mythic tale focused on the exploits of male characters who are forced to atone for their crimes against women. The 'Wife's Tale' extends Alvita's previous discussion regarding her relationship with husband number five and his insistence on the wickedness of women and employment of examples from ancient Greek and Roman literature as evidence. In this section in 'The Wife of Bath's Tale', Chaucer marries Arthurian lore with Ovidian myth. Stories from the *Metamorphoses*, Jason and the Argonauts, King Midas and possibly Perseus appear in this section. While the legend of King Arthur was well known to medieval audiences, a brief synopsis may be necessary for the contemporary reader.

King Arthur was a real historical figure but, with time, stories about his magnificent feats became more folklore than real. The myth of King Arthur was popularized prior to and during the medieval period and spurred numerous versions. Commonly accepted was the story of a Celtic king who, along with his Knights of the Roundtable, fought men (the Saxons), witches, and monsters, and sought after the holy grail. In Chaucer's 'The Wife of Bath's Tale', rather than fighting beasts, witches or armies, as seen in other archetypal quest narratives featuring Jason and the Argonauts or Perseus, the Knight's quest is focused on a less dangerous mission, but perhaps equally important battle. When a knight sexually assaults a maiden he is faced with a death sentence. A powerful queen, who is evocative of the Sphinx, spares him on the condition that he finds the answer to the question: 'What thyng is it that wommen moost desiren' (Chaucer 1947: 299). Upon producing the answer his life will be spared. The knight goes on a journey and along the way encounters women who try to provide answers, but he does not learn the answer he seeks. Eventually, an old crone offers to help if he will accept her as his bride. Begrudgingly, he agrees and is rewarded with her metamorphic transformation from a hag to a beautiful woman. The moral to Chaucer's story: men do well to yield to the power of women.

Smith's recreation of Chaucer's version of the Arthurian legend blends British myth with Jamaican and Greek mythology. It is only fitting that Smith's modernized tale is set in Jamaica and her Queen is Nanny of the Maroons and her knight is a soldier from Maroon Town. Although earlier Smith claims, 'A proviso: it's not my tale. I just / Copied it down from the original. / I could make stuff up and rewrite all / But that would surely defeat the purpose' (Smith 2023: 10), here there is a substantial difference. Smith presents a metamorphosis of her own and transforms Chaucer's white male hero (King Arthur) 'Of which that Britons spoken greet honour' (Chaucer 1947: 298) with the legendary Queen Nanny of the Maroons, 'who Jamaicans love to the nth degree' (Smith 2023: 73). Nanny's story is primarily preserved through folklore and a few written accounts. She was believed to have been a woman of Ghanaian descent who led her army of Maroon warriors against the Spanish and the British. From 1720 to 1739, Nanny and her Maroons fought in what was known as the First Maroon War and resisted the colonial forces who sought to strip them of independence. Eventually, despite the Maroons' inferior weaponry, under her leadership and strategic thinking the British were defeated. They were forced to end the war with a treaty that gave Nanny and the Maroons 500 acres of land. Nanny's name lives on. In Jamaica she is a Jamaican national heroine, a symbol of strength and resistance, appearing on the Jamaican five hundred dollar bill; and annually she and her comrades are celebrated on Maroon Day. Smith's incorporation of Nanny's story makes sense for a character proud of her heritage, and who mirrors her own characteristics of strength and autonomy, fighting for independence from male dominance. Taking on a postcolonial approach to Chaucer's story, Smith writes Nanny within the lore of the British literary tradition and puts her on equal footing with the historical and literary master narratives of the British canon. While a medieval audience would have known of Arthur, contemporary audiences outside Jamaica are much less familiar with Nanny, even though she is tied to British history. Smith avoids recounting the backstory of Nanny and her exploits. Instead, she uses props to announce Chaucer's story has been reworked. Two large banners proclaim: 'Transferred from Arturian Camelot / to Maroon Town, Jamaica' (73) and 'Featuring Queen Nanny / Famed rebel slave and leader of the peoples!' (73). Additionally, the fairies of Arthur's tale are traded for Jamaican mythology. First, The Ol Higue (Old Hag), a witch who feasts on human flesh and has the ability to transform into an owl, is added to Smith's Maroon tale. Next, she introduces 'River Mumma,' a mermaid-like creature who entices people to join her in the deep river by leaving her golden comb on a rock. Those who are lured by greed and curiosity are drowned by Mumma. Wiser individuals admire the comb from afar and are blessed with good luck. Finally, one of the most significant alterations is the portrayal of the knight. Smith's knight is one of Nanny's Maroons. What is of interest in Smith's reworking of the hero's quest within a Jamaican context is the emphasis on what women want, and also the question of autonomy and freedom of the body – both for Black women and men.

In Smith's story, the young girl who is violated is of Ghanaian descent (a member of the Akan tribe). The crime occurs in Cudjoe's Leeward Land, free land of the Maroons claimed by Cudjoe who fought alongside Nanny against the British. The land represents protection and freedom for the Maroons. Thus, the Maroon/knight's assault of the Akan on sacred land is egregious because he desecrates the land and defiles the legacy of the Maroons and their fight against domination. As a descendant of formerly enslaved people, the Maroon should know better than to capture and to deny the young Akan he violates control over her body. However, as the tale illustrates, despite his own history of colonial oppression he is no different from the Knight. He abuses the girl because he has the power to do so. Later, he is forced to acknowledge the privilege of his own bodily autonomy. In keeping with Chaucer's story, the Maroon is aided by an old ugly woman – the Old Higue. She tells the Maroon he must honour the agreement to marry, but he baulks at the suggestion and pleads for an alternative arrangement. He tells her, 'I am a maroon. We're imperious / people: we control our own destinies.' Of course, as all stories in the *Metamorphoses* show, he is wrong, for it is the gods who have dominion over man and determine their fate, and eventually he yields. In keeping with Chaucer's tale, the Maroon submits, but receives no punishment; instead, he is rewarded with a beautiful wife.

King Midas

Within the recounting of the Arthurian legend is Ovid's story of King Midas, which is invoked to prove women's indiscretions, but Chaucer's appropriation of the tale creates a different meaning. The story is presented here in its entirety to give context to the discussion that follows. King Midas was a foolhardy man and his greed and poor judgment results in bodily transformations that lead to deformity and immobility. Midas' fable begins with Bacchus (god of wine) and his band of satyrs. Silenus, Bacchus' tutor, accompanies the group, but after consuming too much wine strays from his party into unknown territory. He is discovered by the Phygians who send him to Midas for safety. Midas, a devotee of Bacchus, graciously welcomes Silenus and, in the spirit of bacchanal, fetes Silenus for ten days of merriment. On the eleventh day, Bacchus reunites with Silenus and in gratitude to Midas for his hospitality, grants him a single wish. Motivated by greed, Midas, 'never too judicious, answered: /"Grant that whatever I touch may turn to gold!"' (Chaucer 1947: 262). Immediately Midas begins experimenting, turning to gold everything within reach, from twigs to apples. Very quickly, he realizes although his touch can produce vast amounts of gold or wealth, there are limitations to possessing such an awesome power. The startling revelation that neither food nor water can pass his lips without turning to gold forces Midas to beg the gods to be released from the spell. Bacchus shows mercy and Midas is instructed to put his head and hands in the River Pactolus to be cured. Later, misfortune falls upon Midas again when puts himself in a dispute with the mountain god Tmolus. When Midas' friend, Pan, boasts about his superior musicianship and concedes he plays the reed pipe better than

Apollo played the lyre, Apollo challenges him to a public contest to determine who is the better talent. Tmolus is appointed to judge. Tmolus declares Apollo as the more talented player and others who are present agree: 'All except Midas, who began to argue, / Calling it most unfair' (Ovid 1955: 264). His contrariness, which appears to be based on loyalty to Pan, rather than objectivity, angers Apollo and results in Midas' punishment. 'Such stupid ears Apollo thought, were surely less than human' (1955: 264) and so he made them 'the ears / of the slow-going jackass' (1955: 265). Midas' ears are transformed as punishment for misjudging the contest and thus his poor hearing and bad decisions make him 'as stupid as an ass'. Mortified, Midas tries concealing his shame with a turban, but the disfigurement is discovered by his barber. Racked with the weight of the secret the barber whispered the secret in a hole and buried it, so it would remain hidden. Unfortunately, reeds grew in the place of his secret and in perpetuity spread the story in the breeze whispering 'Midas has ass's ears!' (Ovid 1955: 265). Thus, the barber for all his effort fails and the secret is revealed for all to hear Midas' shame forever.

Chaucer takes licence to rework the story and give it a different meaning. First, he truncates the story, starting *in medias res* and ending the tale prematurely. His tale commences with Midas' bestial transformation and the subsequent shame he experiences from the deformity. He provides no context, so readers cannot determine why or how Midas has the ears of a donkey. Moreover, he concludes the story without Ovid's ending, which explains how the reeds spread the secret of Midas' ears.

Chaucer's most significant alteration to the story is replacing the barber for a new character, King Midas' wife. She too is forced to carry the burden of his shame, and like the barber her attempt to conceal Midas' misfortune by unburdening her secret in the river also fails and is carried with the wind. Chaucer deliberately omits the ending and instead directs readers to the library for a full accounting. Scholars offer different interpretations of Chaucer's adoption of the Midas story. According to Pelen (1994), Midas' wife is Alisoun's alter ego, and her haste to be relieved of Midas' secret is about her desire for her own metamorphoses as character and storyteller. Lee Patterson on the other hand says, 'Alisoun uses the tale as a testing to see if her mostly male audience is really listening' (Patterson 1983: 657–8). Smith determines there is a subtext to Ovid's tale, which is deeper than a story about disloyal wives or gullible husbands.

Smith doesn't make it explicit to the unobservant reader that Midas is either husband number five (Ryan) and Alvita is his wife, or Alvita is Midas. For Smith, in either case, the story is problematic, especially in regards to Ryan's treatment of abuse which carried over from the prologue. She critiques Chaucer's appropriation of Midas' story with stage directions and authorial interruptions. To more clearly establish the thread between the prologue and 'The Wife's Tale' and Alvita with Midas' story, Smith has characters reenact the story, but they are presented as fictional characters. Ryan plays Midas and Alvita plays Midas' wife. Smith's objective is to highlight the heinous abuse suffered at the hands of husband number five, which she deems is treated too cavalierly by Chaucer. Although Alvita has been in charge of telling her story, at this point Smith intervenes. She is not confident the reader/audience can derive full meaning from Chaucer's text, and takes over Alvita's role. First, she adds a note to help guide the audience through Chaucer's iteration of Ovid's tale (Smith 2023: 82):

> *Throughout the next section, RYAN plays King Midas. We may get the sense, as the story progresses, that ALVITA is talking less about Midas' dirty secret as much as Ryan's marital failings, principally his domestic abuse, which is a secret, of course, that Alvita has refused to keep ... And as they tell the apparently frivolous story of Midas, we sense a serious subtext beneath.*

Smith's statement intimates her belief that without language to directly address Ryan's violent attacks the reader may miss the point. Furthermore, when Smith comments sarcastically, '*And as they tell the apparently frivolous story of Midas*' (82) the choice of language further emphasizes her critique of Chaucer's mishandling of Ovid to address the severity of domestic violence. As a woman telling this story in the twenty-first century, she needs to clarify that Ryan's behaviour is deplorable and unamusing. To ensure readers understand Ryan's role in this reenactment she casts Ryan as Midas and gives him a speaking role that exposes his desire for Alvita to protect his secret. Through the delivery of these lines, Ryan is forced to admit to his crime and expose his misdeeds.

Once readers know Ryan's role, they might interpret the story to mean he is an ass/donkey because he trusted Alvita would not disclose his violence. However, when Smith's directions say, '*we sense a serious subtext beneath*' (Smith 2023: 82), she points to other possible readings of Chaucer's Ovidian tale. To detect alternative interpretations, an observant reader would have to know Midas' story in its totality and deduce the symbolic representation of gold in the Wife's Tale and in the earlier portion of Midas' tale. Moreover, a reader would also discern how it came to be that Midas' ears were (disfigured) and then make the association between Midas' ears and the references to ears/hearing in 'The Prologue'. Most importantly, Smith persuades the audience to acknowledge, although Ryan is equated with Midas, the allusions to gold/greed and deafness are associated more with Alvita than Ryan.

References to both the gold and loss of hearing are detected throughout the prologue (and in the tale), but only the attentive reader, one who knows the story, would pick up on its significance. Smith adds a number of clues precluded in Chaucer's version. In both Chaucer's and Smith's tales, in many instances gold connotes negativity. In 'The Wife's Tale' there are two references to gold. Smith's addition of the Caribbean River Mumma and her golden comb provides another cautionary folktale about the danger of gold. The story warns that those who give in to the temptation to touch River Mumma's gold comb are befallen by a fate even worse than Midas'. Also, if the Arthurian story alludes to Perseus, the story would also be relevant because he was born of gold but conceived in violence, and as the prologue details, gold and violence are synonymous. In 'The Prologue' there are several mentions of gold. First, Smith modifies Chaucer's text by adding a description of Alvita's jewellery. She is described as wearing multiple faux gold chains. Her adornment of gold jewellery makes an explicit link to Midas, but alone it has no pertinence. Unlike Midas, her chains are artificial and lack value and she derives no power from her own plentiful array of necklaces, but her desire for gold is equally as apparent and self-destructive. The real gold she seeks is Ryan's love, the clichéd 'heart of gold'. Ryan's oppressive golden love is antithetical to loving. Just as Midas learns that gold diminishes the quality of his life, Alvita experiences the same outcome. Ryan's presence in her life is dangerous. In the second example, Alvita has frequent nightmares of Ryan trying to kill her. She depicts herself lying in blood-soaked sheets, which stain her body with evidence of Ryan's crime. The dream should serve as a cautionary tale to free herself from Ryan's violence, but Alvita thinks she can change him, transforming 'his base love to gold' (Smith 2023: 48). Later, even Alvita admits her delusion – the idea of blood being a symbol for gold, 'and a good sign' is a lie, and an ominous foreshadowing of what transpires – Ryan's beatings.

A third association with gold invokes the Greek story of Eriphyle and Amphiaraus. Here again is a tale equating gold and trauma. Eriphyle takes a bribe in order to encourage her husband to fight the Thebans. In exchange for her betrayal she is given the necklace of Harmonia, which was made from gold and precious jewels (Chaucer simply says she is given a brooch). Chaucer concludes the story here. What Eriphyle doesn't know, and what Chaucer does not share, is that the necklace is cursed and her decision will cause the loss of her life. According to Greek legend, those who donned it experienced misfortune. Amphiaraus dies in the war. Foreseeing his death, he commanded either of their sons, Alcmaeon and Amphilochus, to kill Eriphyle. Ten years later, Eriphyle accepts another bribe to send her son Alcmaeon to the same war. But this time the necklace Harmonia directs the order. After fighting the Thebans, Alcmaeon carries out his father's directive and slays his mother. Consistent with the Greek rendering of Eriphyle's tale, Smith redirects readers to the necklace Harmonia. While the necklace is not mentioned by name, she explains that Eriphyle receives a gold necklace. Furthermore, to ensure the gold necklace is highlighted, Smith presents Eriphyle asking the colluders for the gold chain. Similar to Alvita, Eriphyle's bad decision (and lust for gold) results in death – which, with Ryan's violent beatings – could be the outcome for Alvita. Thus, Smith is more effective than Chaucer in emphasizing the symbolic nature of gold and the significance of this story. In the examples provided, Ryan is disassociated with Midas' lust for gold. Instead, Ryan represents the gold itself – the curse that befalls those who are blinded by its preciousness.

In addition to the references to gold tying back to the characters, several mentions of ears and hearing also correlate with Midas' tale. Alvita's hearing impairment and Ryan's hand in the damage is stressed three times. Twice, Alvita very casually mentions: 'See this ear? I am now deaf / In it, cos he smacked me in my head / For tearing a page from a book he'd just read' (Smith 2023: 55). While Ryan openly admits to the act of domestic assault, he puts the onus on Alvita, citing 'it was sort of your fault' (67). Again, similar to the references to gold, the focus on Alvita's ears/deafness connect Midas to Alvita, not Ryan.

Ultimately, assessing these references together, Alvita is Midas. Smith invites us to question Chaucer's appropriation of Midas. If Alvita is Midas, what is her flaw? Is she punished for her own greed, especially since she admitted marrying the first three husbands for money. Moreover, why are her ears transformed? Is it because she will not take the cues from the books Ryan reads about being a dutiful wife and must be punished for failing to listen and submit? If both scenarios are true, it would mean Chaucer is blaming the victim and thus, Smith calls him out. These textual clues are added to a stage direction explaining Ryan's failed attempt to strike an assertive Alvita who grabs his wrist to intercept the blow. Furthermore, Alvita holds up Ryan's hand so everyone can see his shameful behavior. Thus, Smith refers to Ryan's hand as the 'shameful object' (Smith 2023: 83), perhaps to redirect the reference to Midas' ears to Ryan's hands, more specifically, his abuse. In this way, Smith underscores the problematic nature of the toxic relationship between Ryan and Alvita. She does not treat the incident with levity; instead, she treats the abuse with the seriousness it deserves. Ultimately, Smith makes changes to Ovid's story in order to reinforce the main point of Alvita's quest for female autonomy – the power of her voice, why she must use it, and why she must tell the tale.

Reading Ovid in conversation with Zadie Smith uncovers several parallels. Similar to Ovid she illuminates through her characters the importance of authorship and women controlling their own narratives; she highlights the woman's perspective in marriages; and lastly, she recentres the woman in the master narratives which historically relegated women (and people of colour) to the margins. Ovid is just one example of how to excavate Smith's work to identify the many ways she reworks classical mythology. Alternative examinations might include an investigation of her appropriation of the epic or allusions to other classical works. The task to unearth the intertextual references may not be as apparent as they are with *The Wife of Willesden*, but it will be worth it to discover Smith's contribution to Graeco-Roman revision; the possibilities are endless.

CHAPTER 17
A CONTEMPORARY MEDEA: ALICE DIOP'S *ST OMER* (2022)
Fiona Cox

In 1986 the novelist Marie Cardinal published a translation of Euripides' *Medea*, declaring that the play seemed to her to speak directly of her own experiences of family life:

> Je reconnaissais les personnages, certains vivaient chez moi, dans ma maison, d'autres avaient vécu avant, dans cette même maison ou ailleurs, dans des contrées dont je connaissais chaque arpent.
>
> L'histoire des miens se transmettait de génération en génération: histoires d'amours, de drames, de violences. Ma mère m'appelait souvent par mon nom de famille 'Cardinal', le nom de mon père, le nom de son mari qu'elle haïssait; chaque fois qu'elle m'appelait comme ça, c'était un crachat qu'elle lui lançait en pleine face.
>
> Cardinal 1986: 13

> [I recognized the characters – some of them lived in my household, in my house; others had lived there previously in that same house or elsewhere, in lands where every acre was familiar to me.
> My family's story was passed down from generation to generation: love stories, dramas, violent outbursts. My mother would often use my surname to address me – 'Cardinal' – the name of my father and of the husband whom she loathed. Every time that she used this name for me it was as if she were spitting in his face.][1]

Cardinal finds in *Medea* a model for thinking through the painful relationships between mothers and daughters – her own adolescence was catastrophically scarred by her feeling of being unloved by her mother. She articulates her grief over this failed bond in her autobiographical novel *Les Mots pour le dire*, an account of her breakdown and her experience of psychoanalysis. However, it is not solely through the representation of damaged and damaging maternity that Cardinal finds her family history, but also in the depiction of alienation. Cardinal was born and brought up in Algiers and came to France during the Algerian War of Independence. In the *Avant Propos* to *Médée* she writes about her experiences as a *pied noir*, people of European descent who were born in Algeria during the period of French rule (1830–1962). Many *pieds noirs* came to France after 1962:

Il m'arrive souvent de penser au comportement des pieds-noirs, en France, depuis qu'ils sont rapatriés. Le million que nous étions s'est intégré sans faire beaucoup d'histoires. Mais je crois qu'en s'intégrant il a introduit dans le corps du pays une semence subversive ... La Patrie ne nous a pas reconnus. Et pour cause: depuis le temps, le fond avait changé, transformé par le mélange des sangs, la chaleur, la nourriture, la terre, les musiques, et surtout par la fréquentation quotidienne, depuis cent trente ans, de l'islam ... Nous ne fûmes pas bien accueillis: nous étions soi-disant responsables de ce conflit pour lequel les petits gars de France avaient donné leurs vies.

Cardinal 1986: 19

[I often find myself thinking about the behaviour of the *pieds noirs* in France, after they were repatriated. There was a million of us and we slotted in without very much fuss. But I think that as we did so, we introduced a subversive element that began to germinate within the fabric of the country ... The Fatherland did not recognize us. And there was a good reason for that – over time our core had changed, had been transformed by mixed blood relationships, warmth, food, the land, music and above all by daily exposure over a hundred and thirty years to islam ... We were not warmly welcomed. We were, apparently, responsible for this conflict for which the ordinary lads in France had given their lives.]

I have turned to Marie Cardinal as a way of introducing a chapter focusing upon Alice Diop's *St Omer* in part because Marie Cardinal's relationship to the story of Medea bears striking resemblances to Diop's two protagonists – Laurence, who is accused of murdering her daughter, and Rama, an academic writing a book about Medea entitled *Médée naufragée*. Both of Diop's protagonists come from families who have had to negotiate arrivals in France from Senegal, thus experiencing life as outsiders within French society, and both women have painfully difficult relationships with their mothers. There is, however, a further important dimension to Marie Cardinal's work; the current surge of interest in the classics on the part of women creatives might risk obscuring the fact that women writers have long been producing works that employ classical myth as a way of thinking through tensions due to immigration, the pain of fractured family relationships and the frustrated rage that is, sometimes, a part of female identity.[2] A translation of *Medea* produced in 1986 from one of France's leading novelists both foreshadows elements of Diop's work, but also alerts us to a female-produced classical tradition that has long been shaping women's writing in France.[3]

Alice Diop's film *St Omer* (2022a) has a strong literary heritage. Diop (born 1979) has established a reputation for producing documentaries that explore the stories of those who belong to marginalized communities within France. She is particularly well known for *La Permanence* (2016), *Vers la tendresse* (2016) and *Nous* (2020). In an interview at the Villa Médici she observed:

Je pense que mes films sont des autoportraits de ce que je suis, de ce que je pense, de ce que je revendique, de ce que je défends. Je suis une femme noire, je suis une femme noire qui a grandi en France [. . .] qui vient d'un milieu populaire, qui a été traversé par l'expérience de l'exil de ma propre mère … J'avais la conviction politique, en tout cas la nécessité politique, que ces histoires soient le plus largement diffusées, le plus largement partagées.'

Diop 2022b[4]

[I think that my films are self-portraits of what I am, of what I think, of what I claim and what I defend. I am a Black woman; I am a Black woman who has grown up in France, who comes from a working-class background, that is shaped by my own mother's experience of exile … I had the political conviction – at any rate the political necessity – that my films should be screened and shared as widely as possible.]

In *St Omer* Diop explores the challenges facing those whose families have come from Africa and who have built a life for themselves in France, examining tensions that are similar to those articulated by Cardinal in the avant-propos to her translation of *Medea*. At the same time Diop is fashioning a portrait of a twenty-first century Medea, is exploring how her story might help us to understand the rage and the pain of an isolated immigrant, who is wholly dependent upon her older lover and who feels neglected and unsupported by him. It is unsurprising that it should be literature that shapes Diop's portrayal of Laurence Coly, the woman who engineered the death of her infant, since literature exerts a far greater influence on Diop than any other art form (Romney 2023).[5] Literature and life coincided very powerfully for Diop, when she attended the trial of Fabienne Kabou in St Omer in 2016. *St Omer* is based upon Kabou's story – indeed Diop points out that the scenes within the law court are transcribed verbatim from Kabou's trial.[6] The newspapers were already presenting Kabou as a contemporary Medea – in *Le Monde* Pascale Robert-Diard observed:

Fabienne Kabou est entrée en Médée et ressortie en malade de la cour d'assises du Nord, à Douai qui jugeait en appel cette mère accusée d'avoir tué sa fille, Adélaïde, âgée de quinze mois, en la laissant se noyer sur une plage de Berck-sur-mer, un soir de novembre 2013.

2017

[Fabienne Kabou entered the courtroom in the North, in Douai, as Medea and left again as a patient. The court was judging the appeal of this mother accused of having killed her daughter, Adélaïde, who was fifteen months old, by leaving her to drown on a beach at Berck-sur-mer one November evening in 2013.]

Diop attended the trial because she was fascinated by the story of this woman with whom she shared a French-Senegalese heritage. In the film Rama performs the role of

Diop. Ostensibly she is following the trial because she is working on a study of *Medea*, but she becomes increasingly unsettled by the links and parallels that bind her story to that of Laurence Coly, especially as we discover that she is pregnant (as, indeed, was Diop, when she attended Kabou's trial). Moreover, both women have to navigate the experience of life in France for those with a Senegalese family background. Perhaps, therefore, it is unsurprising that Diop should have collaborated with the novelist Marie Ndiaye when writing the screenplay of *St Omer*. Ndiaye is a French novelist, born to a Senegalese father who returned to Senegal when she was one, leaving her and her mother in France. Ndiaye's novels have both explored the position within France of migrants from Senegal and have deployed extensive classical imagery while doing so. Shirley Jordan has written compellingly about the Homeric intertexts that colour Ndiaye's presentation of hospitality throughout her work and, in fact, Ndiaye has written her own response to *Medea* through her novel *La Femme changée en bûche* (1989).[7] As Diop observed Kabou's demeanour in court and listened to the educated register of French in which she spoke, she felt very powerfully as if Kabou had walked straight out of a Marie Ndiaye novel:

> Tout de suite je me suis dit, la première phrase que je me suis formulée c'est que cette femme était une héroïne de Marie Ndiaye. Le mystère, la complexité, la puissance de cette femme me renvoyaient en fait à ce qui m'intéresse dans la littérature de Marie . . . c'est à quel point elle travaille à partir du mystère de l'âme humaine et qu'elle invente une langue très spécifique pour approcher ce mystère.[8]
>
> *Diop 2022b*

[Straightaway I said to myself, the first line that came to my mind, was that this woman was a Marie Ndiaye heroine. The mystery, complexity, and power of this women put me in mind precisely of what interests me in Marie's books . . . – and that's how much she works from the basis of the mysterious human soul and that she creates a very specific language in which to address this mystery.]

Diop was intent upon preserving the literary aura of Kabou and instructed Guslagie Malanda, who played the part of Coly to aim 'to speak as if she was reading Marguerite Duras' (Zemler 2023). Duras (who also emigrated to France having been brought up in French Indochina) is an important presence within *St Omer*. Before Rama leaves to attend Laurence Coly's trial, she teaches a class to university students on *Hiroshima mon amour*, for which Duras wrote the screenplay. The students observe the degradation and humiliation of *les femmes tondues*, the women punished in the aftermath of the Second World War for relationships with German soldiers. This intertextual presence ensures that, right from the start, *St Omer* is underpinned by depictions of barbarism within a society that needs to think of itself as civilised. But the educated cadences and register of Kabou's language also point to her distinctive heritage: 'Because of the colonization by the French in Africa, the French they speak is not everyday French,' Malanda explains. 'It's closer to literature in a way. And in the case of Fabienne Kabou, it's clearly a style she gives to herself. It became a singularity. She's a bit like an alien with this language' (Zemler 2023). Diop explores the way in which language heightens the isolation experienced by Coly within the film. Coly explains that her mother forbade her to speak Wolof, believing that an ability to speak perfect French would serve as a passport to a better life for her daughter: 'elle voulait que je parle parfaitement français et uniquement français' (she wanted me to speak French perfectly and exclusively) (Diop 2022a); this was a feature of her upbringing which isolated her from other children in Dakar. This inability to integrate within society in Senegal was exacerbated by her student years in Paris. Coly remembers returning to Dakar for her beloved grandmother's funeral, complaining that she was shunned by members of her community: 'Tout le monde se comportait bizarrement avec moi. On me traitait de toubab' (Everyone behaved weirdly towards me. People treated me as if I were white) (Diop 2022a). Unfortunately Coly was unable to find acceptance within the university community in France either; it became a place where she experienced racism at the hands of a supervisor who disapproved of her choosing Wittgenstein as the topic of her dissertation, declaring that she should have chosen a topic that was closer to her own culture. Yet, Coly harnesses a French belief in reason and lucid thought when she declares 'Je suis cartésienne' [I am a Cartesian] (Diop 2022a). It is a supremely poignant statement given that it is uttered within a courtroom bent upon excavating the reasons for a crime that is so terrible as to defy comprehension.

Though Coly identifies with French culture when she describes herself as 'cartésienne', the differences between African and European cultures are explored in court as a possible explanation of the crime. The lawyers invite her to defend herself by drawing upon a background in which a belief in sorcery, in being cursed, could be proposed as an explanation. 'Je l'invite à puiser dans sa propre culture pour essayer de l'expliquer' [I'm inviting her to draw upon her culture in order to explain it]. 'Mme Coly, n'ayez pas honte de votre culture si cela peut nous aider à comprendre votre geste.' [Mme Coly, have no shame of your culture if that can help us to understand your actions.] (Diop 2022a). Indeed Coly's mother, Odette, takes the stand and declares that her daughter had been cursed by a malevolent spell from the moment that she had arrived in France. Coly herself veers between deep confusion and distress, when she is unable to recall events coherently and when she remembers periods of illness and hallucination, moments when she insists on reason and the clarity of her thought, and moments when she considers sorcery as a possible defence for her crime.[9] She is reported to have said in prison that 'Le juge, il croit au maraboutage' [The judge believes in sorcery], while also observing that 'Je ne suis pas la mère infanticide normale. Ça les embête.' [I'm not their run-of-the-mill infanticidal mother and that bothers them.] (Diop 2022a). It is hard to know how Coly might imagine a run-of-the-mill infanticidal mother to appear, but she perceptively identifies the strategies employed, perhaps unwittingly, by a legal system eager to highlight her otherness, to suggest that the urge to kill one's child stems from a foreign culture, that it is alien to the values of France. As Coly's lawyer observes: 'C'est plus commode pour nous de la voir comme un monstre. Un monstre, il faut le vaincre.' [It's more convenient for us to see her as a monster. Monsters need to be vanquished.] (Diop 2022a).

The myth of Medea risks becoming a glib invocation in cases of infanticide that are reported in the press, as if the cultural heft of classical tragedy can become the focal point of the story as opposed to the horror of the act of killing a child, one's own child. It is striking that when Diop looked upon Kabou, she immediately thought of her in literary terms, thought of her as a Marie Ndiaye heroine. She explained in an interview that what she found particularly compelling in Kabou's narrative was the sense that it was underpinned by myth:

> I went there under the magnetic pull of an obsession that for a long time I couldn't put into words. There was this psychoanalytic and mythical dimension underlying the way she explained her actions. She said: 'I laid her on the sand, thinking the sea would carry her body away.' Somehow that put the horror of the crime to one side: I was hearing something else. I found myself making a story more beautiful, more acceptable than the real one, about a women offering her child to a sea which could care for her.
>
> *Romney 2023*[10]

This is an important declaration, because it points to the way in which Diop has used classical reception to wrest Coly's story away from the exploration of a child's murder to investigate the complexities of the mother's personality, while creating a 'story more beautiful, more acceptable'. The horror of a lost child becomes part of a classical tragedy in which the perpetrator is the heroine and the focus moves from child to mother. The idea that the sea might care better for the child than her own parent establishes a parallel between 'mer' and 'mère', which is explored throughout the film. The film opens with the image of a Black woman carrying a child by night along a beach to the mesmerizing soundscape of the waves rising and falling. At the end of the film we hear the same sound, but this time it is the laboured breathing of Rama's unwell mother, as she allows her daughter to hold her hand in a rare moment of connection and love between the two of them. When Laurence Coly depicts for the courtroom this walk along the beach on the last day of her daughter's life, she does so in highly literary terms, a manoeuvre that angers the prosecuting lawyer. She states: 'C'était l'heure de la haute marée. La lune se dresse devant moi comme un projecteur, comme un appel de phare.' [It was the right time for high tide. Ahead of me the moon was rising like a spotlight, like a lighthouse beckoning me.] The lawyer shuts her down: 'Vous n'êtes pas sur la scène de je ne sais quel théâtre; vous êtes dans un cour d'assises.' [You're not on the stage in some theatre; you're in a criminal court.] (Diop 2022a).[11] Through Diop's film, of course, the protagonist takes her place both within the courtroom as well as in the drama being screened. Diop heightens the literary quality of the scene when she shows Rama, whose book about Medea is entitled *Médée naufragée* [*Shipwrecked Medea*] watching Pasolini's *Medea* (1969) in which Maria Callas plays the title role. The clip from the Pasolini version shows the moonlight streaming through the window, after Medea has tenderly cradled her son before killing him, while the sound of the sea can be heard in the background. Seascape and moonlight connect these two responses to *Medea*, both of which deploy the myth as a way of exploring the complexities of maternity.[12] It is striking that Diop should select the work of a white male to contrast with her own depiction.

Yet by looking back to Euripides we can see that there are several elements of the play that are highlighted, if we explore them through a sense of alienation within society. Edith Hall argues that it was indeed Euripides who created in Medea a woman who was different, was other, within Corinthian society:

> From an Athenian perspective Medea's ethnicity must have cast doubts even on the legitimacy of the union's unfortunate offspring. Medea's difference from the women of Corinth must have been emphasised moreover, by her clothing and appearance; Euripides was almost certainly the first poet to turn her from a Corinthian into a barbarian.
>
> *Hall 2008: xvii*

Hall emphasizes the fact that contemporary interest in ancient Greek drama, and in Euripides in particular, might be driven in part through recognition of his interest in multi-ethnic societies. In the Introduction to a recent translation of some of his plays, she claims that: 'This ethnic pluralism perhaps finds expression in the 'multi-ethnic' casts of tragedy: the present volume alone introduces Egyptians in *Helen*, Black Sea barbarians in *Medea* and an Amazon's son in *Hippolytus*.' (2008: xxv). As Euripides' Medea laments her fate she highlights the desperation of her loneliness, the bleakness of looking around to recognize no answering face, nobody at all to see and accept the person she is. 'You have this city, your father's house, a fulfilled life and the company of your friends, while I, a desolate woman without a city, shamefully injured by my husband who carried me as plunder from a foreign land have no haven from this disaster: no mother, no brother, no relative at all' (2008: 8). Though Medea laments the condition of her womanhood, and contrasts it with the freedom and agency of Jason, it is her isolation which causes her added suffering. As Natalie Haynes points out, however, her isolation is exacerbated because she automatically becomes an object of suspicion through being educated and bright. We might remember, here, Coly's observation that she troubles the legal system because she cannot be pigeonholed as typical of the sort of woman to commit this crime – she is too educated, too intelligent. And we might remember the irritation expressed by her university tutor that she has failed to know her place, has had the temerity to think that she might be welcomed to write a dissertation on a topic of her choice, a European philosopher. Haynes' characterization of Medea elaborates those qualities that are shared by Coly:

> As we saw with Clytemnestra, there were few things more alarming to ancient Greek men than the machinations of a clever woman, and Medea is the cleverest of them all. If Clytemnestra is the worst wife in Greek myth, Medea can lay a strong claim to being its worst mother. But before she becomes that (in the second half of the fifth century BCE), she is already a dangerous figure: clever, female, foreign and magical.
>
> *Haynes 2022: 230*

But the loneliness experienced both by Medea and by Coly is deepened through their dependence upon just one person. We hear at the trial how Coly's contacts within France fell away one after the other; she moved in with her aunt, and it didn't work out, so she left. She moved in with one of her cousins, but they fell out. Her relationship with her mother was strained and infrequent. She was unable to establish connections with fellow classmates. By the time she met Luc Dumontet it seemed inevitable that he would become the centre of her life, even as he kept her on the periphery of his world. Once she has moved in with him, the deep depression into which she sinks isolates her still further from the world, rendering her and her child supremely vulnerable. Her lawyer depicts her tragic descent:

Élise est morte parce que sa mère est folle et parce que dans sa folie sa mère croyait ainsi la protéger. Imaginez les deux extrêmes de son parcours, si vous le voulez bien. Imaginez cette jeune demoiselle pleine d'ambitions et d'envies qui débarque à Paris et posez-vous la question – comment est-elle devenue cette femme enfermée, invisible, qui ne sort plus de l'atelier de son compagnon?

[Élise died because her mother is mad and because, in her madness, her mother thought that she was protecting her like this. I invite you to picture the two ends of her journey. Imagine this young woman full of ambitions and longings, who came to Paris and just ask yourselves – how did she become this woman who was locked away, who became invisible and no longer left her partner's studio?]

Diop 2022a

Coly's desperate loneliness in twenty-first-century France alerts us to the terrible isolation also experienced by Euripides' Medea. Separated by thousands of years the two women are nevertheless kindred spirits. Her nurse describes the terrible condition to which Medea has been reduced, through the mistake of relying on one person alone:

She will not look up, will not lift her face from the ground, but listens to her friends as they give advice no more than if she were a rock or a wave of the sea – save that sometimes she turns away her pale, pale neck and bemoans to herself her dear father and her country and the home which she betrayed to come here with the man who how holds her in dishonour. Schooled by misfortune, the poor woman has learnt what it is to be parted from one's fatherland.

Euripides 2008:2

Medea links her isolation explicitly to her gender, declaring: 'Of everything that is alive and has a mind, we women are the most wretched creatures . . . As for a man, when he has had enough of life at home, he can stop his heart's sickness by going out – to see one of his friends or contemporaries. But we are forced to look to one soul alone' (Euripides 2008: 7). And we might have hoped that these lines might lose their pertinence in a

Western country in the twenty-first century, and yet Coly is estranged from her own family, utterly dependent upon Luc Dumontet financially, unwelcome at the family events to which he regularly disappears and left to care for her child as best she might.[13] Her lawyer points out, bleakly: 'Laurence Coly a appris être mère sur Internet. Elle a essayé de faire ce qu'il fallait, elle a tenté de lutter, de tenir, mais elle a perdu. Il n'y avait personne pour l'aider.'[14] [Laurence Coly learned how to be a mother on the Internet. She tried to do what needed to be done; she tried to struggle and to hang on, but she lost. There wasn't anyone to help her.] (Diop 2022a).

It is interesting that the defence lawyer starts her summary of the case in classical terms: 'C'est l'histoire . . . d'une femme fantôme, une femme que personne ne voit, que personne ne connaît. C'est l'histoire d'une lente disparition, une tragique descente aux enfers dans laquelle une mère a mené son enfant.' [It's the story . . . of a ghost woman, of a woman whom nobody sees and whom nobody knows. It's the story of a slow disappearance, a tragic descent into hell on which a mother led her child.] (Diop 2022a). By framing her defence in this way the lawyer highlights the classical imagery, almost as if she is inviting us to identify Coly with Medea. She chooses to confront directly the question of monstrosity, but does so by emphasising the bonds linking mother and child, bonds that scientifically metamorphose a mother's body and bonds which defy the loss of a child. Furthermore, she is talking about a scientific phenomenon that is universal to all mothers; she does not quite spell out the logical conclusion to her argument where she seems to suggest that any one of us might succumb to monstrous urges if trapped within a succession of desperate situations, and that we are collectively responsible for the unremitting loneliness and isolation that drove Coly towards this terrible act:

> Laurence sait que sa fille sera toujours avec elle. Elle est en elle. Ce que je vous raconte là ce n'est pas la poésie, c'est la science. On sait que lors d'une grossesse les cellules et l'ADN maternelles migrent vers le fétus. Ce que l'on sait moins c'est que l'échange se fait dans les deux sens. Les cellules de l'enfant fuient aussi vers les organes de la mère. Elles se logent dans tout son corps, de son cerveau jusqu'aux orteils. Même après un accouchement, même si la grossesse n'est pas menée à terme, ces cellules persistent parfois pendant toute la durée de la vie d'une femme. Une mère et son enfant sont ainsi imbriqués l'un dans l'autre de manière inextricable. On n'y peut rien, c'est de la biologie. Savez-vous comment les scientifiques nomment ces cellules? Les cellules chimériques. Comme la chimère, le monstre des mythes. Un être composite constitué de nombre d'animaux différents, la tête d'un lion, le corps d'une chèvre, la queue d'un serpent. Alors, messieurs et mesdames du jury, je me dis que nous les femmes nous sommes toutes des chimères. Nous porterons en nous les traces de nos mères et de nos filles qui, à leur tour, porterons les nôtres. C'est une chaîne infinie. Nous sommes quelque part toutes des monstres mais des monstres terriblement humains.
>
> *Diop 2022a*

[Laurence knows that her daughter will always be with her. She is in her. And what I'm telling you isn't poetry, but science. We know that a mother's cells and DNA enter the foetus during pregnancy. What is less well known is that it is a two-way exchange. The child's cells also enter the mother's organs. They lodge themselves throughout her body from her brain to the tips of her toes. Even after the mother has given birth and even if the pregnancy does not go full term, these cells nevertheless survive, in some cases for the rest of a woman's life. And so a mother and her child are inextricably embedded in one another. It's biology and that's all there is to it. Do you know what scientists call these cells? Chimera cells after the chimera, the monster from myth. The chimera was a composite creature made up of a number of different animals, with the head of a lion, the body of a goat and a snake for a tail. And so, ladies and gentleman of the jury, I'm left with the conclusion that we women are all chimeras. We will bear within us the traces of our mothers and of our daughters who, in turn, will bear our traces. It's an infinite chain. Somehow we are all monsters, but monsters who are terribly human.]

This is a vital passage in the film and, indeed, as part of Coly's defence. It is the speech in which the defence lawyer wrests the idea of monstrosity away from the myth of Medea and attempts to tame Coly's monstrous qualities, by arguing that she shares them with all of the rest of us, paradoxically by evoking the image of the wild and weird chimera. Coly is no longer the furious, maddened Medea, but a mother who longs to keep her child close to her, to cherish a bond that can survive death. It is striking that her lawyer not only establishes a parallel between Coly and all women who have fallen pregnant, but also that her speech closes with the assertion that Coly shares our fallen and flawed humanity.[15]

Yet even in this speech that attempts to distance Coly from the image of the murderous witch, Medea, the lawyer emphasizes the links that bind generation to generation in images that serve effectively as a way of thinking through literary heritage. She laments the fact that Coly is unseen and unknown – and yet the myth of Medea swamps the film, making it impossible for us to see Coly just as herself rather than as a twenty-first-century incarnation of Medea. Coly is a ghost woman – a ghost who houses echoes of Euripides' Medea, of Cardinal's Medea, of Marie Ndiaye's Medea, of Toni Morrison's *Beloved*, of Pasolini's *Medea* and, indeed, of Fabienne Kabou. Loss after loss after loss haunts the language that she uses to depict her despair, her loneliness and her rage. She disappears within the host of the Medeas who are her ancestors. And yet there is a sadder disappearance than this. All of the questions that this tragedy provokes – how can we understand this crime? Is the act a response to France's colonial past? Is it a consequence of poorly managed immigration and integration policies? Is it witchcraft? Is Laurence Coly mad – can we make ourselves feel safer through othering her? – all of these questions lose sight of the little girl who lost her life on a November night in 2013. The little girl disappeared through death, but disappears once again because of the connections between her mother and Medea. This little girl was not Élise, nor was she the mythical child of Medea, but she was the daughter of Fabienne Kabou – Adélaïde.

Diop's film is an extraordinarily powerful exploration of loss, of mothers and daughters, of exile. As well as offering a compelling reading of *Medea*, it is a significant contribution to a distinctive female-authored classical reception in the francosphere, which has focused greatly upon issues of migration and displacement.[16] It also intensifies an important trend developing within francophone cinema whereby exile is explored through the lens of classical myth. This is an area where female directors are playing a significant role, as evidenced in recent years by Pascale Ferran's *Bird People* (2014), Céline Sciamma's *Portrait de la jeune fille en feu* (2019) and Sophie Deraspe's *Antigone* (2019). The waves of women-authored creations, flowing distinctively from different corners of the globe, continue to pound the shores of classical reception.

Notes

1. Translations from French are my own unless otherwise indicated.
2. Sébastien Fevry has identified a trend in recent francophone film of deploying myth in order to probe issues arising from immigration. 'In films like *Eden à l'Ouest, Film Socialisme* or *Métamorphoses,* mythological memory reconnects Europe to a Mediterranean world that includes not only European nations but also non-European nations like Egypt (Godard) or Algeria (Honoré), countries from which many refugees originate or where they have lived for many years.' (2017: 29)
3. There is much to be learned from analysing the different forms of women's reception that emerge from different nations. France has not seen the explosion of feminist myth fiction that has dominated classical reception in anglophone countries, but there have been groundbreaking translations produced outside academe by prominent women writers. Cardinal's *Médée* is one instance of this. More recently the most significant translation of Ovid's exile poetry in recent times was Marie Darrieussecq's *Tristes Pontiques* (2008) and of the *Metamorphoses* was Marie Cosnay's *Les Métamorphoses* (2017), which won the prix Bernard Hoepffneer (2017). It is also worth noting that in 2001 the feminist writer Annie Leclerc was already rewriting the *Odyssey* from Penelope's perspective through her novel *Toi Pénélope*.
4. See also an interview with Jonathan Romney, 'For fifteen years, I've been making films from the margins, with a political intention of filming those margins – the *banlieue,* people who have been silenced, because those are the people I come from. That's my territory, my history.' (Romney 2023).
5. In this interview Diop also observes that *Nous* presents a series of short stories, in a style inspired by James Joyce's *Dubliners*.
6. 'Everything that happened as far as the trial is concerned is practically a verbatim transcript of the trial', Diop explains, speaking over Zoom with the help of a translator. '[Kabou's] style of language and her interaction with the prosecutor and the people in the court was so amazing to me, and that is in the film also. The film was born of the texture of that exchange and the quality of the dialogue that I could not have made up even if I was the greatest dialogist.' (Diop quoted by Zemler 2023).
7. Ndiaye 1989. For a reading of the Ovidian presences in Ndiaye's best known work *Trois femmes puissantes* (2010) see Cox (2023: 242–62). See also Jordan 2016. On Ndiaye's use of Medea see J. P. Little (2000).

8. See also Zemler 2023: 'Diop was particularly interested in working with Ndiaye because she felt that Kabou's story had a novel-like sensibility. In fact during Kabou's trial, which resulted in a twenty-year prison sentence, many remarked on her unique quality of speech and unusual cadence.'
9. The *Guardian* article on 20 June 2016 by Kim Willsher reporting from the trial is entitled 'French woman accused of murdering daughter on beach blames witchcraft'.
10. The suggestion that the child might be better cared for in death aligns the narrative with Toni Morrison's *Beloved,* another response to the myth of Medea.
11. The parallels between a criminal court and ancient theatre are striking. Both arenas accommodate narratives in which spectators are acutely aware of the terrible way in which the story ends and are helpless to intervene to step back in time and to alter the course of events.
12. Susan O. Shapiro states that scholars have recently interpreted Pasolini's *Medea* as having an anti-colonial message, though points out that this is somewhat unnuanced. 'Recent scholarship on the film has stressed its anti-colonialist message. Jason is seen as a Western colonial power, while Medea represents an indigenous people, vulnerable to conquest and exploitation, symbolized by the theft of the Fleece. On this view, Medea's murder of her two children represents her revenge against the colonial power' (2013: 96). Later in the chapter Shapiro cites Pasolini himself: '*Medea* is the confrontation of the archaic universe, which is hieratic and religious, with the world of Jason, which is, on the contrary, rational and pragmatic. Jason is the hero of the present . . . the emotionless 'technocrat' whose search is directed solely towards success . . . [But the story of Medea could] just as well be a history of the people of the Third World, of an African people, for example, who know the same catastrophe of contact with Western, materialistic civilization.' (2013: 111).
13. Her lawyer points out that when she moves in with Luc Dumontet: 'Laurence Coly est sans ressources, elle n'a plus de compte en banque, pas de sécu, pas d'inscription à l'université. Elle commence à entendre des voix. Elle a des hallucinations, des rêves effrayants, des signes étranges qu'elle peine à déchiffrer.' [Laurence Coly has nothing; she no longer has a bank account, she doesn't get benefits, she isn't registered at the university. She begins to hear voices. She experiences hallucinations and terrifying dreams, has strange signals that she struggles to interpret.]
14. See also Haynes' comments on Medea's complaints about her womanhood: 'It's harder still for her, Medea continues, because she is foreign and you'd need sorcery to understand how to treat a man under new laws and customs. If it all works out, terrific. Otherwise, it's better to die. A man, if he gets bored at home, can go out and make his own fun. We have to stay at home with one man. And sure, men will tell you that they have to fight in wars. Well, I'd rather stand three times in the front line than give birth to a single child.' (2022: 240–1).
15. See Zemler (2023) where Diop observes: 'It was as if all of us women on the set were constantly haunted by the presence of our mothers and children and we were having this dialogue all the time with these ghostlike ideas . . . It is as if all the things that we would not have dared to tell our mothers, the things we had thought, the things we were afraid of, all these things were coming up for us. It was like a collective psychotherapy.'
16. See Cox (2023).

REFERENCES

Introduction

Alexander, C., trans. (2015), *The Iliad: Homer*, New York: Ecco.
Atkinson, T. (2011), *Catulla et al*, Newcastle: Bloodaxe Books.
Beard, M. (2017), *Women and Power: A Manifesto*, London: Profile Books & London Review of Books.
Canevaro, L. G., M. Canevaro, B. Mazzinghi Gori, H. Stead and E. B. Williams Reed (2024), 'Class in Classics', https://www.pure.ed.ac.uk/ws/portalfiles/portal/411204893/CanevaroEtal2024ClassInClassics.pdf.
Cox, F. (2011), *Sibylline Sisters: Virgil's Presence in Contemporary Women's Writing*, Oxford: Oxford University Press.
Cox, F. (2018), *Strange Monsters: Ovid's Presence in Contemporary Women's Writing*, Oxford: Oxford University Press.
Cox, F., and E. Theodorakopoulos, eds (2013), 'Contemporary Women Writers', special issue of *Practitioners' Voices in Classical Reception Studies* 4.
Cox, F., and E. Theodorakopoulos, eds (2019), *Homer's Daughters: Women's Responses to Homer in the Twentieth Century and Beyond*, Oxford: Oxford University Press.
Deane, M. (2022), *Wrath Goddess Sing*, New York: William Morrow.
DeJean, J. (1997), *Ancients against Modern: Cultures Wars and the Making of a Fin de Siècle*, Chicago: Chicago University Press.
Evaristo, B. (2001), *The Emperor's Babe*, London, New York: Penguin.
Fradinger, M. (2023), *Antígonas: Writing from Latin America*, Oxford: Oxford University Press.
Goff, B. (2022), 'Do We Have A New Song Yet? The New Wave of Women's Novels and the Homeric Tradition', *Humanities* 11 (2): 49.
Hanink, Johanna (2017), 'It's Time to Embrace Critical Classical Reception: Disciplinary Action', *Eidolon*.
Hartman, S. (2019), *Wayward Lives, Beautiful Experiments: Intimate Histories of Social Upheaval*, New York: W. W. Norton.
Hauser, E. (2019), 'When Classics Gets Creative: From Research to Practice', *Transactions and Proceedings of the American Philological Association* 149 (2): 163–77.
Hauser, E. (2023), *How Women Became Poets: A Gender History of Greek Literature*, Princeton: Princeton University Press.
Hoberman, R. (1997), *Gendering Classicism: The Ancient World in Twentieth-Century Women's Historical Fiction*, New York: SUNY Press.
Holmes, B., and K. Marta, eds (2017), *Liquid Antiquity*, Athens: DESTE Foundation.
Kang, H., ([2011] 2023), *Greek Lessons*, trans. D. Smith and E. Yae Won, London: Hogarth.
Kaveney, R., (2018), *Catullus. The Poems of Gaius Valerius Catullus: Some English Versions*, Bristol: Sad Press.
Kinetic Light (2018), 'DESCENT' [Dance performance] Dir. Alice Sheppard, New York Live Arts, 22–4 March.
Knowles, Z. (2024), 'Tell Me Again: Retellings of 2023. Ancient Mythology Continues to Appeal', *The Bookseller*, 19 Jan: 23–4.
Miller, M. (2011), *The Song of Achilles*, London: Bloomsbury.

References

Moyer, I., A. Lecznar and H. Morse, eds (2020), *Classicisms in the Black Atlantic*, Oxford: Oxford University Press.
Porter, J. I. (2008), 'Reception Studies: Future Prospects', in L. Hardwick and C. Stray, eds, *A Companion to Classical Receptions*, 469–81, Oxford: Wiley-Blackwell.
Prins, Y. (2017), *Ladies' Greek: Victorian Translations of Tragedy*, Princeton: Princeton University Press.
Ranger, Holly (2023), 'Critical Reception Studies: the White Feminism of Feminist Reception Scholarship', in M. Ward and M. Umachandran, eds, *Critical Ancient World Studies: the Case for Forgetting Classics*, 213–33, London: Routledge.
Rich, A. (1972), 'When We Dead Awaken: Writing as Re-Vision', *College English* 34 (1): 18–30.
Rivera, L., (2020), *Never Look Back*, London, New York: Bloomsbury.
Silverblank, H., and M. Ward (2020), 'Why Does Classical Reception Need Disability Studies?', *Classical Receptions Journal* 12 (4): 502–30.
Stevenson, J. (2008), *Women Latin Poets: Language, Gender, and Authority from Antiquity to the Eighteenth Century*, Oxford: Oxford University Press.
Taylor, H. (2024), *Women Writing Antiquity: Gender and Learning in Early Modern France*, Oxford: Oxford University Press.
Taylor, H., and F. Cox, eds (2023), *Ovid in French: Reception by Women from the Renaissance to the Present*, Oxford, Oxford University Press.
Tempest, K. (2021), *Paradise* [Theatre production] Dir. Ian Rickson, National Theatre.
Walters, T. L. (2007), *African American Literature and the Classicist Tradition: Black Women Writers from Wheatley to Morrison*, London: Palgrave Macmillan.
Wilson, E., trans. (2017), *The Odyssey: Homer*, New York: W. W. Norton.
Wyles, R., and E. Hall, eds (2016), *Female Classical Scholars: Unsealing the Fountain from the Renaissance to Jacqueline de Romilly*, Oxford: Oxford University Press.
Zuckerberg, D., (2019), *Not All Dead White Men: Classics and Misogyny in the Digital Age*, Cambridge, MA: Harvard University Press.

Chapter 1

Aneziri, S. (2009), 'World Travellers: the Associations of Artists of Dionysus', in R. Hunter and I. Rutherford, eds, *Wandering Poets in Ancient Greek Culture: Travel, Locality and Pan-Hellenism*, 217–35, Cambridge: Cambridge University Press.
Berman, D. W. (2010), 'The Landscape and Language of Korinna', *Greek, Roman, and Byzantine Studies* 50: 41–62.
Bowra, C. M. (1938), 'The Daughters of Asopus', *Hermes* 73 (2): 213–21.
Cagnazzi, S. (1997), *Nicobule e Panfila. Frammenti di storiche greche*, Bari: Edipuglia.
Calame, C., D. Collins and J. Orion (1997), *Choruses of Young Women in Ancient Greece: their morphology, religious role, and social function*, Lanham MD: Rowman & Littlefield.
Campbell, D. A. (1982), *Greek Lyric, Vol. I: Sappho and Alcaeus*, Cambridge, MA: Harvard University Press.
Campbell, D. A. (1992), *Greek Lyric, Vol. IV: Bacchylides, Corinna, and Others*, Cambridge, MA: Harvard University Press.
Clayman, D. (1993), 'Corinna and Pindar', in R. M. Rosen and J. Farrell, eds, *Nomodeiktes: Greek Studies in Honor of Martin Ostwald*, 633–42, Ann Arbor: University of Michigan Press.
Collins, D. (2006), 'Corinna and Mythological Innovation', *Classical Quarterly* 56 (1): 19–32.
Daux, G., and A. Salać, eds (1932), *Fouilles de Delphes, III. Épigraphie-Inscriptions depuis le trésor des Athéniens jusqu'aux bases de Gélon*, Vol. 1.1, Paris: de Boccard (= *FD*).
DeJean, J. (1989), *Fictions of Sappho, 1546–1937*, Chicago: University of Chicago Press.

References

Diehl, E. (1917), *Supplementum Lyricum; neue Bruchstücke von Archilochus, Alcaeus, Sappho, Corinna, Pindar, Bacchylides*, 3rd edition, Bonn: A. Marcus and E. Weber.
Hauser, E. (2023), *How Women Became Poets: A Gender History of Greek Literature*, Princeton: Princeton University Press.
Heath, J. (2017), 'Old Wives' Tales', *Harvard Studies in Classical Philology* 109: 83–130.
Henderson, W. J. (1995), 'Corinna of Tanagra on Poetry', *Acta Classica* 38: 29–41.
Hunter, V. J. (1982), *Past and Process in Herodotus and Thucydides*, Princeton: Princeton University Press.
Kelly, A. D. (2020), 'With, or without, Homer: hearing the background in Sappho', in A. Rengakos, P. Finglass and B. Zimmermann, eds, *More than Homer Knew – Studies on Homer and His Ancient Commentators*, 269–92, Berlin, Boston: De Gruyter.
Kelly, A. D. (2021), 'Sappho and Epic', in P. Finglass and A. Kelly, eds, *The Cambridge Companion to Sappho*, 53–64, Cambridge: Cambridge University Press.
Lardinois, A. (1994), 'Subject and Circumstance in Sappho's Poetry', *Transactions of the American Philological Association* 124: 57–84.
Lardinois, A. (1996), 'Who Sang Sappho's Songs?', in E. Greene, ed., *Reading Sappho: Contemporary Approaches*, 150–72, Berkeley, Los Angeles and London: University of California Press.
Larmour, D. H. J. (2005), 'Corinna's Poetic *Metis* and the Epinikian Tradition', in E. Greene, ed., *Women Poets in Ancient Greece and Rome*, 25–58, Norman: University of Oklahoma Press.
Larson, J. (2002), 'Corinna and the Daughters of Asopus', *Syllecta Classica* 13: 47–62.
Larson, S. (2007), *Tales of Epic Ancestry: Boiotian Collective Identity in the Late Archaic and Early Classical Periods*, Stuttgart: Franz Steiner.
Lefkowitz, M. (2012), *The Lives of the Greek Poets*, 2nd edition, Baltimore: Johns Hopkins University Press.
Lobel, E. (1930), 'Corinna', *Hermes* 65 (3): 356–65.
Mackil, E. M. (2013), *Creating a Common Polity: religion, economy, and politics in the making of the Greek koinon*, Berkeley and Los Angeles: University of California Press.
Marinatos, N. (2022), 'The Myth of Troy Turned into History: Thucydides' Archaeology', in M. Christopoulos, A. Papachrysostomou and A. Antonopoulos, eds, *Myth and History: Close Encounters*, 119–30, Berlin, Boston: De Gruyter.
McPhee, B. D. (2018), 'Mythological Innovations in Corinna's Asopides Poem (fr.654.ii–iv *PMG*)', *Greek, Roman, and Byzantine Studies* 58 (2): 198–222.
Mueller, M. (2023), *Sappho and Homer: A Reparative Reading*, Cambridge: Cambridge University Press.
Nagy, G. (2007), 'Lyric and Greek Myth', in R. D. Woodard, ed., *The Cambridge Companion to Greek Mythology*, 19–51, Cambridge: Cambridge University Press.
Obbink, D. (2016), 'The Newest Sappho: P. GC. and P. Sapph. Obbink: Text, Apparatus Criticus, and Translation', in A. Bierl and A. Lardinois, eds, *The Newest Sappho: P. Sapph. Obbink and P. GC inv. 105, Frs. 1–4*, 13–33, Leiden, Boston: Brill.
Page, D. L. (1953), *Corinna*, London: Society for the Promotion of Hellenic Studies.
Page, D. L. (1962), *Poetae Melici Graeci*, Oxford: Clarendon Press. (=*PMG*).
Plant, I. M. (2004), *Women Writers of Ancient Greece and Rome: An Anthology*, Norman: University of Oklahoma Press.
Plant, I. M. (2015), 'Women historians of ancient Greece and Rome', *Ancient History: Resources for Teachers* 41-44: 77–92.
Power, T. (2020), 'Sappho's Parachoral Monody', in M. Foster, L. Kurke and N. Weiss, eds, *Genre in Archaic and Classical Greek Poetry: Theories and Models*, 82–108, Leiden: Brill.
Rayor, D. J., and A. Lardinois (2023), *Sappho: A New Translation of the Complete Works*, 2nd edition, Cambridge: Cambridge University Press.
Rosenmeyer, P. A. (1997), 'Her Master's Voice: Sappho's Dialogue with Homer', *Materiali e discussioni per l'analisi dei testi classici* 39: 123–49.

References

Rutherford, I. (2009), 'Aristodama and the Aetolians. An Itinerant Poetess and her Agenda', in R. Hunter and I. Rutherford, eds, *Wandering Poets in Ancient Greece Culture: Travel, Locality and Pan-Hellenism*, 237–49, Cambridge: Cambridge University Press.

Scodel, R. (2021), 'Myth in Sappho', in P. Finglass and A. Kelly, eds, *The Cambridge Companion to Sappho*, 190–202, Cambridge: Cambridge University Press.

Siekierka, P., K. Stebnicka and A. Wolicki (2021), *Women and the Polis: Public Honorific Inscriptions for Women in the Greek Cities from the Late Classical to the Roman Period*, Berlin, Boston: De Gruyter.

Skinner, M. B. (1983), 'Corinna of Tanagra and her Audience', *Tulsa Studies in Women's Literature* 2 (1): 9–20.

Tsagarakis, O. (1977), *Self-Expression in Early Greek Lyric: Elegiac and Iambic Poetry*, Wiesbaden: Franz Steiner.

West, M. L. (1970), 'Corinna', *Classical Quarterly* 20: 277–87.

West, M. L. (1990), 'Dating Corinna', *Classical Quarterly* 40: 553–7.

Chapter 2

BnF ms. français 1718. Available online: https://gallica.bnf.fr/ark:/12148/btv1b90591885/f59.item (accessed 26 January 2024).

Alciato, A. (1536), *Livret des Emblemes*, Paris: Chrestien Wechel. Available online: https://www.emblems.arts.gla.ac.uk/french/emblem.php?id=FALa074 (accessed 26 January 2024).

Alighieri, D. (1999), *Inferno*, ed. and trans. R. M. Durling, New York; Oxford: Oxford University Press.

Archibald, E. (2001), 'Sex and Power in Thebes and Babylon: Oedipus and Semiramis in Classical and Medieval Texts', *Journal of Medieval Latin* 11: 27–49.

Atwood, M. (2005), *The Penelopiad*, Edinburgh: Canongate.

L'Aubespine, M. de (2007), *Selected Poems and Translations: A Bilingual Edition*, ed. and trans. A. Kłosowska, Chicago and London: University of Chicago Press.

Baudelaire, C. (1991), *Les Fleurs du Mal*, ed. J. Dupont, Paris: GF-Flammarion.

Boccaccio, G. (2003), *Famous Women*, trans. V. Brown, Cambridge, MA: Harvard University Press.

Brown, P. R., and J. C. Peiffer II (2000), 'Heloise, Dialectic, and the *Heroides*', in B. Wheeler, ed., *Listening to Heloise: The Voice of a Twelfth-Century Woman*, 143–60, London: Palgrave Macmillan.

Le Cabinet satyrique ou recueil parfaict, des vers picquans et [g]aillards de ce temps (1618), Paris: Antoine Estoc.

Champier, S. (2007), *La Nef des dames vertueuses (1503)*, ed. J. Kem, Paris: Garnier.

DeVos, J. (2023), 'Madeleine de l'Aubespine's Translation of *Heroides 2*', in H. Taylor and F. Cox, eds, *Ovid and Women Writers*, 44–66, Oxford: Oxford University Press.

Du Pré, J. (2007), *Le Palais des nobles Dames (Lyon, 1534)*, ed. B. Dunn-Lardeau, Paris: Garnier.

Endres, N. (2012), 'Horses and Heroes: Plato's *Phaedrus* and Mary Renault's *The Charioteer*', *International Journal of the Classical Tradition* 19 (3): 152–64.

Fleuret, F., and L. Perceau, eds (1924), *Le Cabinet satyrique: première édition complète et critique d'après l'édition originale de 1618*, 2 vols, Paris: Fort.

Harty, K. J. (1987), 'Ionesco and Semiramis', *CLA Journal* 31: 170–7.

Haynes, N. (2017), *The Children of Jocasta*, London: Mantle.

Haynes, N. (2022), *Stone Blind*, London: Mantle.

Hornblower, S., and A. Spawforth, eds (1996), *The Oxford Classical Dictionary*, Oxford: Oxford University Press.

References

Jones, A. R. (1981), 'Assimilation with a Difference: Renaissance Women Poets and Literary Influence', *Yale French Studies* 62: 135–53.

Juvenal (2014), *Satires*, in *Juvenal and Persius*, ed. and trans. S. M. Braund, Cambridge, MA: Harvard University Press.

Kłosowska, A. (2008), 'Erotica and Women in Early Modern France: Madeleine de l'Aubespine's Queer Poems', *Journal of the History of Sexuality* 17: 190–215.

Labé, L. (2004), *Œuvres complètes*, ed. François Rigolot, Paris: GF-Flammarion.

Labé, L. (2006), *Complete Poetry and Prose: A Bilingual Edition*, ed. and trans. D. L. Baker and A. Finch, Chicago: University of Chicago Press.

Larsen, A. R. (1990), '"Un honneste passetems": Strategies of Legitimation in French Renaissance Women's Prefaces', *L'Esprit Créateur* 30: 11–22.

Levick, B. (1990), *Claudius*, London: Batsford.

Miller, M. (2018), *Circe*, London: Bloomsbury.

Moss, A. (1982), *Ovid in Renaissance France: A Survey of the Latin Editions of Ovid and Commentaries Printed in France before 1600*, London: Warburg Institute.

Navarre, M. de (1547), *Suyte des Marguerites de la Marguerite des Princesses*, Lyon: Jean de Tournes.

Navarre, M. de (2000), *L'Heptaméron*, ed. N. Cazauran, Paris: Gallimard.

Navarre, M. de (2004), *The Heptameron*, trans. P. A. Chilton, London: Penguin.

Navarre, M. de (2008), *Selected Writings: A Bilingual Edition*, ed. and trans. R. Cholakian and M. Skemp, Chicago: University of Chicago Press.

Navarre, M. de (2012), *L'Histoire des Satyres, et Nymphes de Diane; Les Quatre Dames et les quatre Gentilzhommes; La Coche*, ed. A. Gendre, L. Petris and S. de Reyff, Paris: Champion.

Ovid (1955), *Metamorphoses*, trans. M. M. Innes, London: Penguin.

Ovid (1995), *Amores I*, ed. and trans. J. Barsby, London: Bristol Classical Press.

Pisan, C. de (1999), *The Book of the City of Ladies*, trans. R. Brown-Grant, London: Penguin.

Renault, M. ([1944] 2014), *The Friendly Young Ladies*, London: Virago.

Renault, M. ([1953] 2013), *The Charioteer*, London: Virago.

Reyff, S. de (2012), 'Introduction', in M. de Navarre, *L'Histoire des Satyres, et Nymphes de Diane; Les Quatre Dames et les quatre Gentilzhommes; La Coche*, ed. A. Gendre, L. Petris and S. de Reyff, 17–54, Paris: Champion.

Sannazaro, J. (2009), *Latin Poetry*, ed. and trans. M. J. Putnam, Cambridge, MA; London: Harvard University Press.

Sayers, D. L. (1946), *Unpopular Opinions*, London: Gollancz.

Scève, M. (1971), *Œuvres poétiques complètes*, ed. H. Staub, 2 vols, Paris: Union générale d'éditions.

Sowers, B. P. (2000), *In Her Own Words: The Life and Poetry of Aelia Eudocia*, Washington DC: Center for Hellenic Studies.

Sprague, R. K. (1997), 'Dorothy L. Sayers and Aristotle', *VII: Journal of the Marion E. Wade Center* 14: 33–43.

Sterritt, D. E. L. (2005), 'A Latin Legacy in Louise Labé: Imitation of Tibullus 1.2.89–94', *French Forum* 30: 15–30.

Stewart, V. (2011), 'The Woman Writer in Mid-Twentieth-Century Middlebrow Fiction: Conceptualizing Creativity', *Journal of Modern Literature* 35: 21–36.

Stone, D. (1993), '"La malice des hommes": "L'Histoire des satyres" and the *Heptameron*', in J. D. Lyons and M. B. McKinley, eds, *Critical Tales: New Studies of the 'Heptameron' and Early Modern Culture*, 53–64, Philadelphia: University of Pennsylvania Press.

Taylor, H. (2024), *Women Writing Antiquity: Gender and Learning in Early Modern France*, Oxford: Oxford University Press.

Yourcenar, M. ([1951] 1974), *Mémoires d'Hadrien*, Paris: Gallimard.

Yourcenar, M. (1981), *Anna, soror . . .*, Paris: Gallimard.

References

Chapter 3

Aristotle (1926), *The Art of Rhetoric* in E. M Cope, ed., *Aristotle in 23 volumes*, vol. 22, trans. J. H. Freese, Cambridge, MA and London: Harvard University Press. Available online: http://www.perseus.tufts.edu/hopper/text.jsp?doc=Perseus:text:1999.01.0060 (accessed 23 November 2021)

Aristotle (1921), *On the Art of Poetry*, trans. I. Bywater, Oxford: Clarendon Press.

Behr, F. D. (2018), *Arms and the Woman: Classical Tradition and Women Writers in the Venetian Renaissance*, Columbus, OH: Ohio State University Press.

Behr, F. D. (2021), 'Female Audiences and Translations of the Classics in Early Modern Italy', in J. Decker and M. Kirkland-Ives, eds, *Audiences and Reception in the Early Modern Period*, 252–77, New York, NY: Routledge.

Behr, F. D. (2022), 'Philosophy, Religion, and the Praise of Women in Lucrezia Marinella', in E. Brizio and M. Piana, eds, *Idealizing Women in the Italian Renaissance*, 137–61, Toronto: Centre for Renaissance and Reformation and Studies.

Boillet, É. (2021), 'Aretino's "Simple" Religious Prose: Literary Features, Doctrinal and Moral Contents, Evolution', in M. Faini and P. Ugolini, eds, *A Companion to Pietro Aretino*, 303–28, Leiden: Brill.

Bonfini, A. (1516), *Flavii philostrati De vitis Sophistarum libri duo, Antonio Bonfino Historico Interprete*, Strasburg: N. Gerbel.

Christiansen, Nancy Lee (2019), 'Revisioning Stylistic Analysis and Renaissance *Elocutio*', *Style* 53 (2): 157–84.

Cox, V. (2011), *The Prodigious Muse: Women's Writing in Counter-Reformation Italy*, Baltimore: Johns Hopkins.

Delcorno, C. (1987), 'Dal *sermo modernus* alla retorica Borromea', *Lettere Italiane* 39: 465–83.

Demetrio (2007), *Lo stile*, ed. and trans. N. Marini, Roma: Pleiadi.

Driscoll, S. (2012), 'Aristotle's A Priori Metaphor', *Aporia* 22 (1): 1–30.

Ferrari-Schifer, V. (2002), 'La Teologia della bellezza di Lucrezia Marinella (1571–1653) in tre delle sue opere', *Annali di Studi Religiosi* 2: 187–207.

Fumaroli, M. (1980), *L'Âge d'Éloquence: Rhétorique et 'res literaria' de la Renaissance au seuil de l' épôque Classique*, Genève: Droz.

Giunta, F. (2012), '*Il Predicatore* di Francesco Panigarola: Un nuovo modello di eloquenza sacra per il Seicento', *Acta Neophilologica* 45 (1–2): 109–18.

Goldhill, S. (2006), *The Invention of Prose*, Oxford: Oxford University Press.

Guastini, D. (2005), 'Aristotele e la metafora: ovvero un elogio dell' approssimazione', *Isonomia* 3. Available online: https://isonomia.uniurb.it/vecchiaserie/guastini/guastini2004.pdf

Hankins, J. (2006), 'Religion and the Modernity of Renaissance Humanism', in Angelo Mazzocco, ed., *Interpretations of Renaissance Humanism*, 137–53, Leiden: Brill.

Iglesias-Crespo, C. (2021), '*Energeia* as Defamiliarization: Reading Aristotle with Shklovsky's Eyes', *Journal for the History of Rhetoric* 24 (3). Available online: https://www.tandfonline.com/doi/full/10.1080/26878003.2021.1975465

Marinella, L. (1602), *Life of the Virgin Mary, Empress of the Universe described in Prose and Ottava Rima (La Vita di Maria Vergine imperatrice dell' universo, descritta in prosa e in ottava rima)*, Venezia: Barezi. Available online: https://www.digitale-sammlungen.de/en/view/bsb10788498?q=%28marinella+lucrezia%29&page=4,5

McManamon, J. (1996), *Pier Paolo Vergerio the Elder: The Humanist as Orator*, Tempe, Arizona: Center for Medieval Studies and Renaissance Studies.

Mongini, G. (1996), 'Nel cor ch'è pur di Cristo il tempio La vita del Serafico et glorioso S. Francesco di Lucrezia Marinelli tra influssi ignaziani, spiritualismo e prisca teologia', *Archivio Italiano per la storia della pietà* 10: 359–453.

Moran, R. (1996), 'Artifice and Persuasion: The Work of Metaphor in the *Rhetoric*', in A. O. Rorty, ed., *Essays on Aristotle's Rhetoric*, 385–99, Berkeley: University of California Press.

References

Newman, S. (2002), 'Aristotle's Notion of "Bringing-before-the-Eyes": its Contribution to Aristotelian and Contemporary Conceptualization of Metaphor, Style, and Audience', *Rhetorica: A Journal of the History of Rhetoric* 20 (1): 1–23.
O'Malley, J. (1979), *Praise and Blame in Renaissance Rome: Rhetoric, Doctrine, and Reform in the Sacred Orators of the Papal Court, c. 1450–1521*, Durham, NC: Duke University Press.
O'Malley, J. (1983), 'Content and Rhetorical Forms in Sixteenth-Century Treatises on Preaching', in J. Murphy, ed., *Renaissance Eloquence: Studies in the Theory and Practice of Renaissance Rhetoric*, 237–52, Berkeley: University of California Press.
Philostratus, Eunapius (1921), *Lives of the Sophists. Eunapius: Lives of the Philosophers and Sophists*, trans. W. C. Wright, Loeb Classical Library, Cambridge, MA: Harvard University Press.
Piantoni, L. (2009), 'Mirabile cristiano ed eloquenza sacra', in E. Ardissino and E. Selmi, eds, *Poesia e retorica del Sacro tra Cinque e Seicento*, 435–45, Alessandria: Edizioni dell'Orso.
Prodi, P. (1991), 'Controriforma e/o riforma cattolica: superamento di vecchi dilemmi nei nuovi panorami storiografici', in V. Branca and C. Ossola, eds, *Crisi e Rinnovamenti nell'Autunno del Rinascimento*, 11–21, Firenze: Olschki.
Ricoeur, P. (1996), 'Between Rhetoric and Poetics', in A. Rorty Oksenberg, ed., *Essays on Aristotle's Rhetoric*, 324–84, Berkeley: University of California Press.
Shklovsky, V. (1990), *Theory of Prose*, Elmwood Park, IL: Dalkey Archive Press.
Shuger, D. (1988), *Sacred Rhetoric: The Christian Grand Style in the English Renaissance*, Princeton: Princeton University Press.
Sigonius, C., M. A. Maioragius and G. Marinelli, eds (1584/5), *Aristotelis Stagiritae Rhetoricorum Ad Theodecten Libri III*, Venice: Nicola Moretti.
Trinkaus, C. (1970), *In our Image and Likeness: Humanity and Divinity in Italian Humanist Thought*, Chicago: University of Chicago Press.
Vickers, B. (1983), 'Epideictic and Epic in the Renaissance', *New Literary History* 14 (3): 497–537.
Weinberg, B. (1951), 'Translations and Commentaries of Demetrius, *On Style* to 1600: a Bibliography', *Philological Quarterly* 30 (4): 353–9.
Worcester, T. (2001), 'Catholic Sermons', in L. Taylor, ed., *Preachers and People in the Reformation and Early Modern Period*, 3–35, Leiden: Brill.
Zimmermann, J. ed (2017), *Re-Envisioning Christian Humanism: Education and the Restoration of Humanity*, Oxford: Oxford University Press.

Chapter 4

Alcott, L. M. (1873), *Work*, Boston: Roberts.
Anderson, N. F. (1987), *Woman against Women in Victorian England: A Life of Eliza Lynn Linton*, Bloomington, IA: Indiana University Press.
Aristophanes. (1998), *Acharnians. Knights*, ed. and trans. Jeffrey Henderson, Cambridge, MA: Harvard University Press.
Bicknell, P. (1982), 'Axiochos Alkibiadou, Aspasia and Aspasios', *L'antiquité Classique* 51: 240–50.
Browning, E. Barrett (2010), *The works of Elizabeth Barrett Browning*, London, Pickering & Chatto.
Child, L. M. (1836), *Philothea: A Romance*, Boston: Otis, Broaders.
Child, L. M. (1845), *Philothea: A Grecian Romance*, New York: C. S. Francis.
Comet, N. (2013), *Romantic Hellenism and Women Writers*, Basingstoke: Palgrave Macmillan.
D'Angour, A. (2019), *Socrates in Love: The Making of a Philosopher*, London: Bloomsbury.
Duquès, M. E. (2017), 'Women of Colour, Politics and the Plague in Lydia Maria Child's *Philothea: A Grecian Romance*', in Annika Bautz and Kathryn Gray, eds, *Transatlantic Literature and Transitivity, 1780–1850: Subjects, Texts, and Print Culture*, 93–111, Abingdon: Routledge.

References

Felton, C. C. (1837), 'Philothea, a Romance. By Mrs Child', *North American Review* 44: 77–90.
Fuller, M. (1845), *Woman in the Nineteenth Century*, New York: Greeley & McElrath.
Glenn, C. (1994), 'Sex, lies, and manuscript: Refiguring Aspasia in the History of Rhetoric', *College Composition and Communication* 45 (2): 180–99.
Glenn, C. (1995), 'Rereading Aspasia: the palimpsest of her thoughts', in J. F. Reynolds, ed., *Rhetoric, Cultural Studies, and Literacy: selected papers from the 1994 Conference of the Rhetoric Society of America*, 35–44, Hillsdale, NJ: L. Erlbaum Associates.
Grote, G. (1849), *History of Greece*, vol. 6, London: John Murray.
Gustafson, S. M. (2011), *Imagining Deliberative Democracy in the Early American Republic*, Chicago: University of Chicago Press.
Henry, M. M. (1995), *Prisoner of History: Aspasia of Miletus and her biographical tradition*, Oxford: Oxford University Press.
Kennedy, R. F. (2014), *Immigrant Women in Athens: Gender, Ethnicity, and Citizenship in the Classical City*, Abingdon: Routledge.
Kennedy, R. F. (2015), 'Elite Citizen Women and the Origins of the *Hetaira* in Classical Athens', *Helios* 42 (1): 61–79.
Landon, L. E. (1836), 'The Banquet of Aspasia and Pericles', *The New Monthly Magazine* 47: 176–8.
Levy, A. (1881), *Xantippe and other verse*, Cambridge: E. Johnson.
Lynn, E. (1848), *Amymone: A Romance of the Days of Pericles*, London: R. Bentley.
McClure, L. (2003), *Courtesans at Table: gender and Greek literary culture in Athenaeus*, London: Routledge.
Plato (1929), *Timaeus. Critias. Cleitophon. Menexenus. Epistles*, trans. R. G. Bury, Cambridge, MA: Harvard University Press.
Plutarch (1916), *Lives, Volume III: Pericles and Fabius Maximus. Nicias and Crassus*, trans. Bernadotte Perrin, Cambridge, MA: Harvard University Press.
Poe, E. A. (1836), 'Critical Notices: Philothea: A Romance', *Southern Literary Messenger* 2 (10): 659–62.
Roberts, A. (2015), 'Walter Savage Landor and the Classics', in Norman Vance and Jennifer Wallace, eds, *The Oxford History of Classical Reception in English Literature Vol. 4: 1790–1880*, 365–84, Oxford: Oxford University Press.
Robitzsch, J. M. (2017), 'On Aspasia in Plato's *Menexenus*', *Phoenix* 71 (3/4): 288–300.
Streeter, R. E. (1943), 'Mrs. Child's "Philothea": A Transcendentalist Novel?', *New England Quarterly* 16 (4): 648–54.
Sullivan, K. S. (2007), *Constitutional Context: Women and Rights Discourse in Nineteenth-Century America*, Baltimore, MA: Johns Hopkins University Press.
Winterer, C. (2007), *The Mirror of Antiquity: American Women and the Classical Tradition, 1750–1900*, Ithaca, NY: Cornell University Press.

Chapter 5

Albert, N. (2005), *Saphisme et décadence dans Paris fin-de-siècle*, Paris: Éditions de La Martinière.
Albert, N. (2009), *Renée Vivien à rebours*, Paris: Éditions L'Harmattan.
Albert, N., and B. Rollet, eds (2012), *Renée Vivien: une femme de lettres entre deux siècles (1877–1909)*, Paris: Honoré Champion.
Bartholomot Bessou, M.-A. (2004), *L'imaginaire du féminin dans l'œuvre de Renée Vivien*, Clermont-Ferrand: Presses universitaires Blaise-Pascal.
Blavatsky, H. (1892), *The Theosophical Glossary*, New York: Theosophical Publishing Society.
Boyd, C. (1999), 'La « 'femme nouvelle ». Une étude thématique de *La Dame à la Louve*', Phd thesis, University of Alberta.

References

DeJean, J. (1989), *Fictions of Sappho (1546-1937)*, Chicago and London: University of Chicago Press.
Dupont, F., and T. Eloi (2001), *L'érotisme masculin dans la Rome antique*, Paris: Belin.
Fabre-Serris, J. (2016), 'Anne Dacier (1681), Renée Vivien (1903). Or what does it mean for a woman to translate Sappho?', in R. Wyles and E. Hall, eds, *Women Classical Scholars: Unsealing the Fountain from the Renaissance to Jacqueline de Romilly*, 78–102, Oxford: Oxford University Press.
Nisard, C., trans. (1887), *Venance Fortunat. Poésies mêlées*, Paris.
Smith, W. (1842), *A Dictionary of Greek and Roman Antiquities*, London: Taylor and Walton.
Smith, W. (1849), *A Dictionary of Greek and Roman Biography and Mythology*, London: Taylor and Walton.
Vivien, R. ([1903] 2009), *Sapho, Traduction nouvelle avec le texte grec*, Paris: Alphonse Lemerre.
Vivien, R. (2009), *Poèmes 1901–1910*, Paris: ÉrosOnyx.
Vivien, R. (2020), *The Woman of the Wolf and Other Stories*, trans. K. Jay and Y. M. Klein, London: Editions Gallic.

Chapter 6

Alekseev, V., ed. (1896), *Izbrannye epigrammy grecheskoi antologii*, St Petersburg: Tipografiia A. S. Suvorina.
Burgin, D. L. (1992), 'Sophia Parnok and the Writing of a Lesbian Poet's Life', *Slavic Review* 51 (2): 214–31.
Burgin, D. L. (1994), *Sophia Parnok: The Life and Work of Russia's Sappho*, New York: NYU Press.
Burgin, D. L. (1995), 'Mother Nature versus the Amazons: Marina Tsvetaeva and Female Same-Sex Love', *Journal of the History of Sexuality* 6 (1): 62–88.
Burgin, D. L. (1999), *Sofiia Parnok. Zhizn' i tvorchestvo russkoi Safo*, trans. S. I. Sivak, St Petersburg: INAPRESS. Available online: http://www.ndolya.ru/zhslovo/sv/sp/?r=burgin.
Campbell, D. A., ed. (1982), *Greek Lyric, Volume 1: Sappho, Alcaeus*, Cambridge, MA: Harvard University Press.
Golosovker, Ia., ed. (1935), *Lirika drevnei Ellady. V perevodakh russkikh poetov*, Moscow, Leningrad: Academia.
Healey, D. (2001), *Homosexual Desire in Revolutionary Russia: The Regulation of Sexual and Gender Dissent*, Chicago: University of Chicago Press.
Ivanov, V. (2019), *Alkei i Safo: Sobranie pesen i liricheskikh otryvkov v perevode razmerami podlinnikov Viacheslava Ivanova*, 3rd edn, ed. K. Iu. Lappo-Danilevskii and S. Zav'ialov, St Petersburg: Izdatel'stvo imeni N. I. Novikova.
Louÿs, P. (1894), *Les chansons de Bilitis*, available on Project Gutenberg.
Page, D. (1959), *Sappho and Alcaeus: An Introduction to the Study of Ancient Lesbian Poetry*, Oxford: Clarendon Press.
Parker, H. (2006), 'What Lobel Hath Joined Together: Sappho 49 LP', *Classical Quarterly* 56 (2): 374–92.
Parnok, S. (1979), *Sobranie stikhotvorenii*, ed. S. Poliakova, Ann Arbor: Ardis.
Poliakova, S. (1983), *Zakatnye ony dni: Tsvetaeva i Parnok*, Ann Arbor: Ardis.
Romanova, E. (2005), *Opyt tvorcheskoi biografii Sofii Parnok: 'Mne odnoi prednaznachennyi put''*, St Petersburg: Nestor-Istoriia.
Tsvetaeva, M. (1979), *Mon frère féminin: lettre à l'Amazone*, Paris: Mercure de France.
Veresaev, V. (1963), *Ellinskie poety. V perevodakh V. V. Veresaeva*, ed. S. Apt, M. Grabar'-Passek, F. Petrovskii, A. Takho-Godi and S. Shervinskii, Moscow: Gosudarstvennoe izdatel'stvo khudozhestvennoi literatury.
Zuseva-Ozkan, V. B. (2018), 'Triptikh Penfesileia i obraz devy-voitel'nitsy v tvorchestve S. Ia. Parnok', *Sibirskii filologicheskii zhurnal* 18 (4): 78–94.

References

Chapter 7

Adams, Pauline (1996), *Somerville for Women: An Oxford College, 1879–1993*, Oxford: Oxford University Press.

Alley, Henry M. (1982), 'A Rediscovered Eulogy: Virginia Woolf's "Miss Janet Case: Classical Scholar and Teacher"', *Twentieth Century Literature* 28 (3): 290–301, doi:10.2307/441180.

The Bees: with humblest apologies to the shade of Aristophanes (1904), [Girton College 2nd-Year Entertainment], Cambridge: Metcalfe.

Blodgett, Harriet (1990), 'Cicely Hamilton, Independent Feminist', *Frontiers (Boulder)* 11 (2): 99–104, doi:10.2307/3346832.

Bogen, Anna (2014), *Women's University Fiction, 1880–1945*, London: Routledge.

Carlson, Susan (2000), 'Comic Militancy: The Politics of Suffrage Drama', in Maggie B. Gale and Viv Gardner, eds, *Women, Theatre and Performance: New Histories, New Historiographies*, 198–215, Manchester: MUP.

Chen, Eva (2017), 'Its Prohibitive Cost: The Bicycle, the New Woman and Conspicuous Display', *Journal of Language, Literature and Culture (Australasian Universities Language and Literature Association)* 64 (1): 1–17, doi:10.1080/20512856.2016.1221620.

Clark, Petra (2019), 'The Girton Girl's "academical Home": Girton College in the Late-Victorian Periodical Press', *Victorian Periodicals Review* 52 (4): 659–78, doi:10.1353/vpr.2019.0049.

Cockin, Katharine (2017), 'Formations, Institutions and the "Free Theatre": Edith Craig's Pioneer Players 1911–25', *Key Words: A Journal of Cultural Materialism* 15: 55–71.

Costa, Veronica Pacheco (2018), 'The Use of Irony as a Subversive Element in Suffrage Theatre', *Women's Writing: The Elizabethan to Victorian Period* 25 (3): 362–78, doi:10.1080/09699082.2018.1473020.

Dangerfield, George (1936), *The Strange Death of Liberal England*, London: Constable.

Dolgin, Ellis Ecker (2015), *Shaw and the Actresses' Franchise League*, Jefferson, North Carolina: McFarland & Company, Inc.

Eltis, Sos (2013), *Acts of Desire: Women and Sex on Stage 1800–1930*, Oxford: Oxford University Press, doi:10.1093/acprof:oso/9780199691357.001.0001.

Evangelista, S. (2009), *British Aestheticism and Ancient Greece: Hellenism, Reception, Gods in Exile*, London: Palgrave Macmillan, doi:10.1057/9780230242203.

Fogerty, Elsie (1907), *Tennyson's Princess, Adapted for Amateur Performance in Girls' Schools*, London: S. Sonnenschein.

Gardner, Viv (1985), *Sketches from the Actresses' Franchise League*, Nottingham: Nottingham University.

Girton Review, April 1899.

Girton Review, July 1899.

Girton Review, Lent Term, 1904.

Girton Review, April 1922.

Girton Review, Michaelmas Term 1928.

Hall, Donald E. (1991), 'The Anti-Feminist Ideology of Tennyson's "the Princess"', *Modern Language Studies* 21 (4): 49–62, doi:10.2307/3194982.

Hall, Edith, and Fiona Macintosh (2005), *Greek Tragedy and the British Theatre, 1660–1914*, Oxford: Oxford University Press.

Hall, Edith, and Amanda Wrigley (2007), *Aristophanes in Performance, 421 BC–AD 2007: Peace, Birds and Frogs*, London: Legenda.

Hamilton, Cicely, and Christopher (Christopher Marie) St John (1909), *How the Vote was Won: Text of the Play*, 3rd edn, London.

Hayman, Carole and Spender, Dale (1985), *How the vote was won: and other suffragette plays*, London: Methuen.

References

Heilmann, Ann (2005), 'Medea at the Fin De Siècle: Revisionist Uses of Classical Myth in Mona Caird's the Daughters of Danaus', *Victorian Review* 31 (1): 21–39, doi:10.1353/vcr.2005.0004.

Holledge, Julie (2013), *Innocent Flowers: Women in the Edwardian Theatre*, London: Virago.

Hurst, Isobel (2006), *Victorian Women Writers and the Classics: The Feminine of Homer*, Oxford: Oxford University Press, doi:10.1093/acprof:oso/9780199283514.001.0001.

Hurst, Isobel (2009), 'Ancient and Modern Women in the Woman's World', *Victorian Studies* 52 (1): 42–51, doi:10.2979/VIC.2009.52.1.42.

Lawrence, Emmeline Pethick (21 October 1910), 'Lysistrata', *Votes for Women*: 6.

Levitt, Saraah, 'Pomeroy [née Legge], Florence Wallace, Viscountess Harberton', *Oxford Dictionary of National Biography* (online edn), Oxford: Oxford University Press, doi:10.1093/ref:odnb/45796.

Linton, E. L. (1892), 'The Partisans of the Wild Women', *The Nineteenth Century: A Monthly Review, Mar.1877–Dec.1900* 31 (181): 455–64.

Murphy, Patrick J., and Fredrick Porcheddu (2017), 'Eumenides and Newmenides: Academic Furies in Edwardian Cambridge', in *Brill's Companion to the Reception of Aeschylus*, 362–80, Leiden: Brill.

The Newmenides: with all due apologies to Aeschylus (1907), [Girton College 2nd-Year Entertainment], Cambridge: Metcalfe.

Norcia, Megan A. (2013), 'Performing Victorian Womanhood: Elsie Fogerty Stages Tennyson's Princess in Girls' Schools', *Victorian Literature and Culture* 41 (1): 1–20, doi:10.1017/S1060150312000198.

Oxford Magazine, 2 March 1892.

Paxton, Naomi (2018), *Stage Rights! the Actresses' Franchise League, Activism and Politics 1908–58*, Manchester: Manchester University Press, doi:10.7765/9781526114792.

Pedersen, J. S. (2002), 'Enchanting Modernity: The Invention of Tradition at Two Women's Colleges in Late Nineteenth- and Early Twentieth-Century Cambridge', in M. Feingold, ed., *History of Universities*, 162–91, Oxford: Oxford University Press.

Prins, Yopie (2017), *Ladies' Greek: Victorian Translations of Tragedy*, Princeton: Princeton University Press.

Sloan, Kay (1981), 'Sexual Warfare in the Silent Cinema: Comedies and Melodramas of Woman Suffragism', *American Quarterly* 33 (4): 412–36, doi:10.2307/2712526.

Straus, Michael (2018), 'Ritual Aspects of Aristophanes' Birds', *Acta Classica* 61 (1): 125–57. doi:10.15731/AClass.061.07.

Sutherland, Gillian (2015), *In Search of the New Woman: Middle-Class Women and Work in Britain, 1870–1914*, Cambridge: Cambridge University Press.

Swallow, Peter (2023), *Aristophanes in Britain: Old Comedy in the Nineteenth Century*, Oxford: Oxford University Press.

Vicinus, Martha (2004), *Intimate Friends: Women Who Loved Women, 1778-1928*, Chicago, Ill: University of Chicago Press.

Wånggren, Lena (2022), *Gender, Technology and the New Woman*, Edinburgh: Edinburgh University Press, doi:10.1515/9781474416276.

Watling, Sarah, 'The Gender Riots that Rocked Cambridge in the 1920s', https://blog.oup.com/2019/07/gender-riots-rocked-cambridge-university-1920s/, retrieved 01/06/20.

Wood, Elizabeth (1995), 'Performing Rights: A Sonography of Women's Suffrage', *Musical Quarterly* 79 (4): 606–43, doi:10.1093/mq/79.4.606.

Wright, Jane (2015), '"The Princess" and the Bee', *Cambridge Quarterly* 44 (3): 251–73, doi:10.1093/camqtly/bfv016.

Wrigley, Amanda (2011), *Performing Greek Drama in Oxford and on Tour with the Balliol Players*, Exeter: University of Exeter Press.

References

Chapter 8

Bacon, H. (1974), 'In- and Outdoor Schooling: Robert Frost and the Classics', *The American Scholar* 43 (4): 640–9.

Barron, J. N., and E. M. Selinger, eds (2000), *Jewish American Poetry: Poems, Commentary and Reflections*, Hanover and London: Brandeis University Press/University Press of New England.

Beaver News (1953–4 to 1957–8), 'Dean Higgins Announces Appointment of Five Professors to College Faculty', 25 September: 1.

Burroway, J. (2014), 'Maxine Kumin (1926 [sic]–2014). The Chicago Blog', quoting from J. Burroway, ed. (2014), *A Story Larger Than My Own; Women Writers Look Back on their Lives and Careers*, Chicago: University of Chicago Press. https://pressblog.uchicago.edu/2014/02/14/maxine-kumin-1926-2014.html.

Corbett, W. (1993), 'Trailing Robert Lowell to Castine, Maine and Dunbarton, New Hampshire', *Harvard Review* 3: 124–6.

Dalby, A., ed. and trans. (2010), *Cato: On Farming. De Agricultura*, London: Prospect Books.

Doherty, M. (2020), *The Equivalents: A Story of Art, Female Friendship, and Liberation in the 1960's*, New York: Alfred A. Knopf.

Dubrow, J. (2021), 'Maxine Kumin', *The Mezzo Cammin Women Poets Timeline* Project. Available online: https://www.mezzocammin.com/tieline/tieline.php?vol=timeline&iss=20&page=kumin.

Fox, M. (2014), 'Maxine Kumin, Pulitzer-Winning Poet with a Naturalist's Precision, Dies at 88', *The New York Times*, 7 February. Available online: https://www.nytimes.com/2014/02/08/books/maxine-kumin-pulitzer-winning-poet-dies-at-88.html?smid=nytcore-ios-share&referringSource=articleShare.

Galperin, W. H. (2001), Review of Susanne Klingenstein, *Enlarging America: The Cultural Work of Jewish Literary Scholars*, Syracuse University Press 1998, in *Criticism* 43: 116–19.

Glenside News (2024), 'History with Chuck: Remembering Mrs. Binter [sic], CHS Latin/English Teacher who received distinguished award from Yale', 1 March. Available online: https://glensidelocal.com/history-with-chuck-remembering-mrs-binter-chs-latin-english-teacher-who-received-distinguished-award-from-yale/.

Gundersheimer, W. (1985), 'The Way Things Were', *Pennsylvania Gazette*: 26–7.

Hurley, S. (2014), 'Poet Maxine Kumin Has Died at Age 88', *New Hampshire Public Radio*, 7th February. Available online: https://www.nhpr.org/nh-news/2014-02-07/poet-maxine-kumin-has-died-at-age-88Radio.

Klein, J. M. (2015), 'The Progress of Poet Maxine Kumin', Review of Kumin, *The Pawnbroker's Daughter: A Memoir*, in *The Forward*, 25 July. Available online: https://forward.com/culture/317865/a-poets-progress/.

Kumin, M. [Winokur] (1975), *House, Bridge, Fountain, Gate*, New York: Viking.

Kumin, M. [Winokur] (1992), *Looking for Luck*, New York and London: W. W. Norton.

Kumin, M. [Winokur] (2000), 'For Anne at Passover', Text and Commentary, in Barron and Selinger, eds: 91–9.

Kumin, M. [Winokur] (2005), *Jack and Other New Poems*, New York and London: W. W. Norton.

Kumin, M. [Winokur] (2007), *Still to Mow*, New York and London: W. W. Norton.

Kumin, M. [Winokur] (2012), 'Metamorphosis: From Light Verse to the Poetry of Witness', *The Georgia Review* 66 (4): 724–34.

Kumin, M. [Winokur] (2014), 'The Making of PoBiz Farm', in *The American Scholar*. Available online: https://theamericanscholar.org/author/maxine-kumin/.

Kumin, M. [Winokur] (2015), *The Pawnbroker's Daughter: A Memoir*, New York and London: W. W. Norton.

McCarthy, M. (1942), *The Company She Keeps*, New York: Dell Publishing.

Marquard, B. (2014), 'Maxine Kumin, 88; Pulitzer-Prize-winning-poet', *Boston Globe*, 8 February. Available online: https://www.bostonglobe.com/metro/2014/02/08/maxine-kumin-verse-and-prose-pulitzer-prize-winning-poet-captured-family-friendship-and-natural-world/2SaudL6d0uAcZ1DusTBVdN/story.html.

[Philadelphia] *Inquirer* (2014), 'Maxine Kumin, 88, former poet laureate', *Philadelphia Inquirer*, 8 February. Available online: https://www.inquirer.com/philly/obituaries/20140208_Maxine_Kumin_88_former_poet_laureate.html.

Moscaliuc, M. (2008), Review of Maxine Kumin, *Still To Mow*, New York: W. W. Norton and Company, in *Prairie Schooner* 82: 164–7.

Pride, M. (2005), 'PoBiz Farm – Maxine Kumin', *Concord Monitor*, 5 June. Available online: https://maxinekumin.com/life/pobiz-farm-.

Schreiber, J. (2010), 'Farther South than This', Review of Maxine Kumin, *Jack and Other New Poems*, W. W. Norton, 2005, in *Contemporary Poetry Review*. Available online: https://www.cprw.com/Schreiber/kumin.htm.

Shomer, E. (1996), 'An Interview with Maxine Kumin', *The Massachusetts Review* 37 (4): 531–55.

Talbot, J. (2003), 'Robert Frost's Hendecasyllabics and Roman Rebuttals', *International Journal of the Classical Tradition* 10 (1): 73–84.

Wilner, E. (2015), 'Maxine Kumin 1925–2014: The Long Approach: A Life in Poetry', *The Hudson Review*. Available online: https://hudsonreview.com/authors/eleanor-wilner.

Chapter 9

Dahlke, B. (1997), *Papierboot — Autorinnen aus der DDR inoffiziell publiziert* (Literaturwissenschaft, Bd. 198), Würzberg: Verlag Könighausen & Neumann.

Köhler, B. (1991), 'Elektra. Spiegelungen', *Deutsches Roulette*, Frankfurt am Main: Suhrkamp Verlag.

Köhler, B. (2007), *Niemands Frau*, Frankfurt am Main: Suhrkamp Verlag.

Köhler, Barbara (2009), 'Penelope Gewebe', *Die Hören, Zeitschrift für Literatur, Kunst und Kritik* 273 (64): 140–55.

Knott, Marie Luise, (2024), 'Vita', in *Barbara Köhler. Schriftstellen*, 240–4, Berlin: Suhrkamp Verlag.

Paul, G. (1999), 'German Roulette: Poems by Barbara Köhler', *Comparative Criticism* 21: 223–8.

Paul, G. (2004), 'Multiple Refractions, or Winning Movement out of Myth: Barbara Köhler's Poem Cycle "Elektra. Spiegelungen"', *German Life and Letters* 57 (1): 21–32.

Pound, E., and Fleming, R. ([1987] 1990), *Elektra: A Play by Ezra Pound and Rudd Fleming*, ed. Richard Reid, trans. Ezra Pound and Rudd Fleming, New York: New Directions.

Sophocles (2001), *Electra*, trans. Anne Carson, Oxford: Oxford University Press.

Woolf, V. (1925), 'On Not Knowing Greek', *The Common Reader*, London: Hogarth Press.

Chapter 10

Barker, P. (2019), *The Silence of the Girls*, London: Penguin.

Butler, S. (2016), 'Homer's Deep', in S. Butler, ed., *Deep Classics: Rethinking Classical Reception*, 21–48, London: Bloomsbury Academic.

Dué, C. (2002), *Homeric Variations on a Lament by Briseis*, Lanham, MD: Rowman and Littlefield.

Edwards, M. W. (1991), *The Iliad: A Commentary. Volume 5. Books 17–20*, Cambridge: Cambridge University Press.

References

Glendinning, E. (2013), 'Reinventing Lucretia: Rape, Suicide and Redemption from Classical Antiquity to the Medieval Era', *International Journal of the Classical Tradition* 20 (1/2): 61–82.

Hainsworth, J. B. (1993), *The Iliad: A Commentary. Volume 3. Books 9–12*, Cambridge: Cambridge University Press.

Heslin, P. (2005), *The Transvestite Achilles: Gender and Genre in Statius' Achilleid*, Cambridge: Cambridge University Press.

King, K. Callen (1980), 'The Force of Tradition: The Achilles Ode in Euripides' Electra', *Transactions of the American Philological Association (1974–)* 110: 195–212.

Koutserimpas, C., K. Alpantaki and G. Samonis (2017), 'Trauma management in Homer's Iliad', *International Wound Journal* 14 (4): 682–4.

Li, Y. (2022), *Future Fame in the Iliad: Epic Time and Homeric Studies*, New York: Bloomsbury Academic.

Miller, M. (2011), *The Song of Achilles*, London: Bloomsbury.

Miller, M. (2022), *Galatea: A Short Story*, London: Bloomsbury.

Nagy, G. (1999), *The Best of the Achaeans: Concepts of the Hero in Archaic Greek Poetry*, rev. edn, Baltimore: Johns Hopkins University Press.

Shay, J. (2003), *Achilles in Vietnam: Combat Trauma and the Undoing of Character*, New York: Scribner.

van Emde Boas, E. (2004), *Clusters of Hapax Legomena: An Examination of Hapax-dense Passages in the Iliad*, Universiteit van Amsterdam.

Wolf, C. (1984), *Cassandra*, trans. J. van Heurck, London: Virago.

Chapter 11

Balmer, J. (2004), *Chasing Catullus: Poems, Translations and Transgressions*, Newcastle upon Tyne: Bloodaxe Books.

Balmer, J. (2013), *Piecing Together the Fragments: Translating Classical Verse, Creating Contemporary Poetry*, Oxford: Oxford University Press.

Balmer, J. (2017a), *The Paths of Survival*, Bristol: Shearsman Books.

Balmer, J. (2017b), *Letting Go*, Manchester: Carcanet.

Balmer, J. (2020), 'The Library versus the Lyre: *The Paths of Survival* and the Poetry of Textual History', *Synthesis, Synthesis: an Anglophone Journal of Comparative Literary Studies*, 12: 76–95, doi:https://doi.org/10.12681/syn.25266 (accessed 25 January 2021).

Barker, P. (2018), *The Silence of the Girls*, London: Hamish Hamilton.

Barker, P. (2021), *The Women of Troy*, London: Hamish Hamilton.

Carson, A. (2010), *Nox*, New York: New Directions.

Dodd, E., (1992), *The Veiled Mirror and the Women Poet: H.D., Louise Bogan, Elizabeth Bishop, and Louise Glück*, Columbia MO: University of Missouri Press.

Doherty, L. (2008), 'The Figure of Penelope in Twentieth-Century Poetry by American Women', in G. A. Staley, ed., *American Women and Classical Myths*, 181–206, Waco, TX: Baylor University Press.

Gregory, E. (1997), *H.D. and Hellenism: Classic Lines*, Cambridge: Cambridge University Press.

Hurst, I. (2009), '"We'll all be Penelopes then": Art and Domesticity in American Women's Poetry, 1958–1996', in S. J. Harrison, ed., *Living Classics: Greece and Rome in Contemporary Poetry in English*, 275–94, Oxford: Oxford University Press.

Hurst, I. (2019), 'Monologue and Dialogue: The *Odyssey* in Contemporary Women's Poetry', in F. Cox and E. Theodorakis, eds, *Homer's Daughters: Women's Responses to Homer in the Twentieth Century and Beyond*, 177–92, Oxford: Oxford University Press.

Kakridis, J. Th. (1949), *Homeric Researches*, Lund: Gleerup.

Michelakis, P. (2002), *Achilles in Greek Tragedy*, Cambridge: Cambridge University Press.
Miller, M. (2018), *Circe*, New York: Little, Brown.
Murnaghan, S. (2008), 'H.D., Daughter of Helen: Mythology as Actuality', in G. A. Staley, ed., *American Women and Classical Myths*, 63–84, Waco, TX: Baylor University Press.
Murnaghan, S., and D. H. Roberts (2002), 'Penelope's Song: The Lyric Odysseys of Linda Pastan and Louise Glück', *Classical and Modern Literature* 22: 1–33.
Ostriker, A. (1982), 'The Thieves of Language: Women Poets and Revisionist Mythmaking', *Signs* 8: 68–90.
Oswald, A. (2011), *Memorial: An Excavation of Homer's Iliad*, London: Faber and Faber.
Prins, Y. (2017), *Ladies' Greek: Victorian Translations of Tragedy*, Princeton: Princeton University Press.
Rich, A. ([1972] 1979), 'When We Dead Awaken: Writing as Re-Vision', in *Lies, Secrets, and Silences*, 33–49, New York: Norton.
Sommerstein, A. (2008), *Aeschylus III: Fragments*, Loeb Classical Library, Cambridge, MA: Harvard University Press.

Chapter 12

Adewunmi, B. (2018), 'Tayari Jones is Rewriting the Great American Novel', *BuzzFeed News* (8 February), https://www.buzzfeednews.com/article/bimadewunmi/time-for-tayari-jones.
Alexander, M. (2012), *The New Jim Crow: Mass Incarceration in the Age of Colorblindness*, New York: The New Press.
Bereola, A. (2018), 'If I can't cry, nobody cries: An Interview with Tayari Jones', *Paris Review* (8 February), https://www.theparisreview.org/blog/2018/02/08/cant-cry-nobody-cries-interview-tayari-jones/.
Bergren, A. (2008), *Weaving Truth: Essays on Language and the Female in Greek Thought*, Cambridge, MA and London: Harvard University Press.
Callahan, N. (1987), *The Freedom Quilting Bee: Folk Art and the Civil Rights Movement*, Tuscaloosa: University of Alabama Press.
Campbell, J. ([1949] 2008), *The Hero with a Thousand Faces*, 3rd edn, Novato: New World Library.
Collins, P. H. (2000), *Black Feminist Thought: Knowledge, Consciousness, and the Politics of Empowerment*, 2nd edn, London and New York: Routledge.
Cox, F., and E. Theodorakopoulos, eds (2019), *Homer's Daughters: Women's Responses to Homer in the Twentieth Century and Beyond*, Oxford: Oxford University Press.
Felson-Rubin, N. (1994), *Regarding Penelope: From Character to Poetics*, Princeton: Princeton University Press.
Foley, H. P. (1978), '"Reverse Similes" and Sex Roles in the *Odyssey*', *Arethusa* 11.1/2: 7–26.
Fowler, R. L. (2011), '*Mythos* and *Logos*', *Journal of Hellenic Studies* 131: 45–66.
Gardner, H., S. and Murnaghan, eds (2014), *Odyssean Identities in Modern Cultures: The Journey Home*, Columbus, OH: Ohio State University Press.
Hall, E. (2008), *The Return of Ulysses*, London: I. B. Tauris.
Heilbrun, C. G. (1990), 'What was Penelope Unweaving?', *Hamlet's Mother and Other Women*, 103–111, New York and London: Columbia University Press.
Jones, T. (2019), 'Books that made me', *The Guardian* (24 May), in which Jones also observes that 'Every book I have written harks back to the Greeks', https://www.theguardian.com/books/2019/may/24/tayari-jones-books-that-made-me.
Jones, T. (2018), *An American Marriage*, Chapel Hill: Algonquin Books.
Katz, M. A. (1991), *Penelope's Renown: Meaning and Indeterminacy in the Odyssey*, Princeton, NJ: Princeton University Press.

References

Lévi-Strauss, C. (1955), 'The Structural Study of Myth', *The Journal of American Folklore* 68.270 (October–December): 428–44.

Lorde, A. (1984), *Sister Outsider: Essays and Speeches*, Berkeley: The Crossing Press.

Mᶜ Connell, J. (2013), *Black Odysseys: The Homeric Odyssey in the African Diaspora since 1939*, Oxford: Oxford University Press.

Mᶜ Connell, J. (2016), 'Postcolonial *Sparagmos*: Toni Morrison's *Sula* and Wole Soyinka's *The Bacchae of Euripides: A Communion Rite*', *Classical Receptions Journal* 8 (2): 133–54.

Mullen, H. (2002), '"Apple Pie with Oreo Crust": Fran Ross's Recipe for an Idiosyncratic American Novel', *MELUS* 27.1 (Spring): 107–29.

Murnaghan, S. (2011), *Disguise and Recognition in the Odyssey*, 2nd edn, Lanham, MD: Lexington Books.

Pache, C. (2014), '"Go Back to Your Loom Dad": Weaving *Nostos* in the Twenty-First Century', in H. Gardner and S. Murnaghan, eds, *Odyssean Identities in Modern Cultures: The Journey Home*, 44–63, Columbus, OH: Ohio State University Press.

Podlecki, A. J. (1971), 'Some Odyssean Similes', *Greece and Rome* 18: 81–90.

Puhvel, J. (1987), *Comparative Mythology*, Johns Hopkins University Press.

Rankine, P. D. (2006), *Ulysses in Black: Ralph Ellison, Classicism, and African American Literature*, Wisconsin: University of Wisconsin Press.

Rich, A. ([1972] 1979), 'When We dead Awaken: Writing as Re-Vision', in *Lies, Secrets, and Silences*, 33–49, New York: Norton.

Roynon, T. (2013), *Toni Morrison and the Classical Tradition: Transforming American Culture*, Oxford: Oxford University Press.

Segal, C. (1994), *Singers, Heroes, and Gods in the Odyssey*, Ithaca and London: Cornell University Press.

Wilson, E., trans. (2018), *The Odyssey*, New York: Norton.

Winkler, J. J. (1990), *The Constraints of Desire: The Anthropology of Sex and Gender in Ancient Greece*, New York and London: Routledge.

Zeitlin, F. I. (1995), 'Figuring Fidelity in Homer's *Odyssey*', in Beth Cohen, ed., *The Distaff Side: Representing the Female in Homer's Odyssey*, 117–52, New York and Oxford: Oxford University Press.

Chapter 13

Alaimo, S. (2010), *Bodily Natures: Science, Environment, and the Material Self*, Bloomington: Indiana University Press.

Alaimo, S. (2018), 'Trans-corporeality', in R. Braidotti and M. Hlavajova, eds, *Posthuman Glossary*, 435–8, London: Bloomsbury.

Bennett, J. (2009), *Vibrant Matter: A Political Ecology of Things*, Durham: Duke University Press.

Benson, F. (2019), *Vertigo & Ghost*, New York: W. W. Norton & Company.

Bond, S. E. (2017), 'Why We Need to Start Seeing the Classical World in Color', *Hyperallergic*, 7 June. Available online: https://hyperallergic.com/383776/why-we-need-to-start-seeing-the-classical-world-in-color/ (accessed 15 August 2023).

Brehme, K. (2020), 'Disability Arts: An Overview', *Diversity Arts Culture*, 19 June. Available online: https://diversity-arts-culture.berlin/en/magazin/disability-arts-overview (accessed 20 August 2023).

Chen, M. (2012), *Animacies: Biopolitics, Racial Mattering, and Queer Affect*, Durham, NC: Duke University Press.

Deleuze, G., and F. Guattari (1987), *A Thousand Plateaus: Capitalism and Schizophrenia*, trans. B. Massumi, Minneapolis: Minnesota University Press.

References

Derbew, S. F. (2022), *Untangling Blackness in Greek Antiquity*, Cambridge: Cambridge University Press.

dodd, j. (2019), *The Black Condition ft. Narcissus*, New York: Nightboat Books.

Doolittle, H. [H.D.] (1925), *Collected Poems 1912–1944*, New York: New Directions.

Dove, R. (1995), *Mother Love: Poems*, New York: W.W. Norton & Company.

Fromm, H. (1997), 'The "Environment" Is Us', *Electronic Book Review*, 1 January. Available online: https://electronicbookreview.com/essay/the-environment-is-us/ (accessed 11 January 2025).

Funke, J. (2019), 'The Queer Materiality of History: H.D., Freud and the Bronze Athena', in J. Funke and J. Grove, eds, *Sculpture, Sexuality and History*, 221–44, London: Palgrave Macmillan.

Galinsky, K. (1975), *Ovid's Metamorphoses: An Introduction to the Basic Aspects*, Berkeley: University of California Press.

Galinsky, K. (1999), 'Ovid's Metamorphoses and Augustan Cultural Thematics', in P. R. Hardie, A. Barchiesi and S. Hinds, eds, *Ovidian Transformations: Essays on Ovid's Metamorphoses and Its Reception*, Cambridge Philological Society Supplement no. 23, 103–11, Cambridge: Cambridge University Press.

Garland-Thomson, R. (2005), 'Staring at the Other', *Disability Studies Quarterly*, 25 (4). Available online: https://dsq-sds.org/article/view/610/787 (accessed 15 August 2023).

Haraway, D. (1991), 'A Cyborg Manifesto: Science, Technology, and Socialist-Feminism in the Late Twentieth Century', in *Simians, Cyborgs and Women: The Reinvention of Nature*, 149–82, New York: Routledge.

Hartman, S. (2008), 'Venus in Two Acts', *Small Axe*, 26: 1–14.

Hickman, R. (2020), 'Explore the Origins and Evolution of Kinetic Light's Descent', *Northrop Blog*, 23 November. Available online: https://www.northrop.umn.edu/learn-engage/blog/exploring-origins-and-evolution-kinetic-light-s-descent (accessed 1 August 2023).

Hulbert, M., L. Niedermeyer and A. Sheppard (2018), 'Alice Sheppard and Kinetic Light Present NY Premiere of *DESCENT*', *Disabled World*, 4 March. Available online: www.disabled-world.com/entertainment/descent.php (accessed 26 August 2023).

Ingleheart, J. (2008), '*Et mea sunt populo saltata poemata saepe* (*Tristia* 2.519): Ovid and the Pantomime', in E. Hall and R. Wyles, eds, *New Directions in Ancient Pantomime*, 198–217, Oxford: Oxford University Press.

Kinetic Light (2017), '*DESCENT* by Kinetic Light – In Process', *Vimeo/MANCC*, 13 June. Available online: https://vimeo.com/274970635 (accessed 30 July 2023).

Kinetic Light (2020), 'This Week! Our *DESCENT* Film Premiere', 2 December. Email communication (accessed 10 September, 2024).

Kinetic Light (2021), 'A moment from *DESCENT*', 22 July. Available online: https://www.instagram.com/p/CRofO5LAvuq/ (accessed 30 July 2023).

Kinetic Light (2023a), 'Accessibility', Kinetic Light. Available online: https://kineticlight.org/access (accessed 26 August 2023).

Kinetic Light (2023b), '*Audimance*', Kinetic Light. Available online: https://kineticlight.org/audimance (accessed 26 August 2023).

Kinetic Light (2023c), '*DESCENT*', Kinetic Light. Available online: https://kineticlight.org/descent (accessed 26 August 2023).

Kinetic Light (2023d), '*DESCENT* Artist Conversation Guide', 1–13 (accessed 14 December 2023).

Kinetic Light (2023e), '*DESCENT* Artist Convo Transcript', 1–20, (accessed 14 December 2023).

Kinetic Light (2023f), 'DESCENT Online & In-Depth Audience Guide', 1-3, (accessed 14 December 2023).

Kinetic Light (2024), 'About', Kinetic Light. Available online: https://kineticlight.org/about (accessed 10 September 2024).

References

kineticlightdance (2023), Image from *DESCENT*, Kinetic Light, 27 June. Available online: https://www.instagram.com/p/Ct_ry9JOiYH/ (accessed 28 August 2023).

Lada-Richards, I. (2013), '*Mutata Corpora*: Ovid's Changing Forms and the Metamorphic Bodies of Pantomime Dancing', *TAPA* 143: 105–52.

Lada-Richards, I. (2016), 'Dancing Trees: Ovid's *Metamorphoses* and the Imprint of Pantomime Dancing', *American Journal of Philology* 137 (1): 131–69.

Lanier, D. (2014), 'Shakespearean Rhizomatics: Adaptation, Ethics, Value', in A. Huang and E. Rivlin, eds, *Shakespeare and the Ethics of Appropriation*, 21–40, London: Palgrave Macmillan.

Latour, B. ([1991] 1993), *We Have Never Been Modern*, trans. C. Porter, Cambridge: Harvard University Press.

MacLaughlin, N. (2019), *Wake, Siren: Ovid Resung*, New York: FSG Originals.

McCarter, S. (2022), 'Introduction', in *Metamorphoses* / Ovid, xv–xxx, New York: Penguin Books.

McGrath, E. (1992), 'The Black Andromeda', *Journal of the Warburg and Courtauld Institutes* 55: 1–18.

Ovid (1916), *Metamorphoses*, Volume I, Books 1–8, trans. F. J. Miller, rev. G. P. Goold, Loeb Classical Library 42, Cambridge: Harvard University Press.

Ovid (1916), *Metamorphoses*, Volume II, Books 9–15, trans. F. J. Miller, rev. G. P. Goold, Loeb Classical Library 43, Cambridge: Harvard University Press.

Ovid (1924), *Tristia. Ex Ponto*, trans. A. L. Wheeler, rev. G. P. Goold, Loeb Classical Library 151, Cambridge: Harvard University Press.

Ovid (1929), *The Art of Love and Other Poems*, trans. J. H. Mozley, rev. G. P. Goold, Loeb Classical Library 232, Cambridge: Harvard University Press.

Preston, C. (2011), *Modernism's Mythic Pose: Gender, Genre, and Solo Performance*, Oxford: Oxford University Press.

'Ramp/Kinetic Light, with Alice Sheppard and Yevgeniya Zastavker' (2016), abler, adaptation + ability group. Available online: http://aplusa.org/projects/ramp-alice-sheppard/ (accessed 26 August 2023).

Reeve, D. (2012), 'Cyborgs, Cripples, and iCrip: Reflections on the Contribution of Haraway to Disability Studies', in D. Goodley, B. Hughes and L. Davis, eds, *Disability and Social Theory*, 91–111, London: Palgrave Macmillan.

Richlin, A. (1992), 'Reading Ovid's Rapes' in A. Richlin, ed., *Pornography and Representation in Greece and Rome*, 158–79, Oxford: Oxford University Press.

Rodin, A. ([1890] 1987), *The Toilette of Venus and Andromeda*, NC Museum of Art. Available online: https://ncartmuseum.org/art/detail/toilette_of_venus_and_andromeda (accessed 1 June 2023).

Rodin, A. and P. Gsell (1971), *Rodin on Art*, trans. R. Fedden, New York: Horizon Press.

Romack, C., and Y. Malka (2024), *A Sense of Shifting: Queer Artists Reshaping Dance*, San Francisco: Chronicle Books.

Salzman-Mitchell, P. (2005), *A Web of Fantasies: Gaze, Image, and Gender in Ovid's Metamorphoses*, Columbus: Ohio State University Press.

Sandahl, C. (2018), 'Using Our Words: Exploring Representational Conundrums in Disability Drama and Performance', *Journal of Literary & Cultural Disability Studies* 12 (2): 129–44.

Siebers, T. (2005), 'Disability Aesthetics', *PMLA* 120 (2): 542–6.

Siebers, T. (2010), *Disability Aesthetics*, Ann Arbor: University of Michigan Press.

Siebers, T. (2011), *Disability Theory*, Ann Arbor: University of Michigan Press.

Silverblank, H., and M. Ward (2020), 'Why Does Classical Reception Need Disability Studies', *Classical Receptions Journal* 12 (4): 502–30.

TicketTailor (2023), '*DESCENT* by Kinetic Light'. Available online: https://www.tickettailor.com/events/kineticlight/1021305 (accessed 10 September 2024).

Traub, V., P. Badir and P. McCracken, eds (2019), *Ovidian Transversions: 'Iphis and Ianthe', 1300–1650*, Edinburgh: Edinburgh University Press.

Werth, T. J. (2012), 'A Heart of Stone: The Ungodly in Early Modern England', in J. Feerick and V. Nardizzi, eds, *The Indistinct Human in Renaissance Literature*, 181–204, London: Palgrave Macmillan.

Chapter 14

Allan, W., ed. (2008), Euripides: *Helen*, Cambridge: Cambridge University Press.
Andrews, L. (2003), 'Jacob Burckhardt, Clive Bell and the "Equivalents" of Alfred Stieglitz', *History of Photography* 27: 247–53.
Blondell, R. (2013), *Helen of Troy: Beauty, Myth, Devastation*, Oxford and New York: Oxford University Press.
Carson, A. (2019a), *Norma Jeane Baker of Troy*, London: Oberon Books.
Carson, A. (2021b), *Norma Jean Baker de Troya*, trans. J. L. Clariond, Madrid: Vaso Roto Ediciones.
Carson, A. (2021c), *Era una nuvola, Una versione dell'Elena di Euripide*, trans. P. Ceccagnoli, Milano: Crocetti Editore.
Churchwell, S. (2019), *The Many Lives of Marilyn Monroe*, London: Bloomsbury.
Euripides (2017), *Helen*, trans. J. Morwood, Oxford: Oxford University Press.
Gorgias (1982), *Encomium of Helen*, trans. D. M. MacDowell, Bristol: Bristol Classical.
Greenough, S., and M. Greenburg, eds (1995), *In Focus: Alfred Stieglitz: Photographs from the J. Paul Getty Museum*, Los Angeles.
Kouvaros, G. (2002), 'The Misfits: What Happened Around the Camera', *Film Quarterly* 55 (4): 28–33.
Miller, A., and S. Toubiana (2011), *The Misfits: Story of a Shoot*, London: Phaidon Press.
The Mystery of Marilyn Monroe: The Unheard Tapes [documentary film] produced by E. Cooper, USA (distributed by Netflix, 2022), 101 mins.
Ovid (1914), *Heroides*; *Amores*, trans. G. P. Goold and G. Showerman, Cambridge, MA: Harvard University Press.
Peters, J. D. (2015), *The Marvelous Clouds*, Chicago and London: University of Chicago Press.
Plato (2013), *Republic*, trans. C. J. Emlyn-Jones and W. Preddy, Cambridge, MA, and London: Harvard University Press.
Smith, G. (2002), 'Marilyn Monroe, Long Island, New York, 1952', *History of Photography* 26 (III): 228–32.
Suzuki, M. (1989), *Metamorphoses of Helen: Authority, Difference, and the Epic*, Ithaca: Cornell University Press.

Chapter 15

Hernández Arias, Efrén (2020), 'En el intercambio siempre hay hallazgos'. Available at https://dulcear.com/en-el-intercambio-siempre-hay-hallazgos/ (last accessed 12 September 2024).
Kariakin, Kira, Virginia Riquelme and Violeta Rojo, eds (2015), *Cien mujeres contra la violencia de género*, Caracas: FUNDAVAG Ediciones.
Pérez Yebaile, Evlin (2015), 'Lena Yau: «La comida es una de las formas del amor»', Available at https://evlinpy.wordpress.com/2015/07/11/lena-yau-la-comida-es-una-de-las-formas-del-amor/ (last accessed 12 September 2024).
Pulido, José (2020), 'Lena Yau, poeta, narradora y periodista', *Letralia*. Available at https://letralia.com/entrevistas/2020/09/20/lena-yau/ (last accessed 9 September 2024).

References

Valdivieso, Humberto (2015), 'Lena Yau: la literatura, el hambre y la belleza', *El Nacional*. Available at https://www.elnacional.com/papel-literario/lena-yau-literatura-hambre-belleza_251730/(last accessed 9 September 2024).
Yau, Lena (2015a), *Trae tu espalda para hacer mi mesa* [Bring Your Back to Make My Table], Madrid: Gravitaciones; also New York: Sudaquia 2021.
Yau, Lena (2015b), *Hormigas en la lengua* [Ants on the Tongue], New York: Sudaquia, also Tenerife: Baile del sol, 2022.
Yau, Lena (2016), *Lo que contó la mujer canalla* [What the Rotten Woman Said], Madrid: Kaláthos.
Yau, Lena (2018), *Bonnie Parker o la posibilidad de un árbol* [Bonnie Parker or the Possibility of a Tree], Caracas: Utópia portátil.
Yau, Lena (2021), *Bienmesabes* [Youtastegreat], El Taller Blanco; also New York: Sudaquia, 2022.

Chapter 16

Brown, S. A. (2002), *The Metamorphoses of Ovid: From Chaucer to Ted Hughes*, 2nd edn, London: Duckworth.
Chaucer, G. (1947), *The Canterbury Tales*, New York: Henry Holt and Co.
Fabre-Serris, J. (2009), 'Sulpicia: an/other female voice in Ovid's *Heroides*: A new reading of *Heroides 4* and *15*', *Helios* 36 (2): 149–73.
Levins Morales, A. (2017), 'Revision', in J. Browdy, ed., *Women Writing Resistance: Essays on Latin America and the Caribbean*, 15–20, Boston: Beacon Press.
Moraru, C. (2001), *Rewriting: Postmodern Narrative and Cultural Critique in the Age of Cloning*, Albany, NY: SUNY Press.
Ovid (1955), *Metamorphoses*, trans. R. Humphries. Bloomington: Indiana University Press.
Ovid (1971), *Heroides and Amores*, trans. G. Showerman, Cambridge, MA: Harvard University Press.
Patterson, L. (1983), '"For the wyves love of bathe": Feminine rhetoric and poetic resolution in the *Roman de la Rose* and the *Canterbury Tales*', *Speculum* 58: 656–95.
Pelen, M. (1994), 'Chaucer's wife of Midas reconsidered: Oppositions and poetic judgment in the wife of Bath's tale', *FLORILEGIUM* 13: 141–60.
Slade, T. (1969), 'Irony in the Wife of Bath's Tale', *Modern Language Review* 64 (2): 241–7.
Smith, Z. (2000), *White Teeth*, New York: Random House.
Smith, Z. (2005), *On Beauty*, New York: Penguin Press.
Smith, Z. (2018a), *NW*, reprint, London: Hamish Hamilton.
Smith, Z. (2018), 'Some notes on attunement', *Feel free*: 100–16, https://www.bookrags.com/studyguide-feel-free/chapanal004.html#.
Smith, Z. (2018b), 'The I who is not me', *Feel free*: 333–47.
Smith, Z. (2022), 'On discovering the secret history of black England', *The Guardian*, 24 September.
Smith, Z. (2023), *The Wife of Willesden*, New York: Penguin Press.

Chapter 17

Cardinal, M. (1986), *La Médée d'Euripide: Avant-propos et texte français*, Paris: Bernard Grasset.
Cox, F. (2023), 'Il faut raconter mon long parcours: Migration and Ovidian Presences', in H. Taylor and F. Cox, eds, *Ovid in French: Reception by Women from the Renaissance to the Present*, 242–62, Oxford: Oxford University Press.

References

Diop, A. (2022a), *Saint-Omer*, [Film] dir. A. Diop, Srab Films.
Diop, A. (2022b), 'Interview with Alice Diop at Villa Medici', 5 December, https://www.villamedici.it/en/new/saint-omer-alice-diop/.
Euripides (2008), *Medea and Other Plays*, rev. edn, trans. James Morwood, intro. by Edith Hall, Oxford: Oxford University Press.
Fevry, S. (2017), 'Immigration and 'Mythological Memory in French Cinema: How References to Homer and Ovid Refigure the European Perception of Exile', *Image and Narrative* 18 (1): 20–9.
Hall, E. (2008), 'Introduction', in Euripides, *Medea and Other Plays*, Oxford: Oxford University Press.
Haynes, N. (2022), *Pandora's Jar: Women in the Greek Myths*, London: Harper.
Jordan, S. (2016), *Marie Ndiaye: Inhospitable Fictions*, Oxford: Legenda.
Little, J. P. (2000), 'The Legacy of Medea: Mariama Bâ *Un chant écarlate* and Marie Ndiaye *La Femme changée en bûche*', *Modern Language Review* 95 (2): 362–73.
Ndiaye, M. (1989), *La Femme changée en bûche*, Paris: Éditions de Minuit.
Robert-Diard, P. (2017), 'Fabienne Kabou, de l'effroi au diagnostic', *Le Monde*, September 16.
Romney, J. (2023), 'Interview with *St Omer* director Alice Diop', *The Guardian*, 29 January.
Shapiro, S. O. (2013), 'Pasolini's *Medea*: A Twentieth-Century Tragedy', in K. P. Nikoloutsos, ed., *Ancient Greek Women in Film*, 95–116, Oxford: Oxford University Press.
Willsher, K. (2016), 'French woman accused of murdering daughter on beach blames witchcraft', *The Guardian*, 20 June.
Zemler, E. (2023), 'Inside the tale of a real-life child killer so intense it made its director faint', *Los Angeles Times*, January 12.

INDEX

The letter *f* following an entry indicates a page with a figure.

abandonment 178, 182, 228–31
abdelukta 175–6
absence 178, 182, 228–31
access 203
Acharnians (Aristophanes) 17, 56
Achilleid (Statius) 158
Achilles 95–8, 100, 161–4, 167, 174–6
    as the best 155
    Deidamia 159–60
    violence of 156–7, 158
Achilles in Vietnam (Shay, Jonathan) 157
Actresses' Franchise League (AFL) 108
adultery 179, 181, 184
Aeneid (Virgil) 40, 68, 128–9, 130
'Aeolic lyre – as soon as I hear its song' (Parnok, Sofiia) 83–4, 95
Aeschylus 169–70
    Agamemnon 111
    Elektra 141
    Eumenides 109
    Myrmidons 167, 169–76
    Oresteia 111, 138
'Aeschylus' Revision' (Balmer, Josephine) 169–70
AFL (Actresses' Franchise League) 108
Agamemnon 161
Agamemnon (Aeschylus) 111
Agnes, Saint, of Poitiers 71, 75
Alaimo, S. 200–1
Alcaeus 89–90
Alcaeus and Sappho: Collected songs and lyric fragments translated in the metres of the originals by Viacheslav Ivanov (Ivanov, Viacheslav) 79, 81, 83, 86–7, 104
Alcaics 89–90, 97, 105
Alciato, Andrea
    Emblems 31
    'Iusta ultio / Juste vengence' (Just Revenge) 26
Alcidamas 45–6
Alcinoe 20
Alcott, Louisa May
    Work 59
Alexander, Michelle 177
alienation 139, 215, 243, 249
'All of me was twined in vines of memory' (Parnok, Sofiia) 84–5

Alma-Tadema, Lawrence
    Venantius Fortunatus reading his poems to Radegonda VI 71
Amata 72
American Marriage, An (Jones, Tayari) 177–86
Amphiaraus 240
Amr ibnal-Asi 172
'Amr's Last Words' (Balmer, Josephine) 172, 175
Amymone, A Romance of the Days of Pericles (Lynn, Eliza) 55, 62–6
ancient Greece 13
    Athens 58, 60, 63
    Ionia 58
'And straight-up beautiful, shapely youth, are you' (Parnok, Sofiia) 89–90
Andromeda 189–92, 196–7
Andromeda (Rodin, Auguste) 194
animacy 192–3, 194–6, 202, 205 n. 6
Anna, soror ... (Yourcenar, Marguerite) 34
Anstey, F.
    Return of Agamemnon, The 111–12
antelexa 171
Anthologia Palatina (Asclepiades)104
Antigone (Deraspe, Sophie) 253
Antigone (Sophocles) 170
'L'antre des nymphes' (Louÿs, Pierre) 102
Aphrodite (Cypris) 91
Apollonius Dyscolus 16
'Are Women Human?' (Sayers, Dorothy L.) 23
Aristodama 18–20, 21
Aristophanes 107
    Acharnians 17, 56
    Birds, The 107, 109, 110–11, 114, 117
    Frogs, The 110, 120
    Lysistrata 107–8
aristos Achaiōn 155, 156, 157, 162
Aristotle 42–4
    Marinella, Lucrezia 41, 42–3, 10–1
    Poetics 23, 41, 46–7, 51
    Rhetoric 41, 42–3, 46, 50, 51
'Aristotle on Detective Fiction' (Sayers, Dorothy L.) 23, 34
Arnold, Eve 214, 215–16
Ars Amatoria (Ovid), 190, 228, 232
    Parnok, Sofiia 98–9, 100, 101, 102

Index

'*Ars Poetica*: A Found Poem' (Kumin, Maxine Winokur) 127
L'Art (Rodin, Auguste) 194, 201
Arthur (king of Britain) 235–6
Asclepiades
   Anthologia Palatina 104
Asopus poem (Corinna) 15–16
Aspasia of Miletus 55–9, 61–2, 63–6
At Half Voice (Parnok, Sofiia) 80
Athens 58, 60, 63
'Atthis, a tender stalk from far-off Sardis' (Parnok, Sofiia) 104–5
l'Aubespine, Madeleine de 24, 32, 33, 35
   'Enigme' (Enigma) 24, 33–4
audio description 203
Aurora Leigh (Browning, Elizabeth Barrett) 63
Autograph Man, The (Smith, Zadie) 227–8

Baker, Norma Jean. *See* Monroe, Marilyn
Balmer, Josephine 169, 173
   'Aeschylus' Revision' 169–70
   'Amr's Last Words' 172, 175
   Chasing Catullus 169
   'Epilogue' 173
   'Final Sentence' 173
   'Gloss' 175
   Letting Go 169
   Paths of Survival 167–76
   Piecing Together the Fragments 169, 174
   'Victors' 175
'Banquet of Aspasia and Pericles, The' (L.E.L.) 58
Barker, Pat
   Silence of the Girls, The 157, 168
   Women of Troy, The 168
Baudelaire, Charles
   Fleurs du Mal, Les (The Flowers of Evil) 33
   'Sed non satiata' 33
beauty 74–5
bee symbolism 114, 116–17
Bees, The (Girton College) 107, 109, 110, 113–19f, 121
Beloved (Morrison, Toni) 252
beryls 75
best, the 155, 162, 164
bicycles 111–12 *see also* cycling
Bird People (Ferran, Pascale) 253
Birds, The (Aristophanes) 107, 109, 110–11, 114, 117
Blavatsky, Helena 69, 76
   Theosophical Glossary, The 69
'Boatswain's Mate, The' (Smyth, Ethel) 116
Boccaccio 30
body, the 193, 197
   cyborgs 206 n. 17
   disability 189, 197, 199–201, 203, 204
   trans-corporeality 196, 199–202
Boeotia 17

Bona Dea 67, 68, 76–7
   cult of 68–71, 72–3, 75–7
Bona Dea (Vivien, Renée) 67, 68–77
Borromeo, Carlo
   Instructiones predicationis verbi dei 45
Breeze, Jean 'Binta' 233
Briseis 160–2
Browning, Elizabeth Barrett
   Aurora Leigh 63
Bulwer Lytton, Edward
   Last Days of Pompeii, The 60

Cabinet satyrique, Le (The Satyric Cabinet) 32, 33–4
Cambridge 111 *see also* Girton College
Canterbury Tales, The (Chaucer, Geoffrey) 232
Cardinal, Marie 243–4, 252
   Mots pour le dire, Les 243
Carson, Anne 140
   Era una Nuvola, Una versione dell'Elena di Euripide ('It was a Cloud, A version of Euripides' Helen') 218–19
   Norma Jeane Baker de Troya, 213
   Norma Jeane Baker of Troy: a version of Euripides' Helen. See Norma Jeane Baker of Troy: a version of Euripides' Helen
   Nox 169
Cassandra (Wolf, Christa) 156–7
Cathedral, The (Rodin, Auguste) 194
Cato
   De Agri Cultura ('On Farming') 126
Catullus 131–2
   Poem 76 131–2
celebrity 61–2, 213, 215, 217, 218 see also *kleos*
censorship 176
Chaleion 18, 19
'Challenge' (Parnok, Sofiia) 95–6
Champier, Symphorien
   Nef des dames vertueuses (Ship of Virtuous Ladies) 30
Chanson de Bilitis, Les (Louÿs, Pierre) 99
Charioteer, The (Renault, Mary) 34
Chasing Catullus (Balmer, Josephine) 169
chastity 26, 63, 64, 65–6, 72–3
Chaucer, Geoffrey
   Canterbury Tales, The 232
   Legend of Good Women, The 232
   'Wife of Bath's Tale, The' 227, 232–3, 235–6, 237–41
Chen, M. 192, 205 n. 6
Child, Lydia Maria 55–6, 59, 66
   Philothea: A Romance 55, 59–62
chimeras 252
choral performance 14–15, 16, 17, 18, 20
Christianity 176

Index

Cien mujeres contra la violencia de género (One Hundred Women Against Gender Violence) (Kariakin et al.) 224
Circe (Miller, Madeline) 168
Cité des Dames (City of Ladies) (Pisan, Christine de) 30
Cithaeron 15
citizenship 61
Clash by Night (Lang, Fritz) 209, 217
class 6, 63
Classical Association 6
Classics 1–10, 116, 117, 121
    as a discipline 4
Clearchus
    Erotika 73
Clenched Hand, The (Rodin, Auguste) 194
clouds 209–10
colonialism 246–7, 254 n. 12
'Come Aristotle' (Kumin, Maxine Winokur) 133 n. 2
comedy 107–9, 110
    Greek Comedy 110, 111, 115, 121
'commande, La' (Louÿs, Pierre) 102
Comnena, Anna 13
Company She Keeps, The (McCarthy, Mary) 132
competitions 20
    school-age 6
completeness/incompleteness 196
'Conseils à un amant' (Louÿs, Pierre) 100
copy 211, 212, 218, 219 *see also* replica
Corinna 14–17, 20–1
    Asopus poem 15–16
Corinne, or Italy (Staël, Germain de) 60
courtesans 56–7
creativity 2–4
Crimea 79
culture 247
cyborgs 206 n. 17

Dacier, Anne 5
Dame à la louve, La (The woman with the wolf) (Vivien, Renée) 67, 68–77
dance. See DESCENT
Dangerfield, George
    Strange Death of Liberal England, The 107
Daphne 194–5
De Agri Cultura ('On Farming') (Cato) 126
De Elocutione (Demetrius) 45
De uirginate (Fortunatus, Venantius) 71–2, 75
Deane, Maya
    Wrath Goddess Sing 3
'Dedication' (Parnok, Sofiia) 99–100
defamiliarization 52 n. 10
Deidamia 159–60
Delphi 19
Demeter (Bridges, Robert) 113

Demetrius
    De Elocutione 45
Deraspe, Sophie
    Antigone 253
DESCENT (Kinetic Light) 3, 189–91, 193–4, 196–204
Deutsches Roulette (German Roulette) (Köhler, Barbara) 138
dialect 17
Diana (goddess) 24–9, 35
Dictionary of Greek and Roman Biography and Mythology (Smith, William) 67, 68, 70, 72
Diocles
    Shrines of Heroes 18
Diop, Alice 244–5
    Nous 244
    Permanence, La 244
    St Omer 244, 245–53
    Vers la tendresse 244
disability 189, 197, 199–201, 203, 204
disability aesthetics 194
diversity 2–3, 4–5, 127
divied self, the 35
divine forgiveness 28–9
'Do not call upon death' (Parnok, Sofiia) 100–1
domesticity 56, 59, 64
Downes, Juanita 128, 129–30, 131–2
drama 107–11
    Girton College 109, 110, 112f–19f
    Greek Comedy 110, 111, 115, 121
    performance activism 120–1
    suffrage plays 109, 116
    tragedy 140–1
dramatic monologues 171
du Pré, Jean
    Palais des nobles Dames (Palace of Noble Ladies) 30
'Duel' (Parnok, Sofiia) 95, 96–7
Duras, Marguerite 246

ears/hearing 238, 240
Eclogues (Virgil) 24
education 55, 60, 65, 115 *see also* women's colleges
    Girton College 109, 112f–14
    Kumin, Maxine Winokur 128
    Latin 131
    performance activism 120–1
    restrictions 112, 113–14, 120, 121
    riots 112f, 117, 120
Efron, Sergei 89–90, 97
Egypt 212
εἴδωλον. *See* idol
'Either Or' (Kumin, Maxine Winokur) 133 n. 5
Electra (Sophocles) 109, 110, 140
Elegiacs 92
elegy 99

Index

Elektra 138, 140
Elektra (Aeschylus) 141
'Elektra. Mirrorings' (Köhler, Barbara) 138–43
    translation 143–51
elitism 6, 7
Emblems (Alciato, Andrea) 31
empathy 161
Encomium of Helen (Gorgias of Leontini) 41, 211–12
'Enigme' (Enigma) (l'Aubespine, Madeleine de) 24, 33–4
epic, the 156, 164
'Epilogue' (Balmer, Josephine) 173
equality 65–6, 179
Equivalents (Stieglitz, Alfred) 209
Era una Nuvola, Una versione dell'Elena di Euripide ('It was a Cloud, A version of Euripides' Helen') (Carson, Anne) 218–19
Eriphyle 240
'Eros holds the mirror' (Parnok, Sofiia) 102–3
Erotika (Clearchus) 73
ethics 127
ethnicity 249 *see also* race/racism
Eumenides (Aeschylus) 109
Eunostus 18
Euripides
    Helen 209–10, 211, 212–13, 217, 219, 249
    Hippolytus 249
    Medea 243, 245–6, 249–52
    Trojan Women, The 211
Euvres (Works) (Labé, Louise) 29–32, 35
exclusion 1, 2, 4–5, 6

Fable du Faux Cuyder (Fable of False Presumption) (Navarre, Marguerite de) 23, 24, 25–8, 31, 35
Fabre-Serris, Jacqueline 229
family 182, 243, 244
Fasti (Ovid) 72
Fauna 70–1
Felton, C. C. 60
feminism 110
Femme changée en bûche, La (Ndiaye, Marie) 246
Ferran, Pascale
    Bird People 253
festivals, 19, 20–1
    to Bona Dea 68, 70, 73
    to Hera 14
'Final Sentence' (Balmer, Josephine) 173
Fleurs du Mal, Les (The Flowers of Evil) (Baudelaire, Charles) 33
Fogerty, Elsie
    Princess, The 114–15, 116
food 221–4
For the Most Beautiful (Hauser, Emily) 2

Forster, E. M.
    Howards End 227
Fortunatus, Venantius 71
    De uirginate 71–2, 75
    Poésies mêlées 71
France 244, 246–7
Francis, Convers 59
Friendly Young Ladies, The (Renault, Mary) 34
friendship 161–2, 167
Frogs, The (Aristophanes) 110, 120
    Girton College production 121
Frost, Robert 126
Fulgence of Ruspe 71
Fuller, Margaret
    Woman in the Nineteenth Century 63–4

Gardel, Carlos
    'Volver' (To Return) 222
Gates of Hell, The (Rodin, Auguste) 194
gaze 197–8f
gender 5, 169
    divisions 58
    roles 180, 181–3, 185
genealogy 16
Georgics (Virgil) 127
Gilbert, W. S. and Sullivan, Arthur
    Princess Ida 114
'Girl of the Period, The' (Lynn, Eliza) 62
'Girlfriend' (Tsvetaeva, Marina) 98
Girton College 109, 110, 112f–13
    Agamemnon 111
    Bees, The 107, 109, 110, 113–19f, 121
    Classics 116
    Frogs, The 121
    Newmendies, The 109, 110, 116, 120
    Return of Agamemnon, The 111–12
Glenn, Cheryl 56
'Gloss' (Balmer, Josephine) 175
God 49–50
gold 239–40
Gorgias of Leontini 41–3, 46
    Encomium of Helen 41, 211–12
grandiloquence 44
Greek Comedy 110, 111, 115, 121
Greek Orators 41
grief. *See* lament
Grote, George 57–8
Gundersheimer, Werner 131

Halfway (Kumin, Maxine Winokur) 126, 128
Hall, Edith 249
Hamilton, Cecily and St John, Christopher
    How the Vote Was Won 107–8
handicraft 180–1, 182
hapax legomena 156

Index

Hauser, Emily
   For the Most Beautiful 2
Hauser, Emily and Taylor, Helena
   Women Re-Creating Classics 1, 4, 7
Haynes, Natalie 249
healing 162–3
hearing 238, 240
'Heaven as Anus' (Kumin, Maxine Winokur) 127
Heilbrun, Carolyn
   'What was Penelope Unweaving?' 182
Helen (Euripides) 209–10, 211, 212–13, 217, 219, 249
Helen of Troy 211–13, 214
Helicon 15
Helmet Maker's Once Beautiful Wife, The (Rodin, Auguste) 194
Henry or Byzantium Conquered (Marinella, Lucrezia) 40
Heptameron (Navarre, Marguerite de) 28–9
Hera 14
Herodotus 13
Heroides (Ovid) 23, 29, 40, 190, 203–4, 228–32, 235
heroism 155, 156, 164, 174 *see also* best, the
hetaira 57–8, 63, 64
heterosexuality 99
'Highway Hypothesis' (Kumin, Maxine Winokur) 133 n. 5
Hippolytus (Euripides) 249
Hiroshima mon amour (Resnais, Alain) 246
Histoire des Satyres, et Nymphes de Dyane (Story of the Satyrs and the Nymphs of Diana) (Navarre, Marguerite de) 24
historical novels 55
history 3, 13
   ancient Greece 13, 14
   Aristodama, 18
   Myrtis 18
home 185
   returning to 222
Homer 13
   hapax legomena 156
   Iliad. See *Iliad*
   Odyssey. See *Odyssey*
Homeric Hymn 4 to Hermes 82
homosexuality 34, 175–6
honour 161–2
How the Vote Was Won (Hamilton, Cecily and St John, Christopher) 107–8
Howards End (Forster, E. M.) 227
human intellect 50
Humanism 40
Hurston, Zora Neale
   Their Eyes Were Watching God 234
Huston, John
   Misfits, The 214–15

Idaea 224
idols 212, 214, 218, 219
Iliad (Homer) 157, 161–3, 170
   Achilles 156–7, 161, 164, 167
   Agamemnon 161
   Briseis 161
   heroism 174
   kindness 155
   kleos 156
   Patroclus 158, 160, 162–3, 164, 167
   repurposing 23
   retelling 2
   translations 1, 5
   Trojan War 211
incarceration 177, 178, 179, 183
incest 28, 30–1, 34
inclusion 5, 6, 127, 203
incompleteness/completeness 196
independence 63
Index of Prohibited Books 40
infanticide 245–8, 251, 252
infidelity 179, 181, 184
'Inspiration's flower' (Parnok, Sofiia) 81–2
Instructiones predicationis verbi dei (Borromeo, Carlo) 45
intellectual authority 23, 34
intellectual excellence 55
intellectual inferiority 56
Ionia 58
isolation 249–51 *see also* abandonment
'Iusta ultio / Juste vengence' (Just Revenge) (Alciato, Andrea) 26
Ivanov, Viacheslav 79
   Alcaeus and Sappho: Collected songs and lyric fragments translated in the metres of the originals by Viacheslav Ivanov 79, 81, 83, 86–7, 104

Jamaica 236
Jones, Tayari
   American Marriage, An 177–86
Judaism 128
Juvenal 32, 33, 34

Kabou, Adélaïde 252
Kabou, Fabienne 245–7, 248, 252
καιρός 215
Kennedy, Rebecca Futo 57
kindness 155, 156, 157–8, 160, 162–3, 165
Kinetic Light 189, 203
   DESCENT 3, 189–91, 193–4, 196–204
Kitharèdes, Les (Vivien, Renée) 68
kleos 156, 161, 163, 164, 165 *see also* celebrity
knitting 217

281

Index

Köhler, Barbara 137–43
   Deutsches Roulette (German Roulette) 138
   'Elektra. Mirrorings' 138–43
   'Elektra. Mirrorings', translation 143–51
   Niemands Frau (Nobody's Wife) 137–8
Kumin, Maxine Winokur 125–32
   'Ars Poetica: A Found Poem' 127
   'Come Aristotle' 133 n. 2
   'Either Or' 133 n. 5
   farm labour 126
   Halfway 126, 128
   'Heaven as Anus' 127
   'Highway Hypothesis' 133 n. 5
   'Path, Chair' 133 n. 5
   Pawnbroker's Daughter, The 125, 130
   'Sisyphus' 132 n. 1
   'Snarl, The' 128–30, 131
   'Still We Take Joy' 127
   'To Anne at Passover' 128
   Up Country: Poems of New England 126

L.E.L. (Letitia Elizabeth Landon)
   'Banquet of Aspasia and Pericles, The' 58
Labé, Louise 24
   Euvres (Works) 29–32, 35
lament 140–2, 143, 160, 169
Lamia 18
Landon, Letitia Elizabeth. *See* L.E.L.
Landor, Walter Savage
   Pericles and Aspasia 63–4
Lang, Fritz
   Clash by Night 209, 217
language 246–7
Last Days of Pompeii, The (Bulwer Lytton, Edward) 60
Latin 131
Lawson, Laurel 189, 190, 194, 197, 198*f*, 200, 201, 202*f*
Legend of Good Women, The (Chaucer, Geoffrey) 232
lesbian love 72–4, 77, 79 see also *Roses of Pieria*
Lesbos 14
Letting Go (Balmer, Josephine) 169
Levy, Amy
   'Xantippe' 59
Lexicon (Photius) 167, 175–6
Life of Pericles (Plutarch) 56
Life of the Seraphic and Glorious St. Francis (Marinella, Lucrezia) 49
Life of the Virgin Mary, Empress of the Universe described in Prose and Ottava Rima, The (Marinella, Lucrezia) 39, 44, 48, 51
ligoura 17
'Like a small girl you appeared before me, awkward' (Parnok, Sofiia) 91–2
Linton, Eliza Lynn. *See* Lynn, Eliza

literature 245 *see also* poetry
   dramatic monologues 171
   historical novels 55
   revisionary 168–9
Lives of the Sophists (Philostratus) 41–2
Livia (empress of Rome) 72
Lockhart, J. G.
   Valerius: A Roman Story 60
Louÿs, Pierre
   'L'antre des nymphes' 102
   Chanson de Bilitis, Les 99
   'commande, La' 102
   'Conseils à un amant' 100
   'seins de Mnasidika, Les' 102
   Songs of Bilitis 67
   'Thérapeutique' 100
love 29–32 *see also* lesbian love
   age 32
   food 222
   kiss 74
   male 73–4
lust 24, 28, 29, 30, 33, 34
Lynn, Eliza (Eliza Lynn Linton) 55–6, 62, 66
   Amymone, A Romance of the Days of Pericles 55, 62–6
   'Girl of the Period, The' 62
'Lyre' (Parnok, Sofiia) 82
Lysistrata (Aristophanes) 107–8

Maag, Michael 189, 190, 194, 202
McCarthy, Mary
   Company She Keeps, The 132
Macrobius
   Saturnalia 68
male domination 167–8
male love 73–4
Mandel'shtam, Osip
   'Tortoiseshell' 82
Man's Amorous Turn to Divine Beauty (Marinella, Lucrezia) 49, 51
marble 206 n. 9
'March of the Women, The' (Smyth, Ethel and Hamilton, Cicely) 116
marginalization 5
Marinella, Lucrezia 39, 40–1
   Alcidamas 45–6
   Aristotle 41, 42–3, 50–1
   Demetrius 45
   Gorgias of Leontini 41–2, 46
   Henry or Byzantium Conquered 40
   Life of the Seraphic and Glorious St. Francis 49
   Life of the Virgin Mary, Empress of the Universe described in Prose and Ottava Rima, The 39, 44, 48, 51
   Man's Amorous Turn to Divine Beauty 49, 51

Index

Nobility and Excellence of Women and the Defects and Vices of Men, The 39, 40, 41, 44, 45
   style 44, 45, 47–9
   'To Readers' ('A' lettori') 39, 41, 42, 44–6, 48–9, 50
marmoreum 191, 196
marriage 58, 62, 65–6, 113–14, 183–4
   l'Aubespine, Madeleine 32
   infidelity 179, 181, 184
   Ovid 228–9
Marvelous Clouds, The (Peters, John Durham) 209
master–slave dichotomy 74
Meade, L. T.
   Sweet Girl Graduate, The 114
Medea 245, 248–52
Medea (Euripides) 243, 245–6, 249–52
Medea (Pasolini, Pier Paolo) 248–9, 252
medicine 162–3
Mémoires d'Hadrien (Memoirs of Hadrian) (Yourcenar, Marguerite) 34
Memorial (Oswald, Alice) 169
Menexenus 57
Menexenus (Plato) 57
Messalina (empress of Rome) 24, 32–3, 35
metamorphoses 200
Metamorphoses (Ovid) 26, 190–3, 203–4, 227, 228, 235, 237
   Canterbury Tales, The (Chaucer, Geoffrey) 232, 235
   DESCENT (Kinetic Light) 198, 201, 203–4
   Marinella, Lucrezia 40
   Midas (king of Phrygia) 237–8
   Navarre, Marguerite de 25–7, 35
   Rodin, Auguste 191, 194–6
   Sannazaro, Jacopo 24, 25
   Smith, Zadie 228, 235, 237, 241
   Wife of Willesden, The (Smith, Zadie) 235, 237
Metamorphosis of Ovid, The (Rodin, Auguste) 194
metaphors 42–3, 46–9, 51
   God 50
metre 89–90
   Alcaics 89–90, 97, 105
   Elegiacs 92
   Sapphics 98
Midas (king of Phrygia) 237–40
migration 230, 243–6, 253
Miller, Arthur 215
   Misfits, The 214
Miller, Madeline
   Circe 168
   Song of Achilles, The 1, 155–65
Misfits, The (Huston, John) 214–15
Misfits, The (Miller, Arthur) 214
misogyny 65

Mnasidika 103
modesty 61, 63
Mon frère féminin: letter à l'Amazone (Tsvetaeva, Marina) 98
Monroe, Marilyn (Norma Jean Baker) 209, 210*f*, 211, 213–18
morality 181
   moral lessons 26, 27, 28–9, 30, 31
Moran, Richard 47
Morrison, Toni
   Beloved 252
motherhood 15–16, 157, 243, 247, 251–2
Mots pour le dire, Les (Cardinal, Marie) 243
mourning 169 *see also* lament
Mrs Dalloway (Woolf, Virginia) 227
'Much too tightly clamped shut were those lips' (Parnok, Sofiia) 90–1, 95
multiculturalism 228, 233 *see also* race/racism
Murray, Gilbert 120
music
   sex 33
   contest 15
   choral performance/songs 14–15, 16, 17, 18, 19, 20–1
   internationalization, 19, 20
Myrmidons (Aeschylus) 167, 169–76
Myrtis 16, 17–18
Mystery of Marilyn Monroe: The Unheard Tapes, The (Cooper, Emma) 216–17
myth/s 177, 185, 189–90
   Arthur (king of Britain) 235–6
   British 235–6
   Corinna 15, 17
   Jamaican 236–7
   Midas (king of Phrygia) 237–40
   Monroe, Marilyn 218
   Myrtis 17–18
   Sappho 13–14
   Smith, Zadie 235–7
mythologēsai/mythologeusai 14

names 71
Nanny of the Maroons 236
'Narciso in the kitchen' (Narcissus in the Kitchen) (Yau, Lena) 223
Navarre, Marguerite de 24–9
   Histoire des Satyres, et Nymphes de Dyane (Story of the Satyrs and the Nymphs of Diana) 24
   Fable du Faux Cuyder (Fable of False Presumption) 23, 24, 25–8, 31, 35
   Heptameron 28–9
Ndiaye, Marie 246, 252
   Femme changée en bûche, La 246
Nef des dames vertueuses (Ship of Virtuous Ladies) (Champier, Symphorien) 30

Index

'new Jim Crow, the' 177
'New Woman' 112
Newmendies, The (Girton College) 109, 110, 116, 120
Niagara (Hathaway, Henry) 214
Niemands Frau (Nobody's Wife) (Köhler, Barbara) 137–8
'1910' (Smyth, Ethel and Hamilton, Cicely) 116
'No decir' (To Not Say) (Yau, Lena) 224
Nobility and Excellence of Women and the Defects and Vices of Men, The (Marinella, Lucrezia) 39, 40, 41, 44, 45
Norma Jeane Baker de Troya (Carson, Anne) 213
Norma Jeane Baker of Troy: a version of Euripides' Helen 209–11, 213, 216, 217, 218–19
    cover image 214
Norsa, Medea 167, 169, 172
'Not always in the wind it blazes up brighter' (Parnok, Sofiia) 101–2
Nous (Diop, Alice) 244
Nox (Carson, Anne) 169
NW (Smith, Zadie) 227, 228

occultism 76
Ode to Aphrodite (Sappho) 72–3, 91
Odysseus 164–5, 179, 181, 183, 184, 222
Odyssey (Homer) 14
    female handicraft 180–1
    Jones, Tayari 177–83
    Köhler, Barbara 137–8
    marriage 184
    Odysseus 164–5, 179, 181, 183, 184, 222
    Penelope 180–2, 183, 222
    repurposing 23
    reverse similes 178–9, 181–2
    translations 1, 5
    trees 183–4
    Trojan War 211
Oedipus Tyrannos (Sophocles) 111
Om 69
Oma 68–70, 75–6 *see also* Bona Dea
On Beauty (Smith, Zadie) 227, 228, 229, 231–2
'On Not Knowing Greek' (Woolf, Virginia) 140
On the Shortness of Life (Seneca) 228
opera 116
Oresteia (Aeschylus) 111, 138
Orpheus and Eurydice (Rodin, Auguste) 194
Ostriker, Alicia
    'Thieves of Language' 168
Oswald, Alice
    Memorial 169
Ovid 40, 227, 228
    Amores 102
    Ars Amatoria. See *Ars Amatoria*
    Fasti 72
    Heroides 23, 29, 40, 190, 203–4, 228–32, 235

    love poetry 29
    Metamorphoses. See *Metamorphoses*
    Tristia 99, 203
    women in 228–9
Oxbridge 107, 109, 110, 113, 115–16
    performance activism 120–1

Palais des nobles Dames (Palace of Noble Ladies) (du Pré, Jean) 30
Palatine Anthology 14
Palinode (Stesichorus) 211
Panigarola, Francesco 45
    Preacher or Paraphrase, comment and discourses on the book On style of Demetrius
Parnok, Sofiia 79–105
    'Aeolic lyre – as soon as I hear its song' 83–4, 95
    'All of me was twined in vines of memory' 84–5
    'And straight-up beautiful, shapely youth, are you' 89–90
    At Half Voice 80
    'Atthis, a tender stalk from far-off Sardis' 104–5
    'Challenge' 95–6
    in Crimea 79
    'Dedication' 99–100
    'Do not call upon death' 100–1
    'Duel' 95, 96–7
    'Eros holds the mirror' 102–3
    'Inspiration's flower' 81–2
    'Like a small girl you appeared before me, awkward' 91–2
    'Lyre' 82
    'Much too tightly clamped shut were those lips' 90–1, 95
    'Not always in the wind it blazes up brighter' 101–2
    'Penthesileia' cycle 80, 95–8
    'Return' 95, 97–8
    Roses of Pieria 80, 81–105
    'Roses of Pieria' cycle 80, 81–95, 96, 103
    Sappho 79, 80, 81–105
    'Sappho's Dreams (1)' 86–8
    'Sappho's Dreams (2)' 88–9
    'So on different shores' 94–5
    'Time's up' 82–3
    Tsvetaeva, Marina 79, 85, 91, 92, 98
    'Where his arrows are' 102
    'Wise Venus' cycle 80, 98–105
    Vine 80
    'You are drowsing, my girlfriend' 92–4
parody 111
Pasolini, Pier Paolo
    Medea 248–9, 252
'Path, Chair' (Kumin, Maxine Winokur) 133 n. 5
Paths of Survival (Balmer, Josephine) 167–76
Patroclus 155, 156, 157–8, 159–65
Paul, Georgina 138, 139–40

Index

Penelope 180–2, 183, 222
Penthesileia (queen of the Amazons) 95–8
'Penthesileia' cycle (Parnok, Sofiia) 80, 95–8
performance activism 120–1
Pericles 56–7
Pericles and Aspasia (Landor, Walter Savage) 63–4
Permanence, La (Diop, Alice) 244
personal experience 169
Peters, John Durham
    Marvelous Clouds, The 209
Phaedrus (Plato) 34, 50
Phalaereus, The 45
Philostratus
    Lives of the Sophists 41–2
Philothea: A Romance (Child, Lydia Maria) 55, 59–62
Photius
    Lexicon 167, 175–6
photography 209, 215
Piantoni, Luca 45
Piecing Together the Fragments (Balmer, Josephine) 169, 174
pieds noir 243–4
Pindar 16, 17
Pisan, Christine de
    Cité des Dames (City of Ladies) 30
plants, medicinal 70
Plato
    Menexenus 57
    Phaedrus 34, 50
    Symposium 50, 57
Plutarch 17–18, 20
    Aspasia of Miletus 56–7
    Life of Pericles 56
Poem 76 (Catullus) 131–2
Poésies mêlées (Fortunatus, Venantius) 71
Poetics (Aristotle) 23, 41, 46–7, 51
poetry 16, 43, 44 *see also* metre
    elegy 99
    female 20, 21
    internationalization, 19, 20
    love 29
    ornamentation 44
    pastoral. *See* Kumin, Maxine Winokur
    recusatio 96, 98
politics 107–8
Pope, Alexander 5
Portrait de la jeune fille en feu (Sciamma, Céline) 253
Posthomerica (Quintus Smyrnaeus) 95, 96, 97, 98
prayer 25, 26, 27, 28, 35
Preacher or Paraphrase, comment and discourses on the book On style of Demetrius Phalaereus, The (Panigarola, Francesco) 45

presumption (*cuyder*) 24–7, 28–9
pride 161–2
Princess, The (Tennyson, Alfred; adapt. Fogerty, Elsie) 114–15, 116
Princess Ida (Gilbert, W. S. and Sullivan, Arthur) 114
printing industry 41
Procne 194–5
propriety, 42–4, 46, 51, 63
prose 43–4 *see also* rhetoric
    ornamentation 44, 45–6
public sphere 2, 19, 40, 55–6, 61
Puvis de Chavannes, Pierre
    Saint Radegund listening to a reading by the poet Fortunat 71
Pygmalion 192–3
Pygmalion and Galatea (Rodin, Auguste) 194
Pyrrhus 164, 165

querelle des femmes 40
Quintus Smyrnaeus
    Posthomerica 95, 96, 97, 98

race/racism 177, 178, 189–90, 191, 196–7 *see also* ethnicity
    multiculturalism 228, 233
    Smith, Zadie 227, 228
Radegund, Saint 71
rape 159
re-vision 168, 178, 185
reason 50
reception studies 5–6
recusatio 96, 98
religion 19
Renaissance, the 40
Renault, Mary 34
    Charioteer, The 34
    Friendly Young Ladies, The 34
repentance 28–9
replica 212
restrictions 58, 61, 70
    education 112, 113–14, 120, 121
'Return' (Parnok, Sofiia) 95, 97–8
Return of Agamemnon, The (Anstey, F.; adapt. Watson, E. B. L.) 111–12
reverse similes 178–9, 181–2
Rhetores Graeci 41
rhetoric 39–41, 42–3, 48, 50–1
    epideictic 45
Rhetoric (Aristotle) 41, 42–3, 46, 50, 51
Rich, Adrienne
    'When We Dead Awaken: Writing as Re-Vision' 3, 168, 178
riots 112f, 117
Robins, Elizabeth
    Votes for Women 107

285

Index

Rodin, Auguste
   Andromeda 194
   L'Art 194, 201
   Cathedral, The 194
   Clenched Hand, The 194
   Gates of Hell, The 194
   Helmet Maker's Once Beautiful Wife, The 194
   Metamorphosis of Ovid, The 194
   Orpheus and Eurydice 194
   Pygmalion and Galatea 194
   Toilette of Venus and Andromeda 189, 190, 191, 194, 195*f*–6
   Torso of Adèle 194
   Ugolino and His Children 194
Roses of Pieria (Parnok, Sofiia) 80, 81–105
   'Penthesileia' cycle 80, 95–8
   'Roses of Pieria' cycle 80, 81–95
   'Wise Venus' cycle 80, 98–105
'Roses of Pieria' cycle (Parnok, Sofiia) 80, 81–95, 96, 103

St Omer (Diop, Alice) 244, 245–53
Saint Radegund listening to a reading by the poet Fortunat (Puvis de Chavannes, Pierre) 71
Salices (The Willows) (Sannazaro, Jacopo) 24–5
Sannazaro, Jacopo
   Salices (The Willows) 24–5
Sapho, traduction nouvelle avec le texte grec (*Sapho, a new translation with the Greek text*) (Vivien, Renée) 67, 68, 72
Sapphics 98
Sappho 13–14, 79, 93, 96, 229 see also *Roses of Pieria*
   Ode to Aphrodite 72–3, 91
   'To Alcaeus' 90
   'To Atthis' 86–7
'Sappho's Dreams (1)' (Parnok, Sofiia) 86–8
'Sappho's Dreams (2)' (Parnok, Sofiia) 88–9
Saturnalia (Macrobius) 68
Sayers, Dorothy L.
   'Are Women Human?' 23
   'Aristotle on Detective Fiction' 23, 34
school-age competition 6
Sciamma, Céline
   Portrait de la jeune fille en feu 253
sculpture 190–3, 194, 196
   marble 191, 196
seclusion 64
'Sed non satiata' (Baudelaire, Charles) 33
'seins de Mnasidika, Les' (Louÿs, Pierre) 102
Semiramis (queen of Babylon) 24, 30, 35
Seneca 228
   On the Shortness of Life 228
Senegal 246–7
sermons 45
Servius 68–9

sex 30, 33–4, 35, 233 *see also* lesbian love
   chastity 26, 63, 64, 65–6, 72–3
   disability 199
   double standards 63
   heterosexuality 99
   incest 28, 30–1, 34
   lust 24, 28, 29, 30, 33, 34
   Messalina (empress of Rome) 24, 32–3, 35
Sexton, Anne Harvey 126, 128
Shay, Jonathan
   Achilles in Vietnam 157
Sheppard, Alice 189, 190, 194, 196–7, 198*f*, 200, 201
Shot Marilyns, The (Warhol, Andy) 214, 218
Shrines of Heroes (Diocles) 18
Silence of the Girls, The (Barker, Pat) 157, 168
silencing 182
sin 28, 30
'Sisyphus' (Kumin, Maxine Winokur) 132 n. 1
slavery 74, 160
Smith, William
   Dictionary of Greek and Roman Biography and Mythology 67, 68, 70, 72
Smith, Zadie 227, 234
   Autograph Man, The 227–8
   NW 227, 228
   On Beauty 227, 228, 229, 231–2
   Ovid 227–32, 235, 237, 241
   'Some Notes on Attunement' 228
   Swing Time 228
   White Teeth 229–31
   Wife of Willesden, The 227, 228, 232–5, 236–7, 238–41
Smyth, Ethel
   'Boatswain's Mate, The' 116
Smyth, Ethel and Hamilton, Cicely
   'March of the Women, The' 116
   '1910' 116
'Snarl, The' (Kumin, Maxine Winokur) 128–30, 131
'So on different shores' (Parnok, Sofiia) 94–5
social class 6, 63
society 58, 59, 63
Socrates 57
'Some Notes on Attunement' (Smith, Zadie) 228
Somerville College 120
   'What We Have Come to: or the Higher Education of Women' 120
Song of Achilles, The (Miller, Madeline) 1, 155–65
songs 14–15, 16, 17, 18, 19, 20–1
Songs of Bilitis (Louÿs, Pierre) 67
Sophocles
   Antigone 170
   Electra 109, 110, 140
souls 50
spirit guides 194
Staël, Germain de
   Corinne, or Italy 60

Index

Statius
   Achilleid 158
Stesichorus 211
   Palinode 211
Stieglitz, Alfred 209
   Equivalents 209
'Still We Take Joy' (Kumin, Maxine Winokur) 127
Strange Death of Liberal England, The (Dangerfield, George) 107
style 39, 41–5
suffrage 107–9
suffrage opera 116
suffrage plays 109, 116
Swallow, Peter
   'Women's Aristophanes: Old Comedy and the Fight for Gender Equality' 110
Sweet Girl Graduate, The (Meade, L. T.) 114
Swing Time (Smith, Zadie) 228
Symposium (Plato) 50, 57

Tarn, Pauline. *See* Vivien, Renée
technology 199, 201, 203
Tennyson, Alfred
   Princess, The 114
texts, survival of 167, 168, 169, 170, 171–3
Theosophical Glossary, The (Blavatsky, Helena) 69
Theano 73
Their Eyes Were Watching God (Hurston, Zora Neale) 234
Theosophical Society 76
'Thérapeutique' (Louÿs, Pierre) 100
Thetis 163, 164
'Thieves of Language' (Ostriker, Alicia) 168
Thilo, Georg and Hagen, Hermann 68–9
Thucydides 13
Tibullus 31
'Time's up' (Parnok, Sofiia) 82–3
'To Alcaeus' (Sappho) 90
'To Anne at Passover' (Kumin, Maxine Winokur) 128
'To Atthis' (Sappho) 86–7
'To Readers' ('A' lettori') (Marinella, Lucrezia) 39, 41, 42, 44–6, 48–9, 50
Toilette of Venus and Andromeda (Rodin, Auguste) 189, 190, 191, 194, 195*f*–6
Torso of Adèle (Rodin, Auguste) 194
'Tortoiseshell' (Mandel'shtam, Osip) 82
Trae tu esplada para hacer mi mesa (Bring Your Back to Make My Table) (Yau, Lena) 221–4
tragedy 140–1
trans-corporeality 196, 199–202
transition 194–6
translation 138, 139–40, 142–3, 173, 174, 219
Tristia (Ovid) 99, 203

Trojan War 211–12
Trojan Women, The (Euripides) 211
Tsvetaeva, Marina 79, 85, 91, 92, 98
   'Girlfriend' 98
   Mon frère féminin: letter à l'Amazone 98
Turner, Marion
   Wife of Bath: A Biography, The 233
Twentieth Century Fox 218

Ugolino and His Children (Rodin, Auguste) 194
University of Cambridge 109 *see also* Girton College; Oxbridge
University of Oxford 109 *see also* Oxbridge; Somerville College
Up Country: Poems of New England (Kumin, Maxine Winokur) 126

Valdivieso, Humberto 223
Valerius: A Roman Story (Lockhart, J. G.) 60
values 156, 163
Vazlinskii, Mikhail 100–1
veils 61
'Veinte años no es nada' (Twenty Years is Nothing) (Yau, Lena) 221–2
Venantia Paullina 71–6
Venantius Fortunatus reading his poems to Radegonda VI (Alma-Tadema, Lawrence) 71
Venus 190–1, 192, 197
Vers la tendresse (Diop, Alice) 244
Vestals 70, 72
Victorian period 55–6, 58
'Victors' (Balmer, Josephine) 175
Vine (Parnok, Sofiia) 80
Virgil
   Aeneid 40, 68, 128–9, 130
   Eclogues 24
   Georgics 127
Vivien, Renée (Pauline Tarn) 67, 76
   Bona Dea 67, 68–77
   Dame à la louve, La (The woman with the wolf) 67, 76–77
   Kitharèdes, Les 68
   Sapho, traduction nouvelle avec le texte grec (Sapho, a new translation with the Greek text) 67, 68, 72
'Volver' (To Return) (Gardel, Carlos) 222
Votes for Women (Robins, Elizabeth) 107

Warhol, Andy
   Shot Marilyns, The 214, 218
Watson, E. B. L. (Mrs Swetenham) 110–11
   Return of Agamemnon, The 111–12
weaving 180, 182, 216, 217
'What was Penelope Unweaving?' (Heilbrun, Carolyn) 182

Index

'What We Have Come to: or the Higher Education of Women' (Somerville College) 120
'When We Dead Awaken: Writing as Re-Vision' (Rich, Adrienne) 3, 168, 178
'Where his arrows are' (Parnok, Sofiia) 102
White Teeth (Smith, Zadie) 229–31
Wife of Bath, The TV series 233
Wife of Bath: A Biography, The (Turner, Marion) 233
'Wife of Bath's Tale, The' (Chaucer, Geoffrey) 227, 232–3, 235–6, 237–41
Wife of Willesden, The (Smith, Zadie) 227, 228, 232–5, 236–7, 238–41
wife–whore dichotomy 57–8
'Wise Venus' cycle (Parnok, Sofiia) 80, 98–105
Wolf, Christa
   Cassandra 156–7
Woman in the Nineteenth Century (Fuller, Margaret) 63–4
Women of Troy, The (Barker, Pat) 168
Women Re-Creating Classics (Hauser, Emily and Taylor, Helena) 1, 4, 7
'Women's Aristophanes: Old Comedy and the Fight for Gender Equality' (Swallow, Peter) 110

women's colleges 109–10, 112, 113–14, 116 see also Girton College
   Classics 117 see also Classics
Woolf, Virginia
   Mrs Dalloway 227
   'On Not Knowing Greek' 140
Work (Alcott, Louisa May) 59
Wrath Goddess Sing (Deane, Maya) 3

'Xantippe' (Levy, Amy) 59

Yau, Lena 221
   'Narciso in the kitchen' (Narcissus in the Kitchen) 223
   'No decir' (To Not Say) 224
   Trae tu esplada para hacer mi mesa (Bring Your Back to Make My Table) 221–4
   'Veinte años no es nada' (Twenty Years is Nothing) 221–2
'You are drowsing, my girlfriend' (Parnok, Sofiia) 92–4
Yourcenar, Marguerite 34
   Anna, soror... 34
   Mémoires d'Hadrien (Memoirs of Hadrian) 34

www.ingramcontent.com/pod-product-compliance
Ingram Content Group UK Ltd.
Pitfield, Milton Keynes, MK11 3LW, UK
UKHW020737140925
462851UK00006B/42